PERFORMING JUSTICE

PERFORMING JUSTICE

AGITATION TRIALS
IN EARLY SOVIET RUSSIA

ELIZABETH A. WOOD

CORNELL UNIVERSITY PRESS
ITHACA AND LONDON

First published 2005 by Cornell University Press

Printed in the United States of America

Design by Scott Levine

Library of Congress Cataloging-in-Publication Data

Wood, Elizabeth A., 1958–
   Performing justice : agitation trials in early Soviet Russia /
Elizabeth A. Wood.
       p. cm.
   Includes bibliographical references and index.
   ISBN 0-8014-4257-5 (cloth : alk. paper)
   1. Trials (Political crimes and offenses)—Soviet Union.   2. Trials
in literature.   I. Title.
   KLA40.P64W66 2005
   345.47'0231—dc22

                                              2004030153

Cornell University Press strives to use environmentally responsible
suppliers and materials to the fullest extent possible in the publishing
of its books. Such materials include vegetable-based, low-VOC inks
and acid-free papers that are recycled, totally chlorine-free, or partly
composed of nonwood fibers. For further information, visit our
website at www.cornellpress.cornell.edu.

Cloth printing   10 9 8 7 6 5 4 3 2 1

CONTENTS

Acknowledgments   vii

Introduction   1

1. A Question of Origins   15
2. Experimental Trials in the Red Army, 1919–20   37
3. The Trial of Lenin   57
4. Teaching Politics through Trials, 1921–23   68
5. The Culture of Everyday Life, 1922–24   85
6. Melodrama in the Service of Science   105
7. The Trial of the New Woman   128
8. The Crisis in the Clubs and the Erosion of the Public Sphere   150
9. Shaming the Boys Who Smoke Cigarettes   174
10. Fiction Becomes Indistinguishable from Reality, 1928–33   193

Conclusion   208

Appendix   221

Archives Consulted   231

Notes   233

Index   293

ACKNOWLEDGMENTS

With this book I have accumulated a particularly large set of debts, which I can only partially discharge by saying thank you. I must begin by thanking the skilled teachers who began my acquaintance with the language and culture of Russia, Barbara Glickman, Valentin Kameneff, and Bayara Aroutunova. I am grateful to the historians and literature scholars who first taught me to read texts and contexts: Donald Fanger, Jane Burbank, Mary C. Nolan, Richard Pipes, William G. Rosenberg, Ronald Grigor Suny, and Geoff Eley.

I am happy to thank the community of scholars who have made working in this field so rewarding. Several groups have heard portions of the manuscript and given me skilled feedback. These include the American Association for the Advancement of Slavic Studies, the Davis Center for Russian and East European Studies at Harvard, the History Faculty at MIT, the Women's Studies Reading Group at MIT, the history departments at Brandeis University and Swarthmore College, and the Russian Seminar in Zurich, Switzerland.

Warmest thanks go to the following people, who graciously read portions of this manuscript: John Ackerman, Donald Blackmer, Richard Bodek, Chris Capozzola, Laura Engelstein, Heather Hogan, Lynn Mally, Eric Naiman, Ruth Perry, Helmut Puff, Jeffrey Ravel, Harriet Ritvo, Rochelle Ruthchild, Susan Solomon, James von Geldern, Mark von Hagen, Arthur Wheelock Jr., and Jerry Wheelock. Of these, Lynn Mally, Eric Naiman, and Mark von Hagen deserve warmest thanks for their detailed reader's reports on the first manuscript. Special thanks to Julie Cassiday for allowing me to see the manuscripts of her dissertation and book when they were still in progress. I am grateful to others who offered advice and key discussions, including Robert

Argenbright, Aleksandr Badkhen, Fred Corney, Michael David-Fox, Richard Davies, David Engerman, Donald Fanger, Peter Fraunholtz, Natalia Gesse, Loren Graham, Edythe Haber, Peter Holquist, Mark Johnson, Hiroaki Kuromiya, Lars Lih, Edna Nahson, Richard Pipes, Gabor Rittersporn, Sonya Rose, Gabriella Safran, Ulrich Schmid, Peter Solomon, Richard Stites, Marina Swoboda, and Nina Tumarkin.

The archivists Nonna Tarkhova, Vera Mikhaleva, and Kira Mironova from the Russian State Military Archives facilitated this project in every way imaginable, including providing emotional warmth and good cheer on some bitterly cold days. I am also grateful to Andrei Doronin of the foreign department of the Russian State Archive for Social and Political History, as well as to the staffs of the State Archives of the Russian Federation, the Bakhrushin Theater Museum, the Polytechnic Museum, the Russian State Archive of the Economy, the Central State Archive of Moscow Oblast, the Russian State Archive of Literature and Art, the Central State Archive of the October Revolution and Soviet Construction of the City of Leningrad, the Bakhmeteff Archives at Columbia University, and the Russian National Library in St. Petersburg.

Amy Randall, Lauren Doctoroff, Valerii Khartulari, Laura Moulton, Kirill Rossiianoff, Yulia Woodruff, and Kelly Ann Kolar helped with the research. Lev Lurie, Rima, and Sonya provided a wonderful home on two occasions in St. Petersburg while I did research on this book. Elga and Ira Skrebtsova sheltered me in Moscow. Numerous friends in St. Petersburg and Moscow, in Ann Arbor, Cambridge, Weston, and Jamaica Plain have provided an emotional and spiritual home for more years than I can count.

This book would not have been possible without generous support from the International Research and Exchanges Board, the Kennan Institute for Advanced Russian Studies Research Fellowship, the National Endowment for the Humanities, the National Council for Eurasian and East European Research, the Provost Fund, and the Levitan Prize at the Massachusetts Institute of Technology.

There are a few other debts I want to record here with particular gratitude. Zen master Thich Nhat Hanh and his students have taught me how to be present in every moment. Peter Gombosi taught me the difference between useful and destructive criticism. My father taught to me to listen to music, which is not unrelated to listening to language, and my mother taught me to play card games with complicated patterns. My sister Frances has stood by me through many a trial. And my beloved Jerry Wheelock (who is not responsible for any of this book's flaws) has taught me that actions speak louder than words. Finally, my little Arthur has patiently gone to sleep many a night listening to the clicking of his mother's keyboard.

PERFORMING JUSTICE

INTRODUCTION

In 1918 Vladimir Ilich Lenin, the first head of the Soviet government, commented in his notes to himself: "The role of the court = terror + socialization."[1]

Courts in all societies play a complex set of roles. They set an example and appear to grant justice. They teach people (both observers and defendants) the law. They demonstrate the authority and power of the state. Historically they have often served as a focal point for what is usually called "political justice"—the meting out of judgment in high profile cases that have a particular importance to the state (here one thinks of the Nuremberg Trials and the trials of defendants such as Socrates, Martin Luther, Galileo, and Louis XVI).

The book before you examines a set of trials performed as plays in the Soviet Union over the decade and a half from 1919 to 1933. These mock trials, known as agitation trials in Russian (*agitatsionnye sudy*), address issues that still resonate today: sex, murder, medical malpractice, prejudice, hooliganism, social relations, the state.

Lenin's comments highlight some of the internal contradictions inherent even in these fictional trials. Over time they evolved dramatically from socialization to shaming, from dialogue to terror. Whereas the earliest trials were structured in such a way as to elicit dialogue and to acquit the fictional defendants, the later ones relied on humiliation, intimidation, and the collective guilt of all involved.

The form of the agitation trials changed considerably over this period. In the prerevolutionary period they were not a unified genre at all—only a series of experiments being tried in different contexts for different reasons. Beginning in 1919, however, political instructors began developing the format with their soldiers in order to teach them through games and improvisational theater. Doctors began using the form in 1921, now creating full-fledged plays with plausible motivations and struggles. In the second half of the 1920s directors in workers' clubs began encouraging the staging of mock trials as a way to solve some of the problems experienced inside their own institutions: hooliganism, absenteeism, disinterest in cultural programming. Soon the trade unions and the Komsomol were creating trials that were almost indistinguishable from reality: they took serious issues of noncompliance, truancy, malingering and now came up with charges of "malicious nonattendance," "introducing corruption," and "wrecking."

At the heart of this book thus lies a conundrum underpinning all of revolutionary Russian history: how and why did social projects intended to benefit the Russian people end up enslaving them? In this case, how and why did the agitation trial, which, as I will show, began as a form of entertainment and education, give rise to a form of spectacle that demeaned both its subjects and its audience?

Cultural historians have recently attempted to bring new approaches to Soviet history for the study of the 1920s.[2] Yet the question of change over time remains, to my mind, unsolved. Why did intelligentsia efforts that were rooted deeply in humanist traditions end up dehumanizing and undermining the very society they were hoping to create?

Before going on, however, I should explain a bit about the agitation trials and how they worked.

THE FORM OF THE AGITATION TRIALS

These plays had many names. When the form was first being developed, they were known as "public trials," "model trials," "discussion trials," "dramatized trials," even "show trials."[3] As the political authorities gained experience in staging these dramas, they grouped them under the general heading "agitation trials" since their intent was to rouse audiences to become more active in support of the new regime. The mock trial of the White general Baron Wrangel, for example, was supposed to spur Red Army soldiers to defeat him.[4]

When the agitation trials were published, the scenarios were printed in small booklets ranging in length from four pages to seventy. Editions ranged from three thousand to one hundred thousand copies and sold for anywhere from twenty kopecks to a ruble and a half if the edition contained several trials bound together. They were often distributed free of charge among Red Army regiments for performance in their clubs. The titles of these agitation dramas ranged from the simple *Trial of a Cow* to the almost Swiftian *Trial of Citizen Kiselev Accused of Infecting His Wife with Gonorrhea Which Resulted in Her Suicide.*[5]

The trial format permitted relatively easy staging by amateur actors at low

The Trial of a Cow: A Peasant Play. From Leonid Subbotin, *Sud nad korovoi. Krest'ianskaia p'esa* (Moscow, 1925), cover.

cost. All the actors needed was a red cloth to cover a table for the judge, a few benches for the accused and witnesses, plus a few incidentals such as a bell for keeping order and a carafe of water for verisimilitude. Whereas a regular play might cost a drama club sixty to one hundred rubles to mount, an agitation trial might cost only fifteen rubles.[6] Parts could be improvized once the club members had grasped an overview of the plot, thus minimizing rehearsal time. Nor did the parts have to be complicated. Directors could typecast their actors and expand or reduce the number of witnesses, depending on the number of participants available. For extra piquancy, the court could name real people or real situations known to the audience—for example, a known army deserter or an alcoholic in the local factory. Local place names and local customs made the trials seem "real" and engaging to the local community.

Typically the proceedings began with the election of two lay assessors from the audience, followed by the ritual incantation, "All rise; the court is now in session," as the judge and the two laypeople came to take their places behind the table in the middle of the stage.[7] The judge then asked if all the witnesses were present, and the latter took an oath to tell the truth, "without regard for kinship or friendship."[8] The court pronounced the indictment and questioned the defendant or defendants, who, in these dramatized trials, invariably denied their guilt. As instructions for the agitation trials explained, this initial denial of guilt was quite deliberate. A guilty plea would have obligated the court to proceed directly to sentencing, thus bypassing the questioning of witnesses and obviating the entire dramatic interest of the play![9]

Often the performances were publicized as if they were in fact genuine legal proceedings and not dramatizations. Posters announcing *The Trial of a Prostitute,* for example, appeared across Moscow in the summer of 1921 without any indication that this was an amateur theatrical performance.[10] Organizers were heavily invested in creating the illusion of a real trial so audiences would find it dramatic.

Many different authors and organizers tried their hands at writing or improvising these mock trials: librarians and aspiring writers, political instructors in the army, doctors and sanitation inspectors, agronomists, political leaders in the Women's Section and Jewish Section, Komsomol and trade union leaders.

The agitation trials eventually touched almost every aspect of Soviet life. By the mid-1920s a rough taxonomy of trial types had emerged: *literary trials* of fictional characters (a hero in a novel or a play was put on trial as a way of talking about the work of literature itself and also about moral issues); *political trials* organized around specific historical or current events and people (trials of counterrevolutionaries who sought to sabotage the revolution, or conversely, trials of heroes such as Lenin, the Communist Party, and the Red Army); *sanitation trials* of health and hygiene issues ranging from alcoholism, midwifery, and faith healing to venereal disease and pros-

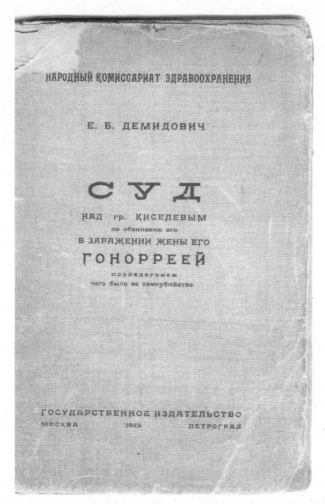

НАРОДНЫЙ КОМИССАРИАТ ЗДРАВООХРАНЕНИЯ

Е. Б. ДЕМИДОВИЧ

СУД

НАД гр. КИСЕЛЕВЫМ
по обвинению его
В ЗАРАЖЕНИИ ЖЕНЫ ЕГО
ГОНОРРЕЕЙ
последствием
чего было ее самоубийство

ГОСУДАРСТВЕННОЕ ИЗДАТЕЛЬСТВО
МОСКВА   1923   ПЕТРОГРАД

The Trial of Citizen Kiselev Accused of Infecting His Wife with Gonorrhea Which Resulted in Her Suicide. From E. B. Demidovich, *Sud nad gr. Kiselevym po obvineniiu ego v zarazhenii zheny ego gonorreei posledstviem chego bylo ee samoubiistvo* (Moscow-Petrograd, 1922, 1923), cover.

titution; *agricultural trials* of poor farming practices such as three-field crop rotation, wooden ploughs, and the smut fungus; *antireligious trials* of superstitious believers and priests; and *production trials* of wreckers, saboteurs, and people who caused accidents.

From the organizers' perspective, the trials had a number of advantages. If well written, they could present heated issues that affected the everyday lives of real human beings (as opposed to abstract issues presented theoret-

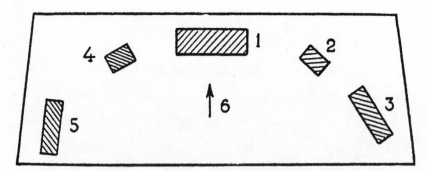

This page. The usual staging: (1) judge's bench; (2) defense; (3) defendants' bench; (4) prose-cution; (5) witnesses; (6) direction the witnesses face in giving their testimony.
Next page. Improved staging: (1) judge's bench; (2) defendants' bench; (3) defense; (4) witnesses; (5) prosecution; (6) table for newspaper correspondents; (7) first entryway; (8) second entry-way; (9) direction for witnesses giving testimony. From V. Vetrov and L. Petrov, *Agitsud i zhivaia gazeta v derevne* (Moscow-Leningrad, 1926), 30, 31.

ically). They contained an element of struggle and sport. If well staged, they kept the audience in suspense as to whether those accused were in fact in-nocent or guilty, what the court would find, and how it would render its final sentence.[11] If the trials were realistic enough, audiences could feel them-selves to be actual participants, sitting in a courtroom helping to decide the fates of the defendants.[12]

Instructions on how to write and stage agitation trials sometimes praised the form as one that would teach "revolutionary consciousness" and Soviet legal consciousness (*pravosoznanie*).[13] In fact, however, the principal focus was on moral and social wrongdoing rather than crimes against the law. The majority of the trials did not even name articles of the law in their indict-ments. Instead they rendered judgments on behaviors that were not, strictly speaking, illegal (prostitution, resistance to three-field agriculture, soiling li-brary books with lard, not building proper fences to keep one's pig from en-tering the neighbors' yard). Often too, especially in the early years, the names of the characters were explicitly allegorical—Slovenly (*Neriashkin),* Consci-entious (*Dobrosovestnyi*), Immature (*Nezrelyi*), Clean (*Chistiakov*)—and alerted the reader or viewer as to what to expect from the character.

The allegorical names, moral topics, and accessible format suggest that these trials functioned in many ways as early twentieth-century morality plays. In the course of the plays the protagonists move from ignorance and sin (if we define "sin" in a social and revolutionary, rather than religious, sense) to confession and redemption in the new postrevolutionary world.

In order to educate the huge population of early Soviet Russia, the new authorities showed a marked preference for forms that were not only edu-cational but also entertaining. Attendance in the army and workers' clubs

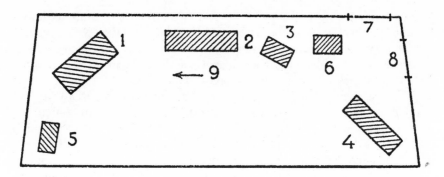

where the agitation trials were staged was at least ostensibly voluntary. The performers and instructors had to appeal to their audiences and draw them in. This they did by playing on the inherent drama of courtroom proceedings, the ritual of the trial, and people's curiosity about the new Soviet order.

The trials drew on topics that organizers hoped would arouse their viewers' passions, questions that were controversial and of local interest. In order to do this, they deliberately focused on topics about which the village or factory was already divided in its opinions and/or about which they felt strongly. They built on everyday concerns with drunkenness, syphilis, and priests who fleeced their parishioners. These were already priority problems in everyday life, problems in which the typical peasant or worker had much more of a stake than he or she did in political matters. As philosopher Julia Kristeva points out, these were *abject* issues, ones that villagers could never fully resolve because they could never fully reject the drunkard, the syphilitic, and the lazy worker. Nor could they fully incorporate them.[14] One of the most brilliant, though perhaps unconscious, strategies of the new Bolshevik leadership was to focus on community issues about which people felt passionately rather than on purely political issues. Through these social and moral dilemmas, individuals and groups were drawn to participate in the new order, taking part in the new rituals without perhaps realizing how political the form of the trial in fact was.

ORIGINS AND DEVELOPMENT

Where did the agitation trial come from? Soviet sources clamored that this was an entirely new form, one that had arisen spontaneously in the army as soldiers responded to political events. In fact, however, the trials had their roots deep in the tsarist past. They drew from religious mystery plays that tried the Sinner; they drew on mock trial practices in law schools; they drew on Silver Age authors' mock trials of each others' poems and stories. By the early twentieth century Russians' obsession with trials of revolutionaries and famous political trials (Alfred Dreyfus, Mendel Beilis, Oscar Wilde) had become so intense as to create an entire *culture* of trials. Open, legal contested trials became the dream of an intelligentsia and indeed an entire nation that had become sick of tsarist arbitrariness and illegality.

Why did the trials take root and spread so quickly in the Red Army and in civilian society? One answer lies in the shared anxiety of intellectuals and political authorities that Russia would never become a "civilized" country, that it would never overcome its backwardness unless the population was awakened and vigorously shaken by means of agitation and propaganda.[15] At root, all the agitation trials focus on *vospitanie,* an untranslatable Russian term meaning "upbringing" or "socialization," and on *kul'turnost',* that is, the quality of being cultured or civilized. Behavior in these dramas is always more important than knowledge or education. Educators of all kinds, both political and nonpolitical, wrote and spoke constantly of their need to find new ways to influence people and move them out of their old habits and ignorance. Without an outside push, they felt, peasants and workers would never give up their outmoded ways; they would never become active citizens of the new order.

The most important actors in the creation and performance of the agitation trials were the mid-level cultural agents of the new state. These included political instructors in the army, directors of workers' clubs in the city, and doctors who penned trials as a way of teaching public sanitation and hygiene to illiterate populations. Each of these groups of professionals or semiprofessionals had a vested interest in simultaneously educating their populations and entertaining them. At the same time the use of trials helped them to convey a certain discipline to their audiences (since all were subject to the judge's commands). Moreover, they could buttress their own authority by demonstrating it concretely with characters in a trial/play. The whole trial might be fictional, but it could serve many purposes in strengthening the hegemony of these new local authorities.

Whereas the earliest trials (in the years 1919–24) reveal their authors' commitment to enlightenment, "criticism" (*kritika*) and "dialogue" (*dialogichnost'*), later ones (from 1925 to 1933) are much more structured around elucidating the "correct" answer. Where the early trials almost invariably acquit the defendants (on the grounds that they have been wronged by tsarist society), later ones typically find them guilty, often of "wrecking" and outright "sabotage." Defense attorneys in the later trials come before the bench to ask only for the court's mercy; they make no attempt to defend their clients. Without a commitment to dialogue and exploration of character motivation, the later agitation trials became increasingly two-dimensional and wooden, and clubs—not surprisingly—became less and less interested in staging them.

Why did the trials become so unforgiving? Politically the collectives staging the trials—for example, the Komsomol, the trade unions, and the so-

СТРОЖАЙШЕ ВОСПРЕЩАЕТСЯ СРЫВАТЬ И ЗАКЛЕИВАТЬ ПЛАКАТ.
ВИНОВНЫЕ БУДУТ ПРИВЛЕКАТЬСЯ К ОТВЕТСТВЕННОСТИ.

СОВЕТ

ТОТ МАЛО
НЕНАВИДЕЛ
СТАРОЕ
КТО РОПЩЕТ
НА НОВОЕ

"The person who grumbles about the new did not sufficiently hate the old" (izdanie Politich-esko-Prosvetitel'nogo Upravleniia Petrogradskogo Voennogo Okruga [1917–22]). The figure on the left points to the soviet building; on the right an old regime Cossack or soldier whips a man lying down. Poster collection, RU/SU 1340, Hoover Institution Archives, Stanford, California.

called voluntary organizations (such as the Society for the Friends of the Navy)—came under increasing pressure in the middle 1920s. The press charged that they were the tools of Trotskyite enemies. These organizations were also facing internal problems with rebellious workers and peasants who engaged in fistfights and refused to come to the clubs. Naturally, trials of hooligans appealed to club directors as a means to establish order in their own establishments.

The Achilles' heel of the agitation trials lay in this cultural divide between the educated and the uneducated and in the elites' deep conviction that they had to inveigle and perhaps even force the general populace to seek new culture and accept new social norms. The trials were deeply rooted in a hatred of the old regime but also in a self-criticism that was unremittingly negative. Though the Bolshevik leadership did not create it, they inherited a culture of blame and censure that proved their eventual undoing. By the end of the 1930s virtually the entire first generation of Bolshevik leaders, the so-called Old Bolsheviks, had either died or been made into defendants in the Moscow Show Trials and executed.

The form of the trial attracted people from a wide spectrum of Soviet so-

Тов. Ленин ОЧИЩАЕТ
землю от нечисти.

Comrade Lenin Cleans the World of Unclean Elements, by V. N. Deni.

ciety who were drawn to fight against illiteracy and to take power as imaginary judges and lawyers. To doctors who had experienced a sense of extreme helplessness in the tsarist era the trials seemed to promise that medicine would attain new authority and expertise. To trade unionists and club managers the trials of hooligans and truants seemed to promise order and control. Ultimately, the trials attracted and encouraged thousands of "little Stalins" who could pronounce sentence from the bench. However idealistic the initial intentions of the authors of the trials may have been, the final results became virtually indistinguishable from the show trials in which Stalin demolished his political enemies.

Stephen Kotkin has written of the process whereby workers learned "to speak Bolshevik."[16] My argument is that at least some workers, peasants, soldiers, political workers, and professionals were learning not only to speak Bolshevik but also to *act Bolshevik,* and that this acting Bolshevik involved not only speech acts but also whole practices of judging and being judged. These new "Soviet" practices were acted out and enacted not so much in the conscious sense of someone "acting a part" but rather in the more complex sense of a parent who tells his or her child to "act your age." To act a part is to act something one knows to be fictional. To act one's age is to adopt a series of behaviors that one feels are appropriate and correct to the situation. In the early Soviet situation, to act Bolshevik meant to try to conform one's behavior to imagined notions of what would please one's superiors. At the same time, for many individuals in positions of some authority (however small) it also meant finding ways to reinforce that authority and reinforce the compliance of one's subordinates (be they readers in a literacy program, patients in a doctor's practice, or soldiers in a drama club).

In his *Prison Notebooks* the philosopher Antonio Gramsci distinguishes between "domination" (direct coercion of the people by the state) and "hegemony" (the obtaining of nonelites' consent in voluntary organizations as part of the fabric of civil society). In a number of places Gramsci shows how the two concepts can be distinguished and yet must be seen as mutually involved in defining and understanding what is colloquially (and in my view insufficiently analytically) understood as "the state." The narrowly defined "politico-juridical" state is sufficient only for understanding some functions of the state as "night watchman." To truly understand the state and political change, one must also examine the state as "educator."[17]

Gramsci assumes that the school has, in his words, "a positive educative function," while the courts have "a repressive and negative educative function." Elsewhere he writes, "Every relationship of 'hegemony' is necessarily an educational relationship."[18] Yet the educational performances of mock trials reveal how productive (in a Foucauldian sense) law and the courts can be as well. In other words, the mock trials were not merely repressing certain behaviors; they were also creating new mini-relations of power in the courtroom.

Perhaps it is time to consider seriously anthropologist Clifford Geertz's notion of a "theatrical state" in the context of early Soviet history.[19] In the agitation trials the new revolutionary authorities in the Soviet Union found a form that combined both positive education functions and repressive functions, both the school and the law court.

Recently, moreover, the eminent anthropologist Victor Turner has argued that every society has its principal form of ritual or theater. This "dominant form of cultural-aesthetic 'mirror,'"as he calls it, is one that then helps the society to see itself and to resolve its conflicts. Relying on decades of research and observation, he claims that preindustrial societies are more likely to foster "immediate context-sensitive ritual," while early industrial societies create staged theater focused on broader problems of the whole society.[20] In the early Soviet Union instructors and agitators developed the agitation trial as a form that was remarkably context-specific (i.e., rooted in local customs and mentalities) and ritualistic. At the same time many of its proponents tried to make it fully theatrical by drawing on drama and character development.

The wide variety of agitation trials and the range of groups involved in their production make this a challenging topic. There appear to have been no central directives explicitly initiating the campaign of mock trials. Yet reports of agitation trials like *The Trial of Wrangel* and even *The Trial of Lenin* were published in army newspapers and in *Pravda* as signals to the rest of the country. Still, the form did not develop entirely "from above." Rather, it emerged in local theaters and children's clubs in the prerevolutionary period; it was seized upon by local army authorities who needed to discipline their troops as well as instruct and entertain them.

Thus at the end of the day, one cannot speak of a unitary "state." The Soviet Union was evolving, with many authorities at many levels. As the interests of these different authorities converged, certain forms, such as the agitation trial, flourished. Other experimental forms died away, including political charades and game playing, pantomimes and pageants. In writing Soviet history, the historian must diligently break open the old notion of "the state," asking always who are the specific actors engaging in particular behaviors at a particular moment in time.

Lenin and the top Bolshevik leadership recognized from the beginning of their rule that political propaganda had to be made concrete, enemies had to have known faces, and people had to be engaged at the level of their daily lives.[21] Trials in general made good press: they excited readers and drew them in.[22] Courts could be used as "lessons of public morality and practical politics."[23] They fostered a sense of "self-discipline" (*samodistsiplina*).[24]

But it was not only the top authorities who had a vested interest in teaching through example and instilling discipline. Local instructors pioneered and developed the form of the agitation trial. They saw many advantages in teaching local soldiers and civilians how to act certain parts, to take on roles as prosecutors, defense attorneys, repentant defendants, and judges. This acting practice, in turn, prepared soldiers to return to their villages and stage trials of so-called kulaks and deserters. For doctors, mock trials provided a desirable venue for influencing patients to pursue medical treatment instead of patronizing local quacks. Agitation trials also helped club directors to discuss the workings of their clubs with the broader membership in a dramatized form and criticize the naysayers publicly if need be.

The agitation trials ultimately set the stage for the party purges and rituals of the 1930s and 1940s when tens of thousands of party members were required to appear before their party cells or other party organizations to have their behavior discussed and judged collectively. These many trials (including the show trials of the 1930s) did not have to be scripted. Instead they could be improvised within certain rules of the genre, rules that the participants learned through observation and practice.

The agitation trials thus provided a template, an empty form, that could be filled with whatever content was currently of concern to a given organizer. Over time different groups picked up the form and developed it in new ways. The spread of the agitation trials reveals the ways in which political power spread not just through decrees and coercion but also through the self-interest, cooptation, and even educational goals of mid-level agents.

The chapters of the book are structured a bit like a musical composition. As new groups became involved in performing agitation trials, they are each introduced into the narrative with their own themes and signature issues. The first chapter ("A Question of Origins") analyzes the prerevolutionary roots of the Soviet-era agitation trials, a subject that has eluded previous researchers because Bolshevik sources insisted on the complete novelty of the form, thus obscuring the religious, bourgeois, and philanthropic origins of the trials. Chapter 2 ("Experimental Trials in the Red Army, 1919–20") then considers the first agitation trials as they appeared in the Red Army with special attention to the role of cultural and political instructors who pioneered the new form.

Vladimir Ilich Lenin is the subject of "The Trial of Lenin" (chapter 3), which takes up the issue of trials in which the defendant is actually the hero who is acquitted and thus vindicated over the course of the trial. Chapter 4 ("Teaching Politics through Trials, 1921–23") returns to the Red Army and the use of agitation trials as a way of teaching politics through drama. Chapter 5 ("The Culture of Everyday Life") discusses the ways in which deserters, slackers, and illiterates become the principal subjects of trials in the years 1922–24.

Between 1921 and 1925 the medical establishment, especially those involved in public health, became centrally involved in the writing and performance of agitation trials (chapter 6, "Melodrama in the Service of Science"). The doctors and health administrators even established special medical-sanitation theaters for the performance of both trials and other kinds of melodramas. In the same period the women's sections (*zhenotdel*) and groups of women delegates began performing agitation trials that focused on their own issues (chapter 7, "The Trial of the New Woman"). These trials tell us a great deal about the subtle messages undercutting the official incantations of gender equality.

By 1925 the clubs that were supposed to serve workers and peasants were experiencing a profound identity crisis as well as increasing problems with hooliganism. In the second half of the 1920s, club directors began putting on mock trials of their own administrations in order to entice new club members and discipline unruly ones (chapter 8, "The Crisis in the Clubs and the Erosion of the Public Sphere").

Chapter 9 ("Shaming the Boys Who Smoke Cigarettes") demonstrates how the anxieties of sanitation inspectors and trade union and Komsomol officials led them increasingly to perform agitation trials of real individuals, thus blurring the distinctions between dramatized agitation trials and show trials. Finally, chapter 10 ("Fiction Becomes Indistinguishable from Reality, 1928–33") examines the changes in the agitation trials as a form after the dramatic Shakhty trial of 1928.

The agitation trials thus give a new perspective on the theatricality of the early Soviet state and the attractiveness of rituals that appeared capable of simultaneously educating, entertaining, and disciplining the general population. The trials fulfilled the desire of top-level ideologues for control over the local population and of local leaders to enlighten, uplift, and discipline the groups in their domain. The trials thus proved to be a crucial venue for the intersection of the Enlightenment ideals of tsarist-era educators, the anxieties and insecurities of early Soviet administrators, and the general population's hunger for drama—above all, for drama that ended in someone else's condemnation and punishment.

A QUESTION OF ORIGINS

In 1904 the Alexander Nevsky Society for Sobriety in St. Petersburg published a four-page drama entitled *The Trial of Vodka*. The judges question Vodka, the primary defendant, who tries to argue that her intention has been to help people. Conscience accuses her of lying and calls in witnesses to show the ways she has ruined their lives. In the end the judges pronounce their sentence: "eternal banishment."[1]

Quite a different "trial" was performed on February 10, 1913, in the city of Krasnoiarsk in Siberia. In this fictional trial a woman named Anfisa is put on trial for the fatal poisoning of her sister's husband, Kostomarev. This mock trial, which was performed in a theater, was a rough adaptation of Leonid Andreev's play of the same title, with a fundamentally reworked ending. Had Anfisa been justified in her poisoning of Kostomarev? the mock trial asked. After the performance the audience voted on whether they ultimately considered Anfisa guilty of murder, given how terribly Kostomarev had treated her and her sister. Some 327 people in the audience voted to acquit Anfisa and condemn Kostomarev. Surprisingly, only 217 found Anfisa guilty despite the proven facts of the murder.[2]

The journalist who wrote up the story, using the pseudonym "Anathema," spoke of this outcome with some horror.[3] Moscow and St. Petersburg had also acquitted Anfisa, he noted. The uneducated public was adamant in their condemnation of the no-good husband: "That's what he deserved," they said after the performance, "the scoundrel, the Lovelace, the dissolute, the traitor." A few of the more educated viewers also justified the acquitting of Anfisa on the grounds that one had to understand her psychology and Kostomarev's guilt.

In part, the journalist concluded, the fault for this outcome lay with the writer Leonid Andreev, who used fantastic symbolism and hypnotic mystification in his original play. In part, though, it was also the journalist's conclusion that the theater public was not yet ready to serve as expert witnesses in such trials since they were too easily swayed by the "irresponsible, pathological state of the defendant" and hence did not see that the acquittal of Anfisa represented a "sad misunderstanding."[4]

Despite the journalist's disapproval of the audience's lack of legal consciousness, he or she expressed hearty approval of the practice of having the masses participate in such public trials (*obshchestvennye sudy*). Here were "visual lessons" that had "enormous usefulness in terms of both socialization [*vospitanie*] and education [*obrazovanie*]." Such "entertainment lessons" (*uroki-razvlecheniia*) should be repeated as often as possible. "The public will learn through them to think through the phenomena enacted on the stage and in a more or less fruitful way will internalize new understandings of the good, justice, beauty and the like."[5]

The key to understanding *The Trial of Vodka* and *The Trial of Anfisa*, as well as the agitation trials to come, lies in the intersection of four distinct but interrelated phenomena in the two decades before the 1917 revolutions: (1) the long history of stories of trials of sinners and even of God in the Russian Orthodox Church and in Judaism; (2) the introduction of jury trials in Russia in 1864 and the ensuing public fascination with trials and courts as dramatic events; (3) the use of theater and dramatics, including dramatized versions of trials, as a tool for popular, extracurricular education beginning in the 1890s; and (4) the symbolist and avant-garde theater's use of mock trials to draw attention to their work in the 1910s and early 1920s.

In the early Soviet era contemporaries insisted that it was impossible to determine the origins of the agitation trials. The tsarist government could not possibly have left a positive legacy in the field of political education since it preferred whips and prisons to active work with the population. Any political education carried on outside the government was hence mired in reactionary views, whether it took the form of religious societies for sobriety or theaters or libraries. Only the revolution had forged new methods of political education.[6]

Instead of explaining the origins of the trials, authors in the 1920s claimed repeatedly that they simply "arose" in the ranks of the Red Army, that "circumstances dictated" their creation, or that they came about "in response to current conditions."[7] More often than not they were described as simply something new. One author, the famous educator D. Elkina, stated that it was impossible to know who was the initiator of these trial/plays because they were "a product of mass collective creativity."[8] Many writers compared the trials to public debates (*disputy*).[9] Others saw them as a combination of the theater and lectures on particular subjects.[10] Others described them as a close replica of contemporary revolutionary tribunals.[11] One contemporary who worked in the agitprop department of the Communist Party suggested that the agitation trials grew out of moot courts practiced in the law schools and out of school plays.[12] Still another said they developed initially "if we are not mistaken" in the ranks of the Red Army.[13]

When the agitation trials did appear in 1919–20, they sprouted up in a variety of places like proverbial mushrooms after a rain *as if everyone already knew what they were.* The challenge for the historian is to go beyond the partial accounts of contemporaries who willfully or accidentally obscured the trials' origins. Mycologists tell us that mushrooms can spring up simultaneously in many places because of the mesh of fine roots under the soil. So in late tsarist Russia we find a rich culture linking truth and justice (*pravda* means both), courts and judgment (*sud* also has a double meaning). This culture was intensified by the widespread feelings of both the intelligentsia and the people that the tsarist system was characterized by vast injustice and arbitrariness (*proizvol*). Revolution, many thought, would bring both justice and a dramatic judgment of the old ways.

THE TRIAL OF PARADISE

In the seventeenth and eighteenth centuries many of the earliest known plays on Ukrainian and Russian soil contained scenes of "The Trial of Paradise," "The Trial of the Sinful Soul," and "The Last Judgment." The Kievan Mohyla Academy and other religious seminaries composed such scenes as parts of larger dramas known as "school plays," which teachers and students performed to convey and reinforce religious and moral values.[14] At the end of the nineteenth century theater historians rediscovered these scenes and began writing extensively about them.[15]

Probably the earliest variation on this theme appeared in a scene known in Europe as "Le procès du Paradis" and in Russian as "Raiskoe prenie," or "Heavenly Arguments." God's Wrath (*Gnev bozhii*) is sent by God to seek vengeance against Nature (*Natura*) for her sins. Compassion (*Miloserdie*) begs that before being punished Nature first be brought for judgment. Judgment (*Sud*) enters, and God's Wrath states the complaint. Judgment questions both sides. Compassion takes up the role of defense; Truth (*Istina*), the role of prosecution. Nature is sentenced to exile from heaven. The Cherubim carry out the decision.[16]

A trial of Adam and Eve that was also discovered in the 1890s imitates the ordinary courts in its structure as well. Adam and Eve are accused of breaking their promise to God and eating from the tree of knowledge of good and evil. Before the trial begins, however, the archangel Michael calls forth all the dead from the grave to be present so they can see that God's judgment does not take place under the influence of Wrath but rather is motivated by fairness. On a scale the Judge weighs two lists, one of the soul's misdeeds, as presented by the devil, and the other of the soul's good deeds, as collected by the angel-protector. The Judge then asks the twelve apostles (the jury) for a sentence. They find him guilty; only John the Baptist tries to throw the soul on the mercy of the Almighty Judge. The Judge finally finds the soul guilty and decrees that he must pay for his sins. Judgment takes place after an equal hearing of the prosecution and defense, the "weighing" of evidence, and the final sentencing based on that evidence.[17]

More judicial ritual can be seen in still another variation, *The Trial of the Sinful Soul* (*Sud nad greshnoi dushoi*), which was published in the journal *Kievan Antiquities* in 1884.[18] According to the notes of an actor who played the Sinner in this play in 1750, the Sinner initially does not believe in the possibility of salvation. Conscience (*Sovest'*) tries to persuade him to repent, even holding before him a mirror so he can see his sins. He turns away but finally is forced to recognize the evidence (*ulika*, a court term) of his sins, and he repents. Conscience publicly reveals the Sinner's wrongdoing (*Sovest' ego oblichaet*). Justice (*Pravosudie*) appears, armed with a sword. The Angel takes up a debate (*prenie*) with the Devil, defending the Sinner against the attempts of the Devil to prove his right to take the Sinner to hell. The Angel responds to the Devil by showing the Sinner's sincere repentance and the compassion of the Almighty. Justice finally resolves the debate and with his sword banishes all devils to the yawning abyss of hell.[19]

At the core of these plays is thus a tension between Good and Evil in human nature. In some trials the sinner is found guilty and taken away to hell, while in others the Angel wins the case and leads the sinner off to heaven. This tension and weighing were also characteristic of seventeenth- and eighteenth-century Russian frescoes of the Last Judgment. While the earliest medieval plays tended to exact harsh judgment, the later ones (in keeping with the frescoes of the same era) tended to acquit the sinner/defendant, thus revealing God's and especially Christ's compassion.[20] (The agitation trials, by contrast, progressed over the course of the 1920s from more merciful to more vengeful.)

That these school plays had a direct influence on the creation of agitation plays (though no Soviet-era source ever admitted it) can be seen in the number of parallels between the two. One Soviet-era play was explicitly called *The Trial of the Sinful Soul*.[21] In both the church-school plays and the early agitation trials the characters are allegorical (though this changes later). "Conscience," for example, a character in an agitation trial, persuades the defendant, "Slovenly" (*Neriashkin*), to repent. Characters with names like Conscientious (*Dobrosovestnyi*) and Clean (*Chistiakov*) play a role in bringing him to that repentance. Secular judges in the agitation trials take over the medieval roles of Justice and Judgment. The defendant's repentance makes the difference between being acquitted and being found guilty.[22]

The Heavenly Tribunal also figures in the East European Jewish tradition. Stories, parables, and aphorisms enjoin mortals to look to the Day of

The Last Judgment. Mid-sixteenth century, from a church in Lviv oblast. From Hryhorii Lokhvyn, *Ukrainskyi seredn'ovichnii zhyvopys* (Kiev, 1976), plate 83.

The Vision of John Climacus. His vision is also known as "The Ladder of Divine Ascent" and shows angels rising on one side, with devils plummeting on the other. Mid-sixteenth century, Russian Museum, St. Petersburg.

Judgment when the Almighty will consider their sins. In some versions a Heavenly Jury will be convened to weigh the sins of those standing before God. In Hasidic lore God himself is sometimes placed on trial for allowing kings and despots to pass laws contradicting His laws and causing His people to suffer. Since God has given humanity the Torah, the rabbis and holy men in these tales claim that it is their right to judge Him according to His law.[23]

In the Soviet era the Jewish Section of the Communist Party created its own trials of the Jewish religion, Jewish schools (the *kheder*), the yeshiva, and even circumcision.[24] These, like other trials of religion and of God, built on the ubiquitous and passionate debates among Russians of every estate and religion at the end of the nineteenth century about religion versus atheism, salvation in the next life versus the building of socialism in this one, the possibility that saints' bodies decayed after death, and so on.[25] While most of the Soviet-era trials of religions were intended to ridicule the priests, rabbis, and mullahs who were made into humorous characters, a few trials were staged as a way of combating popular anti-Semitism and prejudice more generally, as we shall see in the next chapter.[26]

THE ROMANTIC CULT OF TRIALS

As students of tsarist history know well, Imperial Russia had no jury trials until 1864.[27] Until then there were only judges, advocates with extremely limited capabilities (and almost no legal education), and clerks.[28] The courts as a result were extremely corrupt. Vladimir Dal' himself, Russia's most famous lexicographer, reported in 1882 that in all the time he had been collecting proverbs and sayings, only recently had he found one positive reference to trials.[29] All the other proverbs reflected the unfairness of the courts:

> "Take a thief to court, and you'll end up there yourself";
> "Where there's a court, there is falsehood";
> "There are worms in the earth, spirits in the water, stumps in the forest, and chicanery in the courts—how can you ever get away?";
> "Go before God with the truth, but before the courts with money."[30]

For centuries the term *Shemiakin sud* (borrowed from a fictional story of that name) had been synonymous with any corrupt or unfair judicial proceeding. In this seventeenth- century story a poor peasant is brought before Shemiaka, a corrupt judge, for a series of improbable misdeeds but manages to gain his freedom by pretending that he has a bribe for the judge (in reality a rock wrapped in a stone).[31] In the late nineteenth century this story was chosen for dramatization by Nikolai Popov, one of the leading advocates of popular theater.[32] The subject no doubt appealed to Popov because it was universally known and it was picaresque. It also contained a scathing critique of a system that until 1864 had produced only a parody of justice.[33]

In the decade before the reform of 1864, the Slavophile Ivan Aksakov wrote and circulated his own dramatization of the evils of contemporary law courts, based on his negative experience of working there, an experience he considered "the abomination of desolation in the holy place." The play he wrote was called *Office Hours of the Criminal Chambers: Court Scenes from the Notes of an Eyewitness Bureaucrat.* His goal, he stated, was to show "the sad truth" not so much of society's sins (*grekhi*) but rather of its peccadilloes (*greshki*), to provide an exposé (*oblichitel'nyi dokument*) showing the humorous and the vulgar instead of the tragic.[34]

The play opens with a list of the dramatis personae (judges, defendants, witnesses, and guards). The scene is set to look like a real trial, including a table for the clerk covered with a red cloth (like the red cloth in later, Soviet-era agitation trials). The wretched unfairness of the trials comes through in the mournful response of a clerk who comments on a peasant's unsuccessful attempt to appeal his case: "Well, yes, he obviously didn't know that he can appeal only after his punishment, from his place of hard labor . . . ." The judges all show no interest whatsoever in matters of justice and fairness.[35]

When Tsar Alexander II introduced jury trials by law in 1864 (and in practice in 1866), the country was taken by storm, especially the capital cities. Everyone in St. Petersburg and Moscow was talking about celebrated cases. Law students practiced their new professions by reenacting the defense and prosecution used in Western European and Russian trials. Jurists and other members of the intelligentsia had great hopes that open court proceedings (an essential element in the tsar's programs of *glasnost'*) would provide a way to overcome the arbitrariness of the tsarist order, the abuses of power, the daily inequities. If ordinary people would learn to use the courts, the face of the autocracy could be changed. Trials could thus serve as what one historian has called "a school of social morality for the people."[36]

Because defense speeches in public trials could be published in full as official court documents in the press, they became a favored forum for revolutionaries to launch frontal attacks against the regime. Defendants who spoke out against the autocracy even at the risk of long sentences, hard labor, or execution gained the public status of martyrs. Defense lawyers, too, received standing ovations and became heroes of the day.[37] For both revolutionaries and defense attorneys it became a point of pride not to offer a defense but rather to counter the prosecution with a dramatic public indictment of the tsarist social and political order.[38]

During the Revolution of 1905 the pitched battle between the autocracy and the rest of society, especially the radical intelligentsia, continued to take the form of trials. In 1904 the press covered some 84 trials; in 1905 it ran stories on 500 trials.[39] At the same time censorship laws were relaxed, and the liberal intelligentsia began furiously publishing materials on all the major political trials that had taken place in the previous decades. Journals like *Byloe* (The Past) and *Katorga i ssylka* (Hard Labor and Exile) carried documents from public trials in almost every issue. Countless volumes of court speeches were published in periodicals and edited collections, as were histories of forensics and court oratory.[40]

Through the drama and martyrdom of these trials, the intelligentsia, both radical and liberal, hoped to educate and, above all, agitate the broader public concerning the wrongs of the tsarist regime. For at least two generations of Russians, revolution and trials were interconnected in people's minds.[41] As Georgii Plekhanov, Lenin's mentor in the study of Marxism, noted, the revolutionary trials of the 1870s and 1880s were "the great historical drama which is called the trial of the government by the people."[42] For these reasons the big public trials were never just legal events. They were also dramatic. And they were at least quasi-educational (from the perspective of the defense), since they attracted the public to take part as discussants in the nascent public sphere.

The Bolsheviks played a large role in publicizing workers' trials and their speeches as widely as possible. As Lenin put it, "the court is an organ of power. The liberals sometimes forget this, but it is a sin for a Marxist to do so."[43] Lenin, himself trained as a lawyer, offered advice to young revolutionaries and Duma politicians alike who ended up before the courts: "It is time for us to make sure that every such trial [of demonstrators] is turned into a political trial by the accused themselves, so that the government would no longer dare to cover its political revenge with the comedy of criminality!"[44] Those on trial should carefully consider ways "to use the court as a means of agitation."[45]

Meanwhile authors like Turgenev and Dostoevsky avidly followed every trial they could, even going out in the middle of the night to find fellow aficionados who might have the latest word on a particular trial they had missed. Both included trial scenes in their novels.[46] Tolstoy criticizes the courts in "Confession," "The Power of Darkness," and *Resurrection*.[47] Gorky, too, castigates the court and shows the heroism of the defendants in his novel *Mother*.[48] From 1898 the public could follow court cases in an illustrated monthly journal entitled *Court Dramas*.[49]

In 1908 Leonid Andreev (the author of *Anfisa*) published his play *King Hunger*, in which he adroitly combined trial motifs and drama in a parody of the medieval trials of Paradise.[50] The third scene takes place in a courtroom with five judges, presided over by King Hunger himself. Each time they hear the case of a starveling defendant, King Hunger turns to the judges and commands them "to assume a deliberative air." Each time not they but Death, who sits behind them, makes the final decision, condemning the prisoners "in the name of Satan."

A whole group of actors playing the roles of spectators comment on the action in the courtroom as if they were in a theater. After one child comments on the nose of one of the judges, another spectator says of the trial "How interesting! Just like a stage" (54). When it is time for them to take a break, King Hunger announces to the spectators, "Now, ladies and gentlemen, I propose a recess for refreshments. The work of justice is hard and fatiguing" (63). The judges take off their wigs, and all settle down to eating, with much commentary, a huge feast of roast pig, whole mutton sides, and "mountain-like roasts," all this at the "trial" of people who are starving. After this intermission and after condemning several more people, King Hunger makes a final speech: "Ladies and gentlemen! Today you have witnessed a highly instructive spectacle. Divine eternal justice has found in us, as judges and your representatives, its brilliant reflection on the earth." He insists sardonically that the court has been impartial, unmoved by compassion or prayers. After all, only "ruffians" have been hanged. "We showed no mercy to God himself, in the name of the laws of eternal justice." Finally, of the condemned, he says, "They are there; we are here. They are in dungeons, in galleys, on crosses; we will go to the theater. They perish; we will devour them—devour—devour!" All the judges laugh hysterically. The stage directions read: "All is blended into one black, wide-open, savagely roaring maw." The courtroom has become a scene from hell. Yet it is always still a stage. "Death alone is not pleased." He exits, and the curtain falls.

Also around 1908 the Russian Jewish writer S. An-sky (born Shloyme-Zanvl Rappoport, 1863–1920), a prominent Socialist Revolutionary, educational activist, and trained lawyer, took up the Hasidic tradition and penned at least three versions of what he called "God on trial," one in essay form and two in poems. As Gabriella Safran, a literary scholar, has shown, An-sky draws directly from tales of God's trial circulating in Warsaw and the Pale of Settlement more generally at the time. While one of An-sky's purposes was to revive Jewish literature and tradition, he also sought to argue that if God must obey the laws of the land, then the Tsar too cannot be above the laws he has given his people.[51]

An-sky's most famous play, *The Dybbuk*, concludes with a trial scene in which the father of the main female character (Leah) and the ghost of the father of the dead man haunting her are brought face to face in a rabbinical court so that the dybbuk can be exorcised. In carefully legalistic language the trial considers the arguments of both sides, insisting all the while on its own impartiality. When *The Dybbuk* was published posthumously (An-sky died in 1920), literary critics in Vilna and Tel Aviv staged mock trials of the play as a vehicle for discussing its literary merits and demerits.[52]

The line between fact and fiction became blurred in some real trials at the turn of the century as well. In November 1908 Artsybashev's novel *Sanin* was "arrested" in Munich. A month later the publisher, Georg Mueller, was called into court on charges that the novel sinned against morality because of its erotic content. Four months later the book was "freed," emerging as what the publisher called "the complete victor" in the case. Within the year the case with all its legal apparatus (including charges and statements by expert witnesses) was published in Russia as almost a literary work in its own right.[53] The book itself, the publisher, and the expert witnesses are all presented as actors in a drama designed to stir the public's imagination and, of course, to sell more copies of the book.[54]

A PASSION FOR EXTRACURRICULAR EDUCATION

When the Bolsheviks came to power in 1917, they were able to draw on a twenty-year tradition of work in what was usually called "extracurricular education" (vneshkol'noe obrazovanie).[55] This movement focused on work with adults, young people, and children in a variety of settings outside the schoolroom such as libraries, reading rooms, people's houses (narodnye doma), theaters, clubs, tea rooms, and other primarily "recreational" settings.[56] Such projects sprang up everywhere in Russia in the 1890s and, above all, in the years 1905–17. Activists ranged from the most radical left-wing political activists seeking revolution to liberals and even right-wing sobriety societies sponsored by the Russian Orthodox Church.[57]

Despite their political differences these movements had in common a number of features. One was an almost agonizing concern with Russia's "backwardness." As historian Esther Kingston-Mann has shown, Russians in the late nineteenth century were terrified that if they did not somehow become an "England," they would become an "India," a country enthralled to other powers.[58] "Of all the cultured peoples, we are the most uncultured," one activist declared in 1908.[59] Social scientists and social activists disagreed, sometimes vehemently, about the causes and conditions of these problems, but they were united by an almost feverish concern to transform the country and, above all, the people within the country.[60]

Another common feature of these adult education movements was a determination that they could make more progress and reach people more successfully in extracurricular settings than they could in the schools, which were heavily controlled by the state and the church.[61] Independent literacy societies sprang up not only in Moscow and St. Petersburg (from the 1840s), but also in provincial capitals such as Kharkov, where the Kharkov Society for the Spread of Literacy among the People was one of the most radical and highly developed.[62] Often as well, workers' clubs served as a front for left-wing political organizing.[63]

A third and crucial feature of the extracurricular education movement was the intense cross-fertilization taking place among a wide range of activists from all walks of life. Academics, writers, artists, actors and directors, lawyers, doctors, and teachers of every kind joined forces to find innovative ways to mobilize "the people," to teach and activate the broad Russian masses in hopes of changing the society and eventually the state. To take but one example, the roster of attendees at the Kharkov Congress on the Organization of Rational Recreations in June 1915 included 136 teachers, 128 representatives of educational societies, 99 activists in cooperative organizations, 24 doctors, 15 agronomists, and 13 representatives of the church.[64] All these activists were learning from each other, sharing ideas and practices.[65]

The ambitions of many of these extracurricular activists, or *vneshkol'niki*, went beyond encouraging literacy.[66] They hoped that the creative use of what they called "rational recreation" would transform Russia, healing and "civilizing" the nation.[67] Amateur theater in particular, they argued, could go beyond any other art form and certainly beyond mere book learning. The theater could reach illiterate audiences in the way that stained glass windows had reached illiterate audiences in medieval France and Germany, providing visual stories for people who could not read. It could not only teach but also enlighten. The value of a play, theater activists argued, should be the degree of its "influence on the moral feeling and moral consciousness of the viewer."[68] The theater could encourage initiative taking and self-development (*samodeiatel'nost'*). It could draw in audiences so they were not just spectators but actual participants. It was emotionally charged so it could tap into people's moods. It could be created collectively, thus getting away from the authoritarianism of the schools and the state. For some, its value lay in teaching skilled work habits that would foster industrialization in Russia.[69] As one theater historian wrote later, "Only the theatre could serve as primary school and newspaper for the masses thirsting for 'education, enlightenment and knowledge.'"[70]

For many, the use of popular theater also had what one contemporary called important "*applied*" significance.[71] It could be used to teach specific skills and to convey certain bodies of knowledge. Sobriety societies, for example, which had been founded by the Russian government and by philanthropists, sought to develop popular theater programs as a means of attracting people away from the taverns and of teaching values of restraint and "culturedness" (*kul'turnost'*).[72] Doctors associated with the temperance societies began writing and performing plays with and for soldiers and other members of the less educated classes as a means of combating both medical and social evils, especially alcoholism, gambling addictions, venereal disease, and prostitution.[73] The Guardianship of Popular Temperance alone spent some 727,000 rubles on theater productions in 1901, out of a total budget of only a few million rubles.[74]

Soldiers in the tsarist army formed a particular target audience, though Ivan Shcheglov, a leading theater organizer, rued what he called "the thankless task" of trying to "combine two irreconcilable demands, one for free art and one for military discipline (not to mention theatrical!)."[75]

A number of the workers' clubs also supported drama circles focused on medical and sanitation issues. Sociologists such as Mikhail Gernet (1874–1953) gave lectures there on criminality, while doctors lectured on syphilis, tuberculosis, alcoholism, and prostitution. These lectures were particularly valuable from a political point of view because they allowed the speakers to castigate the existing social order without drawing too much unwanted attention from the police.[76]

In the postrevolutionary period the Bolsheviks criticized these philanthropic theatrical efforts as producing "boring, moralizing plays."[77] They did not like the fact that local inhabitants were invited to so-called people's houses to drink tea and read religious-morality brochures while occasionally watching plays and skits. Nadezhda Krupskaia, Lenin, and Maxim Gorky all criticized such clubs as producing plays *for* the people rather than *by* the people.[78]

Between 1905 and 1917 even the mainstream theaters began to dramatize delicate topics such as prostitution. In 1906 or 1907, for the first time ever, the Malyi Theater in Moscow performed scenes from Dostoevsky's *Crime and Punishment,* including a scene between Raskolnikov and the prostitute Sonya Marmeladova. Never before had tsarist authorities allowed a prostitute to appear on stage![79] The writer who described this scene was Boris Bentovin, himself both a venereologist and a playwright, as well as a translator of a German work on theatrical portrayals of prostitution, "The Stage and Prostitution." Bentovin added his own essay to this latter work, an essay entitled "Prostitutes Illuminated on the Contemporary Russian Stage," in which he examined nine different Russian plays that portrayed prostitutes.[80] The tradition of doctors writing plays, especially plays about marginal topics, was to become a rich one in the Soviet era.

DRAMATIZATION IN SCHOOLS IN RUSSIA AND THE WEST

By the early 1900s Europeans, Americans, and Russians were increasingly traveling between continents in order to learn from each other about cultural and education work among the urban poor and among children. Leo Tolstoy went abroad in the years before he began his educational experiments at Yasnaia Poliana. Jane Addams, the founder of Hull House in Chicago in 1889, in turn came to Russia to visit Tolstoy in 1896.[81] In 1899 Petr Kropotkin, the great anarchist, visited Hull House. In 1903–4 a young architect named Alexander Zelenko (1871–1953) also visited Hull House and the University Settlement in New York City. On coming back to Russia, Zelenko brought back practical ideas about how to create such settlements. Together with his close companions and fellow educators, Stanislav Shatskii (1878–1934) and Luiza Shleger (1863–1942), Zelenko helped found the First Moscow Settlement (known in Russian by the odd-sounding name "Setlement"), which then led to the development of a chain of children's clubs.[82] Here they focused on "labor education, self-government for children, satisfaction of their interests, and providing ever needed opportunity for the creative powers of all members."[83]

Educators like Zelenko also brought back the philosophical works and ideas of progressive educators including John Dewey, Maria Montessori, and G. Stanley Hall. As both early Soviet scholars and Western visitors to the Soviet Union noted, an entire generation of prerevolutionary Russian educators and activists was brought up on the ideas of Dewey and his contemporaries.[84] Nadezhda Krupskaia (1869–1939), later one of the leaders of Soviet education, herself wrote extensively about Dewey in her book *Popular Education and Democracy.*[85]

Both Westerners and Russians were becoming smitten with what the British and Americans called "dramatics" and Russians called *dramatizatsiia.* Around 1900 John Dewey began arguing that the games and spontaneous activities of children should be viewed as "the foundation-stones of educational methods."[86] Children at his Laboratory School in Chicago and the Dalton School in New York were putting on plays as part of their curriculum. Jane Addams created boys' and girls' clubs as well as drama groups at Hull House. A huge literature sprang up in the United States, Britain, and Russia on "the dramatic instinct" and the value of drama in education.[87] Plays, these authors insisted, could help children build character, understand the lives of others, and develop the body. Dramatization could also foster civic-mindedness.[88]

In 1914–15 the progressive education journal *Svobodnoe vospitanie* (Free Upbringing) published an article called "Dramatization as a Teaching Method" by an Englishwoman, Harriet Finlay-Johnson,[89] in which she relayed her fifth graders' dramatization of a trial of King Charles I. Rather than simply studying the facts of Charles I's overthrow and subsequent execution, Finlay-Johnson's students took roles in the conflict and acted them out. The children, she found, almost effortlessly learned all the facts of the case, as well as considering the "whys" and "hows," the causes and effects of the overthrow and trial of the king.

In this exercise Finlay-Johnson found exactly what political instructors were to find in the 1920s: namely, that students, soldiers, workers, and peasants all responded to seeing themselves on stage. They were transformed from a passive "class" into active learners who showed initiative and even creativity in putting on this kind of dramatic lesson. For Finlay-Johnson this experiment showed the power of tapping into what she called "the Niagara Falls of children's instincts."[90]

In the Soviet era the new leadership would tap not only into an instinct for dramatization but also into every villager's and town dweller's instincts for gossip and criticism of others' untoward behavior. As we shall see, it was not primarily political crimes that formed the subjects of the agitation trials. It was behaviors that were already marginalized by villagers themselves:

drunkenness, prostitution, letting one's cows wander into a neighbor's fields.[91]

Dramatic instincts lay at the base of other work being done with children and adults in popular clubs across Russia. As V. A. Zelenko (probably no relation to Alexander Zelenko), made clear in his book *How to Create Political Clubs* (1917), historically all the great political revolutions had been marked by the spontaneous developments of clubs. The key, he noted, was "to help people figure out political issues, to enlighten them, give them an opportunity to work out, organize their opinions."[92]

Children's clubs were still a new phenomenon in 1914.[93] Many of them were inspired by Leo Tolstoy's work in his famous, though rather short-lived, colony in Yasnaia Poliana. Rejecting all physical punishment for children, Tolstoy insisted that they learn at their own pace, in their own way. One method that he pioneered was to have his students write plays based on proverbs. He also experimented with student self-government. For Tolstoy schools should be viewed as places for experimenting. Like John Dewey and Maria Montessori, he had come to view education as something that should be child-centered and improvisational: it should respond to the child rather than vice versa.[94]

THE LIBRARIANS' REVOLUTION IN EDUCATION

In the years just before World War I several librarians began working to try to increase literacy and reading among the peasants using these latest methods.[95] Two of them were involved in performances of mock trials both before and after the October Revolution. One was Boris Osipovich Borovich (1883–1943), who lived and worked in and near Kharkov.[96]

Borovich's overriding concern was hooliganism, which he thought had reached "epidemic" proportions. While ancient Russia had long known ignorance and stupidity, he argued, the phenomenon of banditry, unruliness, and senseless behavior was new. Together with colleagues, whom he described as "dedicated to ideas of free upbringing," he sought to create a club as a kind of after-school program for kids in need of "rational recreation." Here they would give the children warmth and kindness. But they would also give them "the rudiments of a civic upbringing" (*nachatki grazhdanskago vospitaniia*). Through such recreation the children and teenagers would, they hoped, develop "energy, independence [*samodeiatel'nost'*] initiative, will, courage, an ability to live collectively and to govern themselves [*samostoiatel'no upravliat'sia*]."[97]

In the yard of a newly founded "Children's Home" (*Detskii Dom*) in an unnamed southern city (probably Kharkov) in the years just before World War I, Borovich described how the teachers used to walk around with a pile of books under their arms as a ploy to interest the children in reading. Finally one of the children would call out, "Hey, what's that you have under your arm? Can you read to us?" The leaders of this after-school program were counting on this kind of curiosity to attract the children, mostly the poorest of the urban poor, to come hear books being read out loud.[98]

One day after reading aloud a story about a boy named Ianko who stole a violin, the instructor (possibly Borovich himself) told the children about juries and how they work. Sometimes, he explained, juries have to face a direct conflict between the facts of a crime and the question whether the defendant should be considered guilty. Should Ianko be considered guilty and did he deserve to be punished? he asked the children. What would you do if you were the jurors? The children thought about it for a bit. Finally after some discussion, they decided that Ianko should not be found guilty and that he should be given the violin to keep.[99] Here was an early form of an improvised agitation trial: a group of young people were encouraged by a teacher to discuss the question of a fictional defendant's guilt or innocence as if they were themselves participating in the court case.[100]

Vladimir A. Nevskii (1888–1974) was another librarian who wrote extensively on extracurricular education work and used examples of courtroom dramas in both his pre- and postrevolutionary writings. For Nevskii the burning issue was workers studying in self-education circles who had had no experience in political work. He was particularly cognizant of the huge importance of workers' clubs and the need to teach "a maximum of knowledge and habits with a minimum of disruption from their ordinary work lives."[101] One central quality needed in all such schools of adults, he insisted with some ferocity, was that they had to be self-governing and self-organizing labor communes. Their work must engage club members in collective creativity and in activities that reflected real-life conditions. They must focus on controversial problems so they could engage people's interest. Finally, they must encompass problems that were really on people's agendas both locally and nationally.

Borrowing explicitly from practices in workers' clubs in England, Nevskii suggested a long list of types of meetings that workers in clubs could organize and dramatize as a way of practicing running them: regional (volost') meetings, local courts (*narodnyi sud*), meetings of cooperative activists, meetings of strikers, meetings of electors, cultural-educational congresses, district (zemstvo) meetings, city soviets, party meetings, and political demonstrations.[102]

Nevskii explained to his readers that this practice had its roots in the late Middle Ages in Jesuit schools, where students and faculty practiced their studies through "mysteries" (plays dramatizing scenes from the life of Christ) and university disputations.[103] Participants in the latter had to quickly respond to propositions put forward by the master with citations from Aristotle, the Bible, and the Holy Fathers. This gave them practice in understanding their opponents' viewpoint as well as their own, thus ensuring that they had really mastered the subject they were studying. In today's world, Nevskii commented, such debates were frequently organized in England in workers' clubs, in universities, and in vocational education schools. Students in these settings would take roles in a mock parliament, some playing ministers striving to pass a particular bill, while others acted out the role of the opposition with its counterarguments.[104]

Nevskii also suggested that workers' adult education classes should stage court cases as a way of thinking about contemporary issues. As an example he suggested the case of a female servant accused of killing the baby she had had out of wedlock by the master of the house where she worked. The students should not just follow the letter of the law in putting her on trial, Nevskii argued. Instead there should be a wholly different conception of who should be the judges and who should be tried. "Should not the court of public conscience [*sud obshchestvennoi sovesti*], the court of the ideals of social justice of the toiling masses, try the master of the house, the fat bourgeois, who obtained the assent of his servant to have extra-conjugal relations after long and pestering harassment, through threats and lying promises?"[105] Here Nevskii explicitly resurrected the older notion of collective responsibility— the notion that the whole group (usually a village in prerevolutionary tsarist taxation practices) should be answerable for implementation of a certain policy. "However much it may be hated by individualistically minded historians," collective responsibility, Nevskii argued, should be applied so that all of bourgeois society could be put on trial for its sexual crimes.[106] The students should meet among themselves and stage a genuine public debate over the social conditions giving rise to this kind of exploitation and harassment. The mock trial could thus serve as a stimulus for a new level of student involvement in public issues.

THE INFLUENCE OF THE AVANT-GARDE MOVEMENT

To support his defense of popular theater, Nevskii cited the leading foreign expert in this area, the French playwright and theorist Romain Rolland.[107] Convinced that theater could attract the masses and draw them in, Rolland wrote "The people will always find itself to be the most magnificent spectacle."[108] Anatoly Lunacharsky, the Soviet commissar of education, took this notion one step further: "In order to feel themselves [*pochuvstvovat' sebia*], the masses must show themselves externally [*vneshne proiavit' sebia*]. And that is possibly only when, as Robespierre put it, they become a spectacle for themselves."[109] Such an appeal to people's egocentrism, their desire to see themselves and their friends on stage, was often cited as one of the reasons for the later success of the agitation trials.[110]

The leading avant-garde directors such as Vsevolod Meyerhold (1874–1940) and Nikolai Evreinov (1879–1953) seem not to have been directly involved in trial performances either before or after the revolution.[111] Yet they influenced agitation trials through their articulation of key principles, including Dionysian collective creativity, the destruction of the fourth wall between actors and audience, the revival of Greek theater, medieval mystery plays, and Italian commedia dell'arte (particularly the practice of improvisation).[112] From these older practices Meyerhold, Evreinov, and other colleagues in the popular theater field came away with a strong interest in rituals and "Ritual Theater" (*Obriadovyi teatr*) (Evreinov's term).[113] Theater activists translated the latest French work on French revolutionary festivals into Russian.[114] They read Nietzsche and Wagner as well as Romain Rolland.[115]

Evreinov at this time developed quasi-anthropological theories of the "instinct for self-transformation." Children's play in all times and places was associated with the desire "to be other than oneself" (*zhazhda byt inym*). From this playfulness came rituals—church rituals, tsarist state rituals, military rituals, wedding rituals, carnivalesque-mystical rituals, and, most interestingly for our purposes, court trials. For many Russian directors Evreinov's theories provided, in the words of one Russian theater historian, "a way out of inertia and passivity toward the activation [*aktivizatsiia*] of the broad viewing masses through the charms of the theater."[116]

That the charms of the theater were indeed working their hold on the broad masses was attested by dozens of observers. They referred to the "theater mania" (*teatromania*) of the day, the fact that the people's theaters were growing in numbers "not by the days but by the hours."[117] During the Civil War (1918–20) drama circles were spreading like an "epidemic of the Spanish disease."[118] For Bolshevik cultural education specialists, this love affair with the theater would prove immensely rich. As Lunacharsky noted, "We are dealing with a *new* public. They have almost never seen the theater. They must see it and reorient its values."[119] This new, fresh relationship to the dramatic meant as well that the viewing public had no resistance to any form of theater. They had no preconceived notions of what theater should and should not be. For the first time in Russian history the theater was truly accessible to the people and they drank it in with every fiber of their beings.

The literary community of the Silver Age went beyond an academic interest in this kind of school play. In November 1920 a group of Symbolist poets including Sergei Esenin and Valerii Briusov staged two mock trials of each others' works and literary styles: "The Trial of the Imazhinisty" and "The Literary Trial of Contemporary Poetry."[120] These were literary debates staged in courtroom format in order to draw a larger audience. As one poet commented, "The verbal skirmishes at the trial went on without end. The audience was pleased, of course. How else could they hear in one evening Briusov, Esenin, Mayakovsky, and the Imaginists, who at the end of the evening began to read their poems?"[121]

Esenin and the Imaginists wanted publicity. "Scandal, especially a beau-

The Trial of Contemporary Poetry. The Polytechnical Museum. "On Tuesday November 16 [1920] at 7 p.m. the All-Russian Union of Poets is holding a Literary Trial of Contemporary Poetry. Defender of contemporary poetry, Valerii Briusov; Imaginist Prosecutor, Vadim Shershenevich; Judge, V. L. L'vov-Rogachevskii; Expert Witnesses, M. A. Aksenov, S. Esenin; Plaintiff, A. Mariengof. Twelve judges will be chosen from the audience." From Sergej Jessenin, *Gesammelte Werke,* Herausgegeben von Leonhard Kossuth, 3 vols. (Berlin, 1995), 2:129.

tiful scandal always aids talent," Esenin told his friend V. Kirillov in 1919.[122] The trial was just one of many forms of publicizing his work and others'. In this same time period he tried to organize a mock duel between the poets Vadim Shershenevich and Osip Mandelshtam, a mock coronation of Velimir Khlebnikov for his "world fame," and a mock funeral of himself to which he invited his friends. "Esenin is dead," he told them, disguising his voice on the phone.[123] A mock trial of their friends and rivals served the poets well: not only did it draw a large audience to the conservatory where it was performed but it also gave them a dramatic forum to draw attention to their views.[124]

It is hardly surprising that Soviet accounts of this early form of agitation theater could not explore the full genealogy of the trials. They could never have admitted that their own form of mass public education had anything in common with the Alexander Nevsky Society for Sobriety and its *Trial of Vodka*. Still less could they publicly admit that Russian Orthodox plays about the Last Judgment could have any relation to their resolutely secular agitation trials. Since they regularly denounced bourgeois dramatists as obscurantists stupefying the masses with cheap entertainments, they could also admit no kinship with the Krasnoiarsk organizers of *The Trial of Anfisa*.[125] Nor did they countenance any connection with the plays of late-nineteenth-century philanthropists and popular theater activists. Nor still, especially after 1930, could any Soviet authorities on agitation trials mention the influence of important Western notions of progressive education since many of those educators (especially John Dewey) were rapidly becoming personae non grata.[126]

Yet the extent of these prerevolutionary roots makes it clear how embedded Soviet-era agitation trials were in the aspirations and practices of the late tsarist period. They were not merely the "hate drama" some historians have construed them to be.[127] Nor were they entirely the "invention" of the Red Army, though we will see that army instructors played an enormous role in the development and spread of this particular dramatic form. Rather, they grew out of many passions of the late nineteenth century in tsarist Russia, especially hatred of the autocracy, hopes in "the people" and its "dramatic instincts," and a fascination, bordering almost on obsession, with public trials as political and social events.

The agitation trials were not themselves a unified, recognized genre in the prerevolutionary period. Rather, they seem to have emerged as an occasional form used by playwrights (*The Trial of Anfisa*, Leonid Andreev's *Trial of the Hungry*), by temperance activists (*The Trial of Vodka*), and by school club organizers (Borovich's jury discussion of Ivanko and his violin, Nevskii's trial of the woman who committed infanticide).

Yet all the elements were in place for a takeoff once the Revolution had taken place and, even more important, once the Civil War had quieted down sufficiently to allow the army units to begin experimenting broadly with new theatrical forms.

Seven prerevolutionary principles of "extracurricular education" dominate the later agitation trials: (1) *aktivnost'*—the notion of involving as many people as actively as possible in all aspects of the production; (2) collective creativity (*kollektivnoe tvorchestvo*)—fostering collective authorship of scripts; (3) independent activity (*samodeiatel'nost'*), meaning grassroots, amateur performances without outside professional supervision; (4) the use of small circles (*kruzhki*) of participants working together on different parts of the production; (5) the conveying of information not so much through lectures as through conversations (*besedy*) and stagings (*instsenirovki*) to engage participants and deepen their understanding; (6) the unity (*sliianie*) of actors and audience; and (7) "localization" (*lokalizatsiia*)—the teaching of abstract material through the use of local examples. Soviet-era agitation trials almost always relied on local geography, local symbols, local problems, even local speech patterns in order to draw in area residents to become active and engaged in the performances.[128]

Initially those committed to creating debates and theatrical trials were not wedded to certain outcomes. As E. Khersonskaia wrote in 1924, in a debate the goal was to create "not only space for disagreement but also the freedom to argue, to work out the given issue later in different directions." Those who are usually afraid to speak in public should be the ones most encouraged, she noted. Above all, Khersonskaia and others were convinced that political education should not rely on set "recipes."[129]

Like all extracurricular education and theater efforts, the agitation trials carried the special burden that they had to attract, even entice, the audience's participation through whatever means possible in order to be able to deliver a certain amount of educational material. In the Red Army, where such trials were first performed in the Soviet era, young instructors drew on every possible device and technique they could find—from grassroots popular theater to those of the avant-garde theater. In addition they recruited many older theater activists to come into their Red Army studios to try to jumpstart the creation of a new, revolutionary, socialist theater.[130] It was in this hothouse environment committed to experimentation and "learning by doing," as John Dewey would say, that all the many tendencies discussed in this chapter came together. As we will see in the next chapters, the pressure on young political instructors in the army fostered the use of a range of different forms of what was soon to be called "political enlightenment" (*politprosvet*), a new name for the much older phenomenon of extracurricular education.

Even before 1917 a warning about the dangers of trials in schools came from an unlikely source. In 1911 Nadezhda Krupskaia spoke out against the creation of school-based disciplinary courts (*shkol'nye sudy*) in which the children or young people themselves acted as judges and lawyers for their peers accused of misdemeanors. Such practices were currently being practiced in progressive education circles in Germany and America. In her view the reason for these school disciplinary courts stemmed from a desire to see children not only participate in self-government but also control themselves and each other as a convenience for the grownups.[131]

Playing at court (*igra v sud*), Krupskaia insisted, was something "extremely unsavory."[132] It would have a deleterious influence on the very children it was supposed to help. Of course, those who defended the notion of "school courts" were convinced that children would gladly play the roles of judges, prosecutors, and defenders, and that in the course of such trials they would display initiative, independent activism (*samodeiatel'nost'*), spontaneity (*neposredstvennost'*), and purity (*neisporchennost'*). But such a "game" always entailed serious adult intervention, she was convinced, which undermined any claim that it was based on genuine independent activism. Furthermore, as Leo Tolstoy had discovered at Yasnaia Poliana, it could well lead to "self-deception and a criminal faith in the legality of the punishment . . . , especially a self-deception that the feeling of revenge becomes just [*spravedlivym*], as soon as we call it 'punishment.'"[133] Moreover, she noted, in such courts the prosecutor would attempt "to make white into black" and the defense would attempt "to make black into white." This, Krupskaia concluded, would "unquestionably corrupt the performers." Before such an innovation of school courts could be introduced into the new schools she was supporting, she insisted, there should be close study whether it would be worthwhile.[134]

Such close study was never done, however, before the agitation trials were introduced, first experimentally and then wholesale, into the army, the workers' clubs, and schools of Soviet Russia.

EXPERIMENTAL TRIALS IN THE RED ARMY, 1919–20

On December 7, 1919, the amateur actors of an army reserve unit in Kharkov performed a play called *The Revenge of Fate* about a wife's murder of her husband after years of his abuse. Immediately afterwards the soldiers staged a revolutionary tribunal of the fictional wife. Should she be found guilty of the murder? The army units sent to see the play elected the court. The judge explained the charges against the heroine. Members of the audience came forward to debate the case as witnesses for the prosecution and defense. In the end the judges acquitted the defendant, a verdict the soldiers approved.[1]

Contemporary accounts claimed that the idea for this kind of trial arose locally in the ranks of the Red Army. The new methods of agitation trials and living newspapers had their beginnings "out in the sticks": "The center did not dictate them from above, but rather the local areas gave a push to the center in popularizing this work."[2] The revolution itself was said to have "forged" and "brought forth" the new methods of political education work.[3]

At root this was a notion that the agitation trials arose "spontaneously" from the masses in the Red Army, that they were a reflection of the soldiers' own *samodeiatel'nost'*, that is, their independent, amateur acting.[4] The historian must ask how much this was the case and how much that *samodeiatel'nost'* was deliberately directed in ways that organizers hoped would appear imperceptible to participants.

As a general phenomenon, "cultural-education work," as it was called, was indeed consciously fostered from above by early political leaders, beginning almost immediately after the October Revolution of 1917.[5] By 1918 the leading authorities both in the army and in the railroad administration had created special instruction courses for those being sent into the field to work with soldiers and railroad workers.[6] In 1919 they held the First National Congress on Extracurricular Education (May 6–19), which resolved to give full support and assistance to "the freely appearing creative amateur activism [*svobodno proiavliaemoi tvorcheskoi samodeiatel'nosti*] of the broad masses of the population."[7]

Herein lay one of the central paradoxes of the Russian revolutionary years: the state and its congresses were telling local leaders to encourage "freely appearing" local initiative while at the same time telling those leaders what kinds of *samodeiatel'nost'* would be most acceptable.

Soviet-era agitation trials did in fact appear in the Red Army before they showed up in the cities. Their exact origins, however, are lost in the confusion of the times. Here were exhausted armies (there were sixteen of them on different fronts during the Civil War), whose soldiers had been "voting with their feet," as Lenin noted, since the middle of World War I and who began to desert once more in large numbers in the spring of 1920 as the war came to an end. Since the armies were in constant motion, no one had time to keep a close record of what was happening, least of all about plays that were improvised in the trenches between battles.

Those most under pressure in this situation were the political instructors (*politicheskie rukovoditeli,* or *politruki,* for short). The mass demonstrations and exhortations that had been used to rouse soldiers to fight the White forces during the first years of the Civil War were no longer effective once the war began to come to an end. The instructors needed to find creative solutions to simultaneously please their superiors and also attract the rank-and-file soldiers who were in their charge.

Barely older than the ordinary soldiers, these political instructors were part of what might be called a "new intelligentsia" — a generation of young men and women born in the 1880s and 1890s who worked to spread the revolution once power had been seized in Petrograd and Moscow. We will never know their exact motivations. It seems clear, though, that as they improvised in response to directives from above, they developed new forms of working with the masses, including (and for our purposes principally) the agitation trial. This was a form that could entertain the troops (thus getting them to come to events that were ostensibly voluntary), educate them (an ideal of both the prerevolutionary intelligentsia and the new military), and discipline them in times of serious change and upheaval. Through this kind of activity this generation of political instructors came to serve as conduits and mediators between the regime and the broader masses.[8]

Fortunately, several instructors later recounted their experiences of improvising agitation trials with their soldiers. They practiced this improvisational theater in Kharkov, Kostroma, and Smolensk, which had been centers of extracurricular education in the prerevolutionary years, and in the northern Caucasus, which was a new focal point for organizing and innovation. The information is sketchy since the skits were played primarily for consumption in the moment; the texts did not survive. Still, there is much one can glean from reading between the lines of the organizers' accounts.

THE FAILURE OF THE OLD METHODS

By the winter of 1919–20 organizers saw clearly that the original "revolutionary" methods for rousing the soldiers were no longer working. Soldiers and civilians alike had grown heartily sick of public rallies in particular. In the first days of the revolution it had been comparatively easy for an orator to hold the attention of a crowd for several hours. Everything was new; people wanted to know who the new government was, what was going on. The leading orators of the party, Lenin, Trotsky, Lunacharsky, and Kollontai, frequently went out to the factories to make speeches. As the Civil War wore on, however, these top-level Bolsheviks shifted their attention from public speech making to the business of running the government. The younger party orators who replaced them had less experience and less charisma, which made it more difficult for them to hold a crowd's attention.[9]

One woman journalist described graphically how the faces of audiences at rallies "froze into positions of unbearable boredom." Listeners waited only for the "sacramental hurrahs" (*da zdravstvuet*) signaling the end of the speeches. They applauded weakly and avoided asking any questions.[10]

Another account maintained that "orateli" (the peasant pronunciation of "orators") had completely lost all respect. When peasant soldiers were asked why they didn't like to go to rallies, they replied, "Oh, those *orateli*. You come to listen, but he [*sic*] won't tell you anything from real life. 'Ations,' 'itions,' 'isms,' 'visms,' and you sit, like a blockhead, and you can't very well leave; the chair [of the meeting] appeals to your conscience. They drive you, as if into a bottle, and there they pickle you [lit., "marinate you"] like a son of a bitch!"[11]

Of course, peasants and soldiers liked to listen to the good orators, their "favorites," those who used simple, concrete language and didn't tell long-winded stories with foreign words. The worst case, the same journalist reported, was that of the *korkodily* ["crocodiles," mispronounced]:

> We had one agitator come to us in the village. "Well," he began, "first of all, comrades, you must wage a struggle against the *korkodila*, because," he says, "that is our first enemy. Who is against the village councils? The *korkodila*. Who leads you into provocation? The *korkodila*. Who can undermine the revolution? The very same infamous *korkodila*! Comrades! Your children, your sons, who are spilling their blood on the fronts of the civil war, they will curse you if you do not eject from your ranks this *korkodila*."

Well, the people don't understand a thing. Some are frankly horrified. But then one old man comes forward and says: "Hey, Mr. Comrade Agitator! The *korkodila* isn't hanging around these parts. We don't have any *korkodily*, and if we did, and if it got going, you know, we wouldn't leave it alive, the rotten scum."[12]

Another experienced lecturer commented frankly that agitators should give soldiers what they wanted to hear: "It is too harsh to force a comrade who has often stared death in the face, who has endured cold and hunger, to listen to what is completely uninteresting to him." The *kul'turnik*, or cultural worker, should give way to what the masses were interested in, should try to learn what they really wanted to know.[13] Nadezhda Krupskaia, Lenin's wife and an important figure in Soviet education, admitted frankly in an unpublished letter that "broken-record, rally-style agitation" had become impossible, and new methods would have to be found: "Purely political rallies are possible now only through deception, by calling them 'lectures,' or by attracting people with big names, or by using expensive props, such as agitation trains or steamships."[14]

Even at the height of the Civil War, instructions from the top had acknowledged that it was better not to hold a rally if there was only a mediocre orator available.[15] Political departments everywhere were now complaining vociferously about the "catastrophic" lack of staff.[16] Even some of the top party leaders such as Evgenii Preobrazhenskii were admitting that an agitator shouldn't be allowed to say that a village was counterrevolutionary just because people laughed at him. No, it wasn't the village that was counterrevolutionary—it was the agitator who was poor.[17]

Civil War agitation had relied on the simplest slogans possible: "Death or victory!" "The Socialist Fatherland is in danger!" As the war came to a conclusion, such black-and-white portrayals of the dangers to the homeland no longer worked to generate enthusiasm in soldiers tired of fighting and campaigning.[18] By the time of the Ninth Party Conference in September 1920, the central authorities were belatedly acknowledging that campaigns such as the "weeks" and "days," which had been the staple agitation form of the Civil War (the "week of aid to the front," the "day of the wounded soldier"), should be held on a national scale only in exceptional cases.[19] Gradually, as new resources became available, army authorities began to seek new methods of reaching the population.[20]

THE NEW ROLE OF THE POLITICAL INSTRUCTOR

In October 1919 the army high command created the position of the political instructor (*politruk*) to "enliven" political work and help make it more systematic.[21] It was now the instructor's responsibility to make the peasant soldier into a "conscious warrior," to help him understand what he was fighting for.[22] Each instructor was to serve as "not only the political supervisor, but also the tutor [*vospitatel'*] of the soldiers." He had to become "the closest friend of each soldier in the company."[23] Peasant soldiers themselves asked in question-and-answer sessions, "What is the difference between the political instructor and the priest?"[24] Evidently they saw the political instructor as taking on many of the moral and cultural functions of the pre-revolutionary army chaplain.

The central dilemma facing the instructors was that they had to use persuasion rather than force to induce their charges to undertake political or social activities. Instructions from above enjoined them "to make an exact account of all the leisure time of each Red Army soldier" and "to fill it with rational and useful diversions close to the soldiers' barracks." At the same time they were to try to make sure that such entertainment was not overly formal or burdensome and obligatory.[25]

Political departments often used cultural events as a way of reducing the incidence of drunkenness, violence, and looting since they kept the troops occupied. They were also supposed to divert the masses from religious spectacles.[26] When, for example, the southern city of Rostov-na-Donu was liberated from the Whites in late 1919, the political department immediately organized a series of concerts, rallies, lectures, plays, and film showings as a way of fighting indiscipline among the troops.[27] Later, in 1922 the authorities created the obligatory political lesson (*politchas*), but even then all work in the clubs was voluntary. The soldiers were not supposed to be forced to join in cultural work of any kind.[28] For this reason political instructors set great store by any method that would help them attract and entertain the soldiers.

Those in charge in the clubs and political departments in the army were well aware that they had a more or less captive audience. Here was an easy place to experiment with different forms of political education:

> The conditions in the army are particularly favorable [for political education work]. On the one hand, we have the current military breathing space, and, on the other, the fact of compulsory communal living, concentrations of people, and military discipline.[29]

Following up on a resolution of the Eighth Party Congress (March 1919), cultural education workers insisted that they should "turn the barracks into a real military-political school, creating an atmosphere of constant, lively, principled work, awakening people's inquisitiveness, answering their needs, and filling their leisure, thus raising the general cultural level."[30]

"Cultural-educational work" (later renamed political education [*polit-prosvet*]) was designed to encompass a wide range of functions—literacy programs, general education, public lectures, libraries, reading rooms, and clubs. These organizations were supposed to provide both culture in the broadest sense and a political understanding that was new for most of the soldiers. Above all, they were to combat "the creative propaganda" of the enemy.[31]

The Political Administration of the Army (PUR), moreover, was willing to spend significant amounts of money on cultural and education work on the fronts. In fact, one striking feature of the budget materials available is that virtually all the money was being spent on work at the front rather than on the maintenance of the central apparatus.[32] This may be one more reason why innovations in political education methods were occurring principally in the field rather than in Moscow.

The numbers of schools and clubs in the army grew rapidly over the course of 1919 and 1920. On January 1, 1919, no schools, theaters, or libraries had yet been organized in the army and only 32 clubs. By October 1 of the same year there were 3,800 schools and 1,315 clubs. The number of theaters had reached 250. Libraries had jumped to 2,392 in the same time period.[33] A year later (November 15, 1920) the numbers of clubs had risen to 2,430.[34] By the end of 1921, when local political education organizations (politprosvety) had widely developed their activities, there were some 475,000 people working in political education all over the Russian Republic.[35]

By late 1919 and early 1920 the end of war was in sight. The political arm of the army now claimed a special responsibility to prepare soldiers to return to their villages as representatives of Soviet power. As the First National Congress of Political Workers in the Red Army resolved in December 1919, the Red Army must become "a true bearer of communist culture among the peaceful civilian population."[36] This meant "trying to eliminate sluggishness and passivity among the soldiers and making them into citizens."[37] The returning soldiers would be the messengers of the regime: if they themselves had a bad impression of the new Soviet order, they would convey that to their fellow villagers at home. If, on the contrary, they returned home as organizers with a positive view, they would help villagers overcome their ignorance.[38] They could also organize Soviet-style meetings and institutions in their villages.

The political instructors finally had longer periods of time when the army was stationary and they could try out new methods.[39] Earlier, when units in the field had tried to put on skits for political purposes, they had had to do so between skirmishes and occasionally with bullets flying past.[40]

They now began writing articles and holding conferences discussing new methods they could use with their soldiers. They had already come up with some innovations: posters and woodcuts (lubki) showing deserters, lice, and other "enemies" of the revolution; group readings out loud of army newspapers and leaflets; handwritten wall newspapers (stengazety); staged debates between atheists and priests; lectures, conversations, and readings on topics "of real life" and local conditions such as epidemics, anti-Semitism, and partisan warfare. They also tried more interactive forms of political-cultural education as well: tableaux vivants ("living scenes," which involved acting out historical events and then freezing the action), pantomimes, charades, puppet shows, buffoonery, caricature, red and black boards (indicating those in particularly good favor and those accused of misdemeanors), and, beginning around the same time as the agitation trials, so-called living newspapers (in which participants acted out the news of the day).[41]

The political instructors were concerned to find ways to respond to what they perceived as the psychology of their soldiers.[42] They openly acknowledged that their soldiers shared the general conviction of many peasants in this period that "Bolsheviks" and "communists" were different things.[43] They knew that many—perhaps the majority—of the soldiers were hostile, wishing they had never been torn from their villages.[44] They disagreed as to whether soldiers and workers had a real thirst for knowledge or were instead plagued by "complete indifference." Most agreed, however, that the soldiers wanted principally to learn what was practical.[45] As Trotsky explained, political instruction should begin with the most basic topics such as "correct polishing of boots" and only from there move inductively to more complex reports from the Communist International.[46] Numerous reports from the field rejected "empty phrase-mongering" in favor of more accessibility, more statistics, facts, and diagrams in political lectures.[47] Political education instructors were especially enjoined to organize mass amateur activism (samo-deiatel'nost') in order to raise the cultural level of the soldiers.[48]

Army authorities had concerns as well that the new recruits often had no experience or knowledge of the February and October Revolutions. In 1920–21 the recruits called up had typically been born in 1900–1901, which meant that they had been teenagers in 1917, many of them in regions far from the capital cities. From the point of view of the army command, this "raw, ignorant peasant mass" had somehow to be turned into conscious fighters and citizens. They had to learn to put behind them the superstitions and prejudices, stagnation and passive resistance of the villages from which they had come.[49]

Theater was universally praised by its proponents for its effects on the emotions of viewers. Many Soviet people had never even seen the theater before.[50] Cultural staffs sought to stir up the recruits with new feelings and new thoughts.[51] Many in the army command hoped that the clubs and theater performances would bring order into the soldiers' lives and help to socialize them. Above all, political theater could be used to "work over" [obrabatyvat'] the "inert, unmoving masses who are closed off in their interests and their complacency and who continuously resist [outside intervention]."[52] By the fall of 1920 many railroad political units, for example, were spending more on theater of all kinds than on any other cultural work.[53]

Prosecutor. Shadow woodcut. From E. A. D'iakonova, *The Trial of Smut Fungus* (*Sud nad golovnei*) (Leningrad, 1925), 63.

Agitation trials from their inception seemed an ideal way to get the soldiers involved and active.[54] They were inherently dramatic; they provided a good fight, if only a verbal one, between the prosecution and the defense. The court might give a death sentence to the fictional deserter or acquit him on grounds of his ignorance. Either way such a trial involved a contest. Even when peasant soldiers were tired from their military training and despite their short attention spans, they could understand and be drawn into a trial.[55] They loved too to see their fellow soldiers on stage.[56] Trial organizers were proud of the fact that they could draw in their viewers and through vivid visual examples help them come to particular conclusions that they might not otherwise have come to on their own.[57]

Trials could also be used to draw soldiers away from light, amateur plays on frivolous topics, which drama circles in all the units seemed to be performing in a veritable "theater epidemic."[58] Amateur theater was growing up like a weed, and some theater authorities were not happy with this at all.[59] Mock trials could bring a political dimension to the performances of these drama groups and get them involved in discussions of what organizers considered more serious issues of the day.

In staging agitation and propaganda at the end of the Civil War, it was no longer sufficient to simply beat up fat puppets representing capitalists and imperialists. Now the army and civilian authorities were committed to a much more serious socialization and education process. The trials emerged during this sea change as a didactic tool, a way of reaching the masses, presenting them with new ideas, and teaching them new ways of thinking, all while engaging and entertaining them.

Defense. Shadow woodcut. From E. A. D'iakonova, *The Trial of Smut Fungus (Sud nad golovnei)* (Leningrad, 1925), 66.

KHARKOV, 1919: SOME PRACTICAL LESSONS

A group of soldiers sat around a small, smoky stove. Many of the "students" were absent. Some were on watch; others were on detail. Still others had gone for supplies or out to requisition grain. The leader of the group asked them to act out a meeting of peasants who were organizing cultural work in the village and working on the rules for a new village club. Some played the parts of the proponents of the club; others played the "obscurantists" who opposed it. One played an "old man" (aged fifty!) who stubbornly insisted that his ancestors had had no such tomfoolery and it was not necessary now. The youngsters grew riled up and nearly came to blows.[60]

The organizer was none other than Boris Osipovich Borovich, whom we met in chapter 1. He was now working at the military-instruction courses in cultural enlightenment in Kharkov. For Borovich a principal goal of such a playacted meeting was to have the soldier-students themselves play the leading roles, especially that of the chair of the meeting. Then they could learn from their mistakes. The other players, too, he felt, were freer, less constrained in their playacting when one of their own was chairing. The organizer, by contrast, should play an ordinary person at the meeting. Without intervening too much, he could occasionally make a point of order so as to remind them all how the meeting should be run.

From playacting such a meeting, it was but a short step to putting on a trial. Two weeks after that first skit, Borovich asked the soldiers to think of a subject for a mock trial. They came up with the idea of trying a peasant accused of murdering a grain requisition official. In order to make the trial more dramatic, they gave the fictional murderer two sons, one fighting in the Red Army, the other on the side of the Whites. From the beginning they

Unconscious and His Daughter.
Shadow woodcut. From E. A.
D'iakonova, *The Trial of Smut Fungus* (*Sud nad golovnei*) (Leningrad,
1925), 24.

agreed that the defendant would not deny that he had taken the life of the grain official. Still, the question remained whether he should be punished. Here the students found themselves exploring many of the classic ethical issues of any society. Does society have the right to take a life, even of a murderer? Should the fact that the country was at war affect the sentencing since this was a time of danger? Should, on the other hand, the goal be correction and deterrence, in which case it was not necessary to execute the murderer? What about the fact that he had committed the murder under the influence of strong emotions? Should that have a mitigating effect on the sentence? What about the role of circumstances, the economic inequality of society, and social injustice? To what extent is someone who commits a crime a product of his surroundings and circumstances?

Ultimately the court decided on a conditional sentence, given the circumstances of the crime and the defense mounted by the accused's fellow villagers. His property would be confiscated for the benefit of the family of the murdered man, but he himself would not be executed. The organizers explained, however, that the final sentence did not matter as much as the overall process, the fact that the actors and even the audience were thoroughly engaged in the play. The goal was not to pass high-sounding, abstract "resolutions" (as was common in those days), but rather to begin with a conversation about everyday issues. From what was familiar the organizers felt they could move to what was more general, more abstract. Using abstract terms would only "confuse the untried [*neiskushennyi*] viewer, close his lips." The goal was to help everyone present become involved, to get them to speak out.[61]

Perhaps the most innovative of all the improvised agitation trials in this earliest Civil War period was *The Trial of Jewry,* staged by Borovich and his students. Borovich was himself Jewish, as his students knew. Soon after their first agitation trial, several Jewish soldiers came to him to express their concerns about hidden anti-Semitism in the army and their fears that it might explode one day. They asked to put on a debate as a way to draw out the peasants and get them to express their views. Borovich and the students agreed that it was never worthwhile to "force an ulcer inward." Better to bring it out and have a public airing of everyone's views.[62]

As it turned out, the soldiers had recently been required to read a book called "Mendel' of Gdansk" by Polish author Maria Konopnicka (1842– 1910).[63] Originally they were supposed to have held an ordinary reading of the book. The soldiers soon decided, however, that they would organize a debate around the book in the form of a trial. This would be one of their "show exercises" (*pokazatel'nye zaniatii*).[64]

By the time of the performance they had thirty people involved in the play, some acting as witnesses for the prosecution and others as defense witnesses. They chose every kind of witness they could think of, a Christian businessman, a landlord, a factory owner, a police officer, and many others, all from the tsarist era. In their first discussions of the play, however, they ran up against the problem that no one wanted to play the prosecution witnesses since they did not want to become known as anti-Semites.

Finally, one of the Jewish students broke the ice by agreeing to testify for the prosecution, and others followed suit. The soldier actors could voice anti-Semitic views they knew to be common when they were just playing roles; then they didn't have to appear to be speaking in their own voices. Soon the students had cobbled together an indictment based on prevailing anti-Semitic sentiments (Jews as misers, lovers of easy money, shirkers of military service, profiteers, deceivers). Meanwhile, the defense, which was deliberately made up primarily of Christian students, parried every point made by the prosecution. They showed the terrible lack of rights of the Jews, the hardships of their lives both in and outside the Pale of Settlement, the horrors of the pogroms in Kishinev, Odessa, and Gomel. They demonstrated the underpinnings of anti-Semitism in tsarist policies and the ways the government used it as a safety valve for people's larger discontents.

The audience followed this "single combat" (*poedinok*) with rapt attention. According to Borovich, the defenders of Jewry were stronger intellectually than the prosecution. The audience sympathized with the defense. The organizers were not initially certain, however, that they had won. Given that they had a particular result that they wanted to affirm, they considered holding open voting; in that case, they knew, those who were wavering would vote with the majority, thus confirming the "correct answer." Nonetheless, they were sufficiently confident that they could "read" the audience that they decided to hold secret voting (which would give a more accurate view of people's real sentiments). In prepared written ballots they asked the audience whether they now thought Jews "were guilty of what they were usually charged with"; and if they were in fact guilty, whether they deserved punishment, including and up to pogroms. Of the dozens of ballots returned (the exact number is not given), only eight found the defendants guilty, and not one said they deserved punishment through pogroms.[65]

For organizers like Borovich, the trial form had obvious benefits for work in extracurricular education with uneducated audiences. Lectures were too dry, even when the speakers brought out the latest technology of "magic lanterns" (slide shows). Audiences needed plays that appealed to their emotions, gripped them with suspense, and drew them in.[66] Borovich's account of the origins of the dramatizations, including this *Trial of Jewry*, was that they "appeared among us neither accidentally nor on purpose [*ne sluchaino i ne nadumanno*]. They were somehow born naturally in our lecture-conversations in which the students themselves took an active part."[67]

Other instructors in military-political courses also began staging trials of fictional characters in stories that the soldier-students were reading, though none sound as creative as Borovich's *Trial of Jewry*. Favorite stories for dramatizing trials were Gorky's "Vas'ka Krasnyi," Chekhov's "Zloumyshlennik" ("The Culprit"), Stepan Kravchinskii's "Andrei Kozhukhov," Veresaev's "Strashnaia smert' nevinnogo cheloveka" ("The Terrible Death of an Innocent Man"), Gorky's "V stepi" ("In the Steppe"), Kuprin and Iablonovskii's "Konokrady" ("Horse Thieves"), and Serafimovich's "Strelochnik" ("The Switchman").[68] All were stories that involved crimes and moral dilemmas. When Denis Grigorev from Chekhov's story "The Culprit," for example, was accused of taking bolts from the railway tracks, an action that could have caused a serious accident, the audience at the dramatized story had to consider how an illiterate and politically unconscious villager, however "moral" he might be, could cause untold harm to his village and society through his ignorance.

The literary trials did not spread as far in the army as some other forms of agitation trials because they apparently involved too much "high culture." Peasant soldiers and workers had not always read the stories involved. They were not prepared to engage in critical discussions of the characters and their moral choices, despite their teachers' high hopes.[69] Not until the mid-1920s were such literary trials revived in civilian clubs in what became known as "evenings of worker criticism."

Avant-garde poets and theater activists, however, kept up an interest in literature trials for a longer time. Mikhail Bakhtin, the famous philosopher, put on mock trials in the provincial city of Vitebsk in the former Pale of Settlement in 1919. On several occasions he played the role of defender, managing to win his case both for Khlestakov in Gogol's *Inspector General* and for Katerina Maslova in Tolstoy's *Resurrection*.[70]

In mid-November 1920, as mentioned in chapter 1, a number of poets created trials of each other's work and literary styles: *The Trial of the Imag-*

inists; The Trial of Russian Literature; and *The Literary Trial of Contemporary Poetry.*[71] On November 14, 1921, the Bol'shoi Dramaticheskii Teatr in Petrograd staged a *Trial of Raskol'nikov.* Even though it was panned for its poor acting, it showed how Dostoevsky's protagonist could be tried for murdering the pawnbroker.[72] Sometimes soldiers' and workers' clubs also organized trials around plays that had just been performed.[73]

COLLECTIVE CREATIVITY

Borovich's trials engaged the whole student population, giving them roles to play and positions to take in the ensuing debates. Many educators felt that all exercises in the army should have such a "collective character." By taking issues of the day, the collective could draw its members into active involvement. If they acted out the holding of public meetings, for example, they could learn to grapple with concrete, everyday problems and also learn to work as a group.[74]

One instructor working in Kostroma (a city on the upper Volga), P. A. Bliakhin, used dramatizations widely in the First Soviet School-Commune (a high school) in his lessons on the study of official decrees. The students worked out the plots themselves. They then performed the most successful dramatizations of court trials and of meetings of workers' deputies in local workers' clubs.[75]

Vladimir A. Nevskii, the second librarian we met in chapter 1, now argued forcefully in favor of dramatizations of trials and meetings as a teaching device. In March 1920 he and his students put on dramatizations for the Day of the Paris Commune. For Nevskii, these new methods were clearly preferable to the old: "Given the fact that one can dramatize literally anything and everything, dramatizations have recently begun to be practiced in the place of the rallies and political lectures that everyone is sick of."[76]

Nevskii expected the collective character of exercises to reflect what he called "the reality of social life." Participants should "coordinate their feelings and actions with the feelings and actions of others." This would correspond to the peasant ideal of solidarity, *v mire s mirom,* which meant "with the collective in the world." Students should take up the issues they were most concerned about, especially those in which different points of view came into conflict, from local village problems upsetting one faction of people to "national problems occupying public, political thought." Dramatizing a meeting or a trial, in Nevskii's view, should play the same role as a science experiment.[77] His views continued to resemble those of progressive educators who advocated laboratory schools and experimental methods.

Nikolai Karzhanskii (b. 1879), a contemporary of Borovich and Nevskii, wrote extensively about collective dramaturgy as well, comparing his work to developing a "theater without plays."[78] Beginning in late 1919, several actors founded a dramatic studio linked with the Proletcult movement in Smolensk. Karzhanskii joined them in March 1920 as their "playwright." Together they focused on improvisation. The whole collective composed the plays, not on paper but directly on the set. This was a perfect answer, Karzhanskii and the others felt, to the crippling lack of revolutionary plays.[79] A group of amateur actors, especially a collective such as a group of soldiers serving in one unit, could get together, decide on a central problem, assign roles, and work out the scenes. Improvised trial scenes were among the easiest to put on because the plot and characters followed directly from the nature of the indictment and because the plot had a fixed ceremonial development. This, in Karzhanskii's book, was a perfect framework for "free playacting" (vol'noe litsedeistvo).[80]

In July 1920 Karzhanskii and his amateur actors began working on a Trial of Pilsudskii (the Polish head of state who led the Polish Army against the Bolsheviks in the spring of 1920).[81] Although they never performed their trial, they did work out a range of "types" that each actor would play. Their first priority was to make the play "artistic." Through high-quality acting and audience involvement they felt they could attain their political ends. Karzhanskii was particularly proud of a classic theater trick of having a few actors strategically placed in the audience who appeared to react viscerally to what was happening on stage, booing, hissing, crying out in indignation, thus drawing in the rest of the audience. Although this might have initially been a purely theatrical technique, it was one that political activists and the organizers of later show trials came to employ throughout the 1920s, manipulating audiences to try to bring them to conclusions the authorities wanted them to have.

COLLECTIVE DISCIPLINE

Literary trials and "free playacting" were not the only focus of instructors, however. Desertion was on the rise, and in the spring of 1920 it was at the highest levels Red Army authorities had ever seen. Soldiers were convinced that the war was virtually over, and they saw no reason to wait for formal demobilization. For the authorities, however, desertion was a serious matter. No one worried too much about legal niceties. Any military commissar could arrest and bring someone to trial for desertion.[82]

But if legality was not at issue, education and propaganda were. By order of the Central Commission on the Fight against Desertion (created in December 1918), sessions of the military tribunals (real trials, not fictional ones) examining cases of desertion were held in theaters and other large halls with great ceremony, in order to have the maximum possible educational (*vospitatel'nyi*) effect on those present.[83] In the villages and cities the military authorities organized what they sometimes called *sudy mitingi*, or trial-rallies. The focus of these rallies was not so much on the individual deserters as on the apparent causes of their wrongdoing: their petty bourgeois moods, their ignorance and weakness of will. Once a deserter was convicted in this public forum, he was usually given a conditional sentence so he could be sent off to the front to "expiate his guilt."[84]

Army authorities claimed that these trials were important not so much for the actual punishment of the individual as for the public demonstration of the fact that desertion would not be tolerated. Both those on trial and those in the audience were to be convinced that Soviet power saw the guilty as people who had violated laws because of their ignorance, but who, having repented (*raskaiavshiesia*), would be given a chance in action to make amends for (*zagladit'*) their guilt before the workers' and peasants' state.[85]

A decree of May 29, 1920, moreover, put the political and cultural workers themselves on the spot. They were now told that they would be brought to trial if they were found "guilty of inaction and nonfulfillment of instructions on the fight against desertion."[86] This was repeated during the campaign against Wrangel in the fall of 1920, when all communists were told they had to take part in agitation campaigns or face a party court trial and possible expulsion. The political departments of the armies, moreover, had to report weekly to their superiors on the work they were doing to agitate the troops.[87] In other words, the political instructors now had every incentive to find ways to demonstrate that they, too, were fighting desertion and potential desertion.

Mock trials of deserters also began to be performed at recruitment stations and during agitation campaigns such as The Week of the Front in January 1920. The instructors' stated goal in staging these trials was to "brand with shame" (*kleimit' pozorom*) deserters and their accomplices.[88]

On December 8, 1920, a railway workers' club in Smolensk staged *The Trial of the Deserter*. The fictional deserter in this trial did not get off so lightly as his real counterparts (the ones who were simply sent off to the front to atone). In the account published in a Smolensk newspaper, the elected tribunal of five soldiers voted to condemn the defendant to twenty years' hard labor. "Let him serve time," the soldier judges allegedly commented. "In prison he'll straighten out and understand how a person should live in the Soviet Republic."[89] The soldier actors may, of course, never have said anything of the kind. Yet it is clear that this is the message that the newspapers, acting on behalf of the authorities, wanted to report. Although there is no hard evidence to support this, one wonders if it was in fact easier for political and cultural authorities to stage *fictional* trials, where they did not need any actual legal authority, than to stage court trials, which at least in theory should still have included military judges and some formal procedural defense.

AGITATING THE SOLDIERS

The majority of Civil War–era dramatic trials were premised on *agitating* the audience. Soldiers put on trials of the White Army general Kolchak and trials of the "white-green" (that is, independent resistance) movements in the Caucasus.[90] The cultural authorities who were staging agitation trials wrote of their hope that such performances would "shake up" their viewers and "push the masses out of their inertia." With any luck the trials would be "contagious," sparking discussions that would go on long into the night after the formal performance was over.[91]

At the height of certain military campaigns soldiers and workers were called on to stage trials of enemies in order to rally their fellows. The workers in the city of Tver in western Russia put on a *Trial of Upper-Crust Poland* in June 1920 as a way of blaming the Polish elite and firing up the soldiers to do battle.[92] Karzhanskii, as we have seen, made preparations for a *Trial of Pilsudski* in early July 1920, just when the Red Army troops were beginning their offensive toward Minsk.[93]

The agitation trial that received the most attention, however, was the *Trial of Wrangel*, performed in a Cossack village in the Kuban in the northern Caucasus in the fall of 1920. Several sources reported on this trial, claiming that this was the first attempt to hold "a mass political theatrical performance on a purely agitational topic."[94] It was performed on an outdoor stage with some ten thousand soldiers in the audience.

The story told in the press was that in October 1920 the theater director, Vsevolod Meyerhold, received a letter from the director of clubs and theater in an army division stationed in the northern Caucasus.[95] Several units stationed there had just defeated the White general Baron Petr Wrangel when he tried to land at Novorossiisk.[96] The club director wrote to Meyerhold to tell him that after the defeat of Wrangel, several of his staff had decided to carry out a mass agitation campaign to publicize what had happened. This campaign took the form of a trial of Wrangel with roles improvised by the participants in the recent battle.

Since the trial was not elaborate, participants were directed to work without a prepared script. The audience apparently responded viscerally to the trial and interrupted the actor playing Wrangel with cries of "You lie! You won't fool us, you bloodsucker."[97] The actor claimed he feared for his life in the face of such angry mobs. The final sentence was pronounced as a call to arms: "Wrangel must be destroyed. This sentence is to be carried out immediately by all the toilers of Soviet Russia." Soon other regiments were attempting to perform similar public trials of the man known as the "black Baron."[98]

The political staff involved in the attack on Wrangel included both Dmitrii Furmanov (1891–1926), soon to become famous as the author of the Civil War novel *Chapaev,* and Vsevolod Vishnevskii (1900–1951), a young political officer who was beginning to write plays. Both had worked on revolutionary tribunals and both had loved the theater since childhood; both were just beginning to write works of fiction.[99] A third important figure was Anna Furmanova, Dmitrii's wife (1894–1941), who had been putting on plays in Chapaev's division even when the troops were at the front.[100]

Almost immediately after the first performance of the *Trial of Wrangel,* Furmanov wrote an article on the trial boasting of its virtues as a new form of agitation and propaganda. He called as well for creating more such "public political trials" (*obshchestvenno-politicheskie sudy*) using "fresh events."[101]

Vishnevskii, at the time a political instructor in the Black Sea fleet, explained many years later his sense of why it had been important to stage a mock trial of Baron Wrangel:

> We had to show the Cossacks who Wrangel was. Communists became playwrights and wrote plays. Our hearts were pounding, but we did it. We called in the audience. Who was this audience? 10,000 viewers with their families came on machine-gun carts, on supply carts, armed, with their women. They came to see the Bolsheviks' play.[102]

Wrangel at this time had only about 35,000 troops at his disposal, while the Red Army had grown to five million. It was thus not his military might that the Red Army leaders feared. Rather, it was his potential influence among the Cossacks and other peoples of the region.[103] Throughout the spring and summer Lenin had sent a continuous stream of telegrams to Ordzhonikidze, Stalin, and Smilga, asking about the state of the troops in the Kuban.[104] In early August the Caucasus Biuro, which the party had set up in the spring, reported from Rostov that the whole Kuban had been overtaken with uprisings.[105] Lenin wrote urgently to Dzerzhinskii: "If we have an uprising in the Kuban, our whole politics will collapse. Under no circumstances should we allow an uprising; spare neither people nor efforts."[106] Trotsky, too, was enormously worried about what the Kuban Cossacks would do if Wrangel managed a victory.[107]

Political control in the northern Caucasus region also took on particular importance in 1920 because the area's rich grain resources were among the very few not affected by the bad harvest then overtaking the agricultural provinces of the central Volga region and threatening much of the nation with famine.[108] At the same time White propaganda efforts in the northern Caucasus in the spring and summer of 1920 were intensifying. Not only did Wrangel's army officers encourage troop defections from the Reds; they also made special efforts to train agitators, print newspapers, drop leaflets from airplanes, and distribute proclamations claiming that the Bolsheviks were panicking and giving news of the Whites' recent "conversion" to ideas of land reform.[109]

The Trial of Wrangel allowed the political authorities to play up their military victory and turn it into a political lesson. Furmanov commented that trials of this kind were a way to combat "the whole heavy artillery of our enemies, especially the Mensheviks whose conclusions at first glance so often seem logically based, serious and fair." The best way to crush those conclusions was not with empty exhortations but rather with "the facts of our history of three years of struggle and three years of building."[110]

The following spring (1921) Vishnevskii, who was stationed on the Black Sea only fifty miles from Furmanov's unit, tried his hand at a similar *Trial of the Kronstadt Mutineers* a short time after the real uprising of the Kronstadt sailors outside Petrograd. In a retrospective letter (the date of which is unknown) Vishnevskii described what happened:

> We learned about the Kronstadt mutiny just about the day it happened. The press published government information. In Novorossiisk in the Eastern Sector of the Black Sea we were very anxious. There were lots of sailors in Novorossiisk. . . . We had to immediately influence their moods, introduce clarity, and demonstrate the loyalty of the sailors to the revolution.[111]

On March 28, 1921, he wrote to his father. The Kronstadt uprising, he said, was "Made in France"; foreign agitators were stirring up the sailors. Like Furmanov, Vishnevskii was well aware that his soldiers no longer had any desire to attend rallies: "You can no longer go out [to them] with a ready, fiery, ringing speech. Instead you give a report and they pick it to pieces, with no applause." Staged trials, he told his father, were becoming a normal part of his work as a political instructor, though, interestingly, he still expressed a wish that he were off doing something "more serious."[112]

Vishnevskii had particular reason to be familiar with public trials as one of his duties during the Civil War had been to serve as public prosecutor of the Revolutionary Tribunal of the Black Sea Fleet. Even before that, in 1918, he had worked for the Cheka and had participated in the suppression of a number of uprisings, which also, he claimed later, gave him information for this trial.[113] When the order came from above to create a show trial, he commented that he already knew what he was doing (*ia eto delo znal*).[114]

It is, of course, pure speculation to imagine what was going on in Vishnevskii's mind when his bosses in the political department of the Black Sea Fleet asked him to write something to calm his sailors, who would soon learn of the uprising of their brother sailors in Kronstadt. Still, we know that there had been attacks on political officers during the fighting in the Civil War. Black Sea sailors shared many of the complaints of their northern brothers about the "Commissarocracy," the lack of democracy, and the lack of winter uniforms. The immediate enemy had been vanquished. Wrangel had been pushed into the sea. Why did they need to continue to serve? Vishnevskii's goal, as he told a group of journalists in 1948, was to show his audience what had happened in Kronstadt and to try to get the audience to "condemn that kind of people" (*chtoby auditoriia osudila liudei takogo tipa*).[115]

Unfortunately, the text of the *Trial of the Kronstadt Mutineers* has not survived. It was, by all accounts, Vishnevskii's first play. Vishnevskii, like Furmanov, was anxious to prove his literary talents, to put them to use in the service of the revolution. Yet he must also have been anxious to save his own skin, to present the hardships of the day as the fault of foreign intervention, and to help prevent such an uprising from breaking out in the Black Sea. It is not surprising, then, that he himself played the leading role of a sailor defendant who repents his political mistakes and in the process denounces the foreigners who incited the uprising.[116]

The mid-level political staff in the army and navy—young political instructors like Borovich, Nevskii, Karzhanskii, Vishnevskii, Furmanov, and Furmanova—thus appear to have been the ones who pioneered the adaptation of literary trials to political subjects. They had multiple motivations: conviction, fear (of being attacked by their men, and also of losing their jobs if the political administration of the army [PUR] was disbanded), genuine impulses to creativity, and a sense (however true or erroneous) that this was the kind of propaganda to which the masses would respond. They had to answer to their superiors in the political chain of command, to their commanding military officers, and also, significantly, to their soldiers, who would attend "voluntary" exercises and club events only if the latter were at least minimally attractive and interesting. Through concrete if fictional trials of individuals (rather than of abstract ideas and issues), the *politruki* attempted both to attract audiences and to convey a new vision of politics, as well as of correct moral and social behavior.

The Bolsheviks could beat the White armies militarily. They could even use force against the increasingly numerous peasant uprisings. But they could not win over the population unless they offered them something more than war and hardship. The agitation trials thus presented a moral agenda that involved not just beating the enemy but also showing the collective creativity and discipline of the soldiers themselves.

Ultimately, the trials provided a highly malleable form of political education. As a template they could be filled with different content depending on the current issues of the day. They could be performed at all levels in the armed forces. Above all, they seem to have captured a successful formula of entertainment plus education plus discipline. This in turn allowed them to last throughout the decade of the 1920s while other "new forms" of agitation being tried out in these Civil War years (political pantomimes, charades, puppet shows, etc.) seem to have died out rather quickly. The agitation trials were dramatic, even occasionally melodramatic. They could serve as a forum for new ideas and scientific knowledge. They were inexpensive to perform and required relatively little expertise. Finally, they could be adapted to any issue of concern to the community. Thus, they could both attract audiences because of their inherent drama and satisfy the requirements of the political instructors' superiors that they had to perform a certain number of amateur events each month.

THE TRIAL OF LENIN

On April 17, 1920, the railroad workers in a Moscow suburb held what *Pravda* called a *Trial of Lenin*. It was a Saturday night, the eve of a holiday, and an audience of three hundred came to see what was going on. The court called witnesses for the prosecution and the defense. Local communists brought charges against Lenin and the Communist Party. Ultimately, Lenin was acquitted, and the audience applauded.[1]

The anonymous report in *Pravda* never explicitly states that this was a mock trial. Instead it matter-of-factly describes how the local political organization of the Moscow station on the Vindava railway line "organized" a trial (*ustroili sud*). The report appears not on the front page of *Pravda* under a banner headline but rather on page two, under the rubric "Workers' Lives." No officials of Lenin's government presided over the trial, only the local political organizations of the railroad and the neighborhood. A year later Nikolai Karzhanskii referred to the *Trial of Lenin* as "an ordinary event."[2]

Yet on the other hand, this was clearly a staged performance. The audience clapped at the conclusion of the evening and allegedly listened "with great interest" to this "new form of political conversation." Local communists played the key roles for a noncommunist audience who came after work. Moreover, it was timed so that it coincided with the eve of Easter Sunday, the anniversary of the Lena shootings in 1912, and Lenin's fiftieth birthday.[3] The report in *Pravda* appeared on the very day of his birthday (April 22, 1920).[4]

This mock *Trial of Lenin* was, it seems, a deliberately new kind of spectacle designed to show, through staged polemics, the correctness of the path taken by Lenin and the Bolsheviks. In this sense it was a revolutionary version of what historian Richard Wortman has called a "scenario of power."[5] Through a dramatized (and controlled) contest of wills Lenin and other heroes of the day could dispel rumors and criticisms. Above all, they could demonstrate in ritualized form that the people's court, the voice of the people, vindicated them.

By 1920 the Bolshevik leadership of Soviet Russia had become adept at creating participatory political pageantry. They mounted parades and progovernment demonstrations. They reenacted leading historical events such as the storming of the Winter Palace. They inaugurated public ceremonies around elections.[6]

The agitation trials, which had been created in the Red Army to discuss literary characters and stir up the troops against external enemies, now began to be used to highlight the work of those who had made the revolution. These new trial defendants were given an opportunity to combat the ideas of their enemies in the context of mock court proceedings. They appeared to submit themselves to the will of the people, only to be acquitted and thus ritually vindicated. This by definition helped to elevate them to the status of heroes for all to emulate.

HEROIC TRIALS IN 1920–23

In the months after this first *Trial of Lenin, Pravda* carried reports of a number of mock trials held for agitational purposes: trials of the Russian Communist Party, of the October Revolution, of the Soviet authorities, of Lenin and Trotsky, of the Red Army and Red commanders. While trials of negative role models were also coming to vogue at this time and would eventually become dominant, these early political trials (1920–23) are striking for the large numbers of them that proceeded against the *heroes* of the Revolution.

These heroic trials, as I call them, contain real charges being brought against leading individuals and organizations at the time in popular conversation, in rumors, and in the émigré press.[7] In several trials the Communist Party is charged with illegally seizing power in October 1917.[8] In another trial it is indicted for ruining industry, expropriating factories, closing newspapers, and introducing poor quality, inexperienced management.[9] The Soviet government, in turn, is put on trial for allowing foreigners to lease concessions and in so doing, for "betraying the principles of communism."[10] The "new woman" is charged with betraying the family.[11] The year 1920 is prosecuted in mock fashion for continuing the Civil War.[12] In other words, in this early period of Soviet history genuine complaints and concerns were being given some voice in these staged performances.

Some of the charges brought were quite elaborate. The instruction for one *Trial of the Communist Party,* for example, lists charges against the defendant on three different levels. One prosecution witness charges the party with theoretical matters: the destruction of the principles of democracy, the establishment of a dictatorship over the proletariat, and the incorrect organization of labor. A second brings the "philistine" objections of someone defending only his own interests. A third dwells on cold, hunger, bureaucratism and other hardships in people's lives.[13]

The trials thus stage a contest in which popular grumblings and criticisms could be voiced and then proven false. As one commentator noted in *Pravda,* such mock trials were useful in combating rumors that undercut the authority of the government, especially when many of the factories had ground to a halt. Otherwise workers easily fell under the influence of "the cunning minions of the bourgeoisie, people whispering on the sly."[14]

These early trials made the people's courtroom the legitimating organization for judgments about successes and failures in the political sphere. The workers of the city of Tver, for example, found the Polish upper class and bourgeoisie guilty of attacking Soviet Russia in *A Trial of Upper-Crust Poland.*[15] In the trials of the Russian Communist Party and the Soviet government, the workers of a particular neighborhood in Moscow (Sokol'niki) and the party cell of the Higher Military Chemical School were the ones who passed judgment.

Political instructors began improvising these trials at a time when dissatisfaction was at its highest. The Civil War was coming to a close, yet the population was continuing to experience untold hardships. In February 1921, for example, *A Trial of Lenin and Trotsky* was held in the notoriously volatile province of Tambov, at the very height of the peasant uprisings that soon were to stimulate the party to introduce the New Economic Policy.[16]

If rulers in ancient Rome offered their subjects bread and circuses to distract them, Soviet rulers offered theirs a different kind of "circus," the mock political trial. This political trial could engage the audience, present it with a dramatic contest, and demonstrate that the new rulers had emerged victorious.

MULTIPLE ACCOUNTS OF THE TRIAL OF LENIN

The original *Trial of Lenin,* like many of the first agitation trials, is difficult to evaluate because of the lack of an actual script. Like much agitprop theater at the time, it was improvised by participants who had only a general working outline to go on. Nonetheless, three different accounts of the trial are extant: the newspaper account in *Pravda,* dated April 22, 1920; a handwritten report preserved in the files of the political department of the Vindava railway line, dated April 26, 1920; and a memoir account by a contemporary witness, Sofia Vinogradskaia, published in the reformist journal *Novyi mir* in October 1957.[17]

The *Pravda* account, a mere four paragraphs long, provides only the sketchiest of information. The fact of Lenin's acquittal is stated, but the actual charges are not given. Nor are the speeches of the prosecution, defense, and witnesses reproduced, though the witnesses are listed.

The report from the political department of the Vindava Railroad is written in neat pencil and dated April 26, 1920. It was apparently sent to the head of the railroad political department for this line and to the political arm of the railroads, Glavpolitput.[18] In addition to the information given in *Pravda*, it mentions the names of the six communists who put on the trial. It also introduces a new term, calling the event a "politico-critical trial-debate" (*politiko-kriticheskii sud-disput*). This term suggests the trial's close kinship to public debates (*disputy*), which had been popular since before the revolution on a wide range of subjects, including religion and atheism, morality, and social change. The local report also claims that such a form of agitation enlivened the viewers, "developing in the audience a critical view [*kritika*] of positions put forth by the orators." The political director's report insists that the indictment "was very harshly drawn." The Menshevik witness "went so overboard" (*nastol'ko perestaralsia*) that he "created a strong mood in favor of the prosecution." Only the detailed speech of the defense was able to "unmask the complete hopelessness of the bourgeois order and the shakiness of the policies of the defensists and conciliators."[19]

Sofia Vinogradskaia, the author of the memoir account, was then a young journalist (b. 1904) working in the *Pravda* editorial offices.[20] She claims that the railroad workers "unexpectedly" (*neozhidano*) decided to put on the trial, then sent a report to *Pravda* for publication. When Maria Ulianova, Lenin's sister and managing editor of *Pravda*, received the report, she took it home to Lenin for his approval, after which the newspaper published it.

Vinogradskaia makes much of the fact that the trial took place in the context of Lenin's fiftieth birthday. Lenin, she claims, was threatening to boycott the party planned for him at the headquarters of the Moscow Communist Party. Yet at the same time, evenings (*vechera*) in his honor were "springing up spontaneously" (*stikhiino to i delo voznikali*) all over Moscow. This "trial" was one of them.

The problem with the sources is, of course, that there is no way to verify the authenticity of any of them. My own working assumption is that a trial of Lenin was indeed staged at a small railway station outside Moscow on April 17, 1920. However, the fact that the archival railway report is dated *after* the *Pravda* report suggests that local authorities may have submitted their report only after they saw how the *Pravda* report was phrased. Vinogradskaia's account of the railway workers submitting their report entirely on their own initiative is, I suspect, a fiction designed to emphasize the alleged spontaneity of the event. The very fact of the decision to stage such a trial and to publish a report in *Pravda* suggests that someone at the highest level or some group of individuals considered this a fundamentally important event.

TROUBLE ON THE RAILROADS AND IN THE PARTY

From the Vindava railway archives, it is possible to determine that the communists who appeared in the *Trial of Lenin* had been appointed to work in the political departments of the railway only a few weeks before.[21] One, Umrikhin, was the main commissar of the whole Vindava line; another headed the agitation-education section of the political department of this line, the so-called *dorpolit;* another two were district commissars; a fifth worked for the railway Cheka; and a sixth was a local instructor. As recently as a month before the trial, the agitprop section had complained that they did not have a single staff member for work in agitation. It was not until March 25 that a host of new comrades were appointed, some from Glavpolitput, others from the army's political departments, and a few from other district party committees.[22]

The disciplinary problems on the Vindava line were colossal. Food rations were in short supply, and productivity was declining. On March 1, the workers of the nearby Podmoskovnaia station held an unsanctioned meeting, demanding that all food they collected for the state should be returned to them and distributed among them. They should also receive firewood and work clothes. Overall, local reports emphasized that the mood of the masses was "unsatisfactory"; general meetings were "stormy."[23] Umrikhin, the main commissar of the Vindava line and a participant in the *Trial of Lenin,* wrote on February 12, 1920, that productivity on the line had fallen by 20 percent in just the last month and a half.[24]

The influx of new political staff into this particular railway in the spring of 1920 came about as part of a larger move to militarize the railroads. At the time there were only about ten thousand communists on all the railways (fewer than 1 percent of the total workforce of over one million). The Party Central Committee now ordered the transfer of another five thousand communists into transport.[25] The communists who staged the *Trial of Lenin* were among those now streaming into the railways, often to be greeted by criticisms that they didn't know anything about the railways.

Militarization also meant the imposition of military revolutionary tribunals. Anyone who had ever worked in any capacity in the railways in the last ten years was required to register with the government and report for work in the field of transportation. If they did not, they could be turned over to revolutionary tribunals for trial. The administrative staffs and technical personnel of the railways were also given the right to arrest anyone they suspected of wrongdoing and to impose administrative penalties.[26]

At the same time, however, the top authorities responsible for the railways were making great efforts to find political and, above all, cultural-educational solutions to the discipline problems. Railway strikes, after all, had brought the tsarist regime to its knees. The railways had been a central site of Menshevik and Socialist-Revolutionary organizing even after 1917. And most important, they were the backbone of the whole economy. If the trains did not run, then fuel and food for the country could not be sent to their destinations and the economy had no chance of recovering after seven years of the European and civil wars.

Repressions alone had not proven effective in increasing labor productivity. By April 1920 the agitation-education section of the Vindava railroad line had begun to fill out its ranks and to try a number of new ventures. As Umrikhin noted in a special directive: "It is necessary to remind every commissar that we cannot raise productivity by repressions alone. Instead by means of personal example and heroism in work and agitation, we need to raise the consciousness of the masses of workers."[27] This "Politico-critical 'Trial of Lenin'" undoubtedly was intended to provide just such a "personal example" of heroism.[28]

In 1920 and 1921 the Russian Communist Party faced problems not just on the railroads but in its own ranks. When the Bolsheviks had seized power in 1917, they had been able to ride a powerful wave of antiautocratic, antiaristocratic, and antibourgeois sentiment.[29] Yet by now the myths that had sustained the party through two decades in the underground and through three years of Civil War were becoming stale. Tsarism had been overthrown. The military battles against the White guards were being won. The war was almost over. Yet, as everyone knew, the country was in a shambles. Morale was at an all-time low. There was no common external enemy to unify the country.

Two groups of party members, the Workers' Opposition and the Democratic Centralists, were attacking the party's policies on the grounds that they were leading to a "dictatorship of leaders" and the stifling of free criticism. They detested the introduction of so-called political departments (*politotdely*) as replacements for the party committees, particularly since they were appointed from above rather than elected. Soon, they feared, the Central Committee itself would be appointed. They argued, moreover, that the party was violating decisions taken by the Congress of Soviets, ostensibly elected by the whole nation.

Lenin finally grew so exasperated at this flood of criticisms that he exclaimed at the Ninth Party Congress on March 30, 1920: "If they show that we have violated a decision of the Congress, we ought to be put on trial."[30] The next day, March 31, he opened his "Speech on Economic Development" with a comment in the same vein: "I maintain that you cannot hurl unsupported accusations, very serious accusations, at a Party Congress in that way. Of course, if the Council of People's Commissars has violated a decision of the All-Russia Central Executive Committee, it should be put on trial."[31]

RITUALS TO LEGITIMATE THE REVOLUTION

Writing in July 1921, Nikolai Karzhanskii, who was working in Smolensk, commented that "almost everyone" had heard of *The Trial of Lenin, The Trial of Kolchak,* and *The Trial of Wrangel.* These earliest political trials, he noted, differed little from political rallies with long speeches focused on current events. The only difference was that they were given the appearance of a public trial.[32]

Organizers of the agitation trials had two principal audiences in mind whom they wished to influence through the performance of these dramas. One was the audience sitting on benches in the workers' club or theater. In recounting *The Trial of Lenin,* for example, *Pravda* commented that the audience was transformed from a group that was "dead, expressing itself only in shows of hands" into something "living, thinking."[33] For an illiterate audience, the dramatic, visual presentation of ideas could be far more effective, organizers reasoned, than any long-winded political lecture by a single orator standing at a podium. They hoped that the audience would listen "with bated breath," with "strained attention."[34] They deliberately sought to "capture the mood of the audience," to play to their emotions.[35] The whole point, they noted, was to make sure that "a certain mood takes over the audience, a certain idea penetrates its consciousness."[36]

The second target group for the trials was the participants themselves. As the *Pravda* account of the *Trial of Lenin* noted, the communists who participated gained practice in public speaking. Through this kind of exercise they could learn not just to mumble empty phrases but also to think and argue polemically about the issues of the day. The *Pravda* report proudly claimed that "the comrade communists . . . so entered into their prosecution roles and expressed their viewpoint that they could hardly be reproached with having only a superficial knowledge of their own program and that of their opponents."[37] In a successful trial, another article claimed, "the comrade men and women workers enter deeply into the meaning of the issue they are discussing and hence the types they play [*izobrazhaemye imi tipy*] are so lifelike, so much in relief."[38]

For both the audience and the participants, the trial was a sufficiently lifelike form that it broke down what theater specialists at this time loved to call the "fourth wall," that is, the distance in the theater that normally separated audience from participants.[39] In these plays (which could last anywhere from an hour or two to six or eight hours) the audience and participants in the trial could easily believe that they were not in a club or theater but rather in the midst of a real trial. The ritual of the contemporary revolutionary tribunals and courts was maintained to the minutest degree.[40] The whole courtroom rose when the judge entered. He opened the court session in the name of the Russian Socialist Federated Soviet Republic. Court officials brought in the witnesses and then took them out to another room, where they were sequestered for the duration of the trial. If either a character in the proceedings or someone in the audience spoke out of turn, the judge was equipped with a bell that he could use to reinforce his own authority and to discipline the offending person. In this way the audience and the participants were placed on an equal footing. Both were subject to the power of the state in the person of the judge. Often lines were scripted for an individual or two in the audience as well so that it would appear that the audience was thoroughly engaged and speaking out of its own volition.

Why go to such lengths to put on this kind of political trial? Why choose to ritualize a series of mock trials as a form of interaction with the population, a "political conversation," as it was called in *The Trial of Lenin*? Was this an intentional manipulation of a public that otherwise had no voice in public policy? Or was it an experiment in creating a ritualized space for people to express their negative views, their fears, their criticisms? It seems to have been both. The whole process was obviously illusory. Lenin and the Communist Party were never really on trial. At the same time I would argue the trials served as a genuine, if still manipulated, attempt to create a legitimate ancestry and line of political empowerment for a new ruler and a new system of government.

If we look at the rituals of the trials in terms of what they were designed to present, we can see quite a number of illusions being deliberately fostered: an illusion that all this was real (especially since the trials were performed by ordinary workers, soldiers, and peasants rather than by actors); an illusion that the trials were democratic since it was "the people" who represented the court and who passed judgment; an illusion that "comrade" Lenin could be tried on the same basis as anyone else in the society; an illusion, therefore, that the Soviet state had transcended the arbitrary and venal nature of tsarist justice. Now anyone could be put on trial in a people's court and found guilty or innocent on the merits of the case.[41]

Moreover, the trials were designed to convey a dramatic conflict among differing points of view. The bourgeoisie, the monarchists, and the Mensheviks were given apparently free rein to speak their minds.[42] Instructions on how to stage agitation trials explained that they were more convincing if the defendant's guilt or innocence was less obvious so there could be more genuine conflict.[43] There was even a small chance that the trial would go "off the rails"—that the wrong side might win if the participants forgot their lines or became confused, or if the stronger orators played the anticommunist side, though this was not desirable. That chance of failure gave the trials piquancy for viewers encouraged to think that they were witnessing a real conflict.[44]

This new kind of ritual placement of the sitting ruler and his party on trial in fact filled an important void. Russia, after all, had had no state funeral of Tsar Nicholas II, though it had seen public celebrations of his overthrow in February 1917.[45] There had been no public trial of this hated tsar despite the fact that both Kerensky's and Lenin's governments had seriously considered it.[46] In fact, between 1918 and 1920, the government published numerous pamphlets and monographs on the significance of the trial and execution of a king in the making of revolution.[47] Without such a signal event, one source said, all the revolutions after 1789, including the Russian Revolution of 1905, had been "indefinite, unfinished."[48] Beyond the absence of a trial of Nicholas II, there had also been no inauguration of Lenin as the leader of the nation. The Second Congress of Soviets had endorsed the seizure of power in October 1917, but there had been no formal ceremony installing the Bolsheviks in power.

As James von Geldern has noted, one of the dominant preoccupations of the Bolshevik leadership at this time was to "mark the center," to demonstrate the legitimacy and focus of the revolution and the state.[49] Fred Corney has also demonstrated how the Bolshevik leaders chose to "write" the October Revolution, to create versions that people would "remember" as if they had actually happened.[50] Equally important, I would argue, was the drawing of a sharp distinction between the new order and the old. This new regime was doing something unthinkable in the old tsarist order (and in the later Soviet order as well)—namely, creating mock trials of the ruling head of state, the ruling party, and the government in power.

This was a useful form because it could be contained within certain boundaries. Through its ceremonial opening and closing and through the enforced submission of the actors and audience to a court hierarchy (from the judge to the guards), the trial format placed limits on the central conflict, dictating when it began and ended and how much negative criticism could be voiced.

Above all, such early mock trials ritually expressed genuine conflicts that existed in the society. "The goal of the agitation trials," noted one speaker at a conference in 1923, "is the exposure [*vyiavlenie*] of the negative sides of our life; the agitation trials follow the goal of socializing us [*vospitanie*] in a moral sense."[51] Participants could hear their own voices as expressed in their roles, in their votes for guilt or acquittal, in their discussions after the conclusion of the performance. Through that experience they would be drawn in to the clubs and persuaded to become further involved in public productions. For organizers, this meant local people would then find themselves to be the "object-subjects" [*sic*] of work in the clubs and would increasingly come under the clubs' influence.[52] In short, the trial format both constrained its performers and allowed them a certain amount of creativity in the arguments they made and rebuttals they gave to others' arguments.

The trial format also provided a dramatized rite of passage for Lenin and Trotsky as leaders, marking their transition from an underground party resisting the tsarist order to heads of an inaugurated party in power. In the ritualized form of the trial the leaders are separated from the rest of society. Their ideas are put in the dock and declared open for discussion. Once that discussion takes place and the court acquits them, they are returned to their place at the head of the state.[53]

The clubs liked to put on such trials because, as one observer noted, with a minimum effort they could create a maximum impression on the viewer.[54] As contemporaries were well aware, ordinary citizens were terrified of the courts and avoided any participation in them at all cost.[55] To witness a trial and even to participate in one (audience members were often chosen as assessors or were allowed to vote at the conclusion of the play) made the whole experience of "trying" the leader's policies and then acquitting him all the more dramatic.

The trials legitimated Lenin and his party not only by dramatizing the testing and victory of their ideas but also by positioning them in the long line of great revolutionaries who had been on public trial from the 1860s onward. Lenin, like his entire generation, had been steeped in the heroic cult of those trials and of the defendants who used their trial speeches as virulent attacks on autocracy.[56] Social Democrats had boasted of having transformed the tsarist court into a tribunal to "unmask tsarism's predatory policies."[57] Lenin would also have practiced mock trials as a law student. And he would have been aware that April 17 (the day of his "trial" in 1920) was the date when tsarist-era lawyers annually celebrated the founding of the reformed jury courts.[58]

Such trials of the victors in the revolution lasted only a very few years. They began in 1920 as experiments and seem to have died out by 1924 with only one or two examples after that.[59]

In the end it is impossible to say who authored this *Trial of Lenin* and the other heroic trials. We can, however, say that the authors and producers went to extraordinary lengths to make it look as if these were spontaneous events designed by and for the working masses. Instructors on the railroads and in the army reported on individual performances of agitation trials before they published any formal instructions and methodologies. They regularly called on the party to study their attempts and issue general guidelines for others.[60] The majority of the articles on these trials appeared in *Pravda* as if they were reports from local organizations rather than directives from above.

If Lenin and the Communist Party could be "acquitted" in the court of the people, then they would surely be "vindicated" (which is the same word in Russian, *opravdany*) in the court of history. This tiny trial in a railway station in Moscow with an audience of three hundred was an experiment in finding new ways to mark the revolution and to mark Lenin's identification with that revolution. Whether any of the accounts of this and other heroic trials were actually true in some absolute sense (whether audiences listened "with great interest," whether they applauded, whether they went on to further discussion of the issues raised)—none of this mattered in comparison with the construction of the particular ceremony of marking Lenin's fiftieth birthday and his "coronation" with a trial. Finally, he, too, could have his day in court. He and the revolution could be vindicated not only by the court of the people but also by the court of history.[61]

TEACHING POLITICS THROUGH TRIALS, 1921–23

During the Civil War the Bolshevik government had ruled mostly by armed force and by control of the food supply. Once the war was over, however, the country's leaders needed to find new mechanisms of power. They could no longer shoot all deserters and speculators. They could no longer limit rations to those people supporting the regime. They had now to establish themselves as the single political power in the nation. It was not accidental that throughout this period the new authorities most often referred to themselves as "Soviet power" (*Sovetskaia vlast'*) rather than "the Soviet government."

The country was in a terrible state of disarray, which the introduction of the New Economic Policy (NEP) did not immediately allay. As Lenin once explained in typically concrete language, "There is no bread because there is no coal, and no coal because there is no bread. . . . We have to break through this damnable chain by using our energy, pressure [*nazhim*], and the heroism of the toilers, so that all the machines start turning."[1] In other words, without hard currency, without other forms of capital, with industry and agriculture in disarray, there were few ways to influence the economy other than by appealing to the toilers themselves. Persuading workers, peasants, and soldiers to raise their productivity thus became an imperative for the new regime. That in turn, however, was predicated in the Bolshevik worldview on the toilers' understanding the political importance of what they were doing.

The introduction of the New Economic Policy in 1921 intensified the Bolshevik leadership's quest for legitimacy for a number of reasons. One was that the "retreat" to NEP appeared to confirm the predictions of Mensheviks and others that Soviet Russia would have to go the way of "state capitalism" because it was not yet sufficiently advanced for socialism. If that was correct, then Bolshevik claims to rule single-handedly without assistance from other political groups became suspect. Second, many Bolshevik leaders feared that in bowing to economic pressures, the regime would lose its political and cultural edge. The bourgeoisie would continue to operate and influence the rest of the population.

Lenin and his primary associates in the Kremlin now began an all-out propaganda battle to explain the new political and economic realities and also to combat alternative political influences. For the top Soviet leadership the link that had to be grasped (to use Lenin's favorite metaphor) was culture itself. "The last and decisive battle," as Lenin wrote, would be not against international capitalism but against Russian capitalism. Who would win out? This was the decisive test. "Either we pass this test in competition with private capital, or we fail completely. To help us pass it we have political power and a host of economic and other resources; we have everything you want except ability. We lack ability."[2]

Literacy was crucial. "Without it," Lenin wrote, "there are only rumors, fairy tales, [and] prejudices, but not politics."[3] As Nadezhda Krupskaia, head of the new Main Political Education Committee (Glavpolitprosvet) explained, "We political education workers know that the ideas of communism are absorbed much better and are understood much more deeply, if that propaganda is linked with education work."[4]

The earliest agitation trials in 1919–20 had virtually all been improvised, using what instructors called a "skeleton" plot summary and sometimes relying on what they hoped was the experience of the troops in fighting one or another enemy. The army trials of the years 1921 to 1923, by contrast, were becoming more elaborate, often scripted. They had a predominantly political focus, unlike almost all the other trials, including and especially the later civilian trials, which tended to eschew politics entirely.

These agitation trials demonstrate the combination of coercion and independent activity that was at the heart of this work in the army. On the one hand, the soldiers themselves were to be completely responsible for the organization of the clubs. Yet on the other hand, they were to be (in the words of one report) "forced to show their independent activism [*samodeiatel'nost'*]."[5] In practice this meant they were required to include some high politics in their cultural work, but they could choose from a variety of methods and topics.

NORMALIZATION

Only in 1921–22 did local army authorities begin to issue instructions on agitation trials and how to perform them. In the previous winter (1920–21), *Pravda* had printed some eight examples of dramatized trials, most of which were discussed in the previous chapter.[6] Yet these were clearly experiments, trial balloons, as it were. The only comment that came close to representing a formal endorsement came from a minor writer (Artemii Garin) who stated rather weakly, "Such performances [*postanovki*] should be recommended as the best means of agitation and propaganda. It would be desirable if our Communist Party cells would pay special attention to this kind of agitation, holding trials of a labor deserter, a speculator, etc."[7]

Of course, as Sheila Fitzpatrick and others have shown, the party had many ways of sending signals to its subordinates.[8] In this case, as in so many others, the main way was not to issue an abstract decree but to show by example how such trials could be staged, with specific topics and names of groups involved.

Even without official directives the army was leading the way in creating new trials. In April 1921 a "local news" article in *Pravda* claimed that the Krasnodar Party organization had put on fifty-five living newspapers and thirty-five dramatized trials in clubs, theaters, and factories.[9] It is not surprising that these occurred in Krasnodar, the capital of the Kuban region where Dmitrii and Anna Furmanov were working as instructors in the Ninth Army.

In October 1921 the central women's section of the party sent out one of the first circulars to all the provincial sections recommending that in preparation for the upcoming celebrations of the anniversary of the October Revolution, the sections should organize "political trials, political dialogues with women workers, and revolutionary plays."[10] In 1922 the army political departments finally circulated instructions for the creation and performance of trials. They also listed political and literary trials as one of the "recommended" forms of political education work, along with readings out loud, conversations, oral and living newspapers, excursions, evenings of questions and answers, evenings of reminiscences, illustrated reports, shows, and so on.[11]

By the fall of 1922 the political administration of the Ukrainian and Crimean military region, leaders in the new field of agitation trials, boasted a long list of materials that their units had developed, including both scripts and instructions on how to put them on:

The Technical Organization of Model Trials (Instruction)
Political Trials (Instruction)
Historical Political Trials (Instruction)
The Literary Trial of Vaska Krasny (from Maxim Gorky)
The Trial of the Sentry Who Allowed the Burning of the Collection
    Point for the Tax-in-Kind
The Trial of Neriashkin (Sanitation Education)
The Trial of Those Guilty of the Famine
How to Put on the Trial of an Illiterate
Sanitation Education Work in the Clubs

How to Put on the Trial of White Representatives of Poland and
   Romania
The Trial of Deserters
The Trial of Petliura
The Trial of the Soldier Who Spread Cholera
The Trial of the Kulak Demanding Payment
The Trial of the Scout Who Didn't Fulfill his Duties[12]

In April 1923 the Regulations for Clubs in the Red Army and Fleet specified
six different kinds of agitation trials to be staged as part of "mass work"
among the soldiers: political, military, agricultural, sanitation, historical, and
literary.[13]
   The stated purpose of the trial/plays, as put forth in the new army instructions, was to "take possession of the mood of the audience" and to "inculcate various ideas," such as the wrongfulness of desertion, banditry, and
indiscipline. Potential authors of agitation trials were instructed, moreover,
to *personify* the misdemeanor or crime. In other words, they should structure the trial not around desertion in general but rather around a particular
(fictional) deserter who could exemplify the general problem.[14]
   Internal reports within the army occasionally expressed the purpose of the
agitation trials even more baldly. As several club authorities explained in
1923, the goal of the agitation trials was "to bring out the negative sides of
our lives." They were "to fight unhealthy phenomena, desertion, pillage, in-
stability." Above all, as everyone agreed, they were dedicated to "the moral
upbringing" of the soldier-citizens of Soviet Russia.[15]
   At their most basic level the trials were designed to narrate the failings of
individuals in society, to *perform* those shortcomings for all to see. As theatrical events, they provided dramatic interest because of the inherent power dif-
ferentials between the court and the defendants and because of the audience's
feelings of suspense as to whether the individual defendants would confess and
whether they would be found guilty. That suspense could then be played on
to convey dramatically the "teachings" or parables of the given case.

TEACHING THROUGH GAMES

Instructions for the clubs in the army in the early 1920s suggested that the
agitation trials could be fruitfully employed as a kind of teaching game. The
clubs had strict instructions not to duplicate the military training and schooling that the troops were receiving. Without becoming scholastic, they were
to be interesting and attractive, and to provide "rationally organized leisure"
that the soldiers would attend "on a voluntary basis," "motivated by interest growing out of desire."[16]
   Many in the leadership of the club section of PUR were well aware that

rank-and-file soldiers did not like the clubs, did not go to them, and did not feel connected to them.[17] The task of *attracting* the soldier masses was perceived as a crucial first step for organizations that hoped to influence them.

Above all, the clubs were to help in instilling "habits of *aktivnost'* [literally, activeness]." This *aktivnost'* instructors defined as "an ability to think independently about issues, to study independently and to put into practice the general educational, political and military knowledge" acquired in one's studies. Above all, the club was to be "a place of rational recreation" and "a place of cultural, comradely relations that draw together the commanders and rank and file."[18]

Starting in 1922, military study circles (*kruzhki voennykh zaniatii*) were directed to put on evenings of military reminiscences, sports competitions, charades, and other forms of games. Of course, such "games" were designed to coincide with the political lessons being studied each week in the *politchas*. The games were to illustrate various points in the garrison regulations, in the duties of a soldier, and so on. Yet they were also supposed to carry an element of spontaneity and play.

The members of one study circle, for example, were asked to consider the types of soldiers who they thought brought the most harm to the military. Each person had two or three minutes to prepare. One acted out the sentry who fell asleep at his post; another, the illiterate soldier; a third, the deserter. Then the others decided who had given the best portrayal. These skits were sometimes turned into trials—for example, the trial of the slacker or the trial of the drunkard.[19]

In another military study circle a political instructor began by telling his soldiers the story of a company of soldiers who captured a village that had recently been occupied by rebel Makhnovtsy (anarchists) but who did not take any measures to stand guard. The officer on duty fell asleep; the sentries went off to visit their comrades in other units; and the guard who was supposed to stand watch at the entrance to the village went inside to have dinner with the priest, where, having eaten well, he fell asleep. That night fifteen Makhnovtsy attacked the village and killed almost the whole company of eighty soldiers. In this theater/study exercise the troops were told to break into small groups to discuss different parts of the story and the mistakes made by different members of the company. Then each group dramatized the mistakes through fictional agitation trials to show the mismanagement of the company, the carelessness of individual soldiers, and the lack of discipline of the whole unit.[20]

Trials were sometimes staged "spontaneously" among a group of soldiers who had been resting and reading out loud. Without looking official (or the soldiers would lose interest), the instructors or senior students tried to persuade those present to set up a mock courtroom. Some were asked to play the judges; others, the prosecutors and defense attorneys. Everyone was allowed to play his role as he saw fit without any prior preparation. If one person thought another had not performed well enough in his role, he could intervene as a second prosecutor or a second defense attorney and put forth his own point of view on the case. What mattered was not the technical angle of the trial but rather the chance for each soldier to have an opportunity "to learn to put forth his ideas, to think critically about the reading, and to find ways to prove his point."[21] It is surely not accidental that the author of this particular instruction was head of a club and library division. Some humanist values of learning to put forth one's views (*izlagat' mysli*) and relate critically to reading (*kriticheski otnosit'sia k prochitannomu*) still had a place in club discussions.

Trials could be as informal as events taken from daily life—the trial of a soldier who spit on the floor, who failed to clean his rifle, or who threw his things around. If someone did something that the others thought was against the regulations, then they could explain to him why he should not do it. But if he held out and a heated argument broke out, then they could organize an agitation trial of the person accused. In such a case the sentence of the defendant should require him to do something useful, such as reading a particular book and then telling everyone about its contents.[22]

Trials were used as well as a way of illustrating the political lessons the soldiers were receiving in their "political hours." Under the rubric of "Policies of Soviet Power" they were asked to write and perform *The Trial of a Tax Dodger* or *The Trial of a Soldier Who Sold His Uniform*. In conjunction with the topic of "The Russian Communist Party and Other Parties" they could perform *The Trial of a Communist* or an agitation version of the current, real trial of the Mensheviks and Socialist Revolutionaries.[23]

Particular trials could also convey articles from garrison regulations. One of the best "teaching trials," as these were occasionally called, was *The Trial of the Sentry Who Allowed the Burning of the Grain Collection Site*. In it soldier Knysh is accused of not having a loaded rifle and allowing bandits to burn down the collection site with ninety tons of grain. His commanders, Gaenko and Evdorchuk, are held accountable for not having checked to ascertain whether he knew the regulations and whether his weapon was loaded. The Bureau of Military Propaganda of the Kiev Military Region, which published the trial, and reviewers from the central club department of PUR praised it for covering no fewer than five different articles of the garrison regulations. In the end Knysh acknowledges his guilt before the court and before the republic. Since his infraction was unpremeditated, he hopes the court will forgive him. In gratitude for the clemency of the court he promises to make every effort on behalf of the people and to teach others how to carry out their duties.[24]

CONTENTION AMONG CLUB ADMINISTRATORS

Among army club administrators a major point of contention centered on the question to what extent the clubs in general and the staging of agitation trials in particular should be subordinated to the political and educational dimensions of soldiers' studies. This question tended to crystallize into two main perspectives: a utilitarian view of the clubs on the one hand and a recreational view on the other.

The utilitarian view insisted that the club had to be seen as "the companion of the political hour," to cite the title of an article in the Red Army newspaper *Krasnaia zvezda*. Work among soldiers in the clubs was to be designed principally to help the soldier remember his political lessons by making those lessons "easy to take in."[25] The rule makers, as the utilitarians could also be called, tended to insist that all the work of the theater circles, the art circles, the literature circles, etc., should be designed to complement the particular work of the political lessons at any given moment. They tried to establish a revolutionary calendar (about which I will say more below) and harness all the work of the clubs to moving from holiday to holiday.[26]

Their critics, the recreationalists, countered with the view that "naked politics" would alienate soldiers and workers instead of drawing them in to creating a new world. "The experience of our work has shown," wrote one head of a club section in spring 1923, "that obligatory political general lessons with the soldiers need above all an extracurricular approach. . . . We have bent the stick too far in the direction of naked politics, insufficiently energetically raising the general cultural level of the soldier at the same time."[27] If they could not find the right balance of politics and recreation, he and others wrote, "we will not be able to get close to the soldier; our agitation will seem to him boring, dry and abstract." If they overloaded him with campaigns of every kind, all the work of the club would turn into "senseless agitation mush."[28]

Yet too much recreation was also dangerous. This was particularly a problem in the early NEP years because of government cutbacks in funding and the closing or curtailing of many clubs and other local programs. In response many of the clubs tried to become self-financing by putting on entertainment for a fee. The problem, of course, was that the entertainment that might draw a crowd tended to be dances, vaudeville, musical shows, and popular theater programs, all of which seemed useless or worse in the larger project of "enlightening" and "socializing" the soldiers.

It is a peculiarity of many social revolutions that they are often rather puritanical affairs.[29] The October Revolution in Russia was no exception. Terrified of "crowd pleasers" and "cheap moneymakers" being put on in the clubs, many authorities swung to the opposite extreme, insisting on the need to outlaw paid performances and public dances, to establish strict repertoire committees that would decide what could be permitted and what should be banned.[30] Clubs, many argued, should be used exclusively for agitation and propaganda.[31]

Isaak Korobochkin, head of the club section of the Political Administration of the Army, sought vigorously to find a solution to these problems. Korobochkin himself exemplified the upward mobility that was possible in the new army. Born in 1898, he attended the newly created "school-instruction courses" of the Commissariat of Enlightenment and joined the Communist Party in June 1920. Sent to the Army later that summer, he rose from a simple instructor to head of the political education section of the political department of the Second Cavalry Army, then by March 1922 to head of the club division of the political administration of the Separate Caucasus Army in Tiblisi. By December of that year he was head of the club section of the Political Administration of the whole Red Army.

In the fall of 1923 he issued an important report entitled "The Club on the Path toward a System." It was time now, Korobochkin insisted, to consider the content of the work in the clubs. The question was how to find the middle way between the "academism" of the school approach and the "vulgarization" (*uproshchenie*) of the recreational approach. The answer, Korobochkin suggested, was to focus on military upbringing but to use forms that were attractive and interesting. The problem (and here Korobochkin is surprisingly honest) was that the principle of *samodeiatel'nost'*, namely having the soldiers develop their own programs, seemed to run headlong up against the principle of planning and systematization. Tired soldiers simply could not take in too many lectures and reports after eight hours of drills, political lessons, and military duties. The political staffs felt they needed to direct pedagogical work for the country's defense. Yet the soldiers themselves ("the objects of the upbringing," as Korobochkin called them) responded only if they were able to hear and see events that were interesting to them. Skits and pantomimes of political subjects seemed the obvious answer, especially ones that were close to the everyday lives of soldiers and to current events.[32]

In such an antihedonist climate the agitation trials provided an attractive mix of politics and culture. By staging a trial, the instructor could attract soldiers to the clubs yet also please his superiors. At the end of the month, when he filled out a report on his activities, he had to indicate on a graph how many of which kinds of performances his club had held in the given month. Trials, strictly speaking, were not required of him. Rather, they were listed as one among eight or nine different kinds of performances the clubs could put on.

CREATING A RED CALENDAR

The creation of a red calendar of patriotic revolutionary events seems to have developed initially as part of mass festivals. Their overall goal was to get the people into the streets, to create lively, colorful, and memorable events that would draw audiences and get them interested in learning more about the revolution and the new society in which they were living. If the politics of the government and Communist Party during the Civil War had focused on bread, land, and survival, the army in the postwar period turned to creating public spectacles for its troops and for local civilian populations.[33]

The Soviet mass festivals and red calendar were explicitly modeled on the revolutionary festivals of the French Revolution.[34] French revolutionaries had in turn predicated their efforts on the hope that dramatizing the ideas of the revolution would make them accessible to all adults. Festivals, they argued, were an excellent way to foster a bond of fraternity among citizens and engender in them respect for law while transferring the task of moral education from the church to the state. As a kind of "political religion" and "a great national school," theaters would "purify manners and give lessons of civism." By acting out the parts of virtuous citizens, the French people would, the revolutionaries of 1789 hoped, imbibe the ideals of the revolution and be transformed.[35]

The red calendar established by the Soviet cultural authorities offered ample opportunities for the performance of fictional political trials. By 1922 the list of holidays and corresponding trials had grown quite extensive:

January 9 (the anniversary of Bloody Sunday in 1905): *The Trial of Father Gapon* or *The Trial of Zubatov and Gapon*

February 23 (the February Revolution, which soon ceased to be celebrated): *The Trial of the Coalition [Provisional] Government*

February 23 (Red Army Day): *The Trial of the Red Army by Nonparty Workers*

March 8 (International Women's Day): *The Trial of the Old Way of Life*

March 18 (the Day of the Paris Commune): Trials of the communards and of the Thiers government that suppressed the commune

April 17 (the anniversary of the Lena gold mine strikes in 1912): *The Trial of the Lena Strikers* and *The Trial of Gendarme Rotmistr Treshchenko [one of their executioners]*

May 1 (International Workers' Day): *The Trial of International Imperialism*

October 23/November 7 (the anniversary of the October Revolution): *The Political Trial of the October Revolution.*

In 1922 Petrograd military regional authorities even discussed creating a new holiday for November 18, "The Day of School Agitation," when a number of literary events and plays would be performed, including the crowning event, *The Trial of an Illiterate Soldier.*[36] Public campaigns on various issues could also be embellished with mock trials or plays on such themes as "the slovenly (or illiterate) soldier is an enemy of the republic," "the soldier who doesn't love and know military matters is a poor citizen," and "the worker and peasant who don't know the correct means of managing the economy are doomed to starvation and extinction."[37] *The Trial of Neriashkin* (a slovenly soldier who infected his bunkmate with lice) also worked well for "the week of struggle with lice infestation."[38]

The existence of the red calendar helped army units and their club directors structure their work. An upcoming holiday could provide themes for posters, slogans, and theatrical presentations. When instructors discovered a gap in materials for a particular holiday, they often sat down and wrote new plays and trials to meet their obligations. Even though the army authorities in the Volga region, for example, did not have their own resident dramatist (as some areas did), the central political leaders nonetheless praised them for closely following the political calendar, noting the needed dates, and preparing the appropriate illustrations, theses (for public meetings), and methodological materials.[39]

SHARP CORNERS FOR DEBATE

The early NEP political trials differed significantly from the agitation trials of the late Civil War in that they moved beyond hatemongering and rabble-rousing to somewhat more nuanced discussions of relations between state and society. Admittedly, audiences were supposed to come to the "correct opinion" (*pravil'noe mnenie*) about events such as the October Revolution.[40] Yet a number of writers created trials with substantial dialogue and debate. As Borovich noted in 1923, where it was acceptable in Civil War–era trials for the opposition to remain largely silent (since the goal was to stir up the audience against them), now the agitation trial had to foster discussion. The trial had to "loosen the opponent's tongue, open his mouth. It is necessary to call him into open combat. Otherwise neither he nor those who share his opinions can be made to change their minds." The dramatization should be put together in such a way as to "leave sharp corners for debate."[41]

Political education directors, moreover, were well aware that full-scale debate provided the best drama for their audiences. Dmitrii Furmanov noted that witnesses' testimony should be "varied, full of content and contradictory," that the defense of someone like Wrangel should bring forth all kinds of convincing evidence and conclusions, "which turn out to be myth only when they are knocked down by yet more convincing accusations."[42] The author of the introduction to another trial, Evgenii I. Khlebtsevich, who was himself head of the Library Division of the Political Administration of the Army, also spoke of the trial form as "discussion-oriented and dialogic." Such a form had the great advantage over rallies and lectures of making the material visible, palpable, and hence more engaging.[43]

To a certain extent educators in this period wanted people to express their views so those views could be disproved publicly, as was evident in Borovich's The *Trial of Jewry*. Early postrevolutionary political debates (*disputy*), especially those between religionists and antireligionists, used the same logic. As one committed antireligionist explained in *Pravda*, he and his fellow debaters might as well put on *disputy* because, after all, "the counterrevolutionary mood of our bourgeois, petty store proprietors, homeowners, and so on has to come forth somewhere, out loud and in public!"[44]

The danger, of course, was that a trial with evenly matched sides and real debate could indeed end up going off the rails. The drunkard might be too sympathetic; the villain might seem too well motivated. Nonetheless, many dramatists held that the answer to this problem was more rehearsals and better preparation rather than the suppression of dialogue and debate.[45]

Some of the texts of the trials even named their sources of information, including non-Soviet ones. *The Trial of the Red Army by Nonparty Workers*, for example, lists some twelve different sources for the trial, including *Smena Vekh* (*Changing Landmarks,* an émigré publication arguing that the introduction of the New Economic Policy meant a return to the path foreseen by the Mensheviks), *Rossiia No. 2*, and Wrangel's proposed land reform plan.[46] The authors of *The Trial of Soviet Power* also explicitly noted that they had built their case based on newspaper articles and in opposition to local rumors.[47]

The timing and the forms of the trials—their explicit attempts to refute charges being brought against the Bolsheviks in conversations and publications from Moscow to Paris—suggest that at least some leaders in the government were aware of the need for an escape valve for public discontents. Now that the war was over, Lenin and the top authorities wanted to end not only the military might of the bourgeoisie but also their influence in ideas.[48] Yet to win these battles, to move from the theater of war to that of socialist construction, it was necessary to understand the criticisms of the bourgeoisie in order to disarm them. The new forms of agitation and propaganda were designed to be "factual, full of content and figures," and intended "for a longer term effect."[49]

The Trial of the Red Army, for example, brings suit against a Red commander (Ognev) and his assistant (Sokhin). They are accused of overthrowing the Provisional Government as part of an armed uprising by Red Guard bands. The overthrow has helped to bring the Bolsheviks to power and plunge Russia into anarchy, poverty, and lawlessness. In creating the Red Army, it is alleged, Ognev and Sokhin have been aiding Bolshevik imperialism, which is trying to capture Russia's neighbors, break up the European peace, and draw the European powers into a new war. In propagandizing communism and its creators (Marx, Engels, and Lenin), they are persecuting private property, the church, and the whole moral foundation of the country. Motivated by greed and cruelty, they are inflaming in the dark masses a hatred toward the wealthy classes and are calling on them to plunder the capitalists and landlords. This trial and others voiced (and, of course, refuted) many of the very real criticisms being made in the émigré press and in the underground press in Russia.[50]

Army authorities criticized trial scenarios they considered overly one-sided and lacking real dialogue and debate. This was the case with "The Trial of the Coalition Government," a rather plotless trial in which the Mensheviks, Socialist Revolutionaries, and Cadets, those "devoted lackeys of the bourgeoisie," are sentenced to be isolated and sent to work in their areas of professional specialization. Korobochkin and Kurdiumov, who wrote most of the reviews of the agitation trials sent to the Political Administration of the Army, praised the trial for being "well thought out and in good conscience." Yet they criticized it for having an excessively obvious outcome from the start, for "lacking any interesting factual material," and for "needing great talent on the part of the director and actors if they are to avoid falling into the danger of holding endless rallies that bore everyone." A better trial would be one that embodied "the collision of two worldviews."[51]

The Trial of the October Revolution, by contrast, provides more serious and genuine criticisms of the Bolshevik seizure of power.[52] In the first part of the play (which is in the form of an ordinary dramatic scene rather than a trial), a White Army general criticizes the Bolsheviks for lacking discipline and training in military technology. Mensheviks and Socialist Revolutionaries express outrage at Bolshevik brazenness in disbanding the Constituent Assembly, which was supposed to express the will of the people.

In an intermezzo before the first and second acts, a master of ceremonies tries to explain the significance of the October Revolution. He is interrupted, however, by objections from the audience that he is presenting only his own opinions. The group in the audience demands an immediate trial of the October Revolution "in order to give it a full and objective evaluation." The master of ceremonies accordingly writes down a petition from them for what the account calls "a social-political trial" (*obshchestvenno-politicheskii sud*). Two members of the audience are then elected to serve as judges in the case.

In the trial itself various witnesses repeat the accusations of the first act, followed by the speech of the prosecutor, who calls the October Revolution an "adventurer" and its participants agents of German espionage. The prosecutor insists on its criminal liability for the bloody consequences of the dispersion of the Constituent Assembly, the outbreak of the Civil War, the shooting of the legitimate defenders of the Constituent Assembly, the reversal of the "will of the people," and so on.

The defense advances the desired lesson in Marxism in the final speech, which is augmented by the judges in their sentencing. It turns the tables on Cadet/Menshevik complaints about the Bolshevik seizure of power, saying that the real adventurer was the Provisional Government, which counted on the helplessness and lack of preparation in the masses. The defense also re-proaches the prosecution for being no more than a cog in the great machine of capitalism, a machine that crushes millions of proletarian lives. In the end it is not the October Revolution that must be considered guilty but capital-ism itself.

Another example of a trial that turns the tables is that of Pilsudski, the Polish head of government whom Trotsky, in a fit of pique, once referred to as a "third-rate Bonaparte."[53] The entire five-page typescript of *The Politi-cal Trial of Pilsudski* rests on the contrast between false, bourgeois appear-ances and the "truth" as revealed by a Marxist understanding of the world (without ever naming Marxism itself). Pilsudski falsely presents himself as a socialist. He claims that he is acting for the benefit of the Polish people. He draws them in and fools them with slogans of restoring Poland to its prepar-tition boundaries of 1772. In reality, however, such a move betrays the work-ing masses by playing into the hands of German imperialism. It creates a false hope that Poland will become an independent great power state when in fact Pilsudski is indebted to the French capitalists who are fostering his reckless adventure. Any Polish gains in a war with Soviet Russia, the prosecution tries to show, would benefit the big landlords who hold lands in Ukraine and Belorussia and not the Polish working class and peasantry. Even the Polish soldiers have no idea what they are fighting for, according to one Soviet sol-dier called to the witness stand. *They* (Polish soldiers) think it is all the Bol-sheviks' fault, that it is the Bolsheviks who want to destroy Poland: "The idiots didn't even know that the Bolsheviks kept wanting to conclude a peace, but the Polish nobles refused." The Polish soldiers have not been al-lowed to read newspapers, he argues, in contrast naturally to the Soviet sol-diers, who do have them. Of course, the Polish soldiers have been well equipped with new foreign uniforms that are all French, proving that Poland, far from being independent, is entirely in the pay (and the clutches) of French capitalists.

Multiple trials of the Paris Commune of 1871 give more historical lessons. Sometimes the defenders of the Commune, the so-called communards, are brought to court as heroes of the trial; sometimes the international prole-tariat puts the communards on trial for their failure to bring off their revo-lution; and sometimes Adolphe Thiers himself, the head of the bourgeois government and chief persecutor of the communards, is put on trial.[54]

The (fictional) international proletariat expresses its motivation to bring the Paris Commune to trial on the grounds that "the mistakes and defeat of the Commune are the mistakes and defeat of the working class of the whole world and hence the international proletariat has the full right to judge the Paris Commune for its mistakes."[55] The "lessons" of the Commune are all ones that serve to justify Soviet policies. They illustrate the dangers of being too "soft." Failing to defeat the counterrevolutionary bourgeoisie inside Paris "with strict proletarian decisiveness" and allowing them to publish their newspapers and hold meetings, the communards have brought about their own downfall.

In the end the court acquits the communards on grounds suggested by one of the defendants: "No one taught us workers how to run a government, and so if we made mistakes the fault is not ours." Another worker comments how complicated it has been to run a government. The final sentence praises the communards as "flesh of our flesh, blood of our blood, representatives of the laboring masses." The working class has been too weak and dispersed and hence unable to found its own workers' communist party, which could have led the fight. Ultimately, therefore, the Commune of 1871 should be acquitted and its lessons taken into account by workers of the whole world.

The trials of the communards by bourgeois courts also reveal the opposition between the bourgeois courts (one of which is filled with lorgnetted ladies and whispering crowds) and the brave communards ready to go to their deaths for their ideals. One judge becomes very annoyed. "What is this?" he asks. "They [the defendants] have no fear. They meet death proudly and disdainfully. They are not afraid of the sea of spilled blood. Who are they?" Another version of this trial notes that the defendants have shown "true courage/manliness [*muzhestvo*] and nobility [*blagorodstvo*]" in contrast to the "brazen comedy" of the bourgeois court, which is a weapon in the hands of the governing class to put down and fight against hostile classes.[56] Thus through verbal combat the heroic defendants (be they the October Revolution, the Red Army, or the Paris communards) show that they have been falsely maligned (and even martyred). Now they emerge victorious through the judgment process.

ELEMENTS OF FANTASY

Many of these agitation trials involve a high degree of pure fantasy. Baron Wrangel could be caught and put on trial. The October Revolution could slay the machine of capital. Raymond Poincaré, the head of the capitalist French government, could be put on trial, then shot, and world imperialism crushed.[57] When the French invaded the Ruhr valley in 1923, one club division in the Separate Caucasus Army in Tbilisi wrote a combined trial and play in which Germany rose up in revolution, the Red Army was able to attack and defeat the French, and the French general staff were taken prisoner and then put on trial by the Soviet proletariat.[58] The danger in the last case, the reviewers noted, was that if the events described did not in fact come to pass at some point, the plot would lose its persuasiveness in the eyes of the audience.[59]

In such trials Adolphe Thiers is described as a "dwarf-monster." Pilsudskii is the "evil-intentioned ruler of capitalist Poland." The communards innocently engage in implementing social transformations and organizing elections, while the enraged bourgeoisie, maddened to a bestial state, blinded with rage and thirsting for revenge, carry out vicious attacks and monstrous crimes.

When the villains in these plays try to defend themselves, they reveal the falseness of their class position and their own lowness. While Thiers claims in his own defense that he has been upholding "order, civilization and justice," the trial reveals that he is really defending property and bourgeois class interests. In another trial of the communards, bourgeois local residents come to the judges to petition for an end to the shooting, which they say they cannot stand any more. The corpses, after all, are piling up on the city streets and may cause epidemics! The factory owners also cynically present a petition complaining about the deaths of the workers, which is causing a reduction in their workforce.

In *The Trial of Pilsudski* the Polish magnates claim they have been living peacefully on land that they had gained legitimately over a long period of time. Yet their own words betray them: "But we allow them [Polish peasants] to live on our land. . . . A noble lord cannot work with the plow and in the stables himself, can he?" The nobles' comments could only have been designed to infuriate Russian audiences: "Poland is not irrational Russia. We don't have dirty peasants and serfs at the head of Poland, but rather noble lords."[60] What Russian audience would not have been inflamed by such a comment?

DRAMATIZING REAL SHOW TRIALS

In 1922 the Soviet authorities began a new practice of creating model agitation trials based on real show trials taking place at the time, especially the trial of Orthodox Church leaders that took place from April 24 to May 7, 1922, and the trial of the Socialist Revolutionaries (June 8 to August 7, 1922).[61] Unfortunately for the historian working on this topic, the show trials in this period look substantially like agitation trials. For example, the court trial of Orthodox Church leaders on grounds that they failed to donate church valuables to aid those stricken by the famine of 1921–22 was held at the Polytechnic Museum in Moscow, which had been the site of several fictional agitation trials. The museum was one of the largest lecture halls in Moscow, so it was a natural choice of venue for a public trial.[62] But the fact that the trial was held there must surely have confused at least some members of the audience: Was this a religious and political debate or was it a real trial of real individuals for alleged crimes?

The famine that swept the Volga region and much of the country in 1921–22 gave the authorities an excuse to confiscate church valuables, allegedly to use them to feed the starving. In line with their general policy of *personifying* political events, the authorities created fictional trials not only of the church (as well, of course, as the real trials), but also "of those guilty of the famine" (which will be discussed in the next chapter).

The forces blamed in court for the famine ranged from foreign imperialist nations that refused to aid the Russian provinces to peasant slackers who refused to sow sufficient land. The chief villain, however, became the church itself, which until this time the Bolshevik authorities had not dared to attack directly. During the Civil War, Lenin had, in fact, given specific instructions that agitators were to treat the church with kid gloves so as not to offend believers. From 1922 onward, however, the state and party launched a frontal attack against both religion in general and the Orthodox Church in particular.

No sooner had the official Moscow trial of the church leaders ended on May 7, 1922, than the regional military-political training courses in Samara performed a *Model Political Trial of the Church*, a copy of which they sent to the head of the Political Administration of the Army in Moscow four days later.[63] Almost more a lecture than a play, the trial considers the guilt of the church for almost every ill currently plaguing Soviet Russia, especially the crime of deceiving and stupefying the Russian people.

Just as the agitation trials were devoted to giving soldiers and civilians the correct upbringing (*vospitanie*), so this trial made it clear that it was now a criminal offense to give the wrong upbringing, which was precisely what the Russian Orthodox Church had been doing for centuries. It had not only oppressed and exploited the workers and peasants (among other things, in its capacity as a huge landowner), but it had also taken control of the elementary schools and trained the children to be "obedient slaves," inculcating into them "meekness, submissiveness, and absolute obedience to the power of the ruling class." The church teachings themselves (the Zakon Bozhii) were the main culprit in this, since they killed all will to learn and all striving toward knowledge. The church, moreover, encouraged peasants to be submissive to their landlords yet to go off to war and kill others in defense of "faith, tsar, and homeland." One after another, witnesses showed how the church had blinded the people, while Soviet power, once it had proved victorious, had opened their eyes.

The second great public show trial of 1922 was that of thirty-four members of the Socialist Revolutionary Party, whom the Bolshevik government now felt strong enough to attack openly. The trial attracted not only international media attention but also enormous propaganda coverage within the country.[64] In the fall of 1922, after the show trial's conclusion (at which twelve of the defendants were sentenced to death but had their sentences suspended), a meeting of heads of agitprop sections in the Caucasian Army discussed different ways they could replay this particular trial in dramatic form for their troops. In what was by now becoming a common practice, they decided that the political circle would write the basic political material, the literary circle would create a scenario, the drama circle would stage it, and the art circle would design posters, slogans, and stage decorations.[65]

At some point the central authorities, including Boris Volin, who was on the editorial board of *Pravda,* decided to create a fictionalized version of the trial of the Socialist Revolutionaries entitled *The Path to the Defendants' Bench.* The goal of this agitation trial was obviously to discredit the Socialist Revolutionary Party by showing how they had once been a party of great revolutionaries but now had fallen on hard times and had emigrated to Western cafés, where they existed on the handouts of the bourgeoisie. In a series of carefully documented denunciations of the falsehood of SR policies, their moral fall (*nravstvennoe padenie*), and the reasons for their failure, this fictional trial implies that they have gone over to the side of monarchists and other White forces and are waiting passively for the restoration of the tsar. Their lulling of the peasants and workers to sleep is contrasted with the propaganda of the Bolsheviks, which has called for the people to awaken and take up active participation in their state and society.[66]

The political trials staged in the Red Army in the early 1920s go far beyond the simple hatemongering rally-trials against Wrangel or the Kronstadt mutineers characteristic of the end of the Civil War. Through attention to some of the most important political issues of the day, they give at least some voice to political opponents' criticisms of the regime, however resolutely they then beat down those arguments with apparently superior reasoning and moral standards.

Nonetheless, the Manichaean approach to politics of these trials is striking. One individual or group of individuals is always guilty. Other individuals or groups of individuals, usually connected to the Russian Communist Party and Soviet power, always emerge as the victors. The villains are almost always sentenced to be shot if they are human and to be annihilated if they are ideologies or movements. In this view the very existence of enemies endangers the Soviet regime and its people. As one judge announces at the conclusion of a trial, "The task of proletarian justice must be to sweep away all forces hostile to the proletarian dictatorship of Soviet power. The very existence of active enemies of the workers and peasants threatens the possibility of a new and bloody civil war."[67]

The aim of the agitation trials was thus to teach the audience to think about politics and events from a particular, state-oriented point of view. It was the power of the state (*Sovetskaia vlast'*) that had to be safeguarded. In their turn the agents of the state, particularly the political instructors in the army, would teach and guide the people, showing them the way of revolution.

THE CULTURE OF
EVERYDAY LIFE, 1922–24

As soldiers from the Red Army began to return home in 1921–22, army officials had great hopes that they would serve as a "cultural lever" in the village, bringing with them the political, organizational, and cultural lessons they had learned in the armed forces.[1] Local activists, meanwhile, received instructions to put on mock political trials as a way of "stirring up" [*raska-chivanie*] the conscious layers of the village. In so doing they were told to rely especially on the individuals (primarily young men) who had been at the fronts and gone through political schooling in the army.[2]

The transition to peacetime created a new set of problems in terms of influence and motivation. During the Civil War a deserter could be taken out and shot as a way of deterring other would-be renegades. Once the war was over, however, army club authorities and those working with new recruits were aware that overly harsh punishments were counterproductive for new soldiers who had not been "hardened" at the front; in such cases a moral judgment, they felt, might have more effect than a harsh sentence of imprisonment or hard labor.[3] During the war soldiers had had a direct self-interest in learning to handle a gun, to march in formation, and to develop their physical fitness. Many units also had older soldiers who had fought on the front lines and knew personally the value of closing ranks and fighting in a disciplined fashion. They knew, too, why they hated the old regime. The recruits of 1921, by contrast, had been born in 1901. They did not remember much of the old regime or the world war, especially if they were from the eastern parts of the country. Yet they did have a sense of the Bolshevik regime and its restrictions on peasant trading, its grain requisitions, and above all, the fact that they themselves had been torn from their villages at a time when there was no enemy in sight, no apparent need to defend the motherland. Although ultimately they would benefit from the upward mobility that the army was beginning to provide in the new revolutionary state, they could not know that when they arrived at their new units. Why should such a peasant fresh from the plow want to learn military arts or literacy?

The appearance of peasant soldiers as subjects (and objects) in agitation trials suggests that these courtroom dramas were designed to convey not only political views and military regulations but also social and cultural values. The soldier had to learn to be a citizen and also an administrator of the state. In that capacity he (or more rarely, she) could not be indifferent to politics. Perhaps even more important, he could not carry himself in an "uncivilized" manner.

As Lenin himself had insisted, the main battle in the postwar period had to be focused on the struggle with the world bourgeoisie. The contest was one of ideas and, above all, upbringing (*vospitanie*). Political education (*politicheskoe prosveshchenie*) was essential because it served as a means "to overcome the old habits, the old practices which remain as a heritage of the old order."[4] For Lenin the creation of a new socialist discipline was "more difficult, more tangible, more radical and more decisive than the overthrow of the bourgeoisie, for it is a victory over our own conservatism, indiscipline, petty-bourgeois egoism."[5]

Agitation trials did not merely attempt to inculcate such habits and discipline from the top down, however. The plays also had to meet the peasant soldier and the worker where he or she was, to convey a picture that at least somewhat resembled his or her existing picture of the world. This meant that the agitation trials had to make familiar what was new and strange, especially the unfamiliar Soviet order.

One way to acquaint viewers with the new world they were living in was to rely on comic, known stereotypes of peasants and workers, of priests and NEPmen (the traders and entrepreneurs who had gotten rich during the New Economic Policy). Because the trials were attempting to convey social "reality," they are especially interesting to the historian as a source of information about the points of contact, pressure, and resistance between authorities and citizens.

Another way to create a new "Soviet" civilization was to criticize the old way of life in all its (perhaps contemptible) familiarity and to create what became known as agitation trials of everyday life (*byt*). *Byt* had long been a pivotal issue for the educated elites as it symbolized everything they considered backward and trivial, inert and slavish.[6]

Agitation trials "of the old way of life," of illiteracy, slovenliness, superstition, and selfishness, relied on two key presuppositions. One was the intelligentsia's conviction that peasant and worker "backwardness" was the source of virtually all of Russia's problems. One agronomist, for example— a character in *The Trial of the Bad Peasant*—explains that the reason "for all our misfortunes and troubles is the same—the people's ignorance."[7]

The other presumption was a belief in the power of the community and community values to effect change in the individual. For all the newness of Soviet approaches to issues of social change, this was an old belief with a long pedigree. From at least the 1860s the intelligentsia had been waging a sometimes quixotic battle to persuade the peasant and worker masses to change. The peasantry and proletariat, meanwhile, had been engaged in an equally stubborn battle to accept only those innovations they found to be in their own self-interest.[8] Of course, there had been important examples of converts, of workers especially, who had traveled the long road from peasant to proletarian and to revolutionary.[9] As Peter Kenez has pointed out, the recent convert is often the most ardent teacher of new truths.[10]

The question remains, however, why Bolshevik efforts to inculcate new values and to reeducate the nation succeeded in creating a new Soviet society, while earlier efforts, despite some progress, had failed. Part of the answer lies in the obvious fact that the Bolsheviks had seized both the political power and the economic means of production. With money and resources to distribute, the new state authorities put themselves at the center of the traditionally centripetal power politics of Russia.

That was not the whole story, however. In addition, the Bolsheviks cultivated their hegemony in the country by capitalizing on existing community values. Unlike the expressly political trials addressed in the previous chapter, the trials of everyday life eschewed Marxist language. They avoided mention of the Communist Party and its leading role. They ignored Moscow and official Soviet-ese. Rather, they relied on induction, on moving from the familiar to the more general, on comparing the known and the unknown or not yet known.[11] As Krupskaia explained in 1922, this was because the masses were not used to logical discussions and reasoning. Rather, they thought in images, so the most effective agitation had to be through posters, through music, and through theater.[12]

"All abstraction must be ruthlessly exiled," wrote one director of army clubs in the Caucasus. "We must not forget the psychological particularities of the age of those called up for service and their mental capacities, which are distinguished by the following characteristics: short attention span, distraction, elementariness of perceptions."[13] Other instructions on military club work also explained that peasant soldiers (who, after all, were in the majority in the armed forces) were seriously interested only in what was "real and tangibly concrete," what was "of burning importance." Since so many of the recruits from 1921 onward had been born in 1901 or later, there was hope that they would show particular receptivity to new club methods, particularly if these latter were varied. They might be able to change more easily than could their older comrades, who had become more resistant with age.[14]

The Trial of a Pig: A Play in Three Acts. For performance in people's theaters, peasant cultural centers, and reading huts. By the agronomist–animal technician A. E. Frolov. (The drawing caption reads, "A piglet correctly fed on bacon.") From A. E. Frolov, *Sud nad svin'ei* (n.p., n.d.), cover.

As we will see, the community values on which these trials of everyday life relied included both ones that might be called altruistic (the values of community, generosity, eagerness for education) and others that appealed to baser instincts, the desire to shame and debase others, to lord one's own achievements over the shortcomings of others. The skill of the Bolshevik leaders can be seen in their ability to mobilize the entire repertoire of such preexisting values, both the high and the low, in the service of strengthening an entirely new political order.[15] At every turn they insisted, moreover, that trials of abstract issues should give way to those based on local conditions, on issues familiar to and debated among villagers and workers in their own fields and factories.[16]

FORMS OF INFLUENCE

The agitation trials relating to everyday issues often tell of elaborate attempts to change the defendant's behavior before the outset of the trial itself. These attempts at communal influence, or *vozdeistvie*, had usually taken many forms: demonstration of the resistance and guilt of the fictional individual or individuals; explanations of the distinctions between good and bad behavior; reasoning and appeals to the positive benefits of the desired behavior; scolding and demonstrations of the negative effects of current behavior; public reprimands and regimental discipline; shaming and public humiliation; and finally the "trial" itself in the form of a play in which the (still fictional) defendant is brought before a community of peers to be shown the error of his or her ways.

One Army memorandum considered measures the clubs could take to help soldiers arriving from the village overcome the prejudices of their ancestors against education and book learning. These included political agitation trials of illiterate individuals, as well as plays, skits, posters, satire, and caricatures. In each case the main goal should be to "judge, portray, and ridicule the illiterate person who is vulnerable to ill-intentioned provocation, who doesn't understand his rights and obligations, and who has been a slave of the capitalist order."[17] Audiences were supposed to "laugh at the messy soldier, criticize the soldier who didn't love the military, berate the one who didn't understand his civilian duty, and, on the contrary, show in a good light the peasant-manager, the true red warrior, the fighter for the ideas of the Comintern."[18]

Extracurricular work was to be "built on a psychological basis," and hence could help create "an appropriate mood oriented toward active attention, initiative and critical thinking."[19] Soldiers who were tired from their drills and training could be drawn into propaganda put on in the form of theater and could be influenced because it played on their emotions.[20] Stereotypical characters and familiar forms of pressure helped audiences absorb the explicit messages of the plays, and with them the implicit structures and hierarchies of the new order.

THE RESISTANT PEASANT

One of the earliest (and perhaps the most primitive) scripts of a trial of individual behavior is *The Trial of the Peasant Who Avoided Conscription into the Red Army*. Ivan Ivanovich Nerazumov (whose name means "Foolish") is put on trial for attempting to evade conscription. When the authorities come to his village to recruit peasants, Nerazumov has fled to the city and tried to hide at his relative's house. However, his relative, significantly named Petr Soznatel'nyi (Conscious) chastises him and kicks him out, telling him to go back to his village. Once there he again tries to hide, this time at his father's, but his neighbor Fedor Dobrosovestnyi (Conscientious) denounces him to the chair of the village council and he is arrested. Both Soznatel'nyi and Dobrosovestnyi testify against him during the trial.[21]

Characters, plot, and setting are all underdeveloped in this play. At every turn the characters attempt to persuade and ultimately to force Nerazumov to see the power of the state and his own powerlessness. His relative Soznatel'nyi patiently explains that the state has given the peasants their land and therefore the peasants should serve in the army, which is their only defense against the landlords, who would immediately try to seize back their land if Soviet power ceased to exist. The leading authorities in the trial (the judge, defense, and prosecution) also attempt to reason with the defendant, explaining that there are two kinds of peasants, those who are "conscious" and answer the call of their government, and those who are egotists (*shkurniki* in Russian, that is, people looking out only for their own skin). While the former recognize that Soviet power has given them their land and therefore they should help to defend it, the latter put their own interests above the interests and welfare of all working people; they are used to attaining their own well-being at the expense of others' labor. In the words of the prosecutor, Nerazumov is just such a malicious *shkurnik* with no social conscience.

Allegorically speaking, Nerazumov has two "brothers" among the earliest agitation trials, Nedomyslov (Thoughtless) and Neriashkin (Slovenly). In *The Trial of the Soldier Who Didn't Want to Learn Military Arts*, Arkhip Nedomyslov is accused of failing to attend political literacy classes even though he is perfectly healthy, while in *The Trial of Neriashkin* the protagonist fails to visit the bathhouse, which results in his spreading lice and typhus to his bunkmate, Chistiakov (Clean).[22] If we look at the trials of Nerazumov, Nedomyslov, and Neriashkin, we can see an archetype of the recalcitrant peasant who has to be persuaded by whatever means possible to do what is good for him.

In all three cases the actions of the protagonist are defended on the grounds of his ignorance and his circumstances. Nedomyslov, for example, grew up in a family where he worked as a shepherd and hence could not attend school; his mother took away any books he was reading. When asked why he consistently found excuses to avoid attending drills and literacy classes, he replies, "What do I need that for? I herded cattle and sheep, and in a year and a half I will again be a shepherd. Drills are inconvenient, and I'm not used to them." When he did go to class, he usually sat in the back of the class, where he chewed sunflower seeds or slept. In other trials of illiterate soldiers (of which there were quite a number) the protagonist found he couldn't understand anything in army classes, and his classmates laughed at him.[23] One trial of an illiterate peasant soldier is even subtitled "the political trial of a soldier who did not attend the activities of the *kruzhok* [study circle in a club] because of his laziness and the incitement of ill-intentioned elements and who returned home without having learned anything."[24]

When Neriashkin (Slovenly) refuses to go to the baths, his offense is not just a question of a dirty shirt or lice but the infection of Chistiakov, who contracts typhus and thrombosis in his leg, as a result of which he loses "50 percent of his work capacity." The prosecution insists that the audience must see this as a case affecting all the soldiers of the Twenty-third Regiment. Neriashkin is guilty, the prosecution charges, of endangering not only his own health but the health of the whole regiment. Under tsarism the health of each citizen was an individual affair; each person could say (in a typical peasant phrase) that "his hut was on the outskirts," and therefore he didn't have to worry about communal affairs. Now, however, conditions are different, and "we have the right to demand a different attitude from our citizens." The prosecution demands nothing less than that comrades today should "feel the collectivism and community of their interests with the interests of their comrades." As in the case of Nerazumov the deserter, Neriashkin, by his slovenliness, has gone against community values. For that reason he must be called to account before the larger community embodied in his regiment.

In the end, the collective itself (that is, the audience) votes on the question of Neriashkin's guilt in the matter of spreading typhus in the engineering battalion of the Twenty-third Regiment. Thirty-six find him guilty, while twelve find him innocent. The judge sentences him to three punishments: having his name entered on the "black board" (a board for public censure of those who have committed misdemeanors), expulsion from the Communist Party, and required attendance at military-political courses. Since not taking a bath was not a criminal offense, the court presumably could not render a criminal sentence. Rather (and we will return to the question of legality) the court prescribes moral sanctions (the black board and exclusion from the party). It also, in a move reminiscent of Tsar Peter the Great's forced enlightenment of his nobles in the eighteenth century, sentences Neriashkin to further education, presumably to help him overcome his backwardness.[25] In the Red Army further education also meant deeper exposure to Soviet values and political indoctrination.

DEATH AND TAXES

"You still think that the tax goes to moonshine for the executive committee?" asks the prosecutor in *The Political Trial of the Peasant Evading Payment of the Household Tax.*[26]

"How would I know what it goes for?" answers the accused peasant Timofeev.

"But if the taxes went for a good cause, then you would pay?"

"Who wouldn't?" says Timofeev.

Kolesnikov ("the big wheel"), head of the executive committee, characterizes Timofeev as "a hard-working, business-like peasant, but very stubborn and having a hard time understanding the new customs." In his testimony, Timofeev, like other peasants in these plays, reveals himself to be suspicious and slow to trust but not malevolent. His notion that the executive committee was drinking up all the tax monies came, he testifies, from rumors he heard from the innkeeper. When asked how the innkeeper knew, Timofeev answers that he was judging by his own experience. During the Civil War, when the younger men like Timofeev were away in the army, the innkeepers and others wormed their way into the executive committee. After all, Timofeev testifies, many committees were run by kulaks (rich peasants) who drank and ate well and told the peasants that they were doing so on orders from the central government. However, when the soldiers returned from the army, they quickly kicked all the kulaks off the village councils and set everything to rights. Under the kulaks, the peasants had been more dissatisfied; now everything was more peaceful. When Timofeev is finally convinced that the taxes are going for something concrete and useful—namely, hospitals and schools—he agrees willingly to pay.

Other agitation trials of tax evaders also made a point of explaining what the taxes went for.[27] Not all the defendants were convinced, however. In *The Trial of the Bad Peasant,* Rogoza, a kulak, is accused of everything from moonshine distilling, money lending, and usury to not paying his taxes and sowing less of his land so the authorities would not be able to collect from him. Ukhvatov, the chair of the village council, charges Rogoza not only with not paying the taxes himself but also with inspiring others to say they had less than they did, following his example. Rogoza objects to Ukhvatov's charges: "You don't have the right to call me a kulak." In response the latter modifies his claim to the court: "He's not what you call a really big kulak, just a small one. . . ."[28]

The trial tries to portray the kulak, however small he might be, in the worst possible light by having his fellow villagers call him names during a kind of prologue while they are waiting for the trial to begin: "Look how greedy he is for other people's things, lord have mercy. And what's he to do with it all?" "What's a kulak to do with it all? A kulak's just like a priest: covetous eyes and grasping hands."

During the trial itself one member of the audience can no longer contain himself when the subject of Rogoza's profiteering comes up: "You'll never get out of this, Rogoza. You can't just cheat your brother."

"When did I ever deceive you, you hungry belly, you?"

"If I've a hungry belly, it's because of the likes of you, you spiders; you suck us dry."

In the end the prosecutor compares peasants like Rogoza to locusts. They are insignificant insects in and of themselves, but when they are present in large numbers they are fearsome and dangerous. The greatest danger to the republic now comes not from external enemies, though they are still to be guarded against, but rather from internal enemies, especially the kulaks and popular ignorance. The defense, by contrast, characterizes Rogoza as "an unfortunate person, beaten down, and crippled by an absurd life." All that is good in Rogoza has been suppressed from an early age. The conditions of his prerevolutionary life are to blame for his situation and actions. After a final speech by Rogoza in which he presents himself as one of the insulted and the injured, the judge sentences him to two years' imprisonment plus loss of his electoral rights but then commutes his sentence in response to the amnesties of May 1 and October 22. As for the charges of resisting the grain tax, however, the case is to be transferred with all the investigation materials to the revolutionary tribunal for final adjudication.

In these agitation trials the peasant is presented as stubbornly resistant to the new order but not necessarily dangerous. When political authorities in the army tried to justify the trials, they cited the peasant proverb, "Unless it thunders, the *muzhik* (peasant man) won't cross himself."[29] In other words, strong medicine might be necessary to get the peasants to give up their illiteracy and their traditional ways. Rogoza, the so-called "bad peasant," is described by one of his neighbors as "an old-fashioned, obdurate person, like a rotten stump. He only wants to get rich whether by hook or by crook [literally, "by truth or untruth"]. They say that one spoon of tar can ruin the whole barrel of honey." In his testimony Rogoza bears this out, questioning why children should go to the new school, which has no priest and no church teachings. As for the doctors, he carps, you come to them with a bad back or a headache and they only give you castor oil. But still you have to chop wood for them and feed them and support them.

In the end, it is not the sentence Rogoza receives that is important so much as the verbal drubbing. Through the testimony against him and also his own foolishness, the audience could see why it was better to cooperate with the authorities than to resist them.

FINDING THE GUILTY ONES

The famine of 1921–22 was one of the most traumatic events of the early Soviet period. The contemporary Soviet economist S. G. Strumilin estimated that more people died from the famine and from epidemics than from the whole Civil War.[30] In the spring of 1922 political units in the army created instructions for their local areas to intensify agitation work in conjunction with the removal of church valuables, which the state claimed were to be used to aid the victims of the famine.[31] In this context many local political workers resorted not only to mock versions of the real trial of the church leaders (discussed in the last chapter) but also to harsh portrayals of priests and other recalcitrants in general.

The Volga and eastern Ukrainian provinces were the areas hardest hit by the famine, so it is not surprising that their military club authorities should have been the ones to develop both *The Trial of Those Guilty of the Famine* and *The Model Political Trial of the Church*. There were also two mock trials of priests who refused to comply with the official Soviet decree on removing church valuables to support famine relief: *The Political Trial of the Priest Obiralov* (whose name means "swindler") and *An Unusual Life Event—Father Evlampiia*.[32]

The Trial of Those Guilty of the Famine plays on well-known stereotypes in order to assign blame for the famine. The four main defendants represent four negative "types": a priest who has resisted the donation of church valuables to the famine effort; a Red Army soldier who deserted in order to help his family at home; a rich peasant described as "fat, red-faced and sly" who is accused of making moonshine and not paying taxes; and a careless peasant accused of sowing only half his land and not sorting his seeds (which reduced his yield).

At the sentencing each defendant receives a different punishment. The main enemies of the famine effort are declared to be two off-stage villains, the imperialist European governments, especially France (for not helping in famine relief), and Patriarch Tikhon (who had issued a statement against confiscation). The deserter and the priest are initially each sentenced to five years of forced labor, although the deserter is then included under the amnesty of May 1 because of his low level of consciousness and is sent to join his unit. The kulak is fined triple the amount of the tax he owed and is obliged to help work the land of two Red Army families in his village. The careless peasant is given a public reprimand, obliged to sow all his land in the most effective way practiced in his area, and also required to subscribe to the main newspaper for peasants, *Bednota*.

A more humorous, but in its own way equally damning, trial devoted to this issue of resistant priests is *An Unusual Life Event—Father Evlampiia*.[33] Not only did this resourceful parish priest resist the decree of the Central Executive Committee (VTsIK) to hand over church valuables to be melted down to buy grain for the starving, but he actually attempted to sneak into the church one night to steal the valuables before state authorities could arrive! The peasants in this trial tell long-winded stories. The judge brings them back to order. They forget to address him respectfully and instead stutter as they say "Mister, I mean, comrade judge . . . " Army youths who have returned to the village on leave become the heroes of the story since it is they, we learn, who were sitting on a bench talking one night at 2 a.m. when they witnessed the priest Evlampia, the deacon, and others leaving the church carrying out the most valuable pieces.

Fortunately for the story, the lay reader in the church (*d'iachek*) recants. He tells the judge, "A fierce repentance is gnawing at my soul, even though I am as innocent as the lamb of God, since my actions did not come about through ill intention, but rather through my ignorance and forced subordination to the higher ranks of the spiritual vocation." In order to expiate his guilt, he offers to tell the whole story of how the priest and his attendants had planned and executed the theft. As a result, the priest and his accomplices, but not the lay reader, are all given prison sentences.

The trial of Father Evlampia reveals not only his juridical guilt in disobeying an official decree and his moral guilt in not aiding the victims of the famine but also a stereotype of the greedy priest who does not openly challenge Soviet power but rather secretly sabotages it, at the same time lining his own pockets and overcharging the peasants for church ceremonies.[34]

Resistance and its futility come vividly to the fore in *The Trial of the Women who Refused to Aid the Starving Population in the Volga Region*.[35] In a Cossack village in an undisclosed region four women are accused of resisting the collection of donations that had been decided on by the village meeting. The trial reveals their anti-Soviet and antisocial behavior, as well as their stereotypically "female emotionality." The first woman, a Cossack kulak, refuses even to allow the donation collectors into her house, yelling at them, "Those communists have already brought us to ruin. They will be the end of us. All they do is steal and take away. Under the tsar father everyone lived well and no one went hungry." The second, a peasant woman, claims she is poor and has nothing to give. The third, a village teacher who is representative of the resistant intelligentsia, also, like the Cossack woman, throws the collectors out of her room with invectives: "I'll give to the Constituent Assembly, but not to you. You go away. Anyhow soon you and your band will be finished." The fourth woman, described as a *proletarka* (probably a day laborer in the village), exemplifies the gullible person who goes along with what others are doing. She has refused to give money just because the upper-class Cossack woman and the teacher did not.

In their self-defense the first three women give speeches denying having criticized the government or even having commented on political affairs. The Cossack woman claims she did not give a donation because she thought the newspapers had lied about the famine. The teacher claims the only reason she did not give was that she had no money herself, while the poor peasant woman claims she has always faithfully fulfilled government requirements and would continue to give her last penny to those starving along the Volga. Only the *proletarka* shows proper "heartfelt remorse," saying she refused to donate because she was under the teacher's influence.

The witnesses against the women are all men who in one capacity or another either had witnessed the famine or had helped collect donations. In the final sentencing the kulak woman and the teacher receive the harshest sentences: for the former, public boycott and a requirement to collect food for twenty children over the course of a month, and, for the latter, exclusion from the trade union plus transfer to the Volga region to work as a nurse. The peasant woman meanwhile is required to feed ten children for a month, while the woman day laborer is required to read or listen to the latest news about the situation on the Volga, to tell it to at least ten women in her village, and to collect five hundred pounds of grain.

In the script of the trial the women's original curses and invectives are conveyed, but they do not have a chance to justify or explain their actions, or present their versions of what happened in any kind of final speech. Rather, they are portrayed as immediately conceding and retracting any criticisms of the regime and its policies of collective donations. In the final sentencing all four are explicitly co-opted to aid the Soviet government in its famine relief efforts. Now they must not only make donations themselves but also agitate others to do likewise.

Through a trial such as this one villagers and workers throughout the country could see that donations and aid to the poor were not a private matter but one of state importance. The trial also served to divide and conquer the villagers since some were castigated for their wealth, others for their "liberal" (anti-Soviet) political views, and still others for falling under the influence of anti-Soviet forces.

DIVIDING AND CONQUERING

The Trial of the Women who Refused to Aid the Starving was not the only public agitation trial that divided defendants according to the type of misdemeanor, the degree to which their anti-Soviet behavior was premeditated, and the level of their ignorance and social class background. *The Trial of the Careless Reader* also brings suit against four individuals for their careless handling of books. Mistreating a book was not by law a criminal act; there was no article in the Criminal Code of 1922 that made it a punishable offense (though the play does briefly invoke article 207 of the Code on harming state property). Here the crime lay not in some great evil deed, but in everyday behavior and *nekul'turnost'* (lack of culture). Reviewers in the army praised it for its portrayal of the "barbarian" treatment of books. At its core this trial distinguishes improper from civilized behavior and exposes the false

"Don't read while eating" (Moscow: Izdanie biuro tsentral'noi katalogizatsii i bibliotechnoi tekhniki glavpolitprosveta R.S.F.S.R., 1926). Poster collection, RU/SU 508, Hoover Institution Archives, Stanford, California.

civilization of people who believe they are acting correctly but who in fact lack an understanding of true political literacy and correct behavior.[36]

The accused include a half-literate peasant soldier who gets lard on a book he is reading, a battalion commander who tears out pages for homemade cigarettes, and a supposedly trained political instructor (named Zubrilov, for someone who crams before an exam) who covers a book with underlining and marginal notes. The soldier's defense is that he took the book on political literacy by accident; when he discovered that it didn't have any pictures and had lots of foreign words, he left it on his table, where it eventually began to lose its covers and became covered with grease stains. The battalion commander denies any guilt; he has never done such a thing as rip out pages from a book. The political instructor admits that he made markings in a book but maintains that it was for a good cause.[37]

The character most vividly depicted is the librarian Bogoliubova, daughter of a noble landlord, young (twenty-five) and unmarried, a graduate of a secondary school who has voluntarily enrolled in the Red Army. The so-called facts of her crime are numerous: poor supervision of the reading public, who are mostly soldiers and have virtually no political preparation (she gives them, for example, Karl Kautsky's *Economic Teachings of Karl Marx*,

"Your annotations hinder others reading the book" (Moscow: Izdanie biuro tsentral'noi katalogizatsii i bibliotechnoi tekhniki glavpolitprosveta R.S.F.S.R., 1926). Poster collection, RU/SU 511, Hoover Institution Archives, Stanford, California.

which the court criticizes as way over her readers' heads); rudeness toward the soldiers; ignorance of how to run a library; and her own political illiteracy, which she has failed to overcome.

In the end the soldier is acquitted, while the political instructor is given a reduced sentence and fine. Both have expressed heartfelt remorse. The commander who denied his guilt receives a six-month prison sentence and fines for the cost of the books he has harmed.

In a surprise move Bogoliubova (who denied any guilt) is fired and forbidden future service in the army. The message the trial clearly intended to send was that among those who harmed books (*knizhnye vrediteli*), the most harm ultimately came from the woman librarian, who was of the wrong class background, failed to choose suitable books for her charges, and, above all, failed to give them a proper *vospitanie*, or upbringing, because she didn't explain to them that they should take care of the books they took from the library. To a Soviet reader steeped in Aesopian language (the practice of reading between the lines in order to find an author's true meaning) Bogoliubova must surely have symbolized the failings of the upper-class intelligentsia as a whole. Although she clearly has good intentions to "help" the working class (and implicitly to mother it), her name (which means "lover of God") indicates that she is in fact a descendant of the priestly estate and ultimately a soft do-gooder of the very kind that the revolution with its leather-jacketed commissars has rejected. Such a figure could not provide the kind of upbringing needed to make the "new Soviet citizen."

In these two last examples one can see clearly that the Soviet citizen was required not only to give donations and take care of state property but also to teach others, to participate actively in the upbringing of a whole new nation. As Ivanov, the peasant with lard on his table, explains in his final speech, he had not been able to learn anything from the book with all its foreign words, but he has learned a great deal from the court experience itself. He has especially learned that books should be taken care of, that they are expensive, and that one can learn a great deal from them. From now on he promises to keep any books he takes out of the library under his pillow, so as not to get lard on them and damage their covers.

Treatment of books, like donations to a good cause, was thus far from a private matter. The Soviet citizen was to take the new order to heart and keep its teachings under his or her pillow, where they would be close at hand. While admitting one's guilt did not necessarily bring an acquittal, the converse did hold: not admitting one's guilt, as in Bogoliubova's case, had now come to carry serious consequences. This was a lesson that the (real) defendants in later show trials were to learn the hard way.

PEASANT SELF-DEFENSE

Peasants in these agitation trials defend themselves by invoking their own ignorance and downtroddenness. "We are a dark people," Timofeev, the tax evader, tells his judges. "We don't always understand right away what is what. They make demands on us, but they don't really explain." Once he has understood what is necessary, and what the tax is being used for, then of course he will pay it, and even the fine. Even the prosecution in this trial does not demand a heavy sentence, arguing: "Timofeev is no enemy of the soviets, no enemy of the workers' and peasants' government. His hands are covered with labor calluses." As a middle peasant, he is worthy of the state's support.[38]

Another peasant who tries to defend himself on the grounds of his peasant origins is Ivan Temnyi (whose name means dark or ignorant) in *The Trial of the Illiterate*. Accused of insulting the teacher, Miss Meshchaninova (whose name implies that she is a representative of the petty bourgeoisie), Temnyi claims he cannot answer the judge's question as to whether he considers himself guilty: "Judge for yourself. You can see more clearly, while we are ignorant. What do we know?" Like the shepherd Nedomyslov, Temnyi claims he does not need literacy for his work of mowing hay and plowing.

Besides, as the judges elucidate through their questioning, he is too oppressed by the kulak and the priest to have time to study. His own land has "ceased to give birth," his cattle have gotten the evil eye, and some kind of infection has carried away his wife and children so he has been forced to become a day laborer. It is hard for him to decide whom to believe. "They [unnamed] come in and talk about your being some kind of deserter and they think up some kind of commune, but they don't look to heaven. They'll just bury you and you'll rot like a stump, but the priest promises a golden wreath. So I think to myself to whom should I bow. He [the priest] tells me to bow to him, and now the teacher's come along."[39]

Peasants most often defended themselves by claiming that their social origins meant they didn't know any better. They were too poor to go to school; their families needed their labor as shepherds, cowherds, pigherds. Often there was a mother in the background who was superstitious and opposed book learning for religious reasons. The father was absent for one reason or another and unable to provide a proper role model. Or else he drank and abused them. In the trial of Nerazumov the deserter, the mother does not figure at all, while the father has hidden his son. The prosecution promises that the father will himself be brought to court for providing sanctuary to a fugitive.

In their final speeches the accused in these plays most often confess their guilt and promise never to repeat their infractions. While the agitation trials were one of the most common venues for such public confessions, it is also interesting to note that cases of public confession were also being reported in the periodical press. In 1922, to cite just one example, an army newspaper reported the story of a peasant woman whose husband had been caught deserting from the army. When the authorities took action against him, she roundly scolded all the authorities she could think of. Then, however, she repented (for reasons not explained) and wrote a note to the village council saying she would never again talk back to the authorities. She promised to hang the note by the entrance to her yard so that everyone might see it: "I acknowledge my guilt," the note said, "but I am a stupid woman and in order to expiate my guilt, I agree to hang a copy of this note near my gate so that every citizen of the Soviet Republic may see that I am wrong, and that they may learn not to wag their tongues and not to provoke others against the representatives of village government."[40]

Her self-description as "stupid" and her willingness to subordinate herself to the community saved her from further punishment. At the same time, however, such a "confession" must have reinforced a common village stereotype of women as ignorant and tongue-wagging. In a context where communal values were explicitly placed higher than those of individuals, the publicizing of such public subordination to the will of the group was clearly an important part of the confessional culture emerging in this period.

COLLECTIVE GUILT

Another successful defense strategy often employed by public defenders in these trials was to show that someone else was at least as guilty as the defendant if not more so. This created a kind of collective guilt of everyone concerned.

In *The Trial of the Illiterate*, for example, the kulak and the priest are shown to be at least as guilty as the defendant. They show no remorse that they exploited the poor peasant Ivan Temnyi and gave him no opportunity to learn literacy. "What does someone like him need to learn for?" they ask. Of course, they strive to give an education to their own children and they themselves are literate, but they do not think literacy is necessary for an ordinary peasant. In fact, it is downright dangerous because it might put ideas into his head, and he might rise up against them. A merchant woman named Zhogova, who is heavy-set and sways as she walks into the courtroom, tries to defend the priest on the grounds that he is the "true edifier [*nastavitel'*] of the people," that he tried to enlighten Ivan Temnyi by giving him books on salvation.[41] Other villagers, however, describe the priest as two-faced, appearing like an angel before the upper classes while holding the peasants tightly in his grip. The priest tries vigorously to defend himself by stating that he is loyal to the Soviet state, that he, too, is a worker, that Christ was the first communist, that he taught only about love and even taught the ideas of Lenin. But the audience also hears him mutter his fears that the Bolsheviks will try to catch him in their verbal traps. "You can get rid of the devil with your cross," he comments *sotto voce*, "but there's no way to save oneself from a communist." The court responds by telling the priest that all his teachings "are no good anymore": "You have never loved the people, father, and you will never understand those who do love them." It is the Red Army soldiers who are bringing enlightenment to the village, who are bringing "a passionate desire to aid those who are backward." If only Ivan Temnyi had asked them, they would have explained to him the significance of literacy and why it is impossible to live well without it.

In addition to the kulak (whose name, Zagrebalkin, means to accumulate profits) and the priest Perezvonov (Chimes), the other character who is pilloried in Ivan Temnyi's trial is the Soviet teacher Meshchaninova, who should have been able to help Ivan. But she is too alien for him. "You cut wood for her, bring her water," says Ivan. "You stand at her doorstep, but you aren't anything to her and she isn't anything to you. She has her own set, and with the [ordinary] people 'she wouldn't eat even a goose.' So what should I do?" The judge picks up on the criticism implied in Ivan's comments and excoriates Meshchaninova for teaching in the old bureaucratic style, for relying too heavily on her textbooks, for not becoming a "friend" to her students. As with army political instructors and Bogoliubova, the Soviet state demands that the new tutors of the nation renounce bureaucratism and schoolmarmish ways in the interests of becoming a friend and tutor to the people. Meshchaninova "should be ashamed of herself," says the defense witness, since she is more guilty before the whole people than is Ivan.

The prosecution tries to show that the fault is really Ivan's, that he has deserted the literacy front. He doesn't want to know the new Soviet laws but rather continues to stay in the "kitchen" of his benefactors who exploit him. If he were a true citizen, he would come out of the kitchen and would recognize his liberators, who have banished the dark forces of slavery, deceit, and parasitism. The implication, of course, though this is not stated, is that he should come out of the kitchen in order to be a real man, cutting himself free from the apron strings of the old order. In this context it does not seem accidental that Bogoliubova and Meshchaninova, the librarian and the teacher, are both women who have given the wrong upbringing to their charges and who have not helped to bring them out of the domestic order and into the public world of literacy and participation.

The defense, using the arguments of Ivan Temnyi's ignorance, illiteracy, and lower-class origins, as well as the fact that his employers and mentors in the village made no effort to help him, wins him a reduced sentence. In the end he is merely reprimanded and required to give a solemn oath to eliminate his illiteracy by the time of the tenth anniversary of the October Revolution. Ivan in turn promises "to listen only to those who want to enlighten us, the ignorant."

TRIALS AS RITUALS

Agitation trials such as these were often performed at graduation ceremonies and at the end of conferences. The trials served as a kind of liminal event separating those who had graduated from those who had failed to go forward into the new order. By highlighting distinctions between the literate and the illiterate, the conscious and the unconscious, the authors of the mock trials sought to mark those transformed by the new order and those still clinging to the old order.

On July 15, 1922, for example, the Fifty-third Cavalry Regiment celebrated the graduation from literacy school of seven soldiers by performing *The Trial of an Illiterate Sentry*. In the trial the sentry Andriichuk does not know how to read the passes presented to him at the door of headquarters, where he is stationed, so he simply sticks them on the end of his bayonet and lets people pass. A Romanian spy, noticing that the passes are all printed on blue pieces of paper, obtains a similar piece of paper and presents it, thus successfully penetrating command headquarters and obtaining crucial documents. The spy is apprehended, and Andriichuk is brought to trial since the incursion occurred on his watch. Andriichuk's literacy teacher testifies that he has slept through most of his literacy classes or spent his time hanging out with young women. The defense, however, adduces as mitigating circumstances the poverty of his origins (he, too, grew up a shepherd) and the collective guilt of his commanders, who never asked if he was literate. As punishment Andriichuk receives a suspended sentence of hard labor and is required to attend literacy school.

According to a report on this performance in the newspaper of the Ukrainian armed forces, *Krasnaia Armiia*, the soldiers in the audience "showed enormous interest in the trial and welcomed the sentence with long applause."[42] Whether or not there was such applause, and whether or not it symbolized approval, the political staffs clearly hoped to deploy *The Trial of the Illiterate Sentry* in order to draw a line between those who attended literacy classes and those who failed to do so. They may also have hoped that those who had gained literacy would be persuaded to see their new learning as superior and hence would support such classes in the village and fight against entrenched peasant ignorance.

Newspaper articles also conveyed didactic lessons about the nature of court trials in general. In the same issue of *Krasnaia Armiia* that reported on the performance of *The Trial of the Illiterate Sentry* at the soldiers' graduation, another article described lynchings in the United States and the horrors of black men being burned, beaten, and dragged behind moving cars while crowds of thousands watched. Entitled "Negroes Subjected to 'Lynch Trials,'" the article implicitly contrasted the cruel mob violence of the United States with the orderly and just trials of Soviet Russia, which showed mercy in sentencing a person (even one who allowed a spy to penetrate headquarters) to obligatory schooling rather than imprisonment.[43]

Numerous groups were now holding mock trials at their meetings on issues close to their members' interests. Women's sections of the party held trials of "the new woman," of the woman who had had an abortion, of the woman kulak, of the muslin miss, of the woman delegate, of the poor housewife, of the rich NEPman's wife.[44] Youth groups in the Komsomol held trials of the Komsomol member who violated Komsomol discipline, who led a dissipated life, or who smoked cigarettes.[45] A graduation from a cooperative study group in a club was celebrated with the performance of the *Agitation Trial of a Housewife*, in which the unfortunate housewife bought groceries from the private market instead of the cooperative and ended up with food poisoning.[46]

The form of the agitation trial thus served as a template that could be adapted to address particular topics targeting a particular group of individuals (whether women or youth or soldiers). That template could then be used to mark good and bad behaviors as audiences "graduated" from a women's or youth meeting or army service to their village, school, or workplace.

Any topic that could show resistance, debate, and resolution through confession and judgment could serve as a topic for a trial. And any political activist who was under pressure to perform something in his or her factory, trade union, or reading group could create a trial around the basic roles of defendants, judges, prosecution, defense, and witnesses. The types of witnesses could be varied almost endlessly. If, for example, the topic was labor desertion, the prosecution could call a huge list of witnesses, from the wounded soldier castigating egotists who stinted in their efforts to raise labor productivity to the unemployed worker who brought suit against lazy railway workers who failed to repair the locomotives necessary to bring fuel to reopen his factory. The worker mother could express anger that her children were starving and freezing because of the lack of food and fuel, while the poor peasant could complain that he had no agricultural tools with which to work the land and bring food to the cities.[47]

As we will see in the next chapter, the more intimate the issues and the closer to individuals' everyday lives, the more opportunity the trials presented to overcome resistance, to have actors and audiences consider social issues of the day, and to present solutions that demarcated the old world from the new.

MELODRAMA IN
THE SERVICE OF SCIENCE

On August 14, 1921, *Pravda* reported in its court section that a prostitute named Z. had been tried in the preceding days at the Polytechnic Museum in Moscow. Accused of engaging in prostitution and infecting a Red
Army soldier with syphilis, Z. was found guilty and sentenced to forced treatment in a hospital to be followed by a required job placement by the section
for labor distribution. If she did not then return to "an honest work life,"
she would be incarcerated in a concentration camp for five years.[1]

The *Pravda* article neglected to mention, however, that this was an agitation trial. On August 19 the newspaper printed a retraction, explaining that
the description of the trial should have been placed in the "local events" section rather than in the court chronicle section.[2] A year and a half later, in
late 1922, when Dr. Aleksandr Akkerman published his play *The Trial of a
Prostitute: The Case of Citizen Zaborova Accused of Engaging in Prostitution and Infecting Soldier Krest'ianov with Syphilis*, his friend and senior colleague A. O. Edel'shtein wrote an introduction trumpeting "the illusion of
reality" of such trials, which was so successful that they could be mistaken
for genuine court trials.[3]

The performance of *The Trial of the Prostitute* represented the public de-
but of a new kind of agitation trial, which immediately became known as
the "sanitation trial" because of its focus on sanitation and hygiene issues.
Edel'shtein and Akkerman took pride in publishing the first sanitation trials,
which they contrasted with the political trials in both subject matter and
complexity. These were trials based not on people's experiences at the front
or on simple political events, but rather on specialized scientific topics in
health and hygiene. Among the most elaborate of the agitation trials in terms

of plot structures, these plays provide a window on popular and elite views of science, on notions of truth, judgment, and the role of the state.

As previously noted, the prerevolutionary intelligentsia became involved in education projects in the new regime in part because of their deep sense that Russia's Achilles' heel lay in its backwardness. Backwardness had become almost a code word for all that was wrong with the autocratic order, including all the evils of illiteracy, alcoholism, venereal disease, prostitution, and infant mortality. Not surprisingly, these emerged as the principal topics of sanitation trials.

During the Civil War sanitation had also taken on importance because of the sheer volume of health issues plaguing the country. In January 1920 the head of the army's Political Administration and the head of the literature division wrote directly to Trotsky, head of the whole army, listing the brochures that were their top priorities, given the severe paper shortage: "Who Is Selling out Russia?" "Our Cossack Brothers," "On Relapsing Fever," and "Destroy the Louse." From their perspective the louse and relapsing fever presented problems every bit as urgent as those of Cossacks and White Guard generals.[4]

In October 1920 the political commissar for sanitation in the army wrote a long report on sanitation education in the army and the need to mobilize all the army's cultural forces (club workers, political instructors, and so on) to combat the high rates of epidemic illnesses (typhus, cholera, etc.) and social illnesses (especially venereal diseases) through cultural education and political education methods.[5]

Although sanitation education began in the army, its proponents soon began to preach its virtues for the civilian population as well. In March 1921 sanitation education doctors held their first national meeting and viewed their first agitation trial, "a show trial [pokazatel'nyi sud] of a syphilitic."[6] They now declared that their goal was to "saturate the whole working class" with sanitation enlightenment.[7]

What was sanitation enlightenment? A. V. Mol'kov, one of its greatest proponents, described it as being less about education, in the sense of academic studies, and more about "upbringing, the attainment of a special sanitary discipline in each individual person and in social groups as a whole."[8] In *The Trial of Neriashkin* (the slovenly peasant soldier who transmitted lice to his bunkmate) the prosecutor explains that there are really three different kinds of medicine: medical practice, which helps someone who has already become ill; social medicine, which tries to prevent illness through administrative and social measures so that illness cannot develop and spread; and medical hygiene, which tries to teach the citizen how to prevent illness and how to follow the "rules of hygiene," which, if observed, can help the citizen fend off illness.[9]

This concern with sanitation education was not a Soviet-era invention. Indeed doctors and medical personnel in prerevolutionary Russia from the time of the Crimean War, and especially after the epidemics of the 1890s, had been convinced that they needed to treat not only the illnesses patients brought to them but also the causes of those illnesses, which could be found in the patients' environment and in their habits. As historians Nancy Frieden and John Hutchinson have shown in wonderful detail, they urged this attention to hygiene as part of the process of "making Russia healthy."[10] Yet in the prerevolutionary period they remained profoundly frustrated at their lack of progress in solving crucial medical and social issues.

Involving the whole population in campaigns for sanitation and against epidemics was one of the first goals expressed by the revolutionary government when it came to power in October 1917.[11] Waves of epidemics broke out throughout the Civil War—typhus, typhoid fever, cholera, and Spanish influenza. By the time of the Seventh Congress of Soviets (December 1919) the country and especially the army had been so buffeted by these illnesses that Lenin is said to have commented: "Either the lice will conquer socialism or socialism will conquer the lice."[12]

Toward the end of the Civil War the government created a special Main Military Sanitation Administration (Glavvoensanupr) in the army headed by Zinovii Solov'ev, a leading prerevolutionary activist in the medical community and the Bolshevik underground.[13] A few months later I. D. Strashun was tapped to direct a special sanitation education section within the Commissariat of Health.[14] By 1922 sanitation doctors working in the army and among the civilian population had begun to focus on two main forms of sanitation education: written materials (brochures, pamphlets, newspaper articles, pages in the newspaper, posters, and appeals); and visual methods such as the organization of museums, exhibitions, display windows, slide shows, sanitation films, excursions, and, of course, sanitation trials.[15] As usual, soldiers about to be demobilized were a favorite target for special sanitation education on the theory that they would then take sanitation literacy with them to their villages. The political supervisors working with these soldiers were encouraged, for example, to put on exemplary trials of moonshine distillers in a village environment.[16]

Among the troops themselves sanitation education was designated as one of the "political hours" each week that the troops were required to spend in the classroom. A report at the end of 1922 summarizing the work of the various political units in the Moscow military sanitation administration noted that political agitation trials had not taken hold very well, though other theater work was doing well. Political and sanitation rallies were declining sharply both as an absolute number and as a percentage of agitprop work. In their stead political supervisors were holding more conversations and offering lectures.[17] Some military regions reported better success with sanitation trials, sometimes even coopting local doctors to perform.[18] On the Western front, for example, army units in the summer of 1923 put on trials of a malingerer, a moonshine distiller, a religious believer, a cigarette smoker, a commander who did not take measures to protect the health of his troops, and a prostitute who infected a soldier with syphilis.[19]

ENTHUSIASM FOR SANITATION TRIALS

For sanitation doctors who had been attempting to enlighten peasants and workers for decades before the revolutions of 1917, the sanitation trials seemed like a golden opportunity to present important scientific information in an entertaining form accessible to illiterate audiences who had had limited or no exposure to scientific ideas. Presentations in other forms quickly bored their audiences, even when presenters tried to enliven their material with magic lanterns (an early form of the slide show). Public sanitation rallies, like political rallies in the army, had helped to mobilize local inhabitants to respond to emergencies such as an outbreak of cholera or other infectious disease, but they could not be used for sustained education and enlightenment. Doctors had also tried staging debates around controversial topics (such as prostitution and communist morality), but the number of topics that provided both sufficient controversy and sufficient interest was limited, and such debates required the participation of knowledgeable sanitation education specialists so they would not go awry and convey the wrong information.[20]

Trials, however, could play on the human dimension, on people's emotions and lived conflicts. Sanitation trial authors expressed particular hopes that the audiences, many of whom had never before seen a theater performance, would give themselves up to the performance before them and watch with unbroken concentration. If the illusion of authenticity was not broken by details or episodes that were out of place, the audience could take in the lessons of the trial effortlessly without tiring themselves.[21]

The trials also provided the logical outcome to the enormous frustrations of the prerevolutionary period of tsarist medicine. They were the quintessential public medicine, which provided education, entertainment, and social pressure on the individual to change. By publicizing the costs of risky activities, sanitation doctors hoped to persuade individuals to change their most intimate (and often seemingly intractable) behaviors, especially those associated with the scourges of Russia—venereal disease, alcoholism and distilling, infant mortality, and quack medicine.

In this sense the sanitation trials, and sanitation education efforts in general, provided a continuation of what Stephen Frank has called the intelligentsia's "internal colonization" of Russia in the prerevolutionary period— that is, their efforts to propagandize and disseminate their own notions of "culture" among the masses.[22] They also suggest that community medicine was far from dead, however much émigré doctors might bemoan its passing.[23] Rather, it had adopted new forms to meet new conditions. In part this metamorphosis was possible because of the continuity in medical personnel, many of whom had stayed in Russia after the revolution. Even more important was the continuity in intelligentsia ideals of enlightenment and their faith that the introduction of scientific ideas to replace superstitions would itself go a long way toward healing Russia.

The expert witness played a central role in these trials, quite unlike anything in the earlier army and political trials, where there was no such figure. He (or theoretically, she) provided testimony during the proceedings on the scientific and medical aspects of the case. Since the sanitation trials grew directly out of popular lectures, the expert witness naturally was given a prominent role so that community audiences could ask questions in a context that might be both more appealing and less intimidating than a formal lecture.

At the same time the sanitation trial authors may well have given the expert witness a prominent role in reaction to their own powerlessness in the prerevolutionary period. The trial texts are pervaded by an authorial fantasy that the doctors narrating the etiology of syphilis and other diseases to a public courtroom can demonstrate not only their scientific knowledge but also their power over both the diseases they are describing and the people whose lives their testimony will affect. They now had more power (at least in this mock court setting) to compel people to respect them and listen to their advice, particularly in the case of contagious diseases. In the decades after their tragic failures during the cholera epidemics and riots of the 1890s, when angry mobs had physically attacked medical personnel whom they distrusted, one can imagine how consoling this new role must have been.[24]

Historian John Hutchinson has noted in his study of the nineteenth-century medical profession that there was an increasing tension between what he calls the growing "authority of knowledge" of the medical profession and the traditional "authority of office" of the bureaucrats in charge of medicine in late tsarist Russia.[25] In writing sanitation trials, Soviet doctors could, perhaps for the first time ever, combine an authority of knowledge (particularly in their new understanding of microbes and microscopes) with the authority of office that came from scripting the roles of judges and expert witnesses. This did not mean that they necessarily had any more genuine authority. Nonetheless, they could have the illusion of fulfilling their ideal of selfless service and seeing the population follow their recommendations.

In order to enhance the entertainment value of their plays, the sanitation professionals constructed them in melodramatic form. For present purposes melodrama can be defined as a dramatic form based on simplified character construction, a schematic conflict involving clear representations of good and evil, and heightened emotionalism.[26] The sanitation trials, more than other kinds of agitation trials, are also a distant cousin of what Donald Fanger has called "romantic realism."[27] They are romantic in the sense that they foreground sentiments (even sentimentalism), the plight of the downtrodden, tales of poverty and seduction, threats of suicide, elements of mystery, and coincidences. The women grow hysterical and sometimes faint. The men remain stoic, though close to despair. Characters of both sexes often exclaim that their lives have been ruined.

At the same time the authors of these plays aspired to realism in their settings and use of scientific discourse. In the prerevolutionary period before the opening of the play, the leading female protagonist might have been a servant, but in the recent past she has worked in the cafeteria of a Soviet economic organization. Doctors discourse freely and extensively about the nature and spread of various illnesses.

Of course, these trials are much simpler than the romantic realism of, say, Dostoevsky. The reader or viewer is not given the elaborate, multiple motivations of *The Brothers Karamazov*. Rather, what advances the plot and serves to hold together the romantic, even sentimental, sides of the plot and the scientific, antisentimental characteristics of the medical evidence is the confession of the defendant, who after a prolonged period of resistance, finally admits his or her guilt and the preeminence of science over ignorance. The sanitation trials, like other forms of agitation trials, are thus morality plays, but with more elaborate and ultimately more convincing, full-blooded character and plot developments.

Ultimately the message of the sanitation trials is that melodramatic emotions and solutions to problems were understandable under the old regime but should give way to a new rationality and scientific approach in the new era. In the old world male youths contemplated suicide when they found out they had venereal disease. Young women returned to prostitution when it seemed there were no alternatives. Mothers abandoned their newborn infants in a state orphanage because they felt they could not care for them. But in the new world (one is tempted to say "brave" new world) of the Soviet state, medical science scoffs at the man who considers suicide instead of treatment and insists that the young woman find herself a job and take proper care of her newborn child. Thus the trials implicitly represent not just an individual Bildungsroman of development from immaturity to maturity but also a collective transformation in the whole society from melodrama to science.[28]

The process of change for society as a whole, as for the individual, lies in its acknowledgment of guilt, expression of remorse, and commitment to follow the new paths rather than the old. The goal of the sanitation trials is to create "cultured [i.e., competent] mothers" who know how to care correctly for their children, productive citizens who do not harm their bodies medically and therefore can work effectively, professional doctors (so that midwives and village healers no longer "cripple" the population), and a generally educated population who will turn to doctors and scientists rather than to priests and nonprofessionals. In order to create this new Soviet citizen, however, this educated citizenry must put the old order, the old way of doing things, on trial.

FASCINATION WITH THEATER AND "THEATRICALIZATION"

In 1921 the Health Commissariat oversaw the creation of a new theater workshop known as the Sanitation-Education Drama Studio of the Moscow Military Sanitation Administration under the direction of Olga Rakhmanova. Not everyone was pleased with this idea, however. The publicist Lev Sosnovskii, correspondent for *Pravda,* penned a scathing attack. Soon, he reasoned, an epidemiological-venereological studio in the Commissariat of Education would put on light comedies about syphilis, eczema, and cholera; the Commissariat of Transportation would have a theater on criminal law; and the Commissariat of Justice would have a drama studio devoted to locomotive construction.[29]

Nikolai Semashko, the commissar of health, disagreed. As far as he was concerned, the best work they had done in the health field had been in sanitation education. In a long rebuttal, he commented on the distance they had traveled from the days of lectures and magic lanterns. Muscovites knew, he argued, how popular were the new "show trials" (as he called them). *The Trial of a Prostitute,* for example, had been performed numerous times to full houses in Moscow. He himself had appeared as public prosecutor in a real court trial of a midwife who had carried out illegal abortions that resulted in women's deaths. This practice of putting on trials, both real and dramatized, had to be viewed as a "new form of enlightenment [*prosveshchenie*]." Because the "living material" in the court proceedings is so "vivid" and "concrete," he insisted, it "leaves much more of an impression than a dry report."[30]

The studio organizers were determined, whatever critics like Sosnovskii might say, to establish the studio's legitimacy. In the fall of 1921 they invited the biggest names in the theater world to participate in a public debate on the theater: Anatoly Lunacharsky, Commissar of Education; Vsevolod Meyerhold, the famous director; Aleksandr Iuzhin, a highly acclaimed actor and playwright, now in his sixties; and the stars of the theater world, Konstantin Stanislavsky and Vladimir Nemirovich-Danchenko. They also invited Stanislavsky to write a written review of the studio's work. This he did in July 1921, comparing their work to that of the many other small studios of the day, and praising them for their good beginnings.[31]

As in army education efforts, the key to the success of the small sanitation education studio was the small group of people dedicated to making it work. At the head of this group was A. O. Edel'shtein, who wrote the introduction to a number of sanitation trials, with the close cooperation of Aleksandr Akkerman, Aleksandr Shimanko, and E. B. Demidovich, and with consultations from V. M. Bronner (Russia's leading venereologist) and Health Commissar Semashko himself.[32] All were young (Semashko and Bronner being Lenin's generation, while Shimanko was born in 1888 and Akkerman in 1894). Akkerman, Edel'shtein, and Shimanko had all served on the Western front during the Civil War (no information is available for Demidovich).[33]

The new Sanitation-Education Drama Studio, also known as the Experimental Theater of Sanitation Education in the Commissariat of Health of the Russian Republic, worked under Olga Rakhmanova's direction in fairly unchanged form from 1921 to 1924.[34] In November 1924 a conference of sanitation education professionals in Moscow and Moscow province suggested organizing the Central Sanitation Education Theater. The core of this new troupe initially came from the theater collective of the House of Sanitation Education in the Rogozhsko-Simonovskii neighborhood in Moscow.[35] In 1925 they began performing in the Central Palace of the Peasant in Moscow, which at this time was under the aegis of the sanitation education department of the Moscow provincial health commissariat. In 1928 it was again transferred, this time to the Institute of Sanitation Culture when the latter was formed in the Moscow health department. In July 1938 (at the height of the purge trials) the theater was closed, though it was briefly reopened from 1942 to 1947.[36]

Early postrevolutionary sanitation educators made a particular point of staging dramatizations of Russian and foreign stories and plays dealing with social ills, many of which were so-called problem plays, including Gerhart Hauptmann's *Before Dawn* and *The Weavers*, Henrik Ibsen's *Ghosts*, Octave Mirbeau's *Epidemic*, Eugene Brieux's *Ruined*, Guy de Maupassant's *Port*, Nikolai Nekrasov's *Lost Consciousness*, Leonid Andreev's *The Fog*, and Maksim Gorky's *Children of the Slums*.[37] These works often combined naturalism and sentiment, concern for the lives of the poor and social commentary.

In the early 1920s, Dr. Mikhail Utenkov, a sanitation doctor who had worked in Petrograd and at the front during the European War, wrote a number of nontrial plays for the same Sanitation-Education Drama Studio and published them himself. With titles such as *Stigmatized by Shame, The Accursed Question, Fallen Creatures,* and *The Victim of Dirt,* Utenkov's plays take social issues of prostitution, venereal disease, and cholera, and place them in the context of prerevolutionary Moscow or a foreign port city to dramatize the horrors of "bourgeois" attitudes toward sex and sexuality, the disregard for the feelings of the lower classes and especially prostitutes, and the abject poverty of Russia's lower classes, especially those afflicted with wasting diseases like syphilis.[38]

Given the immediate prerevolutionary fascination with melodrama as a way of dramatizing social evils, it is not surprising that the postrevolutionary writers of sanitation trials should have cast their work in that form, especially given their paramount desire to attract new viewers and entertain them as well as provide scientific information. How, then, did melodrama and science become intertwined in the writing and staging of these plays?

MELODRAMA IN THE SERVICE OF SCIENCE

Even the titles of the sanitation trials are more melodramatic than those of other kinds of agitation trials. They clearly aim at titillating potential audiences. Some characteristic titles include *The Trial of Citizen Kiselev Accused of Infecting his Wife with Gonorrhea Which Resulted in Her Suicide; The Trial of the Moonshine Distillers: The Case of Karpov Tikhon and His Wife Agaf'ia Accused of Preparing and Secretly Trading in Moonshine; The Trial of Midwife Lopukhina Who Carried Out an Abortion Operation Which Resulted in the Woman's Death; The Trial of a Mother Who Abandoned Her Child: The Case of Citizen Tikhonova Accused of Criminally Negligent Behavior Toward her Child, Which Resulted in Serious Illness, and of Abandoning Her Child to the Whims of Fate.*[39]

The plots of the sanitation trials revolve around misfortunes intended to reveal a particular scientific principle or set of principles (the importance of vaccinating one's child, of following a full treatment for venereal disease, of permitting abortions only in state-regulated hospitals). But they are presented in a manner that draws on penny-kopeck styles of melodrama and adventure. They feature innocent young women and evil seducers, haglike village healers, and daring Red Army men. They are never directly pornographic but often delve into closely allied topics of sexuality, alcohol, and addictions.

Even more than other trials in the agitation tradition, the sanitation trials usually, though not always, end in the acquittal of the defendants. By the end of the play they have shown resistance and acted against the interests not only of themselves but also of the community. But they have also repented, and the defense has successfully shown that they are not alone in their wrongdoing. Ultimately, it is the community, and we, the audience, who are guilty of failing to support them in their transition to the new world.

However, there were several pitfalls associated with the sanitation trials, of which their authors were well aware. If a trial had too much caricature or mockery, it could fail to convey the verisimilitude and seriousness necessary for full effect. If, on the other hand, the trial overloaded the viewers with too much scientific information, it could become nothing more than a camouflaged lecture, which would quickly tire audiences and frighten away future viewers. The sanitation trials were also criticized for occasionally falling into sensationalism. A sensational trial might inflame people's curiosity to come to the show, critics argued, but it would attract audiences who were seeking only titillation rather than knowledge and learning. Such sensationalism actually happened in Moscow, according to some reports, when posters announcing *The Trial of a Prostitute* went up everywhere with no indication that the trial was going to deal with serious issues.[40]

Whereas the directors in political agitation trials had sought to cast the most respected members of a community in the roles of judge, prosecution, and defense, those organizing sanitation trials tended to try to give the most important roles to the expert witnesses, especially the doctors. If possible, the role of the doctor was to be played by a regimental doctor, or at least someone with the training of a physician's assistant. When the court recessed before closing arguments, the person who had played the doctor could take questions from the audience to clear up any misunderstandings they might have or to answer any further questions. In the trial itself the doctor was to carry the scientific, knowledge-oriented side of the trial, while the prosecution and defense, as well as the witnesses, were to develop the emotional, dramatic side of the plot. As in other kinds of agitation trials, much of the dramatic interest in the trial depended on the tension between the positions of the prosecution and the defense.[41] Interestingly, the expert doctor, like the prosecutor and public defender, was almost never given a personal name in the published scripts of the trials. His or her name and personality (not to mention gender, social class, and age) were not portrayed as a fundamental part of the story. Rather, what counted was the information that the doctor imparted. This very namelessness may well have been intended to contribute to the doctor's general appearance of impartiality and objectivity.[42]

Finding someone to play the role of the defendant in sanitation trials often presented a difficult casting issue. It was not so hard to find someone to play an army deserter, but soldiers wanted no part of playing a syphilitic, and even less did they want to play a prostitute. Only through patient explanation could the club members be disabused of their prejudices and persuaded to play such a role.[43]

THE FIRST SANITATION TRIALS

In late 1922 the first two sanitation trials—*The Trial of a Prostitute* and *The Trial of Citizen Kiselev Accused of Infecting His Wife with Gonorrhea Which Resulted in Her Suicide*—were published with some excitement in the medical community.[44] Following *The Trial of Neriashkin* (the story of the slovenly soldier who infected his bunkmate with lice), these were the first trials of the new genre and among its most elaborate representatives. They are worth considering in some detail because of the ways in which melodrama and science, truth and judgment are elaborately interwoven.

The Trial of a Prostitute has all the classic markings of a melodrama. A Red Army soldier, Krest'ianov (whose name means "peasant"), has brought suit against a young woman named Zaborova on the grounds that she has secretly been engaging in prostitution and knowingly infected him with venereal disease when he visited her in May 1921. Zaborova's own name comes from the word for fence and may refer to someone giving birth or dying "under the fence," that is, in dire poverty. Twenty-four years old and born in a village 250 miles south of Moscow, Zaborova resides on Sukharevsky Lane, which marks her as poor and most likely a prostitute, since the Sukharevka was a major market associated in literature with fallen women like Dostoevsky's Sonya Marmeladova in *Crime and Punishment.*

Though Zaborova adamantly denies the charges brought against her, the story gradually emerges that she had indeed worked as a prostitute prior to the revolution. From her brother's testimony we learn that after the death of her father she had gone to work as a servant in a rich household. There, true to melodramatic form, she was seduced by the owner's son and cast out when she became pregnant. In order to save the infant child, she takes to the streets as a prostitute. The child dies anyway and she despairs that she has ruined her life for naught. After the revolution a friend finds her a job in a state cafeteria. However, at work she often encounters former acquaintances who deride her for her past. Forced to leave her job because of their sneers, she returns to the streets.

One night she takes in Krest'ianov, persuading him and a fellow soldier to come visit for the evening. Though his friend Kazakov goes back to the barracks, Krest'ianov stays the night. A month later Kazakov discovers that his friend is melancholy, even suicidal. Krest'ianov explains to him that he has contracted venereal disease and that the shame of it makes him feel he can no longer go on living. Kazakov convinces him that his shame is misplaced. Instead of ending his life, he should file suit against Zaborova so she will not infect anyone else.

An equally elaborate tale is depicted in *The Trial of Citizen Kiselev Accused of Infecting his Wife with Gonorrhea Which Resulted in her Suicide.* Pavel Kiselev (whose name means "sour" or "moping") had served in the tsarist army, where he contracted venereal disease. Having failed to treat it completely, he has infected his new wife, who has then given birth to a child who goes blind from the disease and from the fact that the midwife has failed to put silver nitrate drops in its eyes as a precaution against blindness. The wife, distraught over the illness and then death of her child, ends her life by hanging herself in the kitchen. Her mother, Zotova, a former schoolteacher, brings suit against Kiselev, who she claims has destroyed her daughter.

Although the style of the play contains obvious melodramatic tropes—the wife's silent suffering and suicide from despair, the husband's womanizing, and the mother's scolding—the trial is also antimelodramatic and provides a vivid commentary on the bourgeois morals that gave rise to many of the characters' problems in the first place. Because Kiselev was raised in a petty-bourgeois family, he never learned to talk about such "shameful" topics as venereal disease. He went to a "doctor who advertised" (that is, a private physician, not associated with a hospital, who may well have been a quack) who failed to tell him that he needed to complete the full course of treatment even if the symptoms went away. Because "one doesn't talk about such things," he didn't tell his wife that he was ill with the disease even though he had a renewed outbreak of symptoms a mere three months before their marriage. Nor did anyone talk about venereal diseases in his family or high school, for the same reason—namely, that if someone had even mentioned it, he or she would have been expelled for immorality. Zotova (the mother), as a schoolteacher, says that she, too, regrets now that these matters weren't talked about. If the schoolchildren had asked her about venereal disease before her daughter's illness, she would have screamed at them and told them it wasn't the place of children to talk about "such horrible things" (*ob etikh gadostiakh*). "But now I doubt it. . . . It seems to me that one should shed light on the horrors and dirt [*uzhas i griaz'*] which they will encounter as soon as they are mature, to shed light so that they can avoid such dirt." Yet she also laments that she does not herself have the necessary knowledge to teach them; nor, she says, do other teachers she knows.

In both plays the principal drama lies in the double unveiling of, first, the defendants' guilt despite their denials, and second, their own and everyone else's ignorance, and hence their collective guilt, in matters of science and medicine. Zaborova, for example, admits the truth only when her own brother is called as a witness and tells the story of her prerevolutionary past. The "truth" demanded by the court thus prevails over their kinship. The prosecutor castigates her for telling the truth only under pressure from her brother's account. If she had told the truth of her own free will, she would have "freed herself from the lie which weighs on a person like a heavy stone." Telling would have been a way to leave behind the past and to share her sorrow.[45]

In the end the evidence of the case proves that Zaborova has been working again as a prostitute. The question becomes whether she should be considered guilty. This, of course, prompts long disquisitions by the prosecutor and defender on the subject of prostitution, its origins, its role in the spread of venereal disease, and so on. The speeches of these officials occupy about ten pages each, as does that of the medical witness. Yet the author gives Zaborova herself a mere page and a half at the beginning of the play and the same at the end, with a few scattered responses to questions in the middle. Thus while the experts cumulatively occupy thirty pages of written text (which would probably translate into an hour of stage time), Zaborova is barely allowed a small squeak. For Dr. Akkerman and his associates the experience narrated by the prostitute is less important than the competing theories put forward by these various experts as they battle over questions of causality and significance and the long-range effects of prostitution.

The prosecutor focuses his arguments on distinguishing the new world from the old, acknowledging that the environment was responsible in the prerevolutionary period for "turning women into prostitutes." Now, however, "a daughter of the proletariat" such as citizen Zaborova betrays the people when she fails to show sufficient "will" (*volia*) and "steel-like striving [*stal'noe stremlenie*] toward the new life." She quit her job, he claims, because the pay was low; yet millions of other people manage to work in factories and at the plow regardless of their income. "In the name of money and a sated life," Zaborova had "extended her hand to the enemies of the toilers, and abandoned her own people in the moment of threatening battle." In the prosecutor's view the October Revolution "ruthlessly and justly makes a selection [otbor] so as to create those who should have the right to participate in the building of the new edifice of socialism."[46]

One charge against Zaborova is thus a lack of solidarity and failure to close ranks in the face of the hardships of building a new society. The prosecutor also castigates her for her carelessness, the same carelessness (khalatnost') for which political officers in the army often indicted their soldiers in the army trials. By not taking care of her own health, she is infecting "her brother toilers," which undermines the labor power of the whole nation. Despite the fact that the Civil War has ended, military metaphors dominate the prosecutor's speech. The battlefront is now economic, and "the most evil enemies" are illnesses. In spreading disease, the prostitute strengthens the enemy's forces and demoralizes the nation's. The reason for Zaborova's carelessness lies in her weak will, her selfishness in thinking only of herself, in her lack of desire "to look truth in the eye." It is the duty of the court in general to "force people to think about their health." Hiding illness is treason. "We must force each person to live in such a way that his life will not bring a deadly blow to the collective."[47]

The defense, by contrast, begins from the explicit premise (common in many agitation trials) that to understand is to forgive. In the question of environment versus individual failing, the defense places blame on the environment and on those around Zaborova who failed to come to her aid. She is thus a victim rather than a perpetrator. The old life is what needs to be judged, not Zaborova. Now the revolution has killed that old life, but gossips who scorn Zaborova and have failed to see in her a new person have pushed her back into the abyss of prostitution, so it is their fault as well that she has relapsed. Interestingly, the defense places explicit blame on the Russian intelligentsia personified in a friend of hers who is a student. Not only does the student fail to help her morally and physically, but the whole intelligentsia has been "stumbling along . . . with great but barren ideals, general words about the happiness of the people, but also deep emptiness, lack of will, passivity." Ultimately, the defense declares, "it is not Zaborova who is guilty. It is we who are guilty, we who have done nothing for those whom the old life crushed, for whom it is hard to stand on their feet and go forward with everyone."[48]

Zaborova herself pleads for mercy on the grounds that she is not guilty, that "life itself" (the man who seduced her, her pregnancy, the death of her child) forced her onto the street. She speaks at the end of the play not only in her own voice but also for all women in her position: "People look at us. We are cheerful, happy, but we are hiding our woe, not showing our souls

to anyone. In fact we are the most unhappy, injured by life. We live like an-
imals and then death will take you, [lying] under some fence or you'll rot in
a hospital. Judge me, scold me. But you must pity us. Help me. Help me to
get out of this stinking abyss. Help me!"[49]

In its sentencing the court finds Zaborova guilty of engaging in secret
prostitution but not of consciously infecting Krest'ianov. (This follows the
acknowledgment of the expert doctor that while Krest'ianov might have become infected from Zaborova, there is no way to prove conclusively that that
is the case.) As in other trials, the court finds that Zaborova's proletarian origins and her terrible suffering serve as mitigating circumstances, especially
given the "criminal attitudes of those around her." She is to be sent to a hospital for treatment, and the government commissariats responsible for labor
placement are to find her a productive job guaranteeing her a living wage. In
a last-minute announcement the court (following a request made by the prosecutor) turns the tables on the plaintiff Krest'ianov and says that a new case
will be brought against him for patronizing prostitutes and helping to create
a demand for them. The court is thus putting into practice one of the max-
ims of those fighting against prostitution: that the customers of prostitutes
must be held as responsible as the streetwalkers themselves.

In the case of *The Trial of Kiselev*, the prosecution and defense also make
extensive arguments showing the merits of their cases against and for the defendant. In his concluding speech Kiselev himself breaks down and asks:

Comrade judges . . . . Why didn't you judge me earlier? . . . Why are
people like me not brought to court when there are thousands of us?
You did not know me; I did not fall into your hands; you think then
that I knew, knew what I was doing, knew that I was infected with such
an illness. If even once on my path I had heard what I have heard here
today, believe me, I would not today be on the defendant's bench, and
my wife would be alive.[50]

In both trials the prosecution and defense present their cases with great
skill, relying on the facts brought forth by the witnesses. Yet they present ideas
more than people. Kiselev has more of a real character than Zaborova, and
somewhat more agency, since he openly struggles with the question of his
wife's and child's deaths. Still, he mostly personifies ignorance, as Zaborova
does, proving himself more a product of his environment than an actor in it.
Both Kiselev and Zaborova have "fallen" and become, in moral terms, sinners because of their ignorance and failure to speak. Their false shame has
prevented them from being able to resolve the problems in their lives. In the
place of shame and sinfulness, the doctor authors of these trials try to establish a new morality and a new authority based on science and knowledge that
will overcome this ignorance and the crimes resulting from it.

THE CASE OF SCIENCE VERSUS IGNORANCE

The power of the medical profession and the courts is underlined in the ways the judge and leading court personnel address the doctor: "Comrade expert, the court is interested to know how syphilis progresses."[51] The fact that the doctor is addressed as "comrade expert" reminds (and teaches) the viewer that this is someone whom the court respects as an equal. The defendants, by contrast, true to early Soviet form, are addressed in this and other trials as "citizens," showing that since they are under indictment, they have at least temporarily lost their positions as full comrades in the Soviet order.[52]

The doctor's testimony is couched in formal scientific language. He or she presents a "record of medical examination" for Krest'ianov and Zaborova in *The Trial of a Prostitute*. In this testimony, the doctor's knowledge and experience set him apart from other characters as the voice of authority on syphilis and its progression.[53]

The doctor and other court personnel also establish their authority by naming what others can refer to only euphemistically. Kiselev, for example, does not want to tell how he first contracted venereal disease so he dodges the question by saying offhandedly that he came down with it "the same way everyone does." It then becomes the duty of the prosecutor to clarify: "You mean, through association with a woman of free conduct?" Kiselev laments that he had not told his wife because it was so shameful that he felt "powerless" to tell her even though the doctor had asked him to.[54]

The doctor not only is not afraid to name the illness in question, but he also gives detailed, graphic descriptions of syphilis—its symptoms, course, and eventual effects on the human organism if left untreated. He shows no fear or concern about describing his physical examination of Krest'ianov and Zaborova, including the palpitation of a primary chancre "on the end flesh of the [male] sexual member." He can touch the manifestation of a disease that before about 1910 was considered by doctors to be both highly contagious and incurable. Now, however, the doctor quotes a German colleague as saying that, with the arrival of Salvarsan 606 and 914 (arsenic-based drugs that were the most effective cure for syphilis before the invention of penicillin), syphilis is "not only curable but easily curable." Moreover, the drug no longer had to be imported from Europe as it was being produced in two different factories in Moscow itself.[55]

It is not only physical illness that the doctor can observe but also social ills. In general the trial doctors are extremely careful to argue that it is prostitution as a social phenomenon that is at fault, not the individual prostitute, who in the early 1920s was almost invariably portrayed as a victim of her circumstances. Nonetheless, in the minds of the venereologist authors of these early trials, the link between prostitution and venereal disease was so strong that no trial of someone with the disease could appear without a discussion of prostitution, and no trial of prostitution could appear without discussion of venereal disease in one form or another.

Perhaps the most powerful way for the playwright to demonstrate the doctor's authority, and implicit superiority, was to show the ignorance of virtually every other character in these plays. By the end of *The Trial of Citizen Kiselev*, for example, nearly all the characters have proven their ignorance and ultimately their guilt and complicity because of that ignorance. Kiselev failed to pursue the full course of treatment for his gonorrhea, relying on his own sense that the symptoms had cleared up rather than on consultation with a doctor. He and his wife failed to consult with a doctor before their marriage to make sure they had a clean bill of health. The wife failed to talk with her husband or consult with a doctor. Both the mother and the supremely ignorant midwife assumed that the wife's weakness was just "female troubles," that in fact to go to a doctor (presumably male) would mean that Kiseleva, a young woman, would have to bare her body before a male stranger. The midwife and the mother were both ignorant of the value of silver nitrate drops as a preventive for infant blindness and failed to appreciate the contagiousness of venereal disease. Kiselev's friend Karpenko "reassured" him after his first infection that he just had to go to a doctor, get some medicine, and be done with the whole treatment in two weeks.

SYPHILIZATION OR CIVILIZATION

The main issues in the medical debates over venereal disease and the best way to approach this scourge of the Russian countryside can be seen in a play written in 1923 by the sanitation education department of the Central Communist Club of the October Revolution entitled *The Sanitation Trial of a Syphilitic*.[56] The defendant in the trial, Petr Ivanovich Vertikhvostov, a twenty-five-year-old soldier, is accused of premeditated infection of his wife, Anna Petrovna, with syphilis. She has filed for divorce from him in the people's court in the city of Omsk (western Siberia) on the grounds that he infected her and her two small children with syphilis when he returned on leave from the army.[57] The preliminary investigation by the court reveals that indeed the wife and children contracted syphilis sometime after his return from the army and that he himself was also ill with a more advanced stage of the same disease. The case is then transferred to a sanitation tribunal in the army, where Vertikhvostov (whose name means "hussy," a term used, as in English, almost exclusively for women) admits that when he finally received a long-awaited leave to go home to his family, he went out on a drinking spree, during which he met a woman who invited him up "for a cup of tea." Not suspecting that she had syphilis, he went to visit her and contracted it.

Vertikhvostov, his wife, and various witnesses tell the court their perspectives on what has happened, beginning with Vertikhvostov's declarations of his innocence and Anna Petrovna's fury that she has been so cavalierly betrayed by her husband. The trial is unusual in that the prosecutor and expert witness are both doctors, so their debate about Vertikhvostov's guilt contains in microcosm a debate about the nature of syphilis and patient-doctor relations.

The expert doctor, as in the other trials, presents the voice of reason and science. After a long description of the terrible progress of the disease, the doctor talks about the consequences of the spread of the disease for the whole community and ultimately for the whole nation. The French were already worrying about their death rate being higher than their birth rate. Since syphilis was popularly known in Russia as "the French disease," and had even been referred to as such in the course of the play, the doctor implies that the French are now dying out because of high syphilis rates and that the Russians could soon follow suit. This "insidious disease," which can "sneak up on a person" with few perceptible early symptoms, has been responsible, he tells the court, for countless "family dramas," as when a father infected his family and then killed himself from shame. Innocent children are unknowingly infected with the sins of their parents. Everyone risks infection from a syphilitic at work, in a public cafeteria, on a train. In the villages it has even been called "the soldier's disease."

The prosecutor, in contrast to the expert witness, makes no attempt at impartiality. Vertikhvostov, in his opinion, is nothing less than a coward who has lacked sufficient manhood to go for treatment for his illness. Far from being a conscious soldier, he has been overcome by a "false feeling of shame" and the "cowardice of petty bourgeois morality." He, who has taken an oath before the whole nation, has brought this kind of present home to his children. The village, unfortunately, is still full of old superstitions, whisperings, spells, sprinklings from the holy icon corner, and customs of having the sick person ride around on horseback. The danger, according to the prosecutor, is that the disease could infect not only the soldier's own family, but also the neighboring family and the family after that until the whole village becomes infected. Thus would begin the "wholesale syphilization [sploshnaia sifilizatsiia] of the village." From fear and false shame before the opinion of others, Vertikhvostov has avoided going to the doctor. This has made him no less than a criminal. The army tried to sow the seeds of enlightenment and education, but they fell on stony soil. Vertikhvostov's infection of himself and others makes him a criminal before all his fellow villagers and before the nation as a whole.

The defense makes an equally impassioned plea on the contrary to see syphilis not as a crime but as an illness. Given Vertikhvostov's low cultural level, he could not have known that he would infect others. The way to rid the nation of this scourge is to transform basic socioeconomic relations. Someone like Vertikhvostov should be given medical treatment and not punished.

The prosecutor's fear of "syphilization" thus clashes with the experts' hope that Russia will be able to follow the path of "civilization." Will syphilis in Vertikhvostov and others undermine the nation? Or will civilization and enlightenment gain the upper hand? The court in the end asks those present to vote for Vertikhvostov's guilt or innocence. Sixty-eight find him guilty; 212 vote for his acquittal. The court pronounces that because of his ignorance, he cannot be found guilty of premeditated harm to his family. Instead it sentences him to a public rebuke (*obshchestvennoe poritsanie*) with a warning that henceforth he should pay more attention to the political education exercises in the army and should explain to everyone the dangers of seeking treatment from village healers instead of doctors.

The play thus becomes a dramatization of the possible dire consequences of individual misbehavior. Vertikhvostov has not only infected himself through his drinking and sleeping with strange women, but he has potentially undermined the whole effort to build a new society. Ultimately the play is inconclusive as to whether syphilis should be treated as a shameful, criminal illness contracted by a soldier who should have known better, or whether it is a misfortune that must be treated and not punished. Should society, the courts, and the medical profession shame the defendant so he will seek treatment? Or should they show understanding and compassion so that the patient will not be afraid of social censure and will come forward to seek treatment? Whereas Russian doctors from at least the early 1890s had been roundly asserting to all who would listen that false shame was the enemy of treatment, now a few characters in agitation trials such as this one were beginning to consider that some shaming might be useful. Where earlier Soviet-era trials had referred principally to actions (such as falling asleep on duty) and omissions (failing to acquire literacy), now questions of character, manliness, and moral responsibility were coming increasingly to the fore.[58]

VENEREAL DISEASE AND THE LAW

The fact that the earliest sanitation trials focused primarily on venereal disease was not accidental. This was an issue that had seemed particularly intractable to prerevolutionary doctors. Some considered syphilis in particular to be the most widespread single illness in the Russian countryside.[59] There had also been important recent breakthroughs in treatment. In 1905 German doctors Schaudinn and Hoffmann had discovered the spirochete pathogen that caused syphilis, and by 1906 Wassermann had developed the test that bears his name to determine whether the patient was carrying the antibodies to syphilis. By the time of these trials in the early 1920s it seemed that with the help of Salvarsan (discovered in 1910) syphilis could be pretty well treated and had a high cure rate.

The question of the legal treatment of venereal disease was not so easily solved, however. As becomes evident in the trial of Vertikhvostov, doctors themselves faced a dilemma: if they forced treatment on those who lacked "sufficient manhood" to come forward voluntarily, they risked discouraging others from coming forward out of shame.

The legal, as opposed to medical, debates about venereal disease in particular and sexual crimes in general can be seen most easily in another trial about venereal disease and prostitution, *The Trial of Citizen Fedor Sharov, Accused of Spreading Gonorrhea* by Dr. B. S. Sigal.[60] In this trial a twenty-one-year-old worker named Fedor Sharov, who was taking courses in an electrical trade union school, is accused of spreading gonorrhea to a fellow worker in the same factory, Anna Nikolaeva. Both are members of the drama circle in the factory club. In the course of the play the prosecutor tries to show not only that Sharov infected Nikolaeva but that he should be tried as well on charges of rape for getting her drunk and then raping her.

This trial is somewhat unusual in that it is the only one in which the doctor actually has a name (Golovlev). Also unusual is the fact that the two charges brought against Fedor Sharov are named as articles of the Criminal Code: article 155, which prosecuted the transmission of venereal disease to another person, and article 169, rape or attempted rape. Nikolaeva brings charges against Sharov under article 155 on the basis of the fact that she began to discover symptoms of gonorrhea four or five days after Sharov forced her to have sex with him. The prosecutor tries to charge Sharov with rape as well on the grounds that he deceived Nikolaeva and persuaded her to come with him to a bar, where he got her drunk, after which she awoke to find that he had violated her.

Legally speaking, article 155 (infection of another person with venereal disease) did not fall under the category of sexual crimes but rather under the rubric of "bodily harm and violence against the person." Initially (at the time of the publication of the Criminal Code on June 1, 1922) the article had addressed the "knowing infection of another person with serious venereal disease," but in July 1923 it was modified to remove both the words "knowing" (*zavedomoe zarazhenie*) and "serious" (*tiazhelyi*) on the grounds that it was extremely difficult to prove whether someone had knowingly infected another person and to draw a line between "serious" forms of venereal disease such as syphilis and allegedly "nonserious" forms such as gonorrhea.[61]

The Criminal Code of 1922 contained seven crimes under the specific rubric of "sexual crimes," including what in English would be called (1) statutory rape; (2) aggravated statutory rape; (3) corruption of minors; (4) rape (defined as "sexual relations with the application of physical or psychological force or by resorting to the helplessness of the victim"); (5) using a woman's material dependence or dependence in the workplace to force her into sexual relations; (6) forcing someone to engage in prostitution for one's own gain through use of physical or psychological influence; and (7) procuring, maintaining brothels, and recruiting women for prostitution.[62]

In the sanitation trial of Fedor Sharov the central forensic issues are (1) whether Sharov infected Nikolaeva and (2) whether he raped her. As to the infection, he maintains his innocence to the end of the trial, arguing that he thought he had been cured by the local "fershal" (corruption of the word "fel'dsher," physician's assistant) and that in fact it was Nikolaeva who infected him, not the reverse. To prove his point he has even spread rumors in the club defaming her character and suggesting that she has been sleeping around. The defense disproves these arguments by showing the charlatanism of the local healer, who claimed to have learned all he knew in the army during the Russo-Japanese War and who had then hung out a sign with a list of the diseases he purported to be able to cure. Boasting that he had produced his own "revolution" in the cure of diseases by using "miraculous forces," he maintained that gonorrhea was merely the "exiting [from the body] of harmful vapors," a "cleansing of the blood."

The local Komsomol organizer is asked to attest to Nikolaeva's and Sharov's characters so as to disprove Sharov's claim that he had been infected by Nikolaeva instead of vice versa. This allows the Komsomol organizer to present a different kind of expert statement, this time on the correct and incorrect behavior of youth today. Sharov is at fault, according to the organizer Kuz'min (whose name means "blacksmith"), because he has failed to change his attitudes toward women. He still has old views of women and harasses them instead of treating them as comrades. The prosecution, too, inveighs against the "old-fashioned code of rules of the salons" according to which it was all right to "deceive a poor girl," to get her drunk in a bar, and to make her a present of gonorrhea. But in fact this kind of "heavy life drama" could happen because of the "false view" that sexual life among youth should begin at an early age, with a young man's visit to a prostitute, instead of at a mature age after marriage. Instead, the prosecutor moralizes, a young man should look on the young woman next to him as a comrade, not someone to be seduced and ruined.

On the question of rape the court sides with the defense, arguing that Nikolaeva voluntarily went to the beer hall with Sharov during a dance and stayed with him even when he ordered a private room for the two of them. In other words, the judge grants, and even emphasizes, Nikolaeva's autonomy in decision making and her responsibility for own actions. She is "a conscious girl" (*soznatel'naia devushka*), in the words of the defense, and one who should have known better than to go to a beer hall. Nikolaeva herself rues the fact that the young people organized the dance, that it got hot, and that she allowed Sharov to convince her to go next door to the beer hall since strong drinks were not allowed in their club. In this argument young women and young men are to be held to a single standard of moral behavior. Drunkenness is no excuse.[63]

This case, like others we have examined, also plays upon notions of false and true shame. Sharov's friends shamed him as a young man, calling him a sissy (*baba*) when he was reluctant to go drinking and womanizing. "Relax, it's high time you started going to girls. What are you scared of? You're big now." When he realizes afterward that something is wrong with his health, he avoids going to the doctor: "It was shameful [*stydno*] to go to our factory [doctor]. Everyone would have laughed. And I didn't have money to go to a private doctor. So I went to the 'fershal.'"

The judge emphasizes the court's role as arbiter of true and false shame, and truth and falsehood in general. When Sharov doesn't want to say how he first became infected with venereal disease, the judge tells him to try to remember, "and it will go better for you." When Sharov then tells the story of going out drinking as a young adolescent and spending his time with a woman of the streets, the judge is the one to name the event without euphemisms: "So you became infected with gonorrhea from a prostitute, and already ill, you continued to have relations with her. Is that it?" Nor is the judge afraid to invoke shame in dressing Sharov down: "How is it that you, a young conscious worker, a club member here in the Soviet Republic, could find it possible and even acceptable, to have relations at the same time with both a prostitute and a young woman worker?" When Nikolaeva grows upset in several instances during the court proceedings, he tells her to be calm; the court will resolve everything. The court will "establish the truth [*istina*]," he tells Nikolaeva and Sharov when they hotly accuse each other of lying.

In this early period in the 1920s doctors associated with the fight against venereal disease were convinced, as one of them put it, that "the most important part of the battle against syphilis, as is well known, consists in eliminating the representation of this illness as a shameful thing."[64] In 1924 the Moscow garrison actually put on a play in the First Communist Hospital called "Syphilis Is Not a Disgrace [*pozor*], But Rather a Misfortune [*neschast'e*]."[65]

Still, for serious scholars, questions of shame and judgment, particularly in such delicate matters as venereal disease and prostitution, were not easy to resolve. In 1925 Professor Pavel Liublinskii published his *Crimes in the Area of Sexual Relations,* in which he tried to determine, among other things, the relationship between the sex drive and the collective. Obviously influenced by reasoning similar to Freud's *Civilization and Its Discontents* (1930), Liublinskii questioned the role of law and legislation in limiting immoral behavior and sexual crimes.[66] Hitherto, Liublinskii commented, shame itself had been "the most powerful regulator of mass behavior in the sexual sphere." While not everyone had a strong sense of fear before the law, the vast majority had an "innate sense of shame." The best way to limit immorality, Liublinskii argued, was to "evoke and protect a sense of shame" rather than strictly prosecute appearances of immorality in a person's private life. If someone did commit a sexual crime, in the majority of cases the problem was either "vulgar egotism" or the person's "extreme social lack of development." In other words, the person failed to take into account the collective, either because he or she was selfish or because of ignorance, insufficient social upbringing, or mental retardation.[67]

The agitation trials (which Liublinskii does not discuss) seem to have been tailor-made to foster precisely the three forms of restraint that Liublinskii considered most effective in the area of sexual crimes: (1) external restraints in the form of public censure and social propriety; (2) legal restraints and fear of the law; and (3) the individual's internal "moral consciousness" and knowledge of the "rules of sexual morality."[68] They also contain at least traces of the three motivations he noted for governments seeking to enact new legislation: (1) support of existing moral views on sexual life; (2) concerns with low or falling birthrates; and (3) a new concern with eugenics to "protect the nation and race from degeneration."[69]

The questions raised in *The Trial of Fedor Sharov*—whether he could be held responsible for infecting Nikolaeva and whether he was guilty of raping her—are ones that lawmakers such as Liublinskii debated at some length. On the one hand, venereal disease differed from other contagious diseases in that it was most often conveyed through sexual relations—that is, through an act that should by rights have been subject to conscious control (in contrast to other contagions, which could be spread through carelessness or airborne microbes). On the other hand, it was virtually impossible to prove individual culpability because of the need to prove direct transmission (i.e., that there was no other source of infection) and because of the problem of ignorance. It was easy for a person to claim, as Sharov did, that he or she thought the symptoms had passed or that the infectious period of the disease had passed or that he or she had acted in a state of intoxication. How could one prove that a person knew that he or she had venereal disease? In fact, in the majority of cases, at least in 1925, article 155 on infection with venereal disease remained a dead letter in the law because of these exact problems.[70]

This is important for the question of sanitation trials because, at least on the level of spectacle, they could be used in place of real trials.[71] The agitational significance of a mock trial did not depend on whether the defendant was found formally guilty. An agitation trial could teach the dangers of venereal disease and the importance of proper treatment without having to resolve with any finality the ticklish juridical matters of intent and guilt.

From a legal point of view Akkerman's *Trial of a Prostitute: The Case of Citizen Zaborova Accused of Engaging in Prostitution and Infecting Soldier Krest'ianov with Syphilis* is actually formulated incorrectly since "engaging in prostitution" was not itself a crime (though spreading venereal disease was). As fictional dramas, the agitation trials were able to take liberties to illustrate social concerns and also to teach moral, as well as scientific, approaches to everyday life without being tied to the exact letter of the law.[72]

The trials of cases relating to prostitution and venereal disease also delve into moral issues that formerly had been the domain of the church. As Soviet authorities sought to replace the power of the church as a regulating force, they faced particular dilemmas over the best means to reach the larger population and teach new values. They created special interdepartmental commissions to combat prostitution. They debated (and rejected) the idea of creating a special morals police. Inspired at least in part by contemporary legislation on venereal diseases and prostitution being passed in Germany and Czechoslovakia, they chose to empower doctors to determine the presence or absence of venereal disease and the need to forcibly place recalcitrant prostitutes in special treatment asylums known as *profilaktorii.*[73] At the same time they looked for holistic solutions that would limit not only the supply of prostitutes who spread contagious venereal diseases but also the demand from male customers who sought that kind of sexual intercourse. If it was impractical to imprison all the male customers, it was not beyond the powers of the sanitation education drama programs to provide educational trials to combat the situations that gave rise to prostitution—women's downtrodden position and lack of alternatives and men's choices to seek sexual satisfaction outside marriage or long-term relationships.

Most important, the agitation trials dealing with venereal disease and prostitution demonstrated the important place of the physician at the nexus between the body of the individual and the body of the state. The trials of the syphilitic and the prostitute gave the doctor a forum not only to pronounce on matters of individual hygiene but also to make recommendations for government policy concerning public issues such as women's wages as a prophylactic against prostitution and the importance of introducing more educational programs into the countryside.

Only the doctor with a microscope could actually see the microorganism responsible for causing illnesses, and hence only those in the medical profession could adequately diagnose whether a patient had indeed been cured of the dreaded disease. Moreover, the doctor, because of his (or potentially her) medical knowledge, gained access to the most intimate parts of patients' bodies, their sexual organs. It was the doctor—the representative of a new, enlightened Soviet order—who could lift the patient from a fallen state of depression, shame, and humiliation to a redeemed state of knowledge and healthy participation in the social order.

THE TRIAL OF
THE NEW WOMAN

The accusations were flying thick and fast against the defendant. She had pretensions to running the government and meddling in public affairs. She had taken part in strikes and demonstrations. She was trying to put all women on an equal footing with men. She had destroyed her own femininity, ceasing to be an object of beauty and pleasure for men, ceasing as well to raise her children and instead giving them into others' hands. All these things, it was alleged, contradicted woman's very nature, which was to serve as a decoration for men's lives.

The setting was *The Trial of the New Woman.*[1] The prosecution witnesses included a factory director, a lady secretary, a rich peasant, a priest, and a traditional family woman. The court, which was designed to mimic a pre-revolutionary, "bourgeois" court, initially found the defendant guilty, but then workers charged onto the stage, and her judges ran away. Her rights were restored, and she was recognized to be "equal to men in all respects."

Women as main characters appear principally in two types of agitation trials: (1) political trials of women delegates acquitted as heroines and (2) sanitation trials in which women appear as victims and/or villains in the context of motherhood, midwifery, and village healing. *The Trial of the New Woman,* for example, was staged under the auspices of the local women's section of the Communist Party in the provincial city of Voronezh in late February 1921.[2] Women's sections staged a number of other trials of women's issues around the country over the next six years, including another *Trial of the New Woman* in the Great Columned Hall of the House of Trade Unions in Moscow in October 1921.[3] The medical profession wrote and staged most of the plays relating to sanitation and hygiene issues for women.

On the surface, Soviet ideology was unambiguously committed to women's citizenship and full gender equality. Revolutionary laws explicitly eliminated gender inequalities in voting rights, marriage, divorce, property ownership, land use, and labor policies.[4] The central authorities, working closely with the women's section of the Communist Party, created special positions for women as delegates to village and factory councils.

As in much propaganda literature of the early 1920s, trial authors assumed that women were the characters most in need of change. They were the most backward, the most threatening to the revolution if not transformed. Once women became educated, they could educate their children and help in the transmission of new social values to the next generation.[5] Once they became involved in the public sphere, they could clean up nests of corruption and laziness.[6]

The agitation trials in general do contain rather stinging portrayals of certain male types (the priest, the kulak or rich peasant, and the NEPman, or rich trader in the period of the New Economic Policy). However, these male characters are castigated primarily for their incorrect class position and their wrong views rather than for their masculinity.[7] The "baba," or backward woman, on the other hand, is censured for qualities that in the village world were coded as explicitly "female" (passivity, meddlesomeness, unruliness, lack of discipline).

Gender relations in any society cannot just be legislated. Rather, as scholars have increasingly shown, gender relations are something prepared, rehearsed, and even performed, sometimes consciously and sometimes unconsciously.[8] The trials relating to women and gender turn out to be steeped in mixed messages, a combination of explicit, ideological representations of women as equals and competing, ostensibly "traditional" understandings of gender relations that show women in a negative light.[9] As we will see, even the heroines of these trials, the defendants who are valorized for their work in the village or factory, are shown to be in need of special tutelage and assistance.

The messages in these trials were addressed, moreover, as a warning not only to women but also to men. Negative female stereotypes could be used to discipline males just as much as to discipline females. For example, no man in Soviet Russia ever wanted to be called a "baba," just as the majority of English-speaking males would not want to be called a "sissy."

One result of the Bolshevik commitment to radical social transformation was, in fact, a scapegoating of older women, especially midwives and village healers, who are consistently presented in these trials as epitomizing ignorance and superstition.[10] A battle royal takes place in many trials between educated males, who come in from outside the community with new ideas and knowledge, and uneducated females, who resist such outside intervention.

In part this polarization arises from the trial format itself, which makes some characters into prosecution witnesses and others into defense witnesses. In the plays concerning women and women's issues the male characters tend to be primarily experts and judges (with a few male villains thrown in for good measure), and the females tend to be either victims of the wrong influence exerted by others or evildoers who cripple and maim children and others in the village through their ignorance.

Differences of gender and authority reinforce each other in the trials, especially in the roles of the judges and expert witnesses. Since women were already marginal to village politics and especially since it was quite easy to play on ambivalence about their roles as village folk healers, the plays create a kind of power grid in which the court disciplines the whole audience, and males (in their capacities as experts) discipline women who are either new to politics (and hence not yet disciplined) or who are outside politics (in the case of healers).

Not only were women outside the traditional centers of "politics" in the usual sense, but they also (as healers and as mothers) stood closer to illness and bodies and bodily fluids. Because of this, both in the popular imagination and in that of the intelligentsia, they stood closer to what is sometimes called "the abject." Julie Kristeva, the French philosopher, has suggested that the abject is that which can be neither wholly rejected nor wholly incorporated into society. For this reason it exerts a powerful fascination. The fear of defilement and the blurring of boundaries in turn create relations of power. Religion, politics, language, and literature, in Kristeva's view, can all be seen as operating through our horror of and fascination with the abject, which we can never fully expel. The mother, in particular, can give birth and also deny life (through abortion, infanticide, etc.).[11] The healer can then be portrayed as either the good mother or the bad mother.

In short, in the agitation trials discussed here women were both being brought into the public sphere (especially as delegates to public organizations) and being pushed out of it (as midwives and healers who became symbolic of all that was old and uncultured in the new Soviet sense). Yet women could never be entirely drawn in (as we shall see) because of lingering negative female stereotypes (meddling, gossip, indiscipline). Nor could they be entirely ejected, both because of society's needs for mothers (parenthood being coded in essential terms as a female sphere) and because of the medical establishment's insistence that mothers breastfeed their infants to ensure their health and well-being. The solution, therefore, was to persuade women themselves (and also men, but especially women) to recognize their backwardness and their need for tutelage from the new authorities, especially those in medicine.

This chapter is divided into two primary sections. The first half explores trials written by and for the women's sections of the party to illustrate women's continuing struggles to enter the political sphere. The main focus here is on the women's process of becoming delegates (*delegatki*) and the ways in which they are portrayed as essentially unformed and in need of tutelage. Fictional trials of the heroine-delegatka gave playwrights an opportunity to show the obstacles she faced and to turn the tables on her opponents, showing that they were in fact the ones hindering the new order. At the same time, however, these trials reveal rigid new assumptions that until a woman is involved in work in the public sphere, she is not yet "human." She is never portrayed as having already attained full political consciousness and self-confidence as an activist in the new society.

The second half of the chapter focuses on trials of village healers, midwives, and mothers written by doctors in the Commissariat of Health for its Section on the Protection of Mothers and Infants.[12] Here the trial plays reveal women to be backward in stereotypically misogynist ways. The healers are all witches, and the mothers are all innocent victims. The mothers are "redeemable" because they can learn better mothering skills from doctors and other experts. For the healers, however, there is no possibility of redemption, no discussion of retraining or finding a useful role to play in society. Instead the debate focuses on how to persuade the villagers to give up their dependence on the women healers and even to expel them from the village.

OBSTACLES TO EMANCIPATION

In the Moscow *Trial of the New Woman* (October 1921), the defendant, Avdotia Mikhailova, is brought to court on charges that she has so thrown herself into public work as a delegatka that she has been neglecting her family obligations. Her husband, an unskilled worker, claims that his children have been abandoned by their mother. "Is this why I married?" he asks. "So that my wife could go to meetings?"[13]

The prosecution and defense argue heatedly over this issue. The prosecutor, a male, professional lawyer, plays to what *Pravda* calls "women's feelings of pity and love for this poor, benighted husband." He initially appears to be successful in appealing to the female audience's maternal concerns about this poor man, "left alone in his empty and cold family hearth with his abandoned children." By contrast, an inexperienced, female worker takes up the role of Mikhailova's defender and at first appears unsuccessful. Attempting to make a similar, cleverly constructed speech, she fails, stumbling and losing her train of thought. Soon, however, she begins to speak from the heart. Now, the *Pravda* article notes, she is able to move her audience with her discussion of "women's eternally hard lot," reminding them how this husband used to come home drunk and scold the defendant, dragging her around by her hair. The audience begins to vacillate, whispering and even talking out loud. When the judge eventually reads the sentence acquitting the woman delegate, the audience does not even hear it; they drown it out in a storm of applause and stream out of the hall singing a revolutionary song.[14] In the construction of this narrative in *Pravda*, the author (about whom nothing is known) is evidently trying to contrast the way in which women in the audience are swayed by a professional prosecutor who manipulates their feelings of pity, on the one hand, and their deeper identification with the woman worker defender, on the other, who speaks from the heart rather than purely from "reason."

This officially performed agitation trial contains, in fact, an implicit second trial, or at least a judgment. Seated in the audience, after all, were some two thousand women who had chosen to attend the conference rather than to stay home with their children and their husbands. According to *Pravda*, the prosecutor is well aware that his attack on the fictional character of Avdotia Mikhailova contains an implicit accusation against the women in the audience because they, too, are "new women." Initially the audience fails to perceive this implicit charge. When, however, they hear the defense speech, the *Pravda* reporter claims, they realize that they have to kick out their old views of "women's lot."[15]

This second judgment within the play suggests that the trial has a more complex agenda than just showing the difficulties of the woman delegate whose husband brings suit against her. The play also appears committed to teaching women in the audience how they themselves can respond to others' charges that by becoming delegates they are abandoning their families. As a memoir account from the 1950s claimed, "They [trials of women delegates] were all the rage. The trials accomplished their goals—the husbands made peace, and the authority of the women delegates in the village was fortified."[16]

An important tension in the agitation trials with female heroines revolves around this issue of women's public service to the party through their roles as delegates. Introduced in 1919, the delegate meeting was intended to provide a place for women workers and peasants to meet and learn about current political affairs. Larger conferences of local women would elect the delegatki to serve for a year. During that time the delegatki would study political literacy, visit various model Soviet organizations (museums, factories, courts, day-care sites), and support mobilization campaigns that the regime was running. Sometimes they would hold what might be called "office hours" in their factories to hear the problems of other women and try to help them out. At the end of their year of service they were supposed to report back to the constituents who had elected them.[17]

In practice the delegate meetings were entirely insular. In the first place, they were set up only for women workers and peasants with no equivalent for men. Women were deemed to be particularly in need of remedial work in a way that men were not. (While it is true that 86 percent of women were illiterate on the eve of the October Revolution, fully 67 percent of men were illiterate as well.)[18] Second, the meetings were designed primarily for those women considered most illiterate and least involved in public campaigns.[19] In other words, it was not the most capable or committed women who were asked to join these meetings and contribute their skills to political work. Finally, these delegate meetings did not actually report to anyone other than the women who elected them. They were thus not designed to have any serious influence on the political process, even at the most local level. Rather, they were intended primarily to teach a few women a few political skills. Even that training did not usually translate into increased party membership for women or increased political involvement. After their year of service in the delegate meetings, women workers and peasants typically did not join the party, although they might remain working in the kindergarten or public cafeteria where they had done an internship.

The women's section of the party usually took the lead in publishing agitation trials of women delegates. This set of trials tended to focus on the harassment of delegatki and women electors by local men. The stated goal was to show the harm this harassment could do and to vindicate the women, showing that they had triumphed over resistance. In these trials, like so many others, the raw, the old, the pre-Soviet was to be transformed into the modern and the Soviet. The trials showed not so much the utopian "future perfect" as the "past imperfect,"—the ways in which the tsarist system had left a legacy of ignorance, brutishness, and inequality.[20] They were intended to provide citizens a dramatic impetus to push off from those old ways of life into a new Soviet civilization and culture.

At the same time, however, these trials reveal new assumptions that only public work and service made the individual a member of the new order. The woman delegate who is the ostensible heroine of the trials is never portrayed as having already attained full political consciousness. Even when she does break out of the clutches of the domestic sphere to become involved in the public sphere, she is nonetheless depicted largely in terms of traditionally negative 'female' qualities of indiscipline, meddling, gossip, and/or, their opposite, a kind of saintliness.

Several fictional male characters bring suit against women delegates in separate mock trials, for abandoning their husbands and children or, in one case, for allegedly taking bribes and interfering in men's business relations.[21] Women and the courts (in fictional guise, of course) in turn bring two suits against males: one against a factory committee member who has refused to allow his wife to go to a delegate meeting because he wants her to stay home and cook for an upcoming holiday, and the second against a peasant man who has encouraged the other men of the village to lock up their wives so they will not be able to elect one of their own as a delegatka to the village council.[22]

The male characters in these plays express stereotypical peasant misogyny.[23] Politics, for example, "is no women's matter [ne bab'e delo]," says one peasant husband.[24] Another says his wife can't be a boss because he is the boss and because women have "stupid heads." If you let them run things, "you might as well put your head in a noose." If the women want to go off and form their own "women's council," that's okay, but we don't need them in ours. It's also not women's place to wander idly into various reading huts (created by the regime to encourage literacy) and "stick their noses" into newspapers.[25]

Women delegates in these plays themselves subscribe to many of these views. Before being put on trial for not fulfilling her responsibilities as a delegate, Maria Tikhonova herself thought she did not have a good enough head for politics. She was barely literate. She did not really understand that being elected as a delegate meant that she actually had to do work in that role. She thought the woman organizer from the women's section of the party would take care of everything. After all, she noted, people had gotten along fine without women delegates before the revolution. Furthermore, her "female responsibility," as she saw it, was to get home right after work in order to take care of the house and the farming.[26] Her neighbor defends her, saying, "Look, from childhood no one bothered to teach us, so now what are we supposed to do? Once a female [*baba*] always a female."[27]

EMANCIPATION AS A WAY OF MAKING WOMEN "HUMAN"

The way out of this problem ("once a female always a female") was to make women "human," or so the intelligentsia had long believed. In the nineteenth century radical members of the Russian intelligentsia envisaged the solution to the "woman question" as making women into "people," giving each a personality (*lichnost'*), and in the process making them the equals of men.[28] Through careful intervention and tutelage by male members of the educated classes, women could be "brought up to" the level of men. This was the starting point of the early Bolshevik government's stated commitment to women's emancipation, though the new leaders came to this issue somewhat reluctantly.[29]

In the agitation trials, women delegates invariably speak of themselves as having become fully human only through the outside intervention of the Communist Party, which has brought them a new consciousness. On the one hand, this fits well with Lenin's assertions in his famous essay "What Is to Be Done?" that social-democratic consciousness could be brought to the workers only from outside, only by the party itself.[30] Yet this transition from "backward woman" to "human being" also bears striking overtones of a kind of Pygmalion myth. The party will infuse the inert, uninvolved woman with breath in the form of political consciousness, and she will come alive, now able to serve the revolution and society.

In *The Trial of the Peasant Woman Delegate*, the main character, Maria Cherepanova, is accused by her husband of abandoning her household and children in order to attend political meetings. In her own defense at the end of the play she tells why she became a woman delegate. "I didn't consider myself a person," she begins. For years she worked only for her family. But then Soviet power came, and "they" (presumably Soviet authorities) began to explain everything. Instructors came from the women workers' section in the city. "It was as if a bandage fell from my eyes, . . . as if I had been blind and now I saw everything." When they sent in a rural organizer to set up delegate meetings for women peasants, she became involved. "All of a sudden I felt that I was, after all, also a person, really a person, and that I have all the rights; but before that wasn't the case. I felt so good, so joyful."[31]

The main foil to her character, who illustrates someone stuck in the "old" way of life, is her elderly mother-in-law, aged sixty-five. A widow who must live with her children in order to receive support, the mother-in-law complains bitterly of how young people "have become smarter than us," and how it is a "disgrace" that this family conflict between husband and wife has come to court. What kind of a wife and housewife is Maria? she asks. She doesn't listen to her husband; she leaves her children. Of herself, she says that she never tried to teach her husband; and if he beat her, well, then that was his business. "We tolerated everything. You'll never hear of a life more bitter than that of our women. But what can you do? That's our women's lot. It's obviously God's will. It's not made by us, and not up to us to redo it. . . . We suffered, and she should do the same."[32]

Another character who becomes "a person" through the process of a courtroom trial (*The Trial of the Old Way of Life*) is a wife named Anna Grigor'eva who has been beaten by her husband. Although she is portrayed as a "conscious woman worker," she has tolerated her husband's abuse because of the remains of her "old, slavish habits." Once she realizes, however, that the bourgeois ideal of domestic bliss is really an illusion and once she has found the courage to bring suit against her husband, she becomes, in her words, "a completely different person." Where earlier she was terrified to speak out and act, now nothing frightens her. She is the first to arrive at every meeting, lecture, and political discussion circle.[33]

Though the plays speak of "freedom" and even of "rights" (words that do not often appear in later Soviet writings), the freedom and the rights of women are linked irrevocably in these trials to their responsibility to work for the Soviet state and society. The crime of several husbands in these plays is in failing to see that their wives are "conscious" women workers, that they are "respected and trusted comrades at work."[34] Working as a delegatka and in other public spheres becomes "the duty of every honest, conscious woman citizen."[35] Grigor'eva, the wife whose husband has been beating her, also comes to see that "a woman is not a slave, not a bitch for breeding [*samka*], but a free person, engaged just as much in productive labor as the man, and capable of fulfilling the same public work as he is."[36] In saying this, she asks for a divorce from her husband not in order to have some abstract rights or freedoms but so that she can engage in productive labor and public works. She promises that from now on she will engage in fighting for women's emancipation, for public cafeterias, for nurseries, cooperatives, and clubs. While these institutions did help women become more independent, it is clear that Grigor'eva and the other defendants are not being "emancipated" for their own sake either as women or as individuals. Rather, they are being emancipated so they can work for Soviet power.[37]

These plays rely for some of their drama on the contrast between husbands who try to "teach" their wives through beatings and dragging them around by the hair and the new Soviet authorities, especially the women's sections and the local executive committees, who take the women delegates in hand and teach them through example, showing them the new Soviet order. In the old world, God had allegedly created an order that obliged women to submit to their husbands. In the new world, women can divorce their husbands and become involved in building a whole new social order.[38]

Yet the women are always in need of tutelage. The local authorities, especially organizations like the village executive committee, play a crucial imaginary role in "developing" them. Then the women can "be transformed into good workers" (vyrabatyvaiutsia iz nikh i khoroshie rabotniki).[39] Once they are turned into those good staff members, then even the nouns lose their gender designations; the delegatki (a female noun) become rabotniki (a general word for worker or staff member that does not have a gender indication). It is the party and its political organizations that must show women the way. On her own, Cherepanova, for example, is characterized as having only "an instinct, a feeling" (instinkt, chuvstvo) that "makes her feel drawn [to the new life]" (ona tianetsia k nei). She does not have "a clear striving, a knowledge of the essence of this new life." If she's to be sentenced, the defense argues, it should be to a term in school, so she can learn more and gain in knowledge, so she can "sow light among her co-citizens and awaken the peasant women."[40] In none of the agitation trials of women delegates, even of those who are fully acquitted and vindicated as "useful citizens," are they portrayed as fully formed, fully ready to hold positions of leadership.

THE PERSISTENCE OF MISOGYNY: MEDDLERS, GOODY-GOODIES, AND UNDISCIPLINED WOMEN

Ostensibly, the heroines share a common commitment to telling the truth and helping to clean up village life. They appear to be doing good by blowing the whistle on the bad habits of individuals and groups, habits such as moonshine distilling, hindering the new political processes, and failing to implement political directives from the center. Yet at the same time, these heroines come across as not very likeable. The question is, how and why.

The main character in the play *The Trial of the Peasant Woman-Delegatka* is named Maria Gudkova—the whistle-blower (from the Russian word *gu-*

dok).[41] If her actions were being examined in a U.S. court of law today, the case would probably be considered at least partly a libel case, since the male plaintiff claims that she has publicly defamed his character. It is also in part a corruption case, since she is charged with taking bribes. Her accusers, the plaintiffs Kosorotov (whose name means "crooked mouth") and his wife and daughter-in-law, note that she has called Kosorotov a "bloodsucker" (*krovopiitsa*) and a kulak (a derogatory term for a rich peasant). She has even drawn a picture of him with a fat belly on the wall newspaper in the official reading hut. Kosorotov, who admits that he has a history of moonshine distilling, wants the court to free him from her harassment.

In the course of the trial Kosorotov's main charge in the case, that Gudkova took a bribe from a woman moonshine distiller, is proven to be false. A number of prosecution witnesses bring other charges, however. The men claim that she has been stealing their wives, "stirring them up" to become involved in public affairs, making them "contrary" and difficult. Kosorotov's nephew, for example, claims that his wife was just a female (*baba*) like any other. Now, though, Gudkova has "commanded" her to learn to read and write, while he, the husband, thinks her "women's work" should be to tend to the house and fields. Consequently they are quarreling. In his view, Gudkova is usurping his male role: "And I say, who is your husband—me or Maria Gudkova?" He's also upset that his wife might become literate and leave him behind: "Am I supposed to be her fool then?"[42] Even his parents have been upset by all this. His father calls the wife a "bolshevichka" (female Bolshevik), while his mother, on the contrary, wants to follow Gudkova and become a delegatka herself.

The nephew's wife has a different perspective, however. For her, Gudkova is nothing short of a saint.[43] "She takes care of us, showing us the light, teaching us good things," she notes. She helps the downtrodden women of the village while fighting off their enemies, the kulaks who exploit them, say other witnesses. Even the female distiller whom Kosorotov had tried to force to bear false witness against Gudkova recants and rues her own behavior. "Why should anyone do Maria harm for no reason?" she asks. "She does us a good turn, but we do her wrong." The woman communist who is the organizer for the whole region comments, too, that Gudkova is doing her duty in "revealing all falsehoods and wrongdoing, defending the poorest."[44] In her own brief final speech Gudkova declares that she is not afraid of the likes of Kosorotov: "Where something is bad or unjust, I will reveal it, without fearing anyone." Her account of her transformation to a delegatka is dominated by Enlightenment metaphors: "There was a time when I was ignorant [literally "dark" in Russian, *temnoi*] and didn't know what needed to be done in order to make life better, but now I know, and I want to teach all women to fight for the new, bright life under the direction of our Communist Party."[45]

Yet Gudkova's own words are barely recorded in the twenty-nine-page script of the trial. When she does say anything (aside from her final speech, which is a scant one paragraph long), she often does so without permission, interrupting the plaintiff and speaking out of order. In response to this be-havior, the judge disciplines her verbally. "You will speak when you are given the floor," he insists. While the primary motivation of the judge's interven-tions is undoubtedly to show the court's impartiality (even the heroine could be rebuked for not following the court's rules), a secondary effect is to show Gudkova as impulsive and not in control of her own speech. "I know, citi-zen judge," she tells the judge, "but I don't have any patience."[46]

After she has been rebuked for the second time, Gudkova falls completely silent until the judge asks her for her final speech at the very end of the trial. This brief speech begins in fact with Gudkova's confusion: "What should I say?" Ostensibly her question refers to her insistence that she has not done anything wrong. Yet in the context of the judge's rebukes, it also appears that she has in fact been successfully silenced by the court. She may be the dele-gate in the village, the one who can blow the whistle on others' misconduct, but ultimately it is the judge who has the power of speech and the power to determine guilt and innocence.[47]

Nor does the audience learn from her short final speech what her moti-vations were in choosing to become a delegatka and work for the state (aside from her vague comments about darkness and light). The audience is told nothing of her personal situation. We never learn whether she is married or has children, whether she has parents whom she cares for, and whether she has land (though we learn a great deal about the family situations of the other witnesses). Instead she is inscribed primarily as a vehicle to help, and in fact, push, others in the village to find their way to the reading huts, the schools, the cooperatives, and other Soviet institutions.

The image on the cover of the printed scenario reinforces a sense of the saintliness and mediating role of Gudkova. (See figure below.) It pictures a smiling peasant woman posing her hand on a boy's head and showing him the way to the schoolhouse. Above her are the judge with his bell and two people's assessors. Below her stand three peasant men with their fists clenched. With the help of the wise judge above (now a secular figure instead of God), she helps the ignorant peasants, and especially the youth, find their way to the institutions of the new, brighter world.[48]

The contrast between the presiding male judge and the female lay asses-sor in this play is also instructive. The male presiding judge plays the central role of father in Gudkova's trial. He is described as having a gray beard and being very calm. Several characters address him as "my father" (*otets rod-noi, batiushka*). When the female distiller becomes frightened of speaking in court (because of the threat of retaliation from Kosorotov), the judge tells her not to be frightened of anyone. When she bursts into tears saying that Kosorotov (Mr. Crooked Mouth) is really a wolf and not a person and will harm her if she speaks the truth ("He will eat me," she says), the same male

The Trial of the Peasant Woman Delegate. From N. Bozhinskaia, *Sud nad krest'iankoi-delegatkoi* (Moscow-Leningrad, 1926), cover.

judge adopts a reassuring tone: "Don't be afraid. We have good shepherds [to protect you] against wolves." The male judge thus becomes a strong (Christian) father figure who will protect the hapless female (the sheep) against the evil (wolflike) male peasant who threatens to eat her.[49]

By contrast, the female lay assessor who is assisting the judge is, like Gudkova herself, undisciplined in her comments. Several times she breaks into the dialogue to tell other characters how they should live their lives. She angrily instructs one witness that he has to give maternity benefits to his peasant wage laborer despite the fact that she cannot work. She tells another he shouldn't be fighting with his wife. She warns a woman who does not want to send her children to school that if she does not help them attain literacy, "your children will never thank you when they grow up."[50] Unlike the male judge, she lacks impartiality. She intrudes in a meddlesome way that makes her appear to be an interloper instead of an authority figure.

Another moralizing delegatka who threatens to break into all the men's plans appears in the play *The Trial of the Peasant Medvedev Who Wrecked the Election of the Women's Candidate to the Village Council*. From her first appearance in court, the woman delegate Gracheva (whose name means "rook" or "crow"), interrupts other characters, challenging their interpretations of events and procedures. In her first appearance in the scripted court scene, she angrily interrupts Medvedev, the defendant: "Who then instructed the men to hold their women down by the braids at home during the elections?"[51] Gracheva presents herself as having lost all patience with the "gang" of peasants (including a kulak and a priest) who want to keep women out of elections. She wants women to learn to read so they can learn their rights and go after the "new lords," that is, the kulaks who are making money off the people. She, too, thus appears to be protecting the poor and downtrodden, especially women, against the oppressions of their husbands, who want to keep them from even learning to read and write.

The defendant Medvedev and his cronies, however, take a different view of Gracheva's "righteousness": "Why does she stick her nose in with her morality?" asks Zabubennyi, a former chair of the village council and now a freelance scribe (whose name means "unruly" or "dissolute"). He defends a law-and-order perspective on moonshining, arguing that one cannot simply go into any hut and search for illegal stills without a warrant, as Gracheva (according to him) has done. Others criticize Gracheva for tattling to outsiders when they come to visit, telling them everything that is wrong with the village. When she hears unfamiliar words such as "MOPR" (the acronym of an international Soviet propaganda agency) and "Dobrolet" (a Soviet organization dedicated to supporting the extension of the air force), she wants to know what they are and to introduce them into the village council even though the council already has too much work just taking care of the village's own affairs. Nor, they argue, does she know anything about the really important local matters of land divisions, peasants who want to separate from the commune and live on their own, and the running of tractors.[52]

The male defendants obviously need to find reasons to criticize Gracheva in order to protect themselves against the charges that they have hindered the elections of women as delegates. But Gracheva also betrays herself as less than a fully sympathetic character. She addresses her husband in a simultaneously patronizing and threatening manner: "Oh yes, my Akimushka [little Akim], I can abandon you and I can take you to court for beating me. The comrade judge will affirm that for you. But what I find much more painful than your beatings is your ignorance." She berates him for not knowing anything and for letting the rich peasants take advantage of him. She takes a high moral tone, too, in arguing that if the judges were to acquit the defendants, they would be directly attacking her, and with her the whole worker-peasant government. Often she uses the pronoun "we": "We'll figure out who should have their tax lowered and who should have it raised." "It's only too bad we don't respect moonshine," she concludes, making it clear that she has no intention of respecting village traditions. Instead—and this was what the Soviet government was clearly counting on—she is offering to come in and clean up the whole nest of those engaging in moonshining and illegal kickbacks.[53]

In general, the heroines are almost never granted full, flesh-and-blood characters. They can sing the praises of the party and state, but they cannot evince a broader range of interests and desires. They move seamlessly from the "we" of the family into the "we" of the state, extending their "maternal" qualities to the whole collective. But they cannot do so in an authoritative fashion.

Nor do the trials depict the heroines' development. The narrative trope that their eyes "have been opened" and bandages "have been removed from their eyes" is presented exclusively in a passive voice. The women show little agency of their own, never taking actions that are not directed by the party. While the plays do mobilize their female characters into the public sphere, they simultaneously undermine a sense of their competence. Many delegatki are marked by passivity and insecurity. Others show their intemperance, breaking in while other witnesses are speaking. Still others blow the whistle without regard for local customs or even for the law (Gracheva conducts searches without proper search warrants).

Ostensibly the delegatki are presented to the public as victims of harassment by others. Yet they themselves need to be counseled and restrained. The judges emerge as those with the power and the authority to determine who will speak, on what basis, and when. It is they who determine who can be elevated from the status of "citizen" (defendant) to the status of "comrade," one who is equal to those on the bench.[54] The plays thus ultimately *tame* these activist women even as they allow them to have minimal roles as delegates.[55]

The agitation trials essentially present conversion stories. Individuals "see the light." They "find the truth." They recognize Soviet power. In this context women's stereotypical backwardness provides more dramatic interest than would stories of competence and creativity. Soviet power plays a tutelary role, bringing the women delegates up to the level of "becoming human." As Cherepanova notes in her final speech, she fell in love with Soviet power and the party of the communists: "They opened my eyes, taught me literacy, taught me how to work—they made a person out of me."[56]

Once such women delegates become at least partially conscious, then they can begin to teach others. The defense lawyer for Cherepanova praises her for "sowing light among women peasants, as much as she herself has become imbued with it."[57] She should "awaken the women peasants who don't yet understand the truth/justice [*pravda*] of the new life."[58] Individuals, and especially women, who represent this tutelary state can then take over husbands' traditional roles as teachers and enforcers of discipline within the household. Kosorotov, as we saw above, expresses fear that his wife is listening more to Gudkova than to him: "And I say, who is your husband—me or Maria Gudkova?"[59] Emancipating women as citizens-in-training could thus provide a wedge in the conservative household, a way for the Soviet state and the new Soviet order to penetrate the countryside.

The state in these narratives is the ultimate Pygmalion creator, permitting some women and men to attain citizenship while remanding others to Soviet "schools" such as literacy programs and delegate programs for further development and transformation. Ironically, the Soviet state in these plays is itself rather faceless. Though the judges, the prosecution, and the defense do appear on stage, the organizers and party representatives who originally "awaken" the heroines have always appeared before the narrative action of the plays. They are also mentioned in vague terms, without reference to concrete persons, events, or institutions. In this way, too, the narratives illustrate not rules and procedures for attaining citizenship, or even common paths of promotion, but rather indeterminate psychological states of "unconsciousness" and "consciousness."

SCAPEGOATING: DOCTORS AND THE STATE VERSUS THE OLD WOMAN HEALER

The sanitation trials relating to women differ from the political trials of the women delegates in their more blatant misogyny. To be sure, the doctors writing these plays felt strongly that folk healing (*znakharstvo*) was so disastrous that it was destroying the whole of village life, and it may have seemed immaterial that the majority of healers—and in fact, the majority of their patients—were women.[60] What mattered were the healers' "backward" practices and the threat of those practices for civilization itself. Yet the result of these attacks on what had been "women's spheres"—healing, midwifery, and motherhood—served in fact to reinforce the portrayal of women as ignorant and incompetent. Only those female characters who had contact with outsiders such as political and medical authorities were able to transcend their backwardness.

In the trials of folk healers women are portrayed not only as ignorant but as downright evil and witchlike. Two cover illustrations portray women folk healers (*znakharki*) as toothless old women with long noses and fingers. Both are leaning over cauldronlike kettles. In one the old woman might be viewed as merely a grandmother stirring her soup, though very hunched and dour with her downward-turning mouth.[61] In the other picture the znakharka leers at the viewer with enormous, wide eyes and a gaping, all but toothless mouth, as she stares into the cauldron, divining or casting spells in an evil fashion. Her hair is long and stringy. Her brow is wrinkled. She looks powerful and angry.[62]

Kurynikha, this latter figure, reminds the Russian reader of a witch in other ways as well. Her nickname, Kurynikha, means "chicken." Baba Yaga, that most famous witch in all of Russian culture, lives in a house built on chicken legs and is herself sometimes known as the "bony-legged one."[63] Kurynikha's last name is Indiukova, which means "turkey." So she is twice a fowl, inhuman. When she is brought into the courtroom at the very beginning of the play, she crosses herself "furtively." She mutters and spits three times over her left shoulder. A young man from the audience calls out to the judge, "She is casting a spell on you and spitting out the devil who is sitting on her left shoulder."[64]

In the other leading trial of a village healer the defendant Terent'eva (whose name refers to thorns) also walks into the courtroom leaning on a stick and looking out from under her brow. As soon as the judge addresses her, she claims she cannot hear him because she's old.[65] She is deferential almost to the point of servility. Her difficulties in hearing accentuate her difficulty in understanding the new order.

Terent'eva and Kurynikha, the two folk healers, both live in a mental world that is far from that of the judges and doctors and expert witnesses. For the two healers, illness is animate. It has to be "drawn out" or "persuaded" to leave. Without words and spells, it won't "succumb." "It comes from a sorcerer, or an evil spirit, or an evil eye," says Terent'eva. Still, it "fears" her.[66]

Ironically, the trials of the mothers maintain an almost equally "animate" portrayal of illnesses. It is the mothers' carelessness and ignorance that "cause" children to become ill. Germs, poverty, and malnutrition either are not mentioned at all or are given a back seat to the failures of the mothers.[67] A woman peasant who comes forth in one trial, apparently on her own initiative, to tell the court about the dangers associated with a midwife (*babka*) exclaims that the latter "dupes" the whole village; she is "ruining" the whole peasantry.[68] By implication, the peasantry is innocent; it is the babka who cripples the people. Maiming instead of healing, she symbolically inverts motherhood itself.[69]

The Trial of a Woman Healer. From B. Sigal, *Sud nad babkoi znakharkoi* (Moscow, 1925), cover.

The Chicken Woman (The Trial of a Woman Healer). From *Kurynikha (Sud nad znakharkoi)* (Leningrad, 1925), cover.

Both the trials of the folk healers and the trials of the mothers focus primarily on battles between light and dark, battles, as it were, for the souls of the common folk. In all these trials, doctors, Komsomol youths, and occasionally other male authority figures (such as a village correspondent who runs a reading hut) wage war against the ignorance and gullibility of the villagers, especially the women. The primary difference between these experts and the women who are mothers and midwives is that the former know the rules of proper hygiene and medical care, while the latter do not. A "good" mother was not to give the child her breast when the child cried, but rather according to a schedule; she was not to rock the child in a cradle or to swaddle it. Nor was she to keep it in a dark, close room with no light and air.[70]

Most important, though, she was to turn to doctors for advice. The doctors could give her "rational advice" (razumnye ukazaniia) about breast feeding and raising the child.[71] The mothers' chief fault in these plays is that they turn for advice to "various godmothers/gossips [kumushki] and wise women" instead of to doctors. The mothers are defensive at first. "What are we, scientists, that we should know how to take care of children?" one mother on trial asks sarcastically.[72] When her child grows sick (for reasons never explained), she turns to another wrinkled and witchlike midwife named Goriunova, whose name comes from the Russian word meaning "woe" or "sorrow," and who also walks into the courtroom frowning. Goriunova shows no comprehension of what is wrong with the child. It must be the mother's "bad milk," or the fact that little Petka was hungry so he needed nourishment in the form of chewed bread and potatoes, or that he needed to be calmed down by giving him a bit of moonshine, or that he needed prayers, especially from St. Nicholas the Miracle Worker.

A male hero enters the scene, however, to provide more knowledge and insight. A twenty-eight-year-old director of the village reading hut, Grigorii Ostapchuk, tries to persuade the mother to change her ways: "I'm forced to wage a huge battle," he tells the court. The children die "especially because their mothers don't want to learn how to take care of them."[73] When he would walk by the mother's house, which was next door to his reading hut, he often stopped to tell her how to raise her children. In his testimony he seems to feel no qualms about telling her how to run her life, how to take care of her children, though there is not a shred of evidence that he might have any personal experience with children or with child rearing.

Ostapchuk becomes furious, moreover, when he realizes that despite his well-intentioned assistance, the village women keep turning to Goriunova, the babka. Enraged by their behavior, he has written an article to the newspaper. As a result of his activism and his article, the court holds an investigation and finds that Kovaleva, this particular mother, really did keep a dirty household, and that this is how they have become sick with smallpox (rather than because of smallpox germs, which were spreading up and down the region).

RECEPTION AND EFFECTIVENESS

The women's sections of the party and the medical authorities claimed that the agitation trials succeeded in "interesting" and "attracting" wide audiences.[74] In 1921 these were a new form of agitation that could play to the emotions of the viewers as well to their intellects. The very novelty of the form, it was hoped, would attract audiences who otherwise failed to attend lectures.[75]

In order for the trials to really "work" as agitation, the audience had to find the characters believable. The first published trial of a mother was written at the request of the Health Commissariat by a doctor in the State Scientific Institute for the Protection of Mothers, Dr. B. S. Ginzburg.[76] In his preface he claimed that the play was based on an event that had actually occurred at the former Prokhorovskaia factory in Moscow. When the trial was performed at that factory for the first time, Nikolai Semashko, the first national commissar of health, who was reviewing it, reported that women workers who saw the play came up afterward to tell the main actress (who was not a factory worker at all): "We remember you, how you used to work at the factory."[77] For the doctors who were writing, directing, and occasionally acting in these trials, this kind of response was the best proof that the plays were recognizable to their audiences and therefore might have an impact on people's everyday lives. Of course, this audience's reaction may also have been indicative of their complete ignorance of the theater; for them someone who played a factory worker must actually be one.

In another case, a village teacher wrote to a women's journal claiming that after seeing a performance of *The Trial of the Ignorant Mother,* local women promised that they would no longer turn to the wise women of the village since the latter brought harm to "both the child and the state" through their ignorance. In fact, they hoped that the women's section of the party and the health ministry would send more scenes like these for local performance.[78]

One woman worker who signed her name only as Lena wrote to the same women's journal a month later with her reactions to a performance of the same trial of the ignorant mother. "I have never felt so guilty," she wrote, "as during comrade Melenteva [the defense lawyer]'s speech. Her every word burned into me like fire." Before, Lena said, she had never gone to public meetings, thinking that they were useless. When the play was shown, however, it was as if she woke up. Now she wanted to announce loudly: "You must judge me too, for I am still more guilty than this peasant woman. I give my word that what I did not do before I will do now."[79] In other words, *The Trial of the Ignorant Mother* was said not only to have reached those who already knew something about maternity and the need to trust doctors but also to have galvanized newcomers to become active in a new way.

Without independent confirmation it is obviously impossible to determine whether peasant and working women really did change their behavior as a result of seeing such trials. It is clear, however, that such a transformation in attitudes was the great hope of the medical professionals involved in writing and performing them. Fictional mothers who at the beginning of the trials had resisted outside intervention came around by the end of the performances to admitting that they had been wrong. "Now I see that they are right," comments Maria Kovaleva at the end of her trial. The "dokhtur," as she ignorantly refers to the doctor, and Ostapchuk, the head of the reading hut, have been right all along. "We are ignorant, uneducated, and don't see what is to our own advantage."[80] If she had done as they had said, she now sees, her little son would not have died. If the court would only grant her mercy, she begs, then she would devote all her energies to helping organize a local nursery for the children. In this example, which is typical, the mother thus begs for mercy from the court on the grounds that (1) she didn't know any better; (2) she now sees that she should have relied on outside expert advice; and (3) she has now been so completely transformed that she is willing to devote all her energy to the new Soviet institutions.

While the prosecutions in these trials paint a dire picture of evil midwives and ignorant mothers, the defense attorneys tend to extend blame to the whole audience, making the viewers as culpable as the participants. "We are all guilty," several defense attorneys claim in their closing arguments. If the village or factory did not help to establish institutions for mothers and infants, then the whole audience must be held responsible for the fact that the poor mother, who has been suffering physically and morally, has ended up on the defendants' bench; after all, it is the general social conditions that have forced her to abandon her child.[81] In the end, therefore, everyone is shown to be guilty except the nameless (evidently male) judges and the equally nameless (and equally male) doctors, who help the mothers and other characters see their guilt and also help the audience see *its* responsibility to rectify the situation.[82]

It seems quite ironic that in a country where Marxism was considered the reigning ideology and activists in party schools were being taught to look for dialectical materialism in every set of relations, the trials took on a psychological, highly personalized approach to social problems. Authors of trials stated explicitly that it was best not to discuss an abstract idea (for example, the idea of bad motherhood in general), but rather to indict a personification of that idea, as in *The Trial of the Ignorant Mother*. Furthermore, the trials consistently made ad hominem arguments, focusing on who was guilty rather than providing an in-depth analysis of local problems. Rather than showing the extent of village poverty, the absence of males in the countryside in the immediate postwar period, and the shortages of doctors and hospitals, the trials attacked particular fictional characters such as Kurynikha and Goriunova, presenting them as the personification of all that was ignorant and malevolent.

How, then, can one explain the persistence of misogyny in a revolutionary society that was officially committed to gender equality? Ultimately, it seems that gender became not only "a useful category of analysis" (to quote Joan Scott) but also a useful *form of power* in the sense used by Michel Foucault.[83] This worked at the level of both center-periphery relations and intravillage relations. For the central authorities the trials of women delegates, mothers, healers, etc., were an excellent way to gain the cooperation of the intelligentsia, relying on nineteenth-century Enlightenment notions of village needs, and especially women's needs, for medical and scientific knowledge. On the level of power relations *within* rural and urban communities, the trials and their reliance on preexisting, unexamined notions of female backwardness were useful to local representatives of the intelligentsia in establishing their professional (and therefore privileged) position. The mock courtroom replicated and extended judicial hierarchy, discipline, and control to whole new audiences. The scenarios repudiated village superstitions yet reinforced prejudices against women as mothers, healers, and delegatki. This anti-baba rhetoric served both to highlight the new values of the Soviet regime, illuminating the new against the background of women's alleged ignorance and outmoded values, and to increase the power of the professionals scripting the plays. In this way both medical professionals and party activists could count on popular misogyny in everyday life as a way to dramatize the distance between the new Soviet life they hoped to build and the old peasant world of kinship and ignorance they wanted to leave behind. By putting the "new woman" and the "old woman" on trial, they could show the failings of both and demonstrate their own superiority.

THE CRISIS IN THE CLUBS AND THE EROSION OF THE PUBLIC SPHERE

In the mid-1920s club administrators and political authorities became obsessed with one question: Why weren't adult workers going to the clubs? And why were they instead going to the beer halls and the taverns?[1] When workers' strikes broke out in 1925, these questions became highly politicized. The party Central Committee blamed the trade unions, concluding that the strikes were proof of the "alienation" of the trade unions from the masses.[2]

The trade unions had tried for many years to resist the party's insistence that the clubs under their jurisdiction were supposed to deliver political lessons.[3] From their perspective workers needed music, theater, and sports, not politics. Many club leaders were torn between putting on dances and movies, which they knew the workers wanted, and putting on lectures and public debates, which the political authorities mandated.[4] Dances and movies had the additional advantage that they brought income into the clubs, a crucial factor in the early years of the New Economic Policy (NEP), when virtually all social organizations were denied state funding and had to fend for themselves. The unions had found from experience that if they did not provide some forms of recreation in the clubs, they had no hope of persuading workers even to set foot inside their doors.[5]

After years of ignoring the clubs, the party now began insisting that they had to be transformed into genuine centers of mass propaganda.[6] More concretely, the trade unions were now required to give the clubs a fixed percentage of their budgets.[7] The unions and other political organizations also launched a number of journals directed at the clubs.[8] Glavpolitprosvet, under Krupskaya's direction, held its First Congress of Club Workers in July 1924.[9] Proletkult, the proletarian culture organization, was also pressed into service when it was formally transferred in 1925 from the auspices of the Education Commissariat to the trade unions.[10]

In response to the strikes of 1925 party authorities initially claimed that the unions had actually gone too far in the direction of political education work and support for the factory administrations' agendas. They promoted new watchwords of the day for the clubs, including "diversity of approaches," "attraction," "independent activism [samodeiatel'nost'], voluntariness, initiative," and "healthy workers' democracy."[11] Krupskaia and Maria Ulianova both claimed that the clubs were becoming a place "where the public opinion of the workers is being formed." Krupskaia even defended "theatricality" as a way to influence people's emotions and tie their personal lives to the public building of communism. Some entertainment was clearly a good thing.[12]

The civilian clubs epitomized the dilemmas faced by a range of so-called voluntary organizations during NEP. On the one hand, they were supposed to attract the workers without undue emphasis on politics and propaganda. On the other hand, they were required to "socialize" the workers and educate them in socialist values. Agitation trials provided a flexible combination of entertainment, education, and discipline that worked for a variety of different clubs in different settings.

It was easy to see why workers were not going to the clubs. Even supported by resolutions from the party Central Committee, the clubs still faced a host of problems—shortages of space and heating fuel, dingy furniture, and lack of well-trained staffs. They were far from the luxurious "palaces of culture" that Bolshevik education ministers had dreamed of in the early days after the revolution. Fights broke out. Scandals erupted. Outside rowdies tried to come in and cause trouble. And, as one author noted, the clubs were plagued with "endless sunflower seeds," whole buckets of which had to be swept up after every performance put on there.[13]

Disorganization and indiscipline in the clubs were so rampant that many workers were reluctant to attend, let alone bring their nonworking wives and children. "You won't get me to go there, that's for sure!" exclaims one housewife in an agitation trial; " . . . your club is only decadence, that's what."[14] Another defendant claims he won't let his wife go near the club: "The clubs are all debauchery."[15]

Club administrators themselves criticized the study circles (kruzhki) for producing only "hack work." Krupskaia also criticized the mass work of the clubs for being clichéd and bureaucratic, for killing any initiative in the masses, and for alienating audiences by failing to address their real interests.[16]

As has often been the case in Russian and Soviet history, contemporary observers assumed that the fundamental problem lay in the people themselves and their lack of discipline. Cultural staff workers blamed members' "laziness" and their tendency to find excuses, whether family responsibilities, tiredness from work, headaches, or that untranslatable but omnipresent excuse among the Russian peasantry, "My hut is at the edge [of town]" (*moia khata s kraiu*). In other words, I'm not concerned because I live too far away. For all the materialism of official Marxist-Leninist ideology, administrators viewed the problem as one of "lack of organized consciousness, not being used to thinking carefully about serious matters, an undeveloped sense of moderation, a lack of *aktivnost'* [activeness], and a lack of any attempt to see the club as their own, unifying workers' corner." It was not sufficient to hang posters on the wall: "Don't spit seeds"; "Smoking is forbidden." Nor was it effective to deliver paternalistic reproofs and scoldings that went in one ear and out the other. The answer to carelessness, slacking, and mischief making had to be "labor, discipline and order"—Trotsky's famous Civil War slogan, which observers now returned to.[17]

The club journals blamed the staffs as well as the members. The directors of the clubs and kruzhki were alleged to have little or no preparation; their turnover was astronomically high, as they changed six, eight, or even twelve times in a year; many were castoffs from other union jobs whom no one else wanted; many were barely literate; and most were completely ignorant of how clubs should be run.[18]

The disciplinary problems of the club administrators were made all the more difficult in the mid-1920s by the government's decision to decriminalize a number of petty crimes, including home brewing and hooliganism committed as a first offense, making these last the responsibility of police and local officials instead of the courts. Despite legislators' hopes that this would help to stem the tide of hooliganism cases in the courts, the number of such cases in both the courts and the administrative units rose dramatically in these years.[19]

How, then, did a club administrator or cultural worker find a compromise between the workers' needs for rest and recreation, the party's requirements that the clubs become "real centers of mass propaganda," and the administrators' fervent prayers for discipline and an end to hooliganism?

The answer that a number of administrators and organizers settled on was to organize agitation trials. On the simplest level the trials gave a disciplined performance in which the judge could use his authority ex officio and ex cathedra to call the audience to order. If a club member made too much noise or failed to sit quietly, the judge rang his bell or ordered the person removed from the courthouse. In one trial scenario the judge opened the proceedings by formally instructing the audience to maintain the strictest discipline, not to leave, not to smoke, and not to talk while the court was in session; those found guilty of infractions would be held strictly accountable.[20] In many other trials the judge frequently reminded the witnesses and members of the audience to give clear, objective answers without embellishments. When participants (either defendants or witnesses) refused outright or expressed reluctance to answer questions, the judge had the direct authority to compel them to speak.[21]

As cultural organizers and instructors began trying to make their clubs more "cultured," one head of a small railroad club near Kharkov wrote to the leading journal for workers' clubs, *Rabochii klub,* with a request for materials for trials: "I can see that a new stream has poured life into our clubs. If possible, please send the theses of trials (any ones)." The journal editors responded by saying, "Tell us what topics you need trial materials for, and we will send you them as soon as possible."[22] In the eyes of the club director and the journal editors, the exact content of the trials did not particularly matter. Any topic could be used to put on a trial in the clubs.

Club directors, moreover, were now being explicitly trained in the staging and production of agitation trials. In 1923–24 the Moscow trade unions began holding short-term, practical seminars called "course-conferences," with agitation trials as one of their principal subjects.[23] In 1924 the Moscow Provincial Politprosvet Institute (founded in 1920) expanded and reorganized its course offerings to make a three-year national course of study (called the All-Union Higher Political Education Courses). In the third year of study students learned to set up reading huts in the villages using special political education methods that drew on local personnel and local interests, including forms such as conversations, living newspapers, wall newspapers, information bureaus, and agitation trials.[24] Proletkult, too, moved to create courses that formally taught club staffs how to put on trials.[25] Even the State Courses on Public Speaking (Gosudarstvennye kursy tekhniki rechi) published a *Trial of Chiang Kai-Shek.*[26]

By 1926 the leading authorities on clubs were claiming that agitation trials "are one of the favorite forms of club work. They capture critical life issues and in this way attract the attention of the working masses. What is intriguing is the fact that someone's fate is being decided, albeit a fictional person's."[27]

Raisa Ginzburg, a leading Proletkult activist in the field of trade union clubs, wrote that the agitation trial was a particularly desirable form of activity for the clubs during the summer months because "like any contest between two sides, it is extremely absorbing for the audience, and at the same time allows serious discussion of any issue." For these reasons it could be used to replace lectures. Even the process of preparing the trial could involve a large number of participants, which would be beneficial. Of course, because such trials were fairly complicated to organize, she recommended that this form not be used more than two times per month, and then only in clubs "with a cadre of politically strong staff workers."[28]

In 1924 a study of 517 productions put on in 102 clubs revealed that agitation trials constituted 19 percent of the so-called new forms of work that club members were performing (including living newspapers and dramati-

Table 1. Activities Offered in Twenty-two Clubs on the Moscow–Kursk Railway Line in 1923

Club Activity	Number	Average Audience
Plays (free and charging entrance)	1,094	367
Lectures	1,003	224
Films (free and charging entrance)	461	477
Concerts (free and charging entrance)	280	403
Ceremonial meetings and demonstrations	272	548
Excursions	110	263
Children's performances (free and charging entrance)	75	465
Club evenings	47	423
Living newspapers	40	469
Agitation trials	32	402
Christenings (*oktiabriny*)	10	323
Evenings of questions and answers	5	248
Political lottery	2	445
Other performances	138	457
Total	3,569	

zations of reports) and 11 percent of all forms (new and old, including plays and concerts).[29]

Local statistics (undoubtedly chosen by the authorities from among the most successful and active clubs) show that while trials were not the dominant form of activity in the clubs, they were an accepted and widespread form of activity. A study of the clubs on the Moscow-Kursk railway line, for example, found that agitation trials were roughly tenth in order of number performed and average audience size (see table 1).[30] A study of the Karl Liebknecht club in Saratov (also a railway club) from August 1924 to April 1925 showed similar results (see table 2).[31] Both studies demonstrate that while the clubs were not staging huge numbers of agitation trials, the latter nonetheless drew good-sized audiences.

THE CLUB ON TRIAL

Club directors and educators praised agitation trials in the clubs for their ability "to attract workers' attention to the club and show them visually the main tasks and character of club work."[32] The rank-and-file club member would surely be willing to play a small role in a trial performance if there were a series of conversations about them, reasoned M. Rastopchina, a leading cultural education figure and director of a club in Kostroma.[33]

One use for agitation trials was to mark rites of passage in the clubs. The literary circle of the Union of Municipal Workers, for example, put on a "trial of the reader" when a special "council of the friends of the library" (*sovet druzei biblioteki*) was formed.[34] Cultural workers could find topics in almost every issue of *Rabochii klub* to help them deal with problems in their

Table 2. Activities Offered at the Karl Liebknecht Club,
August 1924–April 1925

Club Activity	Number	Average Audience
Films	328	38
Lectures	44	117
Plays	41	785
Excursions	16	50
Demonstrations	5	760
Living newspapers	4	1,500
Evenings of reports (*otchety*)	3	1,333
Political trials (*politsudy*)	2	1,000
Concerts	2	700
Total	445	

organizations: trials to elucidate why adult workers were not visiting the clubs, trials of workers carrying out agitation against the clubs, and trials of so-called passive (nonparticipatory) members of the club.[35]

Soon civilian clubs were building on what they had learned in the army. They took the club itself and put it on trial (just as the army had created trials of itself and its officers). However, unlike the army trials, which relied primarily on allegorical characters, the new club trials focused on allegedly real problems in the clubs themselves.

The problem for the clubs, as they themselves recognized, was that putting their own organizations on trial required a delicate balancing act. On the one hand, cultural staffs and club administrators needed to find a means of dramatizing the current problems of the clubs and their failings as a way of encouraging members to become more involved. On the other hand, when they highlighted club problems and failings, they risked giving club members additional excuses for being passive and avoiding club work.[36]

One humorous trial presents the defendant as "our old, bald club, dressed in rags," and the witnesses as the library, the school, the piano, and various circles (*kruzhki*) (drama, music, trade union, physical education, and political literacy).[37]

"Do you believe in God?" the court officials ask the old club.

"What God? When the young Pioneers and the physical educationalists [*sic*] get together, there's no room even for the devil."

"Well, what about the kruzhki, have they been meeting?"

"Oh yes, so well that the glass cutters haven't had time to put the windows back in."

When the music circle gives evidence against it, the old club gets very angry: "Don't you believe that broken old balalaika. She's fibbing. She's been lying around all summer, just rusting her strings, and she's only learned to play one song."

In the end the prosecutor attacks everyone, including the narrator, who is the club director. When the defense tries to call for the old club's acquittal, the latter bursts into tears and says farewell to its charges: "I'm sorry, my children, that you have to leave my walls. But it's okay. I will be reborn next summer and will take up new work then." Abramov, the article narrator, concludes from this that the workers have in fact learned to enjoy themselves in the clubs, thus implying that the crisis of attendance after all is not so bad as many would have it.

One of the purposes of the trials of clubs and club activities was to get workers to "reveal" their true opinions about the clubs and to get more involved. *The Trial of Six Factory Workers Who Agitated against the Club*, for example, revealed six different reasons for nonattendance in the clubs, ranging from an illiterate worker's fears that the club would "try to make him into a communist" to a young man's view that there weren't enough amusements at the club and a woman worker's complaint that she had no time for the club because of her two children. The minimalist description of the unnamed witnesses corresponds to the qualities the reader or viewer would have expected of such a person. An older cottage worker who works at home and trades on the market finds he has no time for the club and would rather go to the beer hall. A skilled worker, by contrast, makes more politically acceptable criticisms that the clubs are too "official," there is "no comradely unity," there are no "interesting new forms of work" (which, of course, could mean an implied criticism of the lack of agitation trial performances).[38]

But *The Trial of Six Factory Workers* does more than reveal the perspectives of ordinary workers. It also allows the club a certain amount of free advertising. The witnesses for the defense talk about how their work in the club has helped them overcome their former prejudices against it. Some have even been elected as delegates and members of the factory committee. *The Trial of Six Workers* thus implicitly contrasts "bad agitation" (that of the ignorant workers who laughed at people going to the club) and "good agitation," such as the trial performance itself. It castigates the whole audience for its "passivity" and failure to aid in making the club a better place. As the judge explains, the point of the trial is not so much to determine the guilt or innocence of the six defendants as to address the hundreds of other workers who have failed to understand the significance of the clubs. The trial's sentence "will open their eyes to their error." The final sentence obliges everyone to participate in the club and orders the club administration and cultural commission to eliminate deficiencies in the club's organization.[39]

TRADE UNION TRIALS AND THE EROSION OF THE PUBLIC SPHERE

In 1924 Moscow trade unions pioneered a new kind of agitation trial, the "trade union trial" (*professional'nyi sud*) and "production trial" (*proizvodstvennyi sud*). Such trade union trials, proponents argued, should focus on something that "has happened in reality" and that the audience knows well. The subject should also be something that was not a one-time event but rather a type of incident that happened regularly. If organizers picked a topic that was "a sore subject," then workers would be more likely to come and participate: "Grumblings and cries of pain will come to the surface, as will practical wishes and business-like criticisms of the work of the trade unions." Workers would express their "real views" on, say, the financial practice of their factory committee.[40]

The trial, like all agitation trials, should never be of open-and-shut cases, such as that of the union member who failed to pay his union dues (and who therefore would simply be excluded without a trial). Rather, it should involve an apparently trivial case with nonetheless important consequences for the union and even the whole economy. An example would be a whisper campaign initiated by a union member who did not want to come out and make positive criticisms in public. A mock trial of such a whisperer would help the audience develop its "habits of proletarian public-mindedness [obshchestvennost']."[41]

In other words, "public" forums (commissions, debates, and trials) were being systematically encouraged but only at the expense of individual liberties and private discussions. The individual could voice criticisms but only in public contexts created and controlled by local authorities.

In production and trade union trials the cardinal sins were not just actions committed but those omitted. A number of trials bring suit against defendants for failing to pay their union dues and for failing to join the union. Five women are brought to trial for failing to attend general meetings. Another six factory workers are charged with agitating against the club and exhibiting "passivity." Still another six workers are accused of not paying their union dues on time.[42]

The contrast between the trials of the early 1920s and those of the late 1920s is demonstrated in one of the very first production trials, which still remains within the humanist model of educating the audience and debating genuine dilemmas. *The Trial of Factory Committee Member N. I. Egorov* (published in 1924) is a trial of a man who commits several misdemeanors yet who also has good qualities. In 1924 charges are brought against him as a member of the factory committee on the basis of a visiting instructor's report claiming (1) that Egorov has been preventing his wife from attending delegate meetings because he wants her to stay home and cook for an upcoming holiday, (2) that he has failed to give meeting space to the Komsomol (the allocation of rooms is his responsibility in the factory committee), and (3) that he has discouraged workers from taking part in a political demonstration and from giving donations to a campaign for workers in Japan.[43]

In every other respect Egorov is a model factory committee member. He pays attention to his fellow workers and tries to make sure they receive much-needed housing and heating fuel. He resists going to the political demonstration but only because the factory has a production deadline to meet. Egorov's defense attorney reminds the court that it is not a person's thoughts that should be judged but rather his or her actions and the consequences of those actions.

This trial thus provides a foil for many of the later ones, as we shall see. In the first place Egorov, as previously suggested, is a multifaceted character facing genuine dilemmas in an era dedicated to raising productivity and "rationalizing" industry. In the second place the trial presents a forum for a multiplicity of voices and opinions. Egorov's wife, for example, whom he prevents from going to meetings, is torn between her loyalty to her family and her loyalty to her women colleagues who elected her as a delegate. Voices from the crowd interject that she is not the only one who did not want to go to a meeting because of domestic preparations for a saint's day. The voices also express different perspectives on the Komsomol and whether it is a true vanguard of the proletariat or "a bunch of hooligans." Toward the end of the play three different groups of workers hold short conversations about whether it is worth sending grain to the Japanese since they have not taken previous shipments, whether the men in the company are wasting their time going to beer halls, and whether the women should find a way to have all the men put on trial, or at least one man as an example.

This 1924 trial can be summed up as having certain qualities of "dialogic imagination" (to use Bakhtin's phrase), which soon after this begin to disappear almost completely.[44] The characters, including the crowds, are multivocal and provide a balance of positive and negative views; the characters have complex biographies and hints of lives before the time frame of the play; they express dissenting points of view; the defendant is not all bad and the prosecution witnesses are not all good; the accusations are concrete and potentially refutable or at least defensible.

The public defender, moreover, gives Egorov a full defense on the grounds that he is still half-peasant and therefore ignorant, that he has been overworked with other duties in the factory committee, and that the factory is missing the main element that could have helped him—namely, a club for the workers. Because of the absence of a club, Egorov has not been exposed to the variety of political work he should have been, the lectures, political plays, agitation and political trials, study circles, and so on, that would have attracted him and "imperceptibly" educated him. In the end Egorov is given an amnesty, sentenced to a public reprimand, and required to attend a political school for six months. The defense has thrown out the main challenge: "If it is necessary to find someone guilty, then we should find not only comrade Egorov but all of us who are sitting here guilty. And we should ask: what have you done to give comrade Egorov that political literacy which he is missing?"[45]

As the decade progressed and the party became increasingly insensitive to diverse points of view, the dialogic qualities evident in the *Trial of Factory Committee Member Egorov* began to disappear and to be replaced by their opposites: vagueness, indeterminacy, hostility to the defendant and inattention to his or her voice, pettiness, exaggeration of danger, declining attention to mitigating circumstances, weakening role of the defense attorney, and an overall increase in levels of anxiety and suspicion.

CONTROL FROM BELOW

One of Lenin's most cherished notions had been that society and the state would be able to run themselves. Control and supervision would come from below. Through the Workers' and Peasants' Inspectorate (which was created in 1923) ordinary workers, especially the least educated, were supposed to inspect and supervise the workings of enterprises from the lowest soup kitchen to the most complicated machine-building factories.[46]

In the second half of the 1920s trade union authors began to imagine trials in which the machines put the workers on trial and the workers put the bosses on trial. The shop floor worker could be put on trial for being lazy, "a time waster," someone guilty of absenteeism. The boss could be put on trial for his neglect of his duties, his selfishness, his nepotism, his extravagance, his carousing with NEPmen (rich businessmen) at the expense of the factory.[47] The production commission could be put on trial for "failing to draw the working masses into economic work," while the factory committee could be put on trial for allowing a strike.[48]

When the machines are put on trial for low productivity, the agitation courts show that the fault lies with the workers who do not handle them well, do not take good care of them, and do not organize production well. The language of the trials takes on an infantilizing tone. Signs placed on the machines are used as props in the plays:

- Please don't leave me alone with no work. I am ashamed before my comrades who are working.
- Wipe me off, so that I can be clean, since I have no arms to clean myself, and I don't like being dirty.
- Oil my moving parts; unoiled parts rub and heat up. When I become hot, I get sick and have to be treated.

Of course, the guilty parties in these trials are not the machines, but those who do not know how to take care of them.[49]

Anyone connected with the factory training schools could also be put on trial—the factory director, head of the school, chair of the cultural commission, main engineer, foreman, provincial school representative, slacking students, and Komsomol representatives. The list of possible misdeeds seems daunting: failures of oversight and effort, failure to provide public activism (which now had its own name, *neobshchestvennost'*), and failure to proceed in a disciplined manner.[50]

By the end of a long list of possible variations on the trial of the factory school, its author concluded that the trials had shown "with incontrovertible clarity" that "the defendants did not understand the responsibility which each of them bore in their own area for the work of the factory school." This "incontrovertible clarity" in fact reveals an obsession with insufficiency and inadequacy. The director "failed to understand the interests of Soviet production"; the factory committee "did not show sufficient energy" in preparing skilled workers through the school; the engineer and foreman exhibited an "unsocial (*neobshchestvennyi*) approach" toward the students since they failed to give generously of their time; the students revealed their "lack of consciousness" in their careless attitudes toward their studies and their misdemeanors (such as drinking and hooliganism), which were "unworthy" of working class youth; and the provincial vocational education authorities exhibited only "weak supervision" of the school.[51]

In almost every case the solution proposed was to have the director, the factory committee chair, or the student give a special report to their respective organizations on the value of the factory school. In this way the guilty person could overcome and expiate his or her sins by making a public presentation in favor of the very organization he or she had neglected or undermined.

The trials thus were intended to show (in however artificial a manner) the justice of the system. Trials of high prices, the recent scissors crisis, the closing of a shop and unemployment, the tariff system, the tariff-setting bureau—all these could be used to "bring out the main sore spots" (*vyavit' samye glavnye "boliachki"*) in the life of the factory.

Some trials of the factory school apparently fell flat and turned into nothing more than a series of speeches accusing and defending the school with a bit of discussion at the end. In other trials the heads of the school showed resistance to the whole undertaking. As one commented, "What on earth are you going to judge us for when we have poured so much energy into the school?" But other schools reported great success in their trials. "All the positive and negative sides, all the abnormalities came to the surface [*vyplyli naruzhu*]."[52] For the students, one can imagine what a field day such a trial represented. Since they were the ones to perform the trial, they had an opportunity to say everything they thought about their teachers. As one report noted, "as a result of the trial, the students became aware of their power; the teachers changed in front of their very eyes. 'How sweet they've become,' the young people commented."[53] Reading the report on this trial, it is not difficult to understand the origins of the generational conflict that later exploded during the Cultural Revolution at the end of the 1920s.[54]

CRIMES OF OMISSION AND PRESSURE ON "VOLUNTARY" ORGANIZATIONS

In the middle 1920s the party was not only pressuring the trade unions (which were themselves "voluntary" organizations—officially, at least, no one was required to join) but also consciously creating new voluntary organizations. These "public" (*obshchestvennyi*) groups included societies such as Down with Illiteracy (Obshchestvo Doloi Negramotnost', 1923–1936), the Friends of the Air Force (Obshchestvo Druzei Vozdushnogo Flota, 1923–1925), the League of the Militant Godless (Souiz Voinstvennykh Bezbozhnikov, 1924–1947), and others.[55] Each of them published trials as a way of stating their new missions and creating a collective identity for their organizations.

In 1924 Stalin stressed the significance of these "free" (*vol'nye*) (as he called them) organizations. Peasant correspondents to the newspapers, he insisted, as well as committees of mutual aid and even trade union cells in the village, must "be in the business of denouncing [*oblichenie*] and correcting [*ispravlenie*] the shortcomings [*nedostatki*] in our Soviet society." This was, he said, "more effective [literally, more serious, *mnogo ser'eznee*] than the force of administrative pressure."[56]

With time these organizations provided another pressure point for the party to direct and control the citizenry. Mock trials had always been easiest to put on where a group of individuals worked in what one lecturer called "compact collectives [*kompaktnye kollektivy*]." These were collectives where audiences were "organized," such as army divisions, schools, and women's sections. The collective identities of the audiences facilitated the work of putting on a trial since they shared certain values and reasons for being together. The collectives performing the trials were also used to working together. Furthermore, the groups all had their own issues that could be the subject of performances, particularly their concerns with collective discipline.[57] Above all, they each had an organizational interest in fostering their own identity and disciplining their members.

Although the use of such "compact collectives" had long been the norm, in the middle 1920s these groups began to experience entirely new pressures. The trade unions were now being severely criticized for insubordination. The Komsomol meanwhile was being charged with "Trotskyism."[58]

In this context these allegedly "voluntary" organizations became acutely conscious of their members' behavior. Though the agitation trials had originally been used as educational forms designed to inspire debate and critical thinking, now their organizers focused on disciplining both their subjects (the defendants, witnesses, and other characters) and their audiences.

In 1925 the Society of Friends of the Air Force (ODVF) published an "aviation agitation trial" of two men, a worker and a peasant, who had declined to join the society, and a priest who actively incited people against it. Toward the end of the trial, after many humorous scenes of peasants who do not understand the judge, who cross themselves accidentally in front of Karl Marx, and so on, a liberal defense attorney appears on the scene, ostensibly from the audience. Even the judges do not know him, but he claims he wants to provide a defense for the defendants. His defense is undermined, however, by the fact that he is a representative of the old intelligentsia and that he argues against even the premise of the trial. How, he asks, can a person be brought to trial for nonmembership in a *voluntary* society? Or for speaking out against membership when in the Soviet Union everyone has freedom of speech? The prosecutor answers these charges by saying that not to join a society such as the ODVF harms not only the individual in question but also the whole working class because of the importance of airplane construction. Although he recommends that the cases against the worker and peasant be dropped because of their ignorance and their full confessions, the prosecutor does not admit that such a case might be inadmissible in a real court of law. Instead he gives a long disquisition on the military and peacetime benefits of aviation to workers and peasants.[59]

Like many trials, this one is important not only for whom it officially brings to court but also for whom it pillories during the course of the trial. Not surprisingly for anyone who knows the literature of the NEP period, the classic male villains, the priest and the kulak, are castigated for turning people against Soviet institutions (in this case the ODVF). The kulak in fact has attempted to join the society but only in order to hide his true colors, to make himself look more like an upstanding citizen. The prosecutor and judges, however, pride themselves on ripping off the false masks of the kulak and priest. In the end, the priest, Ikonostasov, is not acquitted (unlike his co-defendants) but instead is accused of "meddling in public matters" that are not his business. The separation of church and state means that he is (magnanimously) to be allowed to continue teaching scripture but not to pronounce on a temporal, public matter such as the air force. Meanwhile the kulak, the prosecutor concludes, should under no circumstances be allowed to join the Society of Friends. "For such an 'element'," the prosecutor insists, "the doors to society are closed and will never open. . . . There is no place for them among true friends; there is no place for wolves in sheeps' clothing, nor should there be."[60] As had been the case with the *lishentsy* (those denied electoral and other rights from the beginning of the revolution), the priest and the kulak are explicitly excluded from membership, however much they themselves might have wanted to join.[61]

CRITICISM AND SELF-CRITICISM IN THE KOMSOMOL

The quintessential "voluntary" organization in the Soviet Union was the Komsomol, or communist youth organization. From the time of the founding of their organization in 1918, Komsomol organizers viewed their mission as one of *winning over* youth. As Nadezhda Krupskaia told the Sixth Komsomol Congress in July 1924, "We must strive to bind our private life to the struggle for and the construction of communism."[62] For many the Komsomol represented "the young guard of the proletariat," the replacements for the older warriors. "Work in the Komsomol from a young age teaches proletarian civic consciousness [*priuchaet k proletarskoi obshchestvennosti*], creates a new human being—the disciplined activist, the party or professional worker."[63] The agitation trials were now commissioned to serve as vehicles for those qualities.

Throughout 1924 the Komsomol was involved in dozens of minor agitation trials: numerous trials of the Bible (especially in conjunction with the so-called Komsomol Easter), trials of wall newspapers, and trials of people who abused books.[64] All of these were fairly innocent. They retained the quality of a debate in which different arguments for and against, say, the Bible, were brought up in the course of the trial. Sometimes they used humor and slapstick to make the audiences laugh.

Around 1924, however, the Komsomol leaders also began to script and organize trials that used more local material and relied more heavily on humiliating of the defendants. At this time the Komsomol as an organization was under fire in the press for alleged "Trotskyist" sympathies.[65] The leaders now had to prove their orthodoxy and their vigilance, and trials were one way to do so. The mass influx of new Komsomol members also strained the club organizers, who found it difficult to control them. Trials, as we shall see, proved an attractive way of fighting against hooliganism and disruptive behavior in general.

Komsomol organizations contributed to the evolution of the agitation trials by shifting their focus almost exclusively to discipline with little attention to entertainment and education. The trials still stressed moral upbringing (*vospitanie*), while education (*obrazovanie*), in the sense of book learning and the development of critical thinking, now receded entirely from the scene. Though Komsomol leaders appear not to have written many trial scripts, the ones that are available convey the disciplinary focus that became the hallmark of trials of the second half of the 1920s.

In the preface to one of the first Komsomol trials, *The Trial of the Komsomolets or Komsomolka Who Has Violated Komsomol Discipline* (1924), author Boris Andreev explains that the final indictment has deliberately been left open in the script so any Komsomol organization can use the text as a template for discussing its own real discipline problems.[66] Andreev illustrates this with the example of a trial of a Komsomol member indicted for failure to attend meetings and for using bad language on the street, but he makes it clear that the ideal variant would be a kind of impromptu trial, one that was drawn from observed infractions by the target population.

In his notes Andreev emphasizes that before staging a trial, its organizers should convene a general meeting during which, working together, the participants can expose all the troublesome problems that have come up in their organization and that might be reflected in one way or another during the trial. "After such a form of self-criticism [*samokritika*]," Andreev notes, "the Trial [*sic*] will have deeply socializing [*vospitatel'noe*], publicly organizational, and disciplinary significance."[67]

For Soviet citizens "criticism and self-criticism" was rapidly becoming a familiar phrase ritually pronounced at almost all collective meetings, whether of schoolchildren or factory committees, the Komsomol, or high party congresses. Most Western historians date it from the famous "Appeal to All Party Members and All Workers on the Development of Self-Criticism" in June 1928, followed by a speech by Stalin a few weeks later.[68] Most Soviet studies, by contrast, treat it as an almost timeless philosophical concept with its roots in Lenin's writings and its full development under Stalin.[69]

Criticism and self-criticism as a practice did not, in fact, originate in 1928. Stalin was using the term already in 1924, when he named self-criticism as one of the four main methods of what he was now calling "Leninism." As he explained it, "self-criticism of the proletarian parties" could be defined as their "education and moral upbringing on the basis of their own mistakes, for only in this way can one bring up genuine cadres and genuine leaders of the party."[70] He gave an example of what he considered appropriate criticism and self-criticism in October 1924 when he hauled the party as a whole over the coals for its poor work in the countryside and launched specific attacks against the secretaries of party cells with whom he was meeting.[71] A few days later he held up his own "ruthless criticism of our party work in the village" as an example for others, arguing that unless the party criticized itself and allowed nonparty members to criticize it, external actors such as peasants in rural uprisings (Kronstadt, Tambov, etc.) would do the criticizing and that would be worse.[72]

In *The Trial of the Komsomolets or Komsomolka Who Has Violated Komsomol Discipline,* Andreev's defendant is charged not only with neglecting his or her duties, but with *consciously* and *maliciously* evading them. The defendant's nonattendance at lectures on the international workers' youth movement in the Komsomol school is "introducing an element of sabotage and disorganization and compromises the Komsomol." Such harsh language is new to the agitation trials. This is no longer a matter of one individual's behavior. Rather, the effect of that behavior on the whole organization must be examined and judged. Since "the usual measures" (unspecified) have failed to influence the defendant, the collective has declared that if the defendant continues this kind of behavior, he or she will be expelled from the Komsomol and the case will be handed over to a "public Trial [*obshchestvennyi Sud*] by the workers and Komsomol members" of the enterprise.[73]

Another, allegedly real, case was that of *The Trial of the Young Men Who Did Not Enroll in the Komsomol.* The defendants, according to this account, are active club members who have shown their knowledge of communism and their commitment to its ideals but who nonetheless have not joined the Komsomol. They are respected and are considered honest and well socialized (*perevospitavshiesia*). Yet no amount of persuasion has brought them into the Komsomol. The prosecution and defense try to show what the Komsomol has done for them and why they and all others must join if they want to fight against the bourgeoisie. The final sentence divides the four defendants into two who are "more conscious" and two who are "less conscious." The former are simply ordered to join the Komsomol within two weeks, while the latter are given two weeks to think about whether they want to join. The trial's organizers considered it a success because it led to lively discussion among young people in the club as to whether the sentence was correct. For the audience it was quite interesting, even titillating, to see their own leading club members on trial.[74]

HOOLIGANISM, ALCOHOLISM, AND SEXUAL DEGENERACY

In 1926–27 the Komsomol and the clubs joined forces to unleash a major campaign against hooliganism, which was said to be on the rise. Nikolai Krylenko, the deputy commissar of justice, commented on the "the process of ceaseless, systematic, noisy growth in the wave of hooliganism" that had taken place from 1924 to 1926. The numbers of cases handled administratively rose from 39,000 in April to June 1924, to 111,386 in the same quarter in 1926. There had also been a rash of high-profile cases involving hooliganism, including the Dymovka case (involving the murder of a village correspondent) and the case of Chubarov Alley (involving an urban gang rape of a peasant woman).[75]

In 1926 club journals began calling for the "healing of everyday life" (*ozdorovlenie byta*) and the rooting out of the main scourges of club life—hooliganism, drunkenness, and sexual license.[76] In earlier years the clubs had tried traditional methods of influence: lectures, debates, discussions, heart-to-heart talks, question-and-answer sessions on alcoholism and campaigns against moonshine, even excursions outside the city to give people fresh air and physical exercise. Some clubs set up special membership commissions to decide who would be included and excluded. They "persuaded" some of the troublemakers to volunteer as guards by threatening to take them to the police. From others the authorities extracted promises and signatures that they would help fight against hooliganism. "Such a signature almost always has a 'magical' influence," wrote one activist. "The former hooligan, embarrassed by the trust shown in him, not only did not violate it but often became an ardent assistant in getting rid of hooliganism."[77] When all else

"The Trial of Drink, December 26." On the left is a table for the defense and on the right, one for the prosecution. In the center under a bottle of beer is the indictment. From *Rabochii klub* 1 (1927): 43.

failed, the clubs brought suit against hooligans in the circuit courts, which traveled out to the clubs. These trials, it was hoped, would have a deterrent effect on any potential hooligans.[78]

It was not always possible to put on "show trials" of real hooligans, however, in which case there were advantages to putting on agitation trials organized by club circles or the club *aktiv* (the group of those most active in the club).[79] If an agitation trial were well staged and well acted (without excessive theatricality), organizers claimed, it could have just as strong an effect as a real court trial. One corrections official in a prison even staged an agitation trial in which the parts were played by prisoners who were themselves incarcerated for violating article 176 of the Criminal Code on hooliganism.[80]

Another agitation trial of a hooligan was performed in an unfinished dormitory in an unnamed neighborhood in an unnamed city. Seated on benches, the audience of seasonal workers watched a play put on by the sanitation education staff. One audience member was skeptical and left the room, saying, "But it's not a real trial; it's made up as an example to others." Others, however, watched the whole trial as the defense tried to show that the causes of the defendant's hooliganism lay in his alcoholic father and downtrodden mother, while the prosecution called for his indictment and punishment. "Who thinks Ivan Lobachev [the defendant] deserves mercy?" the court asked at the conclusion of the performance. Only one woman raised her hand, and was shushed by the others, who commented derisively on "females who take pity." After deliberation the court sentenced Lobachev to three years in exile, but without loss of rights. The sanitation educationists expressed satisfaction that they had done their job in illuminating the medical causes of hooliganism, especially alcoholism. The seasonal workers dispersed to their rooms, supposedly still talking about the trial.[81]

The most elaborate *Trial of Hooligans* was written by Grigorii Avlov, a former lawyer and Leningrad political education expert, who published it with the Down with Illiteracy Society in 1927.[82] The judge in the trial claims that trials like this one are necessary so the working masses can "clearly see the measures being taken in the fight against this ugly phenomenon." As the expert witness notes, "some part of our youth are showing their activism [*aktivnost'*] in deformed hooligan forms." In other words, they are showing the wrong kind of activity, the wrong kind of collectivity.[83] The problem of hooliganism thus resembles other misdemeanors brought to trial, such as incorrect agitation (against the club, instead of for it) and incorrect forms of shame (hiding one's illness instead of treating it). Above all, though, hooliganism reveals an absence of the public-mindedness that Komsomol and other authorities in this period were determined to foster.

"Our social [*obshchestvennyi*] organism is healthy and, like any healthy organism, fights intensively with individual manifestations of illness," notes the expert witness in the trial. What was needed were not only judicial-corrective measures but also "social prophylaxis."[84]

Stepan Smirnov and Pavel Iudin, the two defendants, represent two different types of sons. Smirnov is sarcastic, hardened. He has already been sentenced to two weeks of administrative labor duty for a previous hooliganism offense, and he lies to the court about it. Iudin, by contrast, is melancholy, almost silent, and refuses to defend himself. His nickname is "Pashka the writer." When forced to explain this nickname, he tells the court that he writes poetry. In their closing arguments the prosecution and defense both condemn Smirnov but question how to deal with Iudin. For the prosecutor Iudin is initially a potentially dangerous, chameleon-like figure, hiding his true colors and lying in his confessions of wrongdoing. He concludes, however, that Iudin is not so much dangerous as lacking in will, and he calls for educating his will (*vospitat' ego voliu*) through labor and discipline so that Iudin can become a "useful member of society." The defense focuses on the element of Iudin's fantasy—especially what appears to be Iudin's fantasy of revenge for supposed insults—and, like the prosecutor, concludes that the best means of correction is labor discipline.

These two characters represent in turn two possible threatening paths that working class youth can take. They can follow Smirnov in the path of indiscipline and rowdiness, or they can follow Iudin in the direction of the intelligentsia, vaguely seeking revenge for supposed ills, losing themselves in their own fantasies. To try "to pour one's sorrow into poetry," as Iudin does, and as the intelligentsia does, is not the right solution. Instead of direct action, he "consoles himself" with his poetry.[85] That does not make him a dangerous criminal, even in the eyes of the prosecutor. But it does mean that he needs to be isolated from society for a time and given assistance in learning labor and discipline. By returning a guilty verdict, the prosecutor tells the judges, they will be helping to correct him. An acquittal, on the other hand, could permanently ruin him.

Like many other trials, this one contains an extended fantasy on the possibility of transforming human beings, in this case from the difficult but "muscular" energy of Smirnov and the weak but creative energy of Iudin into correct, upstanding, and honest membership in the working collective.

In another case of self-transformation a woman who was infected with venereal disease by her boss came to "suspect the truth" about the source of her infection after attending a sanitation trial in her local club. Seeing the performance of the trial helped her to decide to take action against her boss, who, in addition to infecting her with venereal disease, had abused his position of authority over her.[86]

The most elaborate trial on the subject of sexuality and transformation, Doctor E. B. Demidovich's *Trial of Sexual Depravity*, was published in 1927 by the Down with Illiteracy Society (Doloi Negramotnost'). The medical community endorsed it by including a preface by Professor A. B. Zalkind, the leading sexologist of the day. The problem with sexuality, according to Zalkind, was that it still tended "to arouse the consciousness of our youth" (*budorazhit soznanie nashei molodezhi*). In Zalkind's view Demidovich's *Trial of Sexual Depravity* was "designed to *sharpen* [*zaostriaiutsia*] the sexual questions." Once those questions were highlighted, the Komsomol members and others would finally sit up and take note of all that the party was doing for them. Zalkind especially wanted this trial to be a model so that local groups would try "to expose [*vyiavit'*] before the juries real facts from the lives and sexual habits [*polovogo byta*] of the given setting."[87]

As Demidovich, the author, explained in his preface, the announcement of the trial was to seem as realistic as possible:

On _____ day of _____ month 192__ in the _____ building an open meeting of the Komsomol cell will be held.

The agenda includes discussion of Komsomolka Vtorova's complaint about citizen Vasilev's sexual depravity.

Two lawyers and an expert doctor will take part in the discussion.

All Komsomol members are required to attend. Nonparty members will be invited. Entrance is free.

The announcement thus makes the discussion as formal as possible and requires the attendance of all Komsomol members. The crux of the play concerns the dilemma whether a man can be charged with abandoning his wife, given the official policy of free marriage and divorce in the USSR. In the course of the trial four different women recount the harm that Vasilev has brought them through his sexual affairs while one defends both his and her right to "freedom" in changing sexual partners. ("I am not a thing, that someone could be said to abandon me," says this last woman.)

By presenting a spectacle, Demidovich clearly sets out to make the whole discussion both more believable and more interesting. The judge explicitly turns to the members of the audience at the opening of the play to explain that they will be the final arbiters. They should arm themselves with pencil and paper, he instructs them, so that they can critically examine all the evidence before coming to a conscious, considered decision at the moment of voting.[88]

In the course of the trial it emerges that Vasilev has harmed all the women by abandoning them when they were pregnant, by spreading venereal disease to them, and by leaving them to have crippling abortions. In his final speech he asks the court to judge him. "I will say in good conscience [po sovesti] that it is only here, in court, that before me has opened up all the evil that I have caused. . . . Judge me in such a way that your judgment can help me stand on the healthy path."[89]

On one level, this Trial of Sexual Depravity remains very much within the classic parameters of the agitation trial. The audience has no idea at the outset whether Vasilev will be found innocent or guilty; the witnesses sometimes contradict each other, creating genuine dramatic conflict; the expert witness explains the workings of sexuality and the dangers of early sex life in "scientific" fashion; the audience is asked to vote at the conclusion of the play (though in this case a sentence is also written up for the judge to pronounce). In other words, it appears to have an open, dialogic structure that would allow some debate.

Yet in a new way the trial actively erodes any notion of privacy. The defense attorney, for example, turns at one point to the defendant and asks if he went to the urology clinic at Moscow State University in November 1924. Later he asks one of the witnesses (the brother of a plaintiff) whether he was at the same clinic on the same day. The latter answers that he was and gives the names of three friends whom he also saw there, including Vasilev. The defense attorney asks if he overheard what Vasilev's presenting complaint was. The witness says that Vasilev had complained of weakening sexual energy (which one of the women had also spoken of). "Do you affirm this, Vasilev?" the defense asks.

"What are you doing, tormenting a person," Vasilev cries; "and you claim to be my defense attorney! There are things into which you have no business meddling [vy ne smeete kovyriat'sia]." The judge then calls citizen Vasilev "to order." It is because the court must investigate "the consequences of your disorderly sexual life" that it must ask these questions, the judge comments. "Citizen defender, continue your questions."[90]

Vasilev's entire sexual history is on the table. His consultation at the urology clinic is reported by his supposed friend. His "weakness as a man" is an open topic for discussion and debate. The expert witness in fact carefully explains that "we have before us a feeble [*tshchedushnyi*] man overstrained [*nadorvannyi*] by early sexual life, a young man aged 26 who has already lost his sexual force." The expert explains for all to hear that engaging in sex at too early an age undermines a person's long-term physical and mental health, while sexual restraint on the contrary confirms them.

The Komsomol press at this time also featured a number of real court cases as a means to dramatize social issues and force discussion among young people. Komsomol youth who exploited their wives, killed their infant children, and engaged in criminal actions such as murder and robbery were brought up in the Komsomol press as examples for discussion. Komsomol cells were expected to hold public discussions of these events so everyone could come to the correct conclusions. Those conclusions focused not only on the impermissibility of certain actions (both the illegal and the immoral) for upstanding members of the youth wing of the party but also on the vital responsibility of Komsomol organizations to discuss their members' affairs and intervene where necessary.[91]

As the trials continued to spread outward as a form of social education, Dr. Boris Sigal even created two trials for the Pioneers (the Soviet equivalent of Boy Scouts): *The Trial of a Pioneer-Smoker* and *The Trial of a Slovenly Pioneer*.[92] They were published together in the series *The Library of the People's Theater*, a series that suggested continuity with the prerevolutionary movement in people's theater.[93] Both trials follow the format of a comrades' court in which all the participants (the judge, prosecution, defense, and witnesses) are members of the same organization, in this case, the Pioneers.

The cases are based on the premise that the behavior of one Pioneer can bring shame on the whole collective (in the case of the Pioneer-smoker) or bring illness and infection (in the case of the slovenly Pioneer). The secretary of the court invokes shaming at the very outset of the trial of the Pioneer-smoker: "Now we will hear the case of Pioneer Vladimir Golovanov accused of smoking. Since his action shames us all [*porochit nas vsekh*], you must yourselves participate in trying this case and passing sentence."[94]

In both cases the boys who are on trial, aged thirteen and twelve, are accused of not breaking with old, decadent habits when they joined the Pioneers. In the first trial (of the boy who smokes) a dichotomy is established between the good Pioneers who know the rules and the bad Pioneers who, although they know the rules, fail to follow them. The good Pioneers express surprise at seeing their fellow Pioneers breaking the rules; they run to tell their supervisors and den mothers of the infraction. The bad Pioneers are sullen and refuse to believe the lectures of doctors and experts on the harmfulness of cigarette smoking. One of the good Pioneers has attempted to shame one of the defendants into changing: "I shamed him [*ia ego pristy-dil*]," he notes, though he admits he was unsuccessful. A goody-two-shoes girl named Pavlova harps on the fact that the lead defendant could never be considered someone conscious (*soznatel'nyi*) since he smokes: "It's shameful for a Pioneer to do that."[95] When the prosecutor asks the head of the troop whether all the Pioneers follow the rules about smoking, the latter answers that they all do: "They themselves watch out for that [*Oni sami slediat za etim*]."[96]

A second, rather rigid dichotomy is invoked between children's behavior that imitates adults to good effect (orderliness, obedience, holding comrades' courts) and behavior that imitates them to bad effect (smoking in order to "look grown-up"). The trial also reveals the difference between good faith (in science and in Lenin's teachings) and bad faith (in the example of one's parents and other adults who smoke). Though it seems common sense to these children that "everyone smokes" so it must be okay, the court strives in every way possible to "beat" into them (that verb is even used by the leaders of the Pioneers) that such imitation is harmful and dangerous. It is because his father does not believe in science that he is ill, the judge tells one of the boys. "But you, as a Pioneer, must believe in science and not become lost in ignorance."

In lecturing the boys on correct behavior, the court establishes an important distance between "you" and "us." You, the defendants, are not to answer out of turn, not to give "superfluous opinions." Nor is the court prepared to accept the defendant's point of view: "We [the court] will determine that [i.e., whether you are right]"; "The court will determine your guilt." The court also has particular powers to elicit confession and truth telling because of the Pioneers' promise to tell only the truth. The wrongdoing of the Pioneer who smokes is compounded by his concealing several incidents from the court. In the end the court declares:

> Remember, you will remain in our ranks only if you prove that you understand the word of a Pioneer. Not to smoke, not to drink alcohol, to maintain cleanliness, to be true to the teachings of comrade Lenin, and to safeguard our health, that is our duty. Whoever does not do that is not with us. If you smoke even one time, you will be removed from the ranks of Pioneers.

The judge gives the boys a conditional sentence, saying that they would be expelled were it not for their promise to reform and not to smoke any more. A second boy who is included as a defendant during the proceedings shows that the trial has successfully converted him from a nonbeliever to a believer. "That is all wives' tales," he had told other Pioneers. In the end, however, he repents and comments that now he believes what the doctors have told them.

Even in this case there is no unconditional acceptance in the trial, however. At any moment, any member of the Pioneers can testify against any other member for any infraction. The power of the courts establishes that all membership is conditional and one's worthiness to belong must be continuously proven by active participation in the group and in society (including reporting others' misdemeanors).[97]

In these trials one can see a sharp shift away from the medical trials' earlier rejection of shame (on the grounds that it would hinder patients seeking treatment) toward the use of both social shame (from peers) and institutional correction through shaming. In Andreev's *Trial of a Komsomolets or Komsomolka,* one of the other Komsomol members comments, "He needs to be knocked down in size. . . . He's gotten completely out of hand. We used to shame him in a comradely way [*my bylo stydili ego po tovarishcheski*], but he didn't accept it."[98]

The offending Komsomolets' father also gives evidence against his son on the grounds that he has gotten out of hand and that he is bringing shame on his father (*otsa pozorit*). The father had himself joined the party during the Lenin Levy (in January 1924) and refers to himself as a "Leninets." His son, however, is "almost a sabotage agent" (*chut' ne sabotazhnikom*). Now the father thinks the court should go ahead and judge his son. "At least let our proletarian court show him the way while it's not too late."[99]

Whereas in the early years of the revolution, especially in the fight against prostitution, the Bolshevik regime had stressed that the individual prostitute or other defendant should never be personally condemned since her actions were the result of larger social conditions beyond her control, the prosecutor in *The Trial of the Hooligan* rejects such an approach. It is not enough, he comments, to try to understand and eliminate the causes of hooliganism (unemployment, homelessness, the low cultural level of the population). That would be "to take a passive, contemplative approach," which would be "criminal." Rather, the authorities and all members in the collective should "demonstrate energetic activity towards those persons who, having the full possibility under the conditions of our lives, our *soviet* lives, to go hand in hand with all their comrades . . . instead prefer to spit in the face of our public life, to hinder peaceful labor and peaceful rest and infect our healthy atmosphere with their breathing."[100] The study of conditions is thus not sufficient; the whole society must begin to work directly on real individuals hindering the changeover to a new order. The timely intervention (*vmeshatel'stvo*) of the Komsomol and trade union organizations, of "the working-class public [*rabochaia obshchestvennost'*]" as a whole, is the most important possible solution to these social ills.[101]

While the clubs were thus striving to increase their membership and establish themselves as viable entities, the party was placing increasing pressure on them to control and discipline their members. The Komsomol was under similar pressure. The cultural directors of these organizations responded by trying to maximize collective pressure through the medium of the agitation trials, forcing protagonists to admit their wrongdoing and the shamefulness of what they had done.

SHAMING BOYS WHO SMOKE CIGARETTES

One day in 1925 a lecturer named Alotin-Elota from the Medical-Sanitation Administration of the Donetsk Railroad arrived in an orphanage for adolescent boys in a town near Kharkov. He noticed that one of the boys had a pack of cigarettes sticking out of his pocket. He struck up a deliberately casual conversation with him. When a small group of boys had gathered around to see what was going on, he turned to the boy with the cigarettes and asked him casually, "So what's that you've got in your pocket?" The boy fell silent. "Cigarettes, cigarettes," the other boys chimed in. "Well, if those are cigarettes," the lecturer continued, "we should discuss the matter. I propose we put him on trial. Do you agree?" he asked the others. "Agreed," they chorused. "Let's hold a trial."[1]

This trial marks the beginning of a new trend in sanitation trials: the staging of mock trials of real individuals known to the audience, or as Alotin-Elota put it, of "a living, real story."[2] These new trials were called "impromptu" trials (*ekspromptnye sudy*) because of the way organizers appeared to organize them spontaneously in response to a given situation. As Alotin-Elota explained, impromptu trials "are more alive, since they include real persons and issues everyone knows. Living people, living facts, living criticism. All that is concrete; there is nothing abstract. After all, it is hard to force a person from the factory workbench or the plow to think abstractly."[3]

This practice of trying individuals known to the local population seems first to have been used on a regular basis by medical students at the Kiev House of Sanitation Education in 1924.[4] As part of their training, they were sent out into the surrounding area to try to "uncover" (*vyiavit'*) defects in sanitation and daily life among the local population. If workers spit on the floor, smoked in the workshop, or didn't wash their hands during the break-fast break, the students were to take notes and then plan local sanitation trials based on the behaviors they had witnessed. This way they could easily "show the population its own negative qualities and habits."[5]

A junior sanitation education lecturer in the army, Dr. M. Belkin, claimed to have been one of the first to try this new method. As his colleagues wrote in nominating him for a prize in sanitation education, "when he organizes a trial, it is not a clichéd one of some nonexistent 'citizen Kiselev,' but rather one of a real person sitting right here on the defendant's bench."[6] One example was a trial "of the dirty soldier from the housekeeping brigade, comrade Shultz." A local military correspondent described Belkin's method, saying even his lectures "were more interesting than any play." He would take local examples and speak in language easily accessible to his audience. Not surprisingly, interest in such a trial was described as "enormous."[7]

In October 1924 the Military Medical Academy in Leningrad also began teaching what they called "real show trials in sanitation education" (real'nye pokazatel'nye sudy v sanprosvete).[8] Explicitly making reference to contemporary psychology and pedagogy, one teacher extolled the American Dalton education method as a way of bringing together "students' active learning" (aktivnost' obuchaiushchikhsia) and their "research orientation" (issledovatel'skoe napravlenie). The first-year students put on some five sanitation trials in the surrounding Leningrad garrisons as part of their course work that fall.[9]

All the organizer of such an impromptu trial needed was an excuse. When someone in the audience had demonstrated "rude sanitation ignorance," Alotin-Elota noted, the lecturer could fix the audience's attention on that fact, making it the subject of a sanitation trial. Any kind of unsanitary behavior would do—spitting on the floor, smoking other people's cigarette butts, drinking from a common cup. Then the organizer who had witnessed the behavior could turn to the audience with a proposal that they try the offender. All this could look entirely spontaneous.[10]

Alotin-Elota gave multiple examples of this practice. On a playground in a railroad station he noticed that many of the children playing had dirty feet. With the assistance of the local physical education instructor, he selected two children from the group, one with the dirtiest feet and one with the cleanest, and had them stand up on a bench. What was the main difference between these two boys? he asked his audience. The children, not surprisingly, had no idea how to answer; they giggled and shifted uneasily. Finally, when the tension had become almost unbearable, Alotin-Elota asked who had dirty feet and who had clean ones. From there it was easy to get the children to say that having dirty feet was bad and to agree that Pavlusha, who had the dirty feet, should be put on trial. "A trial, a trial," the children chanted.[11] Undoubtedly for the children a trial must have seemed far more entertaining than an ordinary gym class or hanging around in the yard.

Alotin-Elota worked trials into his public lectures as well. If an audience was discussing folk medicine and someone commented that it might help, he countered with examples where a woman faith healer (*znakharka*) had left someone paralyzed after treating his boils by putting clay on them. Soon he was able to lead the audience into organizing a trial, not of the healer, but rather "of those comrades who believe in faith healing." Such a trial, he noted, was not a legal matter. Rather, its main goal must be to draw on the *samodeiatel'nost'* of the audience—that is, to make the audience take an active part in organizing their own dramatic production. If the lecturer's questions were properly posed, the audience would find the right answers. By initially addressing the younger members of the audience, Alotin-Elota found he could often draw them out where the older ones showed more resistance.[12]

The dialogue Alotin-Elota used was clearly designed to make his victims as uncomfortable as possible. This is especially clear in the dialogue he wrote for one of his impromptu trials:

"Did you act well, accused?"
"Badly."
"Why badly?"
"I spit on the floor."
"Why shouldn't one spit on the floor?"
"Bacteria, infection."
"How big are the bacteria?"
"Small."
"Like a button in size?"
"(Laughter). Invisible to the naked eye."
"How can you see bacteria?"
"Through a magnifying glass."
"Why didn't you spit in the spittoon?"
"I didn't see it."
"But did you look for the spittoon?"
He falters [*Zamialsia*] . . . doesn't answer. . . .[13]

Again and again Alotin-Elota drew on his ability to confuse and dominate his audience. Both the boy with a pack of cigarettes in his pocket and the children trying to figure out the difference between the two boys lined up on the bench faltered and grew silent out of confusion. Using his authority as a lecturer and sanitation inspector, he could enforce a dramatic performance that put his interlocutors on the spot.[14]

THE APPEAL OF IMPROMPTU TRIALS

Contemporaries explained why this form of "impromptu" trial arose. As audiences grew used to the form of the mock agitation trial, they increasingly lost interest. For many of them the drama lay in the form—that is, the court-room proceedings—rather than the content. Once they knew the trial wasn't "real," it ceased to interest them. If a trial failed and the audience realized that it was all a fictional performance, they were reluctant to come to the next one. They would investigate carefully whether the upcoming trial was "real" or "fake."[15]

With time, audiences were thus beginning to reach a certain tolerance or threshold for the mock trials (as one would with a drug), and organizers had to increase the emotionality and the drama so that the trials would still have an effect. Court scenes alone were no longer sufficiently tension-filled. Now audiences needed to be made to imagine that one of their own, a real person whom they knew, was the subject of the investigation and trial. Soon "methodological bureaus" in the field of sanitation education in Kiev and elsewhere were studying impromptu trials of both adults and children and recommending them for sanitation theaters across the nation.[16] By 1930 Boris Sigal, a leading author of agitation trial texts, was arguing that the best method of sanitation agitation was to stage a "show trial" (*pokazatel'nyi sud*) of a "'real' drunkard, 'one's own'" (*nad 'nastoiashchim', 'svoim' p'ian-itsei*), that is, someone from the workers' own factory or housing unit.[17] Only if that was not possible should one stage a purely fictional trial of an imagined character.

The middle 1920s saw a whole raft of criticisms of and debates about the traditional form of the sanitation trial. The *sansudy* were criticized as too expensive, too hard to put on, lacking in sufficient educational result for the effort they required.[18] Besides, the drama circles in the clubs did not always want to put on sanitation plays. And they often did not have sufficiently ex-perienced directors, so the result was shoddy, overacted, excessively theatri-cal, and so on. Frequently the drama circles had to drop their theater work to take up shock work in the factory or go to meetings, thus making it im-possible to give the trials their undivided attention.[19]

Some sanitation doctors were even questioning the whole notion that ed-ucation and theatricality could be combined. If the players focused primar-ily on the plot and the drama, they often neglected the lessons they were supposed to convey. Sigal, for example, expressed disappointment in a play by L. A. and L. M. Vasilevskii called *The Trial of a Midwife* because of its extraneous subplot of an affair between one of the witnesses and the hus-band of the woman who died from an abortion. This "saccharine melo-drama" left an "aftertaste" that Sigal found distasteful. Besides, he argued, such a twist in the plot "never happens in real life."[20]

The converse was equally true, however. If the sanitation plays concen-trated on conveying medical information to the exclusion of drama, the au-dience would "grow cold" and lose its ardor for the play. The judges' questions to the expert medical witnesses were often too obvious. When the judges came out with such bland directives as "Tell us about the course of syphilis, gonorrhea, etc.," audiences grew bored. Organizers feared that then they would recognize "what many didn't know, namely the 'deceit' [*obman*], [the fact that] the trial is not real."[21]

Many argued that sanitation trials should in any event be based on materials that were not too "musty and outdated" (*zatkhlyi i otzhivshii*). Topics should be of contemporary significance. One solution proposed by a railway sanitation doctor, P. M. Vedernikov, was to take investigatory materials from the state courts as the basis for sanitation trials. Here in the state materials and newspaper articles about the cases, one would find the crime, the charges, the investigative materials, and the final sentence imposed by the courts. Using this material in a collective fashion, the authors could avoid holding numerous rehearsals and requiring elaborate memorization of texts. The participants would be "intrigued" by the creative work involved in staging such real trial materials.[22]

The impromptu trial violated a number of the conventions of the initial agitation trials. Local materials, both people and situations, were still at the heart of the trials. Yet now instead of being general characteristics of the people of the factory or village, the subjects of the trials were known individuals and misdemeanors. Where early trial organizers had laid great emphasis on the elimination of "false shame" (which hindered patients from going for treatment), the later agitation trials began to shame the defendants, both explicitly through name-calling and implicitly through portrayal of their cowardice and confusion in the dock.[23] Where earlier trials had emphasized dialogue and debate, the later ones portrayed the defendants as completely vulnerable and in a position with no exit. Misbehaviors could be treated as crimes. Alotin-Elota, for example, elided the two when he wrote: "The lecturer fixes the attention of his audience on one or another mistake [*pogreshnost'*] and proposes to immediately organize a trial of the person who committed the crime [*prestuplenie*]."[24]

This shaming and criminalizing were accompanied by a corresponding erasure of medical confidentiality and the boundaries between the public and the private. For example, though syphilis and alcoholism as illnesses had long been a subject of sanitation trials, real patients had never before been subjected to the public scrutiny of trials. Now individuals' ideas and beliefs, not just their actions, were on trial (as in the case of Alotin-Elota's impromptu trial of people who believed in faith healing).

DOCTORS' HOPES

Doctors hoped desperately that mock trials would persuade patients to come in "voluntarily" for treatment. Vedernikov, himself a sanitation doctor on the Riazan-Urals Railway, claimed that mock trials of syphilitics had a direct influence on real patients ill with venereal disease. After seeing such performances, sick patients were now willing, he said, to have their names included on lists kept by the medical authorities. They were, in his words, "no longer afraid of the publicizing of their 'shame' [*oglaska svoego 'pozora'*]." In hopes of ridding themselves of their ailment, he claimed, "they have voluntarily given themselves into the hands of medical personnel for special reporting and observation [*pod osobyi uchet i nadzor*]."[25]

L. S. Ioff, a sanitation expert in 1930, tried holding an agitation trial of someone he claimed was a real patient who happened not to be present at the trial. Since he himself worked in a venereal disease treatment center, Ioff suggested that the subject of the trial be someone with venereal disease who was not following the proper course of treatment. The judge was to announce that because of the importance of the case, he wanted the assistance of the audience. Since the accused was ill and the treatment center did not want to cause him unnecessary psychic trauma, it would not bring him forward publicly. Nonetheless, the court insisted to those present that they controlled the fate of this allegedly real patient. Ioff claimed that the resulting trial seemed real instead of theatrical.[26]

The venereological clinics were, of course, in a tough position. They had to rely on public opinion to get people to come in for treatment and then to stick with that treatment. The absentee defendant needed to be put on trial, Ioff insisted, not because he had contracted venereal disease but rather because of his "unworthy behavior" (*nedostoinoe povedenie*) in spreading it and because of his "unconscious attitude toward treatment."[27]

The prosecutor in this case reveals what he insists are "obvious traces of wrecking" (even though he is merely discussing venereal disease). Now that wrecking in industry is being identified and stopped, "wrecking in daily life" (*vreditel'stvo v bytu*) also has to be ended. "That's why it would seem that 'little troubles' in our daily lives ultimately put a brake on the giant growth in socialist construction and why such 'little sores' [*gnoinichki*] must be lanced [*vskryvat'sia*] by the bold surgical hand of our public opinion."[28] The prosecutor is not above implicitly shaming the absentee defendant. While "the rest of us" were dying at the front during the Civil War, he points out, the defendant was off drinking and having sexual relations with prostitutes. Then when the venereal disease clinic offered him assistance, he responded by giving a false address and denying that he was married.

The defense makes the classic arguments of the agitation trial genre: that he should no more be punished than should the alcoholic; that shaming and pointing fingers would never help him obtain treatment; that it is his ignorance and backwardness that have kept him from coming in for treatment; and above all, that the cultural organizations have failed to reach him. "Aren't those organizations which are supposed to carry culture to the masses the guilty ones? Did you, comrade judges, try to talk to him in the factory instead of judging him?"[29]

In the end the judges acquit him on the grounds of his *nekul'turnost'*,—

his lack of culture. But they do issue a reprimand, and more important, they insist that his case be transmitted to the public organization of his factory. Both the factory's public organization and the venereal disease clinic are thus required to keep a close eye on him. In other words, the defendant is not to be "punished" in the classic sense of the word. Yet he is to be subjected to increased surveillance by the factory and by the clinic, all for his own good.

Another fictional character, named Pavlov, is also forced into public repentance. He has resisted going to the baths ("What are we, some kind of children? What do you think, that we don't go to the baths?"). But then he infects another worker in his barracks (whose name, Chumak, means "plague") with typhus. Both Pavlov and the overseer of the dormitory are brought to trial. The latter is found guilty of not checking all the new workers to make sure they are free from illness. Pavlov is required to pay a fine, take a sanitation health course, and, above all, publish the whole trial proceedings in the wall newspaper of the barracks and in the neighborhood newspaper.[30] Though this case resembles the older style of agitation trial, since the defendant is fictional, the public shaming and use of the wall newspaper would have put everyone on notice about the real consequences of not tending to public hygiene.

Vaccinations were another medical area that traditionally had been the subject of immense educational work among the population for obvious reasons: vaccinations were a scary proposition, and they worked best as a public health measure if everyone agreed to them.

In 1933, a doctor on a collective farm (*kolkhoz*) in the Zelenogorsk region near Moscow, I. Kuzmin, decided to hold a "public trial" (*obshchestvennyi sud*) of individual kolkhoz members who refused to be vaccinated. He requested the assistance of the Institute of Sanitation Culture of the Moscow Department for the Protection of Health (Institut Sanitarnoi Kul'tury MOOZ), a group that often helped with theater performances.[31] Having secured the permission of the village council and the kolkhoz chairman, Kuzmin asked the institute to give him posters and also a representative who could play the role of public prosecutor. The trial of two (real) kolkhoz members who refused to be vaccinated was held on July 8 in the local club. The collective farm residents expressed astonishment that this was happening. They had thought that vaccinations were a "private matter" (*delo chastnoe*).

In the public trial no defense was provided for the two defendants. The prosecution insisted that there could be no defense since, as urban factory workers who maintained their residence in the collective farm, they should have been leading the campaign for vaccinations. Had they exhibited the consciousness expected of workers, the whole collective farm would have followed their lead. In the end the judge sentenced them to a public reprimand (*obshchestvennoe poritsanie*) and required them to be vaccinated. The only way they could "correct their mistake," the prosecution argued, was for them to become actively engaged in health work in the collective farm.

Only then could they exculpate their own guilt and draw others into the field of health protection.

Soviet authorities often expanded their influence with local populations by using just such a trick. If a person was caught committing a misdemeanor or an offense, one of his or her best chances of self-defense was to become an activist who furthered the goals of the state. Organizers of such trials thus co-opted not only the fictional characters but also real individuals who were forced to join the local *aktiv,* those working in a particular area of public education. The trial sentence could also maintain the illusion that the entire collective "unanimously" opposed the behavior of any dissenting individuals.[32]

IMPROMPTU TRIALS IN THE CLUBS AND TRADE UNIONS

In 1926 organizers proposed that impromptu mock trials could regularly be used to draw out people's innermost views. Local organizers could, for example, create what they called a "quality report" (*kachestvennyi uchet*) on a club excursion just before the group returned to the city. If not enough people came on the excursion because the administration did not promote the trip well in advance, then that could be discussed. If the excursion was planned for rest and recreation, but the club administration had forgotten to take enough food, then that could be one of the charges. Or there could be discussion of the fact that no one had brought life preservers and someone had almost drowned in the river. The point of this kind of trial was that it could be organized on the spot, up to and including the framing of the indictment, which would depend on people's real experiences of the trip. If people didn't think the trial had been planned in advance, then they would be much more likely to "let their tongues wag." If possible, the audience should have the impression that the first speaker, say, Ivanov, "couldn't hold back and had to speak out." Then others, too, would be more tempted to say what was really on their minds. One or two club members could think about the trial in advance. But under no circumstances should the club administration itself seem to be involved.[33]

Such an impromptu trial, it was argued, "gave a broad field for [club members] to show their initiative." And as in any theatrical performance, it involved a certain amount of deception. Here, though, the deception was not the normal illusion of an audience watching other people playacting. Rather, the illusion was the reverse: the audience members were asked to playact and pretend that their actions could have an effect on the club administration. From the administration's perspective this had the potential benefit of persuading a population of workers to speak who were known for not wanting "to stick their necks out." (Russian proverbs are full of expressions such as the nail which sticks up being hammered down and the person's head which sticks up being chopped off.)

The problem of combining improvisation and staging was by now becoming endemic among trial organizers. While some of them were encouraging genuine acting and improvisation, others relied on pseudo-improvisation and false spontaneity. Two examples may help to clarify this difference between genuine and simulated improvisation. One drama expert, Semyon Dolinskii, who was involved in a number of publications for clubs, suggested that the drama circles take newspaper articles about real court trials and use them as a basis for improvisation and discussion. One case he picked concerned a man who asked a woman to move in with him but then told her to leave because he really couldn't, he realized, support a third wife. What should a man separated from his first wife or wives do? What should a woman do when the man she's been living with asks her to move out? Is she justified in selling some of his belongings (without his knowledge) to pay for a cab to move back to her old apartment? Dolinskii, the author, praised this kind of improvisational work for its "dialogic quality" (*dialogichnost'*) since the original newspaper article had presented realistic verbal exchanges between the man and this new "wife" that could be used almost verbatim in a play. The trial of this "third wife," the dramatist claimed, would allow the audience to come to its own conclusions concerning the marriage code.[34] The trial, as he described it, had no "correct" answer. A sentence was not even suggested.[35]

The false appearance of spontaneity can be seen in a second, contrasting example. The year was 1927 and everywhere trade union organizations throughout the USSR were holding elections for club administrations. In the Donbas region the cultural department of the Stalingrad mining committee decided to hold "trials" of four real club administrators two to four days before the elections in order to evaluate their performance.[36] The organizers referred to these performances as "public, improvised trials"; such trials, they said, had never been held before. Witnesses were chosen from among the club members who genuinely felt (or so it was claimed) that the work of the administrations was weak. Other witnesses were brought forward to explain the "weak organization work" by pointing to "objective circumstances." Everyone was supposed to speak spontaneously, without memorizing their roles. Only the judge, prosecutor, and defender were to have "seriously studied" the actual work of the administration, on the basis of which they drew up a bill of indictment.

Over the course of the trial several "surprises" were set up for the audience. The court, for example, found in several cases that the inspection commission that should have been responsible for overseeing the work of the club administration had been negligent in its work and ordered that it should be brought to trial as well. Upon hearing of their indictment, the members of the inspection commission in one club ran out of the room. In another only the chair of the commission turned out to be in the hall. As ordered, he took his place on the defendants' bench, his face red with embarrassment at this turn of events.

But the real surprise for the audience may have been the discovery that the main goal was to turn the trial of the club administration into "a trial of the whole membership." The organizers were convinced they had achieved this. The court sentences confirmed the weak work of the administration and the inspection commission (no witnesses were brought forth who thought the administration had done a good job); this was then confirmed by a vote from all those present. The need for new elections was thus justified, the old administration was discredited, and a few workers had even stood up "spontaneously" to say "we workers haven't done enough." From this the organizers concluded that such "improvised" trials were better than scripted ones.[37]

The lines between trials of fictional characters and real individuals now began to blur in trade union trials as well. One day in 1927 a sign appeared in a leather factory in Moscow:

On October 11
A Disciplinary Trial of the Truant Terekhin
in the Club

When the trial opened, it was announced that Dmitri Timofeev Terekhin was being brought to trial under article 28, part 2 of the Criminal Code for absenteeism.[38] But the audience, the journal *Rabochii klub* claimed, immediately recognized Terekhin; he was being played by the head of their club, Pozdniakov. Moreover, they knew that the "real truant," Dmitri Timofeev Mikriukov, aged twenty-eight, was sitting in the audience with his head down, embarrassed before his fellow workers in the audience.

This "real truant" even had the same first name and patronymic as the fictional defendant. In the course of the performance the technical foreman testified to Terekhin's missed work days and his defective workmanship when he came to work hung over. The doctor and head of the insurance division testified to his false sick days and self-inflicted wounds to avoid working. The prosecution reminded the court that in these days, when the country was bending all its efforts to construction and defense of the nation, there was no place for parasites and they should be eradicated. The defense in its turn made a familiar plea that "we are all guilty in the crimes of the accused," and hence Terekhin needed to be not excluded but brought more firmly "into the workers' family, under its proletarian direction." Given that the crime was fictional and the performance a play, the court could not sentence the real truant, Dmitri Mikriukov. Instead it sentenced the semifictional defendant, Terekhin, to a conditional sentence of three months' imprisonment and called on all the workers to eliminate absenteeism, malingering, and slackness. In some ways, then, this was an ordinary agitation trial. Yet it differed in that "everyone knew" that Dmitri Timofeev Terekhin was "really" Dmitri Timofeev Mikriukov, their co-worker, friend, and neighbor.[39]

"Send the truants, whiners, and doubters to the black board of shame" [1925–35]. Poster collection, RU/SU 1599, Hoover Institution Archives, Stanford, California.

Kukryniksy, "Send the Christmas truant to the black board of shame" (Moscow, 1931). Below the drunken worker is a leaf from a calendar that says December 25/January 7 with space to list the names of truants. Poster collection, RU/SU 1928, Hoover Institution Archives, Stanford, California.

Agitation trials were now recognized as an effective way of fighting truancy. Iakhnin, the author of one article, came to three conclusions: (1) that agitation trials gave better results in fighting truancy than did other forms of action; (2) that the most effective way of putting on such an agitation trial was to use a real judge or court specialist; and (3) that under no circumstances should trial organizers focus on an abstract topic; rather, they should organize the trial around the particular facts of a given workplace, which all the workers in the audience would know.[40]

To illustrate his point, Iakhnin described a dramatized trial at a factory in Zlatoust in the Ural Mountains.[41] Ten days before the trial, announcements were placed around the shop. The workers were told that the subject of the trial would be quite simple: the head of the rolling mill was to be put on trial for mismanagement in the days after Pentecost, when absenteeism was at its highest. He would be accused of lowering the quality of the work, allowing breakages in the machines, and raising costs, all on the basis of evidence gathered by the foreman and the party secretary of the mill. In preparation for the trial, workers from the shop were asked to take on different roles, with collective discussion of the approach each would take but without a fixed script of what each would say. By chance, Iakhnin noted, the organizers of the trial were able to invite a local judge to preside, a happenstance that they later praised as giving the trial more weight and ensuring more correct proceedings.

What the audience did not expect, however, was that the trial was specifically designed to move gradually from the question of the shop head's guilt to that of the guilt of the truant workers themselves. Because the judge was experienced, Iakhnin noted, he was able "imperceptibly" to move the attention of the public in that direction. Moreover, when a worker (whose role had been planned in advance) gave evidence that he himself had been a truant, the court moved to arrest him. During sentencing, the head of the rolling mill was acquitted, and the administration was required to carry out more production propaganda. The trial ended by recommending that the truant worker be brought to trial. The tables were thus turned. Instead of the management's being found guilty for the poor work and wastage in the period after the holiday, the truly guilty party, the worker, was uncovered and brought to trial.

For the organizers the results of the trial were "unquestionably positive." During the trial workers "hotly discussed" the events of the day. "Crowds" came to read the announcement of the outcome of the trial after it was over. And absenteeism "noticeably declined." Just as Dmitri Timofeev Mitriukhin allegedly sat "burning with shame" in the audience during the performance of the trial of the truant, so workers in the rolling mill shop must have realized that they had little chance of escape. If the real courts did not discipline them, the agitation courts would find ways to bring them to trial.

"Religion is the enemy of industrialization" (Moscow: Aktsionernoe Izdatel'skoe Obshchestvo "Bezbozhnik," [1930–40]). The left image features religious figures coming out of smokestacks that have holes in them, with a drunken worker at the base. The right image features working smokestacks and a well-dressed worker reading *Bezbozhnik* ("The Godless"), an atheist newspaper, while a bad worker (like the devils in medieval icons) is being thrown out of the factory. Poster collection, RU/SU 1916, Hoover Institution Archives, Stanford California.

MALICIOUS NONATTENDANCE

Official Soviet rhetoric in the mid-1920s thus made it more and more difficult for an individual simply to exist and not serve as an active member of a
collective. Gradually the official Soviet public sphere came to dominate to
the exclusion of any alternative public realm where individuals could meet
and talk.[42] Health issues were no longer considered private matters in these
trials. Membership in organizations was not voluntary so much as a duty.
Reporting on others was not a choice but an obligation. Many societies were
not open to all to join but only to the elect. Even if one joined voluntarily,
one could be excluded on the basis of any comrade's testimony at any time.
In practice this meant that membership itself became a much contested and
highly vulnerable sphere of "activity." If one was not allowed to join (because of past class background or present sins), one was vulnerable to dis-
crimination on the grounds of being unreliable. Yet if one was eligible to join,
particularly an organization such as the Komsomol, then one could be held
to a higher, exemplary standard of behavior and charged with failure to meet
that higher standard. In other words, all membership became conditional. It
was not the individual who decided whether to join, but the collective that
decided whether the individual would be allowed to join and allowed to stay.
    Ironically, linguistic vagueness and passive construction of verbs abound
in many of the trial scripts in this period, even as those scripts decry "pas-
siveness" and "lack of consciousness" in members of the working class. The
Komsomolets who violated Komsomol discipline, for example, has twice
"been observed" (*zamechen*) swearing, a fact of which the collective is then
"informed" (*soobshcheno*). When other measures fail to persuade the Komsomolets to stop swearing, the Collective (written with a capital letter) resolves that he is "to be excluded" and "to be handed over" to a public trial
of workers and Komsomoltsy in his factory.[43]
    The language of the accusations is not only passive, however. It also ag-
gressively finds fault with the defendants, exaggerating their misdemeanors
to demonstrate the latter's political significance. The Komsomolets, to continue this example, is accused not only of "a careless attitude toward his
obligations as a member of the Komsomol" but also of "systematic and
malicious nonattendance of meetings of the Collective" and, in his use of bad
language, of "introducing an element of sabotage and disorganization, of
compromising the Komsomol." In other words, he not only failed to attend
meetings (a sin of omission) and used bad language on the street (a sin of
commission) but also did this in a "malicious and systematic" way, and his
actions were to be seen, and judged, in the light of sabotage, disorganization,
and compromising a leading political organization.[44]
    Of course, for the reader of political texts from the 1920s in the Soviet
Union, such language is familiar. Yet if we think back for a moment to earlier trials, we will see that even in the most "political" of trials, against, say,

Baron Wrangel, though the defendant might be hounded with names such as "bloodsucker," nonetheless, everyone in the audience knew where the battle lines were drawn and what Wrangel had done wrong. During the trials of the Civil War, the deserter, the illiterate sentry, and the peasant who stained his library books with lard all had committed crimes and misdemeanors that were immediately recognizable and, in point of fact, verifiable. "Malicious nonattendance" of meetings was something quite different.

Other examples of this new language describing unverifiable transgressions include the following: "complete indifference to the public life of the workers"; "a passive attitude toward their obligations as union members"; a person described as "passive in relation to the life and work of the union."[45] The priest who agitates against the Society of Friends of the Airforce is said to have contributed to the "sabotage of work intended to strengthen Soviet power."[46]

TRIALS OF AUTHORS

As the lines between public and private became increasingly blurred, literature returned as a principal subject of trials. In keeping with the times, however, these were not just trials of characters and books. Now the defendants were living authors known to the reading public.

As in the prerevolutionary period, librarians in the Soviet era encouraged the performance of literary trials as part of "literary evenings" in the clubs. In so-called evenings of workers' criticism an author and a critic would be present and the workers would present their thoughts about the author or work being discussed. Alternatively, when a living author was not present, workers would celebrate one or another jubilee, perhaps Gorky's sixtieth birthday, the fiftieth anniversary of Nekrasov's death, or Tolstoy's hundredth birthday. Literary trials at such evenings were described as "extraordinarily attractive and influential in form," though it was noted that they were "insufficiently used."[47]

At least in theory the libraries and clubs could put on "literary trials of authors or heroes of particular works, of whole works, of a poor reader, of a wrecker of books, of 'friends of the library,' of the library itself." In fact, however, commentators recognized that there were a number of factors inhibiting their production: the complexity of the form, the shortage of personnel to put them on, and the failure of the club administrations to pay sufficient attention in general to the work of the libraries.[48]

Yet literary evenings had enormous virtues. They could "eliminate the gap between the reader and the writer, bring together the producer and the consumer of the book, give much to the reader and the author, and also to 'third persons,' including the critic, the publisher, the librarian, and the workers' club as a whole."[49] In other words, they seemed to offer something for everyone. Above all (though the evidence on this is slim), educators may well have wanted to foster this form as a way of carrying on the intelligentsia tradition of critical reading and discussion.

In its benign form the literary trial was intended to help worker correspondents learn to develop and defend their literary views in public. (Worker correspondents were factory workers who had agreed to write articles for the newspapers but who as yet were usually unskilled in any kind of verbal or written discourse.)[50] In November 1924 the worker correspondents and editors of the journal *Rabochii Zritel'* put on a trial of a play called *Iorgen's Holiday* (*Prazdnik Iorgena*). The correspondents served as witnesses for the prosecution and defense. The purpose of the trial was ostensibly to "shed light on aspects of the theatrical performance that viewers might not otherwise notice." Yet for the worker correspondents who participated as witnesses this was also "their first public exam in criticism." For many this was the first time they had spoken publicly. Although the result was criticized as "rather weak," the author of this particular article was optimistic that future trials would be held with "comrades who are better prepared." In this way the "trial" of a play contained within it a test (was this not also a "trial"?) of worker correspondents who in their semiliterate way were trying to break into the world of writing and publishing for the benefit of the regime.[51]

As long as the authors and actors were allowed to exert some influence over the process of the trial, they could turn it to their advantage. A young writer named V. Ardov did this, for example, in an imagined sketch of a comic trial of Vsevolod Meyerhold's production of A. N. Ostrovsky's play *The Forest* (*Les*). Subtitled "Fantasy" (*Fantaziia*), Ardov's article imagined a trial with Meyerhold at the center defending himself with witty replies to the petty complaints of two drama critics who brought spurious charges. In conclusion Ardov decided that the court sentence did not matter at all. Ardov was clearly enjoying penning a witty debate between a director and his detractors.[52]

Still, the matter was turning serious for established writers. In 1924 the Civil War hero S. M. Budennyi, who had been one of the writer Isaac Babel's models in *Red Cavalry*, attacked him in print, after which a public "debate" was held at the House of Printing in Moscow. Babel was supposed to be the "defendant," while Budennyi was to appear as "prosecutor."[53] Dmitrii Furmanov, the writer, was asked to preside and, as part of his preparation, twice wrote himself notes "to call out [*vyzvat'*]" Babel as in a duel.[54] He then wrote an outline of the leading criticisms of the day to sort out in his own mind all the pros and cons of Babel's writing.[55] In the end, although neither Budennyi nor Babel was present at the debate, the new trend was clear: writers were increasingly being made to answer for their writings before crowds of workers, students, and party hacks.

In May 1926 the training school for border guards (a branch of the Cheka or secret police), put on an "exemplary literary trial" of Babel. This performance, a correspondent for *Rabochii klub* claimed, was designed "as a public show trial [*kak obshchestvenno-pokazatel'nyi protsess*], not dramatized [*instsenirovannyi*] but rather shown in the exact form of an ordinary juridical trial."[56] This time Babel was present, which allegedly made the students all the more attentive. As in the trial in which worker correspondents had to undergo a kind of oral examination, five witnesses for the prosecution and five for the defense were chosen from among students who had supposedly not been prepared in advance. As in the medieval Jesuit-style scholastic debates, these higher-education students were required on the spot to defend their positive and negative views of the famous writer before their teachers and fellow students. Babel was ultimately acquitted but only conditionally. He was deemed valuable as a fellow traveler (*poputchik*) whose work was "artistic" but not "proletarian."[57]

A mere six months after the trial of Babel, the writer Mikhail Bulgakov also found his play *Days of the Turbines* being heatedly discussed in public debates (*disputy*). One such debate, listed as a "trial" at the Press Club on October 11, 1926, was particularly vicious:

The signal for battle to commence was given by Comrade Litovsky. And the trial began! A veritable bath-house lashing! . . . And still they came! Almost all of them arrived fully equipped for battle, armed to the teeth with quotations short and long. . . . Only occasionally did the odd plea for clemency for the theatre and its actors manage to break through.[58]

While numerous newspaper articles carried excerpts from the various speakers' comments, the overwhelming majority were vitriolic, finding little to defend in the author and his work.[59] As this form of the public debate was evolving, it was thus being increasingly used to pillory its subjects rather than to allow a true defense and discussion.[60]

In February 1927 Vladimir Nemirovich-Danchenko, the director and founder of the Moscow Art Theater, where *Days of the Turbins* had been staged, wrote in a letter: "What a hate campaign *The Turbins* has been subjected to. In all this there are elements of sincere conviction, and even some aspects which merit respect. There is also a good deal that is simply venomous . . . or repulsive."[61]

By 1929 Maxim Gorky had become adamant about the dangers of the campaign unleashed against his fellow writers Boris Pilnyak and Yevgenii Zamiatin:

All my life I have fought for a caring attitude towards people, and it seems to me that the struggle needs to be intensified in our time and circumstances. . . . We have developed an idiotic habit of raising people up on a pedestal only to hurl them down shortly afterwards into the dust and dirt. There is no need for me to give examples of this absurd and cruel way of treating people. Everybody knows them. I am reminded of the "kangaroo courts" against petty thieves in 1917–18, which were completely disgraceful dramas staged by philistines. It is just these philistine, suburban, lynch-mob persecutions which come very unpleasantly to mind whenever you see everybody enthusiastically and sadistically setting about a lone individual, in order first to destroy the offender before going on to move into his job.[62]

The motivations for this turn toward the so-called impromptu trials of real individuals seem thus to have been multiple. On the one hand, they were a natural outgrowth of the practice of staging trials devoted to local issues. The distance from a trial of a fictional soldier who had broken garrison regulations to a trial of a real village inhabitant who spit on the floor was not all that great. In both cases the misdemeanors were ones immediately recognizable to local audiences and already somewhat controversial or even repugnant.

On the other hand, the increasing recourse to real trial subjects was deliberately fostered by petty inspectors and instructors who sought extra drama and power for themselves. Stalin and the Communist Party, moreover, were encouraging supposedly voluntary organizations to uncover and denounce wrongdoings. In this sense agitation trials of real individuals were yet another example of a wedge that the authorities could use to divide the community against itself.

For many administrators it must therefore have seemed logical, as it did to the Printers' Club in Moscow, to hold *The Trial of a Hooligan, The Trial of a Drunk,* and *The Trial of a Prostitute* to combat the very hooliganism, alcoholism, and sexual misconduct that seemed to be undermining the clubs' effectiveness.[63]

In the end the club trials, production trials, Komsomol trials, and Pioneer trials must have appealed to leaders of these organizations because such performances increased the authority of those locally in power. Gaining more authority may have appeared to many to be an urgent task, given the dislocation of rapid urbanization and industrialization at the end of the 1920s. As more newcomers poured into the cities, the clubs found it extremely difficult to control their behavior. The trial organizers may have hoped that if rules and, above all, rituals of intimidation were inculcated at an early age, they could have at least some control over their members.

FICTION BECOMES INDISTINGUISHABLE FROM REALITY, 1928–33

The trial that brought the term "show trial" to the English language was the Shakhty trial in May–June 1928. Most sources, including the Oxford English Dictionary, have assumed that it was Eugene Lyons, who worked in Moscow for six years as correspondent for United Press, who first used the term in his *Assignment in Utopia* (1937).[1] In fact, however, *New York Times* reporter Walter Duranty first began using the terms "demonstration trial," "demonstrative trial," and "show trial" (all evidently translations of *pokazatel'nyi protsess*) in the years 1927–29.[2] Of the Shakhty trial Duranty wrote that it was a "trial drama," one that was better than any theater performance, "a marvelous [*sic*] human drama where lives are at stake."[3]

In the Shakhty trial fifty-three engineers, including several Germans, were put in the dock on charges of wrecking and sabotage in the coal-mining industry in the Donbas.[4] This was the first large-scale public trial to seek an indictment on charges of wrecking (article 58.7 of the Criminal Code).[5] Although wrecking had been on the books for a number of years, in January 1928 the USSR Supreme Court ruled that one could be convicted under this article even if one did not have "counterrevolutionary intent."[6]

At the conclusion of the Shakhty trial the prosecutor, Nikolai Krylenko, described what he called "the lessons of the case." "The human documents" of the trial should be published, he claimed, because they showed the contest between "the heroic efforts of the working masses," on the one hand, and "the malicious, destructive, counterrevolutionary work of the engineers and middle technical personnel serving our coal industry," on the other.[7]

As Lyons observed, the hyperbole of the trial rhetoric overshadowed any demonstration of concrete misdemeanors during the trial: "We waited in vain for a genuine piece of impersonal and unimpeachable testimony."[8] In part, of course, the Shakhty trial was lacking in unimpeachable testimony because *there was none*.[9] Finding hard evidence was not the main purpose of the trial. Rather, the purpose of the Shakhty trial, as in the agitation trials, was to show the *character* of the threats facing the Soviet Union and the *characters* of the men involved. In other words, the *personification* of the larger threat had to be demonstrated to the watching public, both those in the courtroom and those in the rest of the nation who were watching newsreels or reading the press.

For Lyons as an eyewitness, the most visible quality of the show trials (both Shakhty and the Industrial Party Trial of 1930) was what he called "the calculated melodrama of the proceedings." "A superb drama, bolstered by confessions and documents," the Shakhty trial in his view was imbued with "the circus spirit of the crowds," "an atmosphere of carnival," "a spirit of festival touched with hysteria—a crowd come to see a righteous hanging." It was "a spectacle of men confessing incredible crimes and embracing death with grandiloquent gestures," "an ordeal of death," and a "Roman circus." "The Shakhty trial offered a tangible object for the hatreds smoldering in the heart of Russia." Ultimately, Lyons concluded, "the melodramatic international plot . . . was largely a figment of their own [the top leaders'] stagecraft."[10]

There was now a direct kinship between the public show trials of the late 1920s and the mock agitation trials of the same decade. Both groups of trials used theatrical methods to convey the feeling of a show presented for all to witness. In the Shakhty trial the Soviet press, radio, newsreels, school announcements, and billboards promoted the trial for weeks and months beforehand. Audiences were given special entrance tickets.[11]

The melodrama was plain for all to see: villains who had undermined the Soviet order; heroes who had uncovered their treachery; a supreme Soviet state, committed to defending innocent citizens. The bill of indictment, published in *Izvestiia* in March 1928, contained a fantastic web of accusations: an organized network of sabotage and espionage that extended beyond the borders of the Donbas region to Moscow, Paris, and Berlin, and was in fact directed from abroad; plans for a catastrophic destruction of all industry in case of foreign intervention as a means of drastically lowering the defensibility of the country; a conspiracy that stretched to other branches of industry; networks of emissaries helping the engineers in the Donbas to communicate with their patrons, owners of expropriated mines who had fled abroad.[12] At the same time there was some unpredictability: Would the accused confess publicly? Would they be found guilty?

The drama was heightened by the lighting and staging. The crews in charge of these technical matters had probably had prior experience with public trials in this very hall, formerly called the "Nobles' Club," now renamed the House of Trade Unions and often called the Hall of Columns because of its impressive Corinthian colonnade.[13]

As in the agitation trials, attention to ceremony was paramount. Even the archival copy of the proceedings of the case carefully documents every time the court returns after a recess and the guard calls out "The court is in session; all rise."[14] Procedural guarantees are ostentatiously noted. The defense attorneys were allowed to state their objections to various proceedings (though admittedly not all the defendants even had lawyers). For the audience, the presence of the microphones and reporters helped, too, to make the rather flimsy charges more convincing.[15] Even if hard facts were never adduced in the trial, factlike fictions were brought forward: written documents, claims about allegedly factual meetings in foreign places, physical evidence like raincoats alleged to have been used to signal that the time was ripe to engage in sabotage.

The crimes of the fifty-three engineers in the Shakhty trial were the types of offenses that could also have been alleged in an agitation trial. They had failed to care for machines; they had ruined the machinery. The hyperbolic charges of wrong membership, evil conspiracies, vast networks, intent to sabotage the Soviet state and lead the people to ruin—all these were the kinds of charges now being made in agitation trials.[16]

Though many historians and other observers of this trial have claimed that the Shakhty trial was "scripted," in fact it was probably more an improvised agitation trial than a scripted one.[17] The principal defendants were probably given only a skeleton version of their parts.[18] They were then expected to improvise on the spot as different questions were thrown their way. It was not memorization that was required of the defendants so much as an apparently "truthful" accounting of why they as wreckers would have acted the way they did.[19] This improvisation and the resulting starts and stops in turn gave the Shakhty and later trials a greater sense of realism than a strictly scripted trial would have had. Confessions were given and retracted and given once again. As in the improvised agitation trials, those very mistakes and retractions gave the trials more of a sense of events that were being lived and not just performed.[20] And, of course, they added to the drama of the trial: Who would win? What would be the outcome?

The show trial had by now become a version of the agitation trial on a larger scale. Even before the defendants appeared in the courtroom in the Shakhty case, the Central Committee of the Communist Party and the Central Control Commission announced that the affair had nationwide significance.[21] As the trial was being prepared and announced in the press, Stalin famously declared: "We have internal enemies. We have external enemies. This, comrades, must not be forgotten for a single moment." In Stalin's mind the case linked these "internal" and "external" enemies. The bourgeois experts had "banded together in a secret group." Yet the party had been able to reveal the plot and recognize the threat to the nation.[22]

The Shakhty trial with its huge wave of attendant publicity intensified the paranoid climate in which the whole country found itself.[23] A *Pravda* editorial at the beginning of the trial spoke of the Shakhty defendants who appeared in court, saying they "were firmly guaranteed the deadly class hatred of the workers and toiling people of the whole world."[24] No sooner had the trial been completed than works appeared in print with titles like *People-Wreckers: The Shakhty Case*.[25] Films were used to distribute information about the trial.[26]

From now on the clubs would be called upon to "prepare public opinion" for such show trials. The "facts" adduced in one trial were often all the evidence produced to prove the guilt of so-called wreckers in the next trial. The trials thus helped to build an increasing pyramid of "evidence," all of it, of course, fraudulent. Each conviction helped to ensure that the next defendants would be found guilty *because the last ones had been*.[27] Class hatred was also whipped up on a daily basis, and show trials were held in theaters in provincial cities to accommodate larger audiences.[28] As one club correspondent noted,

> The existence of broadly conceptualized and organized wrecking serves as proof that the fight against wrecking cannot be *only* the work of the organs of the proletarian dictatorship, the OGPU and the court organs. It is necessary to create the conditions and situations in which wrecking could be revealed [*vyiavleno*], so to speak, "at its roots" [*na korniu*], or, to put it another way, to create a prophylaxis against wrecking. This can be attained through the mobilization of public attention [*obshchestvennoe vnimanie*] and the strengthening of proletarian vigilance.[29]

Political education work was supposed to play the central role in this work.

Trials were thus no longer a place for discussion of social ideas. They no longer featured debate that educators hoped would encourage "critical thinking." The defendants in these real trials were dehumanized and portrayed as pests and wreckers. Above all, they were made into objects of hatred for the rest of society.

A RISE IN TENSIONS AFTER THE SHAKHTY TRIAL

The climate in the clubs now became tenser. Before the Shakhty trial was even quite over, on June 3, 1928, the party Central Committee promulgated its appeal to all party members and workers "On the Development of Self-Criticism [*samokritika*]."[30] Stalin immediately declared *samokritika* to be "an inseparable and permanently active weapon in the arsenal of Bolshevism. . . . Without *samokritika* there is no correct upbringing [*vospitanie*] of the party, the class, the masses. Without the correct upbringing of the party, the class, the masses, there is no Bolshevism."[31]

This was the beginning of Stalin's Great Break and what was often called the new "cultural revolution."[32] In September 1928 the Komsomol and Glavpolitprosvet (the main political education administration) announced their own "cultural campaign," (*kul'tpokhod*), which was "to be directed at the dark sides of daily life [*byt*]—illiteracy, dirt, untidiness, and drunkenness."[33]

The clubs were now designated "the builders of the new culture, the new *byt*." Yet even two years into the campaign, the majority of workers' clubs and youth sections were criticized for being "indifferent to this extremely important campaign."[34] They had waged only small campaigns such as taking photographs of drunken workers and publishing them in the Komsomol newspaper. A few had held lectures on the cultural campaign. But most were still having difficulties attracting adult workers and their families. They were still plagued by dirt and lack of comfort, as well as hooliganism and drunkenness.

In October 1928 the government declared the launching of the First Five Year Plan using language dominated by talk of enemies. Kulaks, drunkards, priests, bureaucrats, Mensheviks, hoarders and wreckers who kept food from the workers, Trotskyites—the list was virtually endless.[35] But it also relied on a notion of self-transformation. "We must all somehow transform ourselves [*peredelat'sia*],"noted Sergei Syrtsov, head of the party's Agitprop section and newly named chair of Sovnarkom (the Council of Ministers of the USSR). "If we don't transform ourselves, we will not correspond to those tasks of socialist reconstruction which are before us. Many of us are still held hostage to the ideology of the reconstruction period [i.e., NEP] with its habits and tempos."[36]

Articles soon appeared in the club press defining the essence of *samokritika* as "flogging" (*bichevanie*). Cultural workers were told they had to respond to "the workers'" increasing demands. The demands being placed on cultural work were diverging from the actual content being provided in a new an unacceptable "scissors gap." It was necessary to "sharpen the masses' attention to the failings of cultural work." "The fire of self-criticism from both below and above would open people's eyes."[37]

Everyone was now in the line of fire. The trade unions were castigated for their "weak oversight," for "just passing resolutions," for too much of a "campaign" approach. They also were not investigating their clubs regularly enough. The trade unions and the clubs could never, it seems, reach a point where their work was considered good enough; they could never relax. Instead they were to "struggle tirelessly for the upbringing and creation of a new type of worker, one who is free from the holdovers of the past, who has overcome backwardness, lack of culture, and who is striving to be an able and dedicated participant in all Soviet construction."[38]

The clubs were supposed to play a special role in *samokritika*. *Samokritika* was supposed to take place in what can only be called a "pseudodemocratic" vein. It was to be organized "irrespective of persons" (*nevziraia na litsa*) with criticism "from top to bottom and bottom to top." The party leadership explicitly emphasized workers' crucial involvement despite any resistance they might show. The whole working mass needed "to be drawn into the work of criticism, castigation and correction of failings [*vtianuta v rabotu po kritike, bichevaniiu, i ispravleniiu nedostatkov*]." Self-criticism needed to become "a kind of habit, so that each person considers it a completely necessary and ordinary matter to open up each and every negative phenomenon, each and every mistake."[39]

Even the self-criticism efforts undertaken so far were deemed insufficient, however. The main failings found by the Central Control Commission included attempts to narrow or limit the work of *samokritika*, failure of some administrations to call their workers to participate in *samokritika*, and attempts by the administrations to fight against the initiatives of the workers. "There have even been attempts at castration [*vykholashchivaniia*] of the creative content of *samokritika*, reducing it everywhere to empty conversations." Both the party and the trade union organizations came in for criticism for not doing enough in the development of *samokritika*. Some people tried to get out of it by having everyone speak "theoretically" without looking at local facts. Some administrations attempted to persecute people for *samokritika*. The clubs came under special pressure to "assist" the party and trade unions in these endeavors. Long lists were drawn up of topics that the clubs should use in *samokritika*: the struggle against violations of labor discipline, drunkenness, falls in labor productivity, truancy, defective products resulting from sloppy work, carelessness toward machines and instruments.[40]

Not surprisingly, these turned out to be the very topics of agitation trials written and performed in this period. Anyone who dared to breathe the slightest genuine criticism of official policy could now be brought before his or her peers in an agitation trial. As one article on propaganda of the First Five Year Plan explained in 1929, "An agitation trial can be organized of the Five Year Plan itself and also of individual persons and groups who do not believe in the Five Year Plan and who brake its implementation whether consciously or unconsciously. . . . The agitation trial can be an extremely alluring [*uvlekatel'noi*] and valuable form of propaganda for the Five Year Plan, but only if it is carefully prepared."[41] It was now sufficient to express skepticism about the Five Year Plan in order to find oneself on trial. Even when a trial of the Five Year Plan was suggested, it listed workers' criticisms, which once voiced, could obviously get the speakers in trouble: for example, "the 'imposition' of tasks beyond our strength, the 'draining' of all our force, the incorrect relationship of heavy to light industry, 'the failure to take into account' our backwardness and lack of culture [the classic peasant and worker self-defense], 'the failure to take into account' peasants' interests and so on."[42]

TRIAL SUBJECTS NO LONGER PERFORMED IN AGITATION TRIALS

Certain kinds of agitation trials were in fact no longer being performed. Whole types of trials had disappeared, as had many particular aspects of earlier agitation trials.[43]

Heroic or reverse trials were the most obvious category of trials no longer performed. No trials of Lenin or the Communist Party appear after about 1923. Stalin, Molotov, Kaganovich, and Beria were never scripted as characters in trials. Leading institutions such as the Red Army were not being presented for discussion through the format of the trial. Occasionally, topics such as rationalization, Fordism (the use of assembly lines), or the First Five Year Plan were suggested for trials, but they appear not to have been actually scripted. The one exception is an excruciatingly boring script for a *Trial of Prefabricated, Reinforced Concrete* held on March 27, 28, and 30, 1933, in Moscow and published by the Permanent Meeting on Prefabricated Constructions of the Ministry of Heavy Industry (NKTP). Designed to show the benefits of concrete, the "trial" consists almost entirely of expert technical testimony by engineers and professors.[44]

One of the reasons for this turn away from heroic trials can be seen as early as 1924 in a review of a new book on mass work in the clubs. The reviewer (probably Raisa Ginzburg, a leading activist in the clubs) scolds the authors for their proposed *Trial of an Atheist*. How can the play's authors pretend, she asks, that it is a Soviet court when the prosecution is bringing charges for disseminating atheist materials, something that would obviously never happen in the Soviet Union? Would a Soviet prosecutor ever say that atheist literature is "poison for the people"? "Not a single worker or peasant," she concludes, "will believe in the possibility of such a trial. Instead of an interesting form of club work, the result is naked agitation sewn with white threads."[45] In other words, fantasy as an element of trials of the heroes of the revolution was now beyond the imagination of even the club activists. Such trials were also impossible because paradoxically they would violate the principle of making agitation trials as realistic as possible. They would entail an impossible suspension of disbelief. Ironically, the highest authorities at this time were beginning to gear up for the most fantastic trials in human history, the Moscow trials of 1936–38, when virtually every charge was to seem beyond the bounds of human comprehension. Small-scale trials in clubs, however, could not be allowed to hear charges that the audience would find implausible.

Another problem with the late agitation trials was that the element of education was becoming uncoupled from the commitment to entertainment. Authors now explicitly contrasted "useful" club evenings [*s poleznym deistviem*) and "recreational" ones (*prednaznachenyi dlia 'razvlecheniia'*).[46] The old extracurricular education activists (*vneshkol'niki*) came under attack as old-fashioned. Club directors told their workers they should not have to rely on "patented extracurricular experts" (*patentovannye vneshkol'niki*) in order to put on plays. Those club directors who insist that young members must know "all the rules of the so-called extracurricular art" before putting on a trial are just exhibiting "sick egotism" (*boleznennoe samoliubie*).[47]

Humor all but disappeared from the agitation trials. On the anniversary of the Sixth Comintern Congress in the summer of 1929, the journal *Klub i revoliutsiia* gave suggestions for performance topics in clubs, saying that for the clubs "this is a crucial political examination, a test of their activism and their ability to serve the paramount political tasks put forth by the Comintern."[48] The clubs were then given a strict program of day-by-day activities for the month ahead. On July 24, for example, they were to perform *The Dramatized Trial of the Social Fascists Who Are Preparing a World War* (*Inst-senirovannyi sud nad sotsial-fashistami podgotovliaiushchimi imperialisti-cheskuiu voinu*). Real foreign leaders were to be the defendants (in absentia), including the American secretary of state, Frank Kellogg, the League of Nations, and the artist George Grosz (for his 1924 painting *Christ in a Gas Mask*). The only vaguely humorous characters are a pair of ordinary guys (*obyvateli*), one of whom "relates passively" to the threat of world war, and the other of whom "falls into a panic" at the news of the threat.[49] It is hard to imagine, however, that a trial of Social Fascists preparing for war would have struck very many viewers as humorous or enjoyable—especially if it was planned as a "political examination" for its performers!

It also could not have been a pleasurable experience when a whole factory shop was put on trial for lagging behind. Such an agitation trial was recommended for the October anniversary holiday in 1930 with the proviso that it be carefully prepared with "all the factual material" demonstrating the shop's violations of the factory's program and leading the whole factory "to the black board," that is, the board of those who had failed.[50]

No one is ever found innocent after 1928. Even the titles presume the defendants are guilty: *The Trial of the Person Guilty of Causing Accidents, The Trial of Those Guilty of Causing Defects, The Trial of Wreckers of Rationalization,* and *The Trial of Truants.*[51]

THE LAST AGITATION TRIALS

The last agitation trials before the form died out almost completely (those published in the years 1930–33) have almost no dramatic interest because the characters are devoid of real personalities and real stories. The scripts still list a cast of characters on the opening pages, but now no descriptions are given of the characters. Previous trials had invariably listed at least a few details about each character's age, appearance, mannerisms, and comportment on stage.

The actions of everyone are ritualistic. The defendants deny they have done anything wrong. A workers' brigade is sent in to investigate what were undoubtedly realistic complaints (a cafeteria that is filthy, has no silverware, subjects patrons to long lines; or a store with insufficient numbers of salespeople, many of whom stand around in an empty department while customers throng to a department that has no one to help them). The head of the cafeteria or store is charged with being insufficiently aware of the significance of his work for raising socialist production and helping workers fulfill the First Five Year Plan. The representative of the investigating brigade finds that the director is of the old school (himself a cook or a salesman), is uncultured, has not learned the new ways, and does not know how to administer the workplace. The only (minimal) defense is that the inspection commissions that were supposed to investigate and keep an eye on this director had themselves not worked up to standard and had failed to recognize his shortcomings.[52]

These late agitation trials reflect the temper of the times. They open with long disquisitions on socialist construction and industrialization, the difficulties of the grain question, the slow growth rates in agriculture, and the tasks of the nation "to mobilize the masses in order to overcome and weaken these difficulties."[53] The trials are said to be taking place "at the most important moment in socialist construction."[54] Art in general can and must be used "in the battle with backward moods of certain groups in the proletariat, in the battle with the holdovers of the old way of life."[55] Even light music such as "gypsy songs" (said to differ from true gypsy folklore), fox trots, shimmies, ragtimes, and all forms of jazz must be put on trial as "hackwork" (*khaltura*) and counter to the Sixteenth Party Congress resolution that all cultural work is to be "saturated with communist content."[56]

The agitation trials took on as well the shrill tone of the Shakhty and Industrial Party trials. Two members of an elected store commission that was supposed to inspect and oversee a cooperative store are brought before the court in an agitation trial on the grounds that they have seriously violated the trust placed in them. Yet the charges against them are picayune. One of the two members of the commission is accused of using a sixty-two-kopeck check she stole from the meat department to buy two hundred grams of soft candies. The other member of the commission is accused of appearing drunk with two friends at the store after closing time when the staff was cleaning up, demanding wine to drink, and causing a row. In addition, both have failed to report and vigorously combat a few minor abuses of the cooperative staff.

In his testimony as a witness, the administrator of the store claims that the staff has "always related to the commission with complete trust," but that the latter's actions "force us" to see them not as members of an elected cooperative organ, but rather as "wreckers of the cooperative."[57] The final sentencing of the two commission members seems completely disproportionate to their crimes: the two are found guilty of "discrediting (undermin-

ing trust toward) proletarian supervision, . . . covering up abuses in the cooperative store and . . . hindering the organization of food supply to the
workers."[58]

Another trial that focused on "abusing the trust" of both the workers and
the administration is that of a group leader of bricklayers.[59] In the final sentence the group leader is accused of "sowing discontent with Soviet power"
because he took measures to make sure the workers did not complain of his
misdeeds and thus he implicitly discredited the government.[60]

By the time of the late trials the defendant is almost never acquitted or
given a conditional sentence. The drunkard in a 1930 trial is sentenced to six
months of forced labor plus forced medical treatment.[61] The members of the
store commission are excluded from membership in the cooperative. The
woman who allegedly stole the check for sixty-two kopecks is to be re-
manded to the people's court, while the man's drunken episode is to be reported to the factory committee at his workplace. The group leader receives
a two-year prison sentence.

The sentences are accompanied by unqualified negative rhetoric. The male
member of the shop commission who shows up drunk does not simply make
a nuisance of himself; he "introduces corruption" among the staff of the
store. The group leader of the bricklayers is also charged with "corrupting"
the workers, with "arming them against Soviet power."[62] A fictional collective farmer who refused to be vaccinated in 1933 and who persuaded his
neighbor to do the same is now branded "a class enemy."[63]

One of the last calls for holding "theatrical comrades' show trials" (to-
varishcheskie pokazatel'nye teatralizovannye sudy) claimed they were an
essential part of the struggle for "the new way of life" and against "crude
backwardness in daily life." All "conciliatory attitudes" must be eliminated,
including those "toward inveterate alcoholism, toward the beating of
women and children, toward religious fanaticism, [and] the rationalization
that this is all a private matter." The trials now rejected any separation of
some matters as "private," any sympathy toward the defendants. Instead
"the concrete names of 'daily life wreckers'" (bytovye vrediteli) should be
"made public" (predavat' glasnost') through all kinds of living newspapers
and dramatizations.[64] Glasnost in this period thus meant publicity in a public sphere where concrete individuals could see their names and their actions
flogged and criticized by other characters in a play and also by an audience
egged on by the presiding officials.

THE DECLINE IN AGITATION TRIALS

Despite such occasional calls for the clubs to put on agitation trials, the latter declined dramatically in quantity as well as quality in the late 1920s.[65]
Although all the statistics on performances must be treated with some skep-

ticism, it is nonetheless interesting to note that whereas some 368 "show trials" (*pokazatel'nye sudy*) were put on in 1925 in the clubs, according to the head of Proletkult, only 51 were staged in 1927. Even in 1925 the 368 show trials represented only 1.3 percent of all performances. Plays were 45 percent of all performances; movies, 28.8 percent; reports, lectures, and conversations, 23.6 percent; excursions, 1.3 percent. By 1927 agitation trials represented 0.61 percent of all performances, while plays were 63 percent; movies, 27.6 percent; reports, etc., 8.3 percent; and excursions 0.4 percent.[66]

Already in 1925 an occasional political education worker was claiming that the earliest Civil War agitation plays needed to be "filed away in the archives" on the grounds that they were "completely antiartistic." Still, he defended agitation plays in general and political trials in particular on the grounds that in comparison with real plays these "require the least energy and produce the greatest effect," by which he meant the greatest impression on the audience. As long as the agitation trials "gave the desired result," they were still a desired form of political propaganda.[67]

By 1927, however, commentators were explicitly criticizing agitation theater for being "extremely primitive in dramatic construction" and "superficial in content."[68] Workers, it was claimed, wanted "more in-depth content and more complicated formal structure"—that is, real plays.

Soviet historians, and to some extent Western ones, have assumed that the decline in the agitation trials was a natural phenomenon, "logically and historically inevitable."[69] The agitation play, contemporaries insisted, "has ceased to interest club audiences. . . . Hence evidently the unstoppable pull at the local level toward the staging of plays."[70] To some extent there probably was a spontaneous movement away from agitation trials toward the staging of plays. The reasons for this were many. For starters, a "new cultural landscape" (Lynn Mally's term) was emerging with its "state-sponsored aesthetic of socialist realism" which demanded more professionalization and less cultural experimentation.[71] The agitation trials, which had always been experimental, now came to seem less desirable.

Many of the clubs, moreover, resisted the endless regimen of campaigns that the party and other organizations forced on them. They would be working on an Ostrovskii play when a directive would come down that they should drop everything to take up a particular issue of the "contemporary moment." They were sick and tired, they complained, "of all those Curzons and Macdonalds" (subjects of agitation trials and other agitation plays).[72] Viewers were sick as well of everything that resembled the Civil War. In the end contemporary dramaturgy was becoming unconvincing because "from the very first moment the audience already knows how [the play] will end. [. . .] The main heroes are inevitably going to be boring. They walk up and down the stage, declaiming wise words about the problem put forth by the author. That is why our plays are so similar to one another."[73] The playwright Aleksei Tolstoi claimed that contemporary plays were so dreary because instead of presenting living people, they pulled formulas out of their briefcases. Not surprisingly, this alienated audiences.[74]

A third reason for the apparently "spontaneous" decline in agitation trials was the fact that the drama circles in clubs had themselves matured enormously over the course of the 1920s. As a one- or two-act play, the agitation trial with its simple structure was often good material for a beginning circle which had only twelve to fifteen members and little experience, no instruction, and few materials. With time, however, the circles began to demand full plays, such as those of Ostrovskii and Gorky.[75]

Competition from the silver screen also eroded club members' desire to put on agitation trials. By 1925 half of Moscow's clubs had their own film projectors; and 70 percent of the "service work" that members were doing was in showing films.[76] Films were easy to show and generated income for cash-strapped administrators. A picture with Mary Pickford was much more attractive than an amateur trial put on by the local drama circle.[77]

The change from agitation trials to plays in the late 1920s was not entirely spontaneous, however. In 1927 a theater meeting held by the Agitprop Section of the Communist Party "decisively condemned the exclusive staging in club dramatic work of small forms and amateur repertoire (dramatizations, agitation trials)." Clubs were to fight against "*liubitel'shchina*" (amateurism).[78] In 1928 a conference on sanitation theater concluded formally that sanitation trials were losing their significance and should be replaced with full sanitation plays.[79] At both these conferences officials stated that workers and club members themselves were spearheading the movement away from agitki and toward plays because of their allegedly increased sophistication. Though this may have been partially true, as has been shown, the fact that agitation and trade union officials were trumpeting this move at every turn suggests the authorities' own deep investment in this move.

The decline in agitation trials surely resulted as well from the ways that the trials themselves as plays had changed over the course of the decade. They had moved from an open-ended form presenting dialogue and contestation of ideas, as well as real inquiry into characters' motivations and defense of them, to a form that served primarily as a forum for the public branding of crimes and misdemeanors. This naturally meant that they had lost much of their drama. The resulting scripts were formulaic set pieces with little attention to character development and plot. For drama circles in the clubs, the late agitation trials must have seemed the antithesis of theater and playacting.

The visible decline in numbers of agitation trials being published and performed must also have resulted from the oppressive weight of the national show trials (Shakhty, Industrial Party, Menshevik Party). The quality of playing and acting in the agitation trials was overshadowed by the fierceness of the prosecution in the real trials. While the agitation trials had successfully worked within a formula of education plus entertainment plus discipline in the early 1920s, that quality had all but disappeared by the end of the decade. Throughout the period audiences could be, and were, bribed to go to didactic morality plays by promises of films afterwards. They were also taken to real trials during their work hours to provide visual proof that the "working masses" condemned wrecking behavior of one kind or another. But amateur drama circles were less and less likely to want to try their hands at the agitation-trial form, which had now become so serious. And it is equally unlikely that cultural organizers and club directors wanted to risk mistakes if amateur dramatists made a slacker too sympathetic or a drunkard too likable. Judgment and trials, rather than providing an opportunity for discussion and debate, were now harnessed almost purely to intimidation and scapegoating. Whereas in the early 1920s to judge had meant to weigh and ponder and often to acquit, now to judge meant to condemn and revile. In such pure condemnation there could be little room for drama and human spirit.

THE AUDIENCE AS PERFORMERS

Of course, it is impossible to say whether the agitation trials were effective in changing individuals' and groups' behavior. Organizers certainly claimed they were.[80] The main pressure was on the audience itself.

In one trial of truants in the Donbas region (1930) virtually everyone present was allowed to speak his or her mind, with the result that the trial allegedly lasted some nineteen hours. This was then claimed as proof that the audience had "played an enormous role" and "the sentence given the truants gave great results."[81]

In the spring of 1929 one of the large cultural halls in Leningrad (Domprosvet imeni Gertsena) organized a month-long campaign combating alcoholism. Each neighborhood was required to list how many alcoholics it had, what had been the consequences of their alcoholism, whether they were in treatment programs, and so on. The "competition-investigation" (*Konkurssmotr*) began on March 20 and had to be completed by April 20. Each housing unit (Zhakt) (which might consist of several apartment buildings) had to (1) organize a special cell of the Society for the Fight against Alcoholism; (2) carry out a survey count of the resident alcoholics and forward the list to the local anti-alcohol clinic (*dispanser*); and (3) organize no fewer than two anti-alcohol mass undertakings and the creation of one anti-alcohol kruzhok. All of these were to be organized "by their own forces [*samodeiatel'nym putem*], by the cultural-daily life commission and by the *aktiv* of the Zhakt residents." All mass amateur evenings had to be organized on the basis of local material, using events, figures, and facts of the given Zhakt and the families in the neighborhood. The results of each Zhakt's efforts had then to be given to the local hall (Domprosvet imeni Gertsena) by April 20. Three prizes were to be awarded, the first for one hundred rubles; the second, seventy-five; and the third, fifty, in the form of textbooks on how to elect participants.[82]

At the conclusion of the campaign/competition, one Zhakt proudly reported that it had registered sixty-five known alcoholics, had held a lecture on "Drunkenness and Alcoholism in the USSR and in our Zhakt," and had shown the film *Alcohol*. In addition the group had held an agitation trial of an alcoholic living in one of their buildings. In a drunken state he had been known to beat his wife, sell her things for drink, abandon her, and go carousing with other women. The trial, the report claimed, "had brought results." The defendant, citizen Maiorov, had promised at the trial to correct his ways (*ispravit'sia*). On the very next day, accompanied by one of the activists, he had gone to the drug and alcohol clinic for treatment. He was soon reunited with his wife and was given his own public work (*obshchestvennaia nagruzka*) to do.[83]

In 1933 Metrostroi, the trade union organization building the Moscow subway, published materials for a trial/play that also mixed imaginary and real defendants. Entitled *The Trial of Violators of Labor Discipline (According to Materials from the Film)*, the play was based on the portrayal of a drunkard in a recent film entitled *Saba*.[84] In the weeks before the actual performance, organizers of the play were instructed to collect a list of the worst drunkards in the union and to try to persuade them to come to the play so their own misbehaviors (wife beating, neglecting their children, showing poor labor discipline) could be discussed and illustrated. Fortunately for them (though doubtlessly not accidentally), not one of them turned out to be in the audience at the time of the performance.[85] Nonetheless, alcoholics were now clearly targets for public agitation and shaming. The regime had declared open season. If a housing unit or work unit was sufficiently pressured by the authorities, most would buckle and put their own alcoholics on trial.

Audiences could be manipulated. Leading questions, proper atmospherics, apparent spontaneity, the participation of other (planted) members of the audience—all could make the trial appear to be real and could lead the audience to certain conclusions. This was of course especially true with younger audiences and those that were less educated. The trials worked best on audiences that had never seen them before.[86] Since most audiences had never seen a trial of any kind, they could easily imagine that the ritual of an agitation trial was the real thing. Since the judge, lawyers, and expert witnesses typically used fancy words and elaborate logic and were drawn from the most educated segments of society, the audience could easily believe that they must know what they were talking about.

Yet audiences were also smart in their own way. When Alotin-Elota put the boy with a pack of cigarettes on trial, the audience allegedly responded by passing a unanimous resolution to stop smoking. They also named a special party cell (*iacheika*) "for the fight against smoking." This, he claimed, was an example of the "brilliant results" that such impromptu trials could give.[87] But was it? Or was it rather an example of the acting that audiences were learning to do? The trials provided thespian training not only to those who participated on stage but also to those who sat in the hall watching. At the conclusion, they learned, they were to applaud vigorously, pass resolutions, then pressure some poor hapless souls into creating a "cell" or a "circle" or an "organizing committee" for a campaign.[88]

Agitation trials from the beginning had been intended to "activate" both the participants and the audience. Through their involvement, both groups, it was hoped, would take a more active role in defending the official values of the regime. In fact, however, the effect was probably to make audiences increasingly passive. Once it was decided to put on an agitation trial, they must have known they were trapped. In response, they as audience members had to resort to their own playacting in the form of sham resolutions so they could escape the "performance" as quickly as possible.

By the early 1930s the use of trials to shame and humiliate defendants had effectively destroyed the humanist impulses of the early revolutionary educators. The show trials of the 1930s might convince some foreign observers that they were witnessing real judicial proceedings, but by this time both agitation and show trials had been divested of any compassion or searching to explore real human motivations. There was no attempt to mete out anything resembling justice. "Truth," or *pravda*, as it is called in Russian, had been sacrificed to *pokazatel'nost'*, or "show."

CONCLUSION

Public trials performed for show purposes went through one last phase of transformation between the Shakhty trial and the famous Moscow Show Trials of 1936–38.[1] The language became more vicious, more polarized than ever. The Moscow Show Trials now returned full circle to the medieval morality plays discussed in chapter 1. The trial had revealed "the bestial countenance of the international brigands," as Andrei Vyshinsky told the court in his summation speech for the prosecution in 1938. This was counterposed to "the new, happy, joyously flourishing Socialist society of workers and peasants."[2] "Two worlds" had come into conflict, "the bloc of traitors, hirelings of foreign capital . . . and the bloc of Soviet patriots, great and invincible in their love for their country." The decisive force in this battle between Good and Evil had been "the wrath and might of the great Soviet country," which "exposed and crushed" the wrongdoers.[3] In this trial, which built on all the previous trials, the perfidy of the evildoers had been revealed and "patriots of the Soviet land" were able to sit in judgment.

In this imagined fairy tale Vyshinsky took pains to show how "a once poor and weak country has become a rich and mighty country, a powerful and invincible country." But the country faced endless waves of enemies who attacked. Through the work of the courtroom it became evident that these enemies were "seeking revenge for the 'lost paradise' of their economic and political domination."[4]

In the trials of the late 1930s the defendants were shown to be inhuman, cunning tricksters who wore masks pretending to be loyal hard-working citizens. Vyshinsky swore the trial of 1938, for example, would be remembered for its ability "to tear the mask of perfidy from the faces of scoundrels." The court had illuminated the "shameful, unparalleled, monstrous crimes committed by the accused," crimes that were worse than the crimes of "the most inveterate, vile, unbridled and despicable criminals."[5]

Enormous villainy merited the most enormous spectacles yet to be played out before the nation. In the course of his concluding remarks Vyshinsky claimed that the truth of all the charges had been demonstrated "with exceptional scrupulousness and exactitude."[6] The trial "proved" that "the Rights, Trotskyites, Mensheviks, SRs, bourgeois nationalists, and so on and so forth, are nothing other than a gang of murderers, spies, diversionists, and wreckers, without any principles or ideals." By his choice of language Vyshinsky stripped the defendants of any possible positive motivations, any service to the nation, any ideals. He cited Stalin as his source for calling them "a gang . . . without principles and without ideals." They were not a political party but rather "a band of felonious criminals, . . . criminals who have sold themselves to enemy intelligence services." Any ideals they might once have had "had long ago vanished and gone rotten in the foul-smelling, abominable underworld of spies." Nikolai Bukharin and the other defendants had been shown to be "rabid counterrevolutionaries." Vyshinsky concluded by appealing to the comrade judges, saying that "our people and all honest people throughout the world are waiting for your just verdict."[7] The verdict, he insisted, would be the "refreshing and purifying thunderstorm of just Soviet punishment." Denying all humanity to the defendants and implicitly rejecting all legality, he closed his speech with the now famous phrase: "Crush the accursed reptiles!"[8]

With these words Vyshinsky and his comrades killed any last vestiges of humanism. Where the authors of the early agitation trials had consciously, explicitly sought to *humanize* certain social problems such as venereal disease and prostitution, the prosecutors in the great show trials *dehumanized* their opponents, characterizing them as "mad dogs," "little dogs snarling at an elephant," and "loathsome creatures."[9] Bukharin, the chief defendant, was in Vyshinsky's words "this hypocritical, false, wily creature; . . . this 'damnable cross of a fox and swine.'" Vyshinsky deliberately chose to quote Maxim Gorky's words about one of the characters from his short story "Those Who Once Were People" in order to underline his contention that Bukharin and his codefendants might once perhaps have been people but were so no longer.[10] The chief offstage villain, of course, was Leon Trotsky, whom Vyshinskii characterized as the "Judas-Trotsky" who had attacked Lenin's ideas with "venomous saliva," implying that he was a snake.[11]

By the second half of the 1930s the show trials had turned the initial values of the agitation trials upside down. Instead of opposing the shaming of the defendants, as the sanitation trials had done, the show trials relied heavily on demonstrating their complete despicability and shamefulness.[12] Instead of seeking to understand the defendants, the trials denounced them with little inquiry into their motivations or their ways of viewing the world.

Instead of placing the blame on the environment, which had failed to protect the individual, they placed the blame squarely on the individual and his perfidious psychology, which failed to recognize the benefits he had received from the Soviet state.

The earliest agitation trials had sought repeatedly to make the defendants' infractions as concrete and locally based as possible. By the time of the late agitation trials the indictment often rested on charges of actions not taken, memberships not upheld, and vigilance not maintained. The line between "public" and "private" matters became increasingly vague as issues of individual health and hygiene, and membership and nonmembership in "voluntary" organizations became subject to public commentary and judgment through the agitation trials. Where the agitation trials initially allowed and fostered polemic and debate, albeit weighted by having the stronger actors play the side that was supposed to win, over time they actively discouraged genuine debate as defense lawyers began to capitulate without putting up a fight. Aleksandr Solzhenitsyn referred to this quality when he sarcastically spoke of the Shakhty show trial as approaching an ideal of a "conflictless trial" because the defense and prosecution were pursuing common ends.[13] Eugene Lyons, too, commented that the defense attorneys in that trial were "timid supernumeraries, an empty concession to appearances," people whose faces "have faded out of my memory."[14]

Throughout the course of the 1920s and early 1930s the agitation trials relied on a dynamic master narrative of the defendants' resistance, their maintenance of their innocence, and the drama of unmasking the individuals' true colors over the course of the trial.[15] Yet the fictional agitation trials differed from the show trials of real individuals in their greater plot development over the course of the story. In 1921 the court in its opening indictment of Zaborova, the alleged prostitute, expressed uncertainty over the charges brought against her. Only through the questioning of witnesses did her reversion to prostitution as a profession become apparent.[16] In other early trials the judges and prosecutors frequently expressed openly their confusion about how to evaluate or judge a person's guilt or innocence. Was Iudin, nicknamed "The Writer," really a dangerous hooligan who camouflaged his true intentions, or was he an example of a weak-willed member of the intelligentsia who needed extra attention and upbringing by the party?[17] Was Zaborova, the woman who had again fallen into prostitution in the Soviet era, "guilty" of taking in Krest'ianov as a client?

The prosecutors in the Moscow Show Trials, by contrast, relentlessly hit home to their audiences the duplicity of the defendants, granting them no quarter for ignorance or error. In the 1938 trial of Bukharin, Rykov, and others, the opening indictment claimed to have uncovered a "chain of shameful villainies."[18] Vyshinsky repeated this claim in virtually identical form in his closing remarks, calling them "a chain of shameful, unparalleled, monstrous crimes."[19] As Walter Duranty observed in watching the Moscow trials, "not only all the plots were one plot, all the oppositions one Opposition but also that the whole business was connected with, and directed by, hostile forces abroad."[20]

The agitation and show trials also carried different understandings of human nature. The agitation trials had tended to assume that people act in fundamentally straightforward ways. If only they were exposed to the correct information and the correct way of understanding their situation (through the medium, of course, of the agitation trial itself), then they would reform and change their ways. The show trials of the late 1920s and '30s, by contrast, consistently portrayed the criminal defendants as complex and devious. They could not be reformed. Instead, the prosecution insisted, they had to be destroyed, "shot like dirty dogs."

Even at the very end, though, the Shakhty and Moscow Show Trials shared certain conventions and moral precepts with the earlier agitation trials. They played, for example, on many of the same "public values." Both appealed to public opinion (*obshchestvennoe mnenie*). In both kinds of trials cultural and political authorities sought to "teach" the public how to understand the trial.[21] All the trials shared a common passion for morality and upbringing. It was a public matter to give everyone, adults and children alike, a proper upbringing (*vospitanie*) through exposure to these trials.

Both the agitation and the show trials contrasted *false* kinship among the defendants with the more "correct" kinship of the new Soviet state and people.[22] They returned again and again to the theme of *membership in the wrong kinds of organizations*—in organizations of foreign capitalists seeking to overthrow the Soviet Union, in fictive organizations such as "the Industrial Party" and "the Union Bureau of Mensheviks."[23] They emphasized the *false shame* of defendants who attempted to retract their confessions and resist the direction of the court inquiry.[24]

Finally, the show trials, like the agitation trials, relied heavily on the *public confession* of the defendants as the only acceptable proof of the latter's integrity. As Viacheslav Molotov told Bukharin at the 1937 Central Committee meeting called to discuss the issues against him (Bukharin), "If you don't confess, that will prove you're a fascist hireling."[25] In his final speech in 1938 Bukharin did give a kind of confession: "Citizen President and Citizen Judges, I fully agree with Citizen Procurator regarding the significance of the trial, at which were exposed our dastardly crimes, the crimes committed by the block of rights and Trotskyites, one of whose leaders I was, and for all the activities of which I bear responsibilities."[26]

Historians and political scientists have made much, of course, of the issue of confession, especially the psychology of the defendants' confessions in many of the leading show trials. Perhaps the most influential treatment of the show trials was Arthur Koestler's portrayal of Rubashov's loyalty to the party and hence his confession in *Darkness at Noon*.[27] Scholars have asked whether the novel provides an accurate portrayal of the situation of Bukharin and other defendants in the Moscow trials.[28]

Torture and threats to their families certainly played the most significant part in the defendants' decisions to confess in court. Loyalty to the party and the requirements of party discipline were undoubtedly additional factors.[29] But why did their capitulation take the form of confessions per se? Why did organizers of the trials *require* the confessions?

One reason Stalin and the party insisted on confessions was that they had no other solid evidence with which to convict leading members of the technical intelligentsia (in the Shakhty case) and leading Old Bolsheviks (in the trials of the 1930s). Stalin's paranoia, too, played an enormous role. For personal reasons he no doubt needed to see his enemies debased.[30]

Confessions were also necessary, however, as ritual markers of membership. Confession was a way of underlining the power and correctness of the larger collective. At the third Moscow Show Trial Vyshinsky hammered away at Bukharin's alleged failure to confess fully on a number of occasions, beginning in 1924. He (Bukharin) had criticized others, but he had failed to criticize himself. He appeared to repent, but then he admitted that his "'repentance' was nothing but a tactical manoeuver, a fraud."[31] Through the requirement that defendants confess, the collectives staging the trials could monitor inclusion and exclusion.[32] These were ostensibly "voluntary" organizations, so individuals' expressions of regret had also perforce to be voluntary. The trial was also, however, a ritual that could, and in fact had to, be repeated again and again since no single confession was ever sufficient.

The agitation trials were among the most elaborate secular, semipolitical rituals the world has ever seen. In that capacity they served a number of functions: to engage the viewers in a process that appeared to stand above everyday life, one that involved the mystery of the power of the state; to bring out (*vyavit'*) conflicts and appear to resolve them; to teach morality and upbringing and thus to reform habits and practices (*byt*); and to uphold the legitimacy of the Soviet state in its role as judge. Trials as a form held out the promise of simultaneously educating, entertaining, and disciplining both participants and audiences.

Initially the ritual of the agitation trial grew out of an attempt to anathematize the old tsarist regime. It was easier to unite the country against Nicky the Bloody (the popular sobriquet for Tsar Nicholas II), capitalist pigs, and White Guard invaders than to unite it for socialism.[33] The Old Bolsheviks had as a group been formed *in reaction against* the Old Regime, both as a political regime and as a way of life. They had some vague notions of what they wanted their new society to look like, but much of what they were proposing, even after 1917, was still defined by—one might even say imprisoned by—its reactive, negative qualities of judging and distancing. Amplifying the broad citizenry's dissatisfactions with the old regime served a useful purpose in agitating them and drawing them into activities sponsored by the new regime. At the same time, however, it created a dynamic of its own in which the regime had always to seek new enemies, new forces to struggle against. Since the party leaders were not entirely united on the positive program they wanted to pursue (one thinks for example, of the party's debates over agriculture, the pace of change, the New Economic Policy, and so on), they had to unite around the persecution of enemies. Since they had a population that had virtually no experience in politics, management, and social reform, it was expeditious to unite them as well around a negative politics of hate and judgment.

The original organizers of the agitation trials seem to have chosen to concentrate explicitly on trials of actions and qualities that were already marginal to society. The principal defendants throughout the whole period were drunkards, syphilitics, prostitutes, hooligans, slackers, and pigs that wandered into other people's fields. These trials did not have to have a political subject at all. The Communist Party, Lenin, and Stalin are never mentioned in most of them. Even when the doctors put on trial midwives and village healers, they drew on popular fears of witchcraft and ignorance. When the trade unions put truants on trial, they drew on timeless village hatred of the *darmoed,* the one who tried to eat for free without pulling his weight. These marginal figures, of course, represented the ones whom the village could never entirely incorporate or truly exile. They had committed no crime, but they were easy to judge.[34]

The producers of agitation trials were themselves people in a vulnerable position vis-à-vis their charges. They were the army instructors who had restless soldiers in their charge whom they were supposed to entertain and politicize in the clubs without being overly didactic. They had a captive audience in their soldiers, who, after all, would not be demobilized until the political authorities agreed to let them go. But they were themselves vulnerable if these restless soldiers decided to rise up against them. The same was true of club directors. By employing the trial form, both groups could hope to entertain their charges and also attempt to instill in them a sense of collective responsibility for the social issues and the individuals being shown on stage.

Staged as a spectacle on important holidays in the new revolutionary calendar and as the culminating moment in graduations and public meetings, the agitation trial involved ritual action that created a sense of heightened seriousness. As a contained form, one with a beginning, middle, and end, the trial was relatively easy for a judge to control through adept use of his disciplinary powers. The court officer's command "All rise—the court is now in session" implicated the audience in the action, making them a part of what was happening at the tables covered in red cloth in front of them. Ritual props such as the judge's bell emphasized both the seriousness of the undertaking and the linking of the audience and the action; the audience fell within the sphere of the judge's discipline.

Ritual phrases and actions separated the witnesses and, above all, the defendants from the rest of the audience. The defendants now entered a liminal space in which their actions were weighed by the judges and by the collective audience, who would then decide whether they could reenter society and under what terms. They were *outside* society until they had received the court's permission to reenter it. They might be reprimanded and/or required to take a particular remedial course (for example, attending literacy classes or working on the village newspaper).

The trial drew in the audience, capturing its attention by its drama and performance. Audiences were fascinated to see their own peers on stage. They were intrigued by the nature of the contest, which usually centered on controversial, local issues. Above all, the audience was given a certain "social responsibility" (*obshchestvennaia otvetstvennost'*) for the outcome.[35]

The fictional defendant initially resisted the correct interpretation by denying his guilt. This denial created a dramatic conflict between the individual(s) and the authorities. The latter would try to incite the former to speak and to admit the error of his ways. Thus a conflict would be created based on real issues of resistance in society, be they desertion from the army, resistance to paying taxes, or resistance to vaccinations. The superior logic and, above all, the superior power of the state would triumph. It was not accidental that the prosecutor Nikolai Krylenko wore hunting clothes in the Shakhty trial. He was seeking to catch his prey in inconsistencies and falsehoods so he could prove their guilt.

The trial was thus a "collusive drama," to use a term developed by anthropologist Catherine Bell, drawing on the work of Barbara Myerhoff.[36] Participants joined forces to pretend that the agitation trial was a "real" court proceeding, one with fixed rules and an apparently uncertain outcome.[37] They were playacting roles and rituals the way children play at being doctors, nurses, and homemakers.

The trial's emotional impact made it especially valuable for all the settings where audiences could not be forced but rather had to be "drawn in." One of the distinctive and innovative features of the Soviet polity in contrast to the tsarist was that it used a wide range of so-called voluntary organizations, such as army and workers' clubs, Komsomol organizations, and women's organizations, to create "compact collectives."[38]

To foster this collusion the trial form was made to seem "natural" and "realistic," often "improvised," rather than something mandated and created by fiat by the regime. "Not only is seeing believing," Barbara Myerhoff has written, "doing is believing."[39] Participants were presented with a conflict that they then acted out and resolved. The conflict re-created in miniature the larger social issues and changes in policy of the Soviet state.

The ultimate mystery of the agitation and show trials is why they took hold, why they proved so powerful in the Soviet imagination. After all, at every moment the authorities had a number of choices of political rituals, many of which they did use. But none expanded into a national phenomenon in the way that the agitation trials grew into the show trials of the 1930s. The answer probably lies at least in part in the larger political culture of the day. These were powerful rituals that could provide a sense of security in times of intense insecurity. Through judgment one could overcome backwardness and ignorance, the twin scourges of the old regime. The Light (Enlightenment, education, active citizenship) could win out over the Dark (ignorance, superstition, passivity). Culture could win out over *nekul'turnost'*, the lack of culture that betrayed itself in spitting on the floor, turning to faith healers, and spreading venereal disease to one's wife and children. In these morality plays, bringing individuals and groups to trial could help them reform and see the way. Politics in this format remained a question of the individual's culpability and reform rather than reform of the system. The nineteenth-century revolutionaries had given readers positive examples of what a social democrat should be like through their autobiographies. The early cultural leaders in the Soviet era gave viewers negative examples of citizens' behavior through the trials. These latter then served as the principal forum for the struggle between the good and the bad, the conscious and the unconscious.

To the extent that this form relied on audience participation—it had to attract viewers—it required stronger and stronger doses as audiences grew immune to the power of the courts. Once they had seen one agitation, or "model," trial, they were not interested in coming to another. They knew that there wasn't a real defendant on trial; they knew that someone was acting; and they knew that the outcome had been fixed in advance. As the distinctions between public and private, voluntary and involuntary eroded, the agitation trial became less and less dramatic. Not only was the outcome fixed but there was no place for the defendant to hide, no defense for him to rely on. For these reasons the genre grew harsher. The defendant's wrongdoing had to be made more melodramatic, more fantastic so there would be at least some drama. The prosecutor had to attack in an increasingly vicious fashion to increase viewers' excitement.

A sociological explanation for the increasing harshness of the trials can be found in the changing profile of the people who staged them. The earliest organizers of agitation trials (especially in the prerevolutionary period but also in the army) had been librarians, educators, and budding writers who sought dramatic conflict in the contained form of the trial format as an end in itself. They did not care about the outcomes of the trials as long as they sparked discussion among their students. They chose the trial format to draw students out, teach them literacy, and give them confidence in public speaking. Holding a trial could teach students how to run meetings, thus preparing them to take a leading role in postrevolutionary society. It could help them to practice critical thinking, weighing the pros and cons of a moral or political issue. It could teach them to see the darkness of tsarist society, which had failed to rehabilitate the prostitute and the syphilitic, thus giving them additional motivation to join the revolutionary society. It could show them the power of the doctor and the agronomist, who were now allied with the Soviet state and whose superior knowledge should be obeyed for the good of the whole society.[40]

Once the new club directors and trade union cultural officers took over the organization of the trials in the middle 1920s, however, the tenor changed. These were people who were themselves factory workers and cooks and shoe-makers by trade.[41] They had neither experience nor education nor incentive to use the trials as debating societies. As Andrei Sinyavsky commented in his *Soviet Civilization,* quoting the philosopher Georgy Fedotov on the 1920s: "Russia is teeming with half-baked intellectuals and semi-learned types, but one rarely meets a 'cultivated' person in the old sense of the word. . . . The old cadres are thinning out and being replaced by a new type: practical-minded barbarian specialists, suspicious of the great cultural riches."[42] For these new directors, the "canned" form of the trial represented an easy means to express the alleged *samodeiatel'nost'*—independent work—of the army or workers' club without risking genuinely uncontrolled performances.[43]

These new directors, moreover, were under immense local pressure in a time of the most rapid urbanization and social change the country had ever known.[44] Workers coming into the factories from the village, especially the young ones, did act in an irresponsible fashion. They broke windows and brawled in the clubs. By the second half of the 1920s many club directors and even ordinary members were undoubtedly only too happy to stage a model trial of a hooligan in hopes of inducing change in their audience. This demonstration function is, after all, a classic function of trials in many times and places.

At the same time the trials demonstrate the intense vulnerability of the middle representatives of the regime. Trade unions and Komsomol groups could be (and were) accused of Trotskyism. If they failed to reform their members, directors and supervisors could find themselves brought into court. Collective responsibility—the ancient Russian practice of holding peasants and workers of all kinds responsible as a group for the payment of taxes, boat hauling, carting, etc.—was alive and well.

The trials obviously benefited the regime itself, both the local politicians and the central ones, by providing scapegoats. As the 1920s wore on and the economy proved resistant to change for the better, the authorities both small and large could provide gladiator contests for the masses to demonstrate that someone was guilty and would be publicly punished. No explanation was then necessary for the food shortages and long lines because actual wrong-doers had been apprehended and publicly tried. The war scare of 1927 pro-vided external enemies and the show trials from 1928 provided internal ones, just as Stalin had noted in his April 1928 speech on the state of the Soviet Union, "We have external enemies. We have internal enemies."[45]

The trial format thus fostered a Manichean outlook in which the world was divided into prosecution and defense, which in turn became identified with good and evil. The role of the good—the state—was to unmask the evil that was masquerading as ordinary, diligent citizens. The evil resided in the Judas-like Trotsky and his cronies, who were ready to betray the revolution at any moment. The confession of the defendants, then, was neither just a "vicious cruelty" nor an "insane preoccupation with a pointless formality" but rather a central point in the weighing of the sinner, a way to underscore the sinners' precarious position between heaven (symbolized by history's positive judgment) and hell (condemnation to the dustbin of history).[46] The confessions were supposed to provide a fundamental admission of moral and even spiritual guilt.[47]

If the deck was so clearly stacked against them, why did the defendants play their parts in the show trials? First, it must be said that not all of them agreed to appear. Marshal Tukhachevsky and the entire top military leadership were shot without ever being brought to public trial. For individuals in the military there was probably no "game" that could be played; treason was clearly spelled out in the legal codes, and they would be shot no matter how they acted in court, whether they played along or denied their guilt. Other leading Bolsheviks, such as Tomsky and Ordzhonnikidze, committed suicide when the danger of arrest appeared imminent.

For those who did appear in the trials a complex calculus must have given them the hope, however illusory, that perhaps they could be acquitted (whether in the immediate courtroom or in the eyes of history).[48] Stalin and Vyshinsky appear to have deliberately fostered the illusion in early 1936 that defendants could be acquitted if they cooperated with the courts.[49] In the summer of 1936 the top leadership promulgated its new "Stalin Constitution," as it was known at the time, which promised justice and legal guarantees for all. Bukharin, soon to be caught in the crosshairs of Vyshinsky's sights, had, of course, served as chief author of the constitution, at Stalin's suggestion.[50]

Robert Tucker and Stephen Cohen have argued persuasively that Bukharin used his final speech as what they call an "anti-trial" in an attempt to show Stalin's guilt and perhaps the Bolsheviks' own culpability in allowing him to seize power. This makes sense in light of the long history of trials as showpieces. The nineteenth-century revolutionaries had demonstrated what they considered the ultimate heroism by agreeing to speak out against the cruel might of the tsarist state. They could not have known that the early tsarist prosecutors would be singularly incompetent in proving their case. Like David against Goliath or the early Christians against lions in the gladiator pits, they willingly pitted themselves against the authorities. Like these earlier revolutionaries, Bukharin and Rykov must have still regarded the public trial as a place for vigorous debate. Vyshinsky, too, like his tsarist predecessor, could be bested in open court. The heroic defendants could show who were the real "counterrevolutionaries."

The antitrial reversed the moral valence of the show trial without attacking its foundations. It attempted to establish that Stalin had subverted the revolution and hence he had to be resisted by the forces of good. Bukharin, who had been known as the "Benjamin" of the Bolshevik Party, was now the youngest son who resisted the pharaoh.[51] Bukharin, as is well known, did not appear to defend himself. Instead he accepted full moral culpability for the crimes he had allegedly committed and used his time in court to heap scorn and blame on the "counterrevolution," i.e., Stalin and those who chose to follow him.

In the end, though, the defendants had no room to maneuver because Vyshinsky and presiding judge, Vasilii Ulrich, controlled almost the entire proceedings of the trial. Bukharin and Rykov could speak at length about the crimes of the state (albeit in Aesopian language), but in the end that state had the power to find them guilty and have them shot. The Soviet state never allowed any chance that the trial would be bungled as it had been in tsarist times.[52]

Ultimately, the state's ability to overcome the sinner/defendant's resistance provided proof of its power. The very resistance in the Moscow Show Trials that viewers sometimes considered a mistake was necessary to prove that the trial was not entirely scripted and that the state had the power to emerge victorious even when the individual resisted.[53]

Even after the show trials of 1936–38 the trial form proved durable because it contained a certain drama, held out an apparently moral solution, and treated what for Soviet society were paramount issues of inclusion and exclusion. In the 1940s and early '50s the trial took on a new form in what historian Arch Getty refers to as "arraignment meetings" of the party and what Alexei Kojevnikov has studied as the "rituals of Stalinist culture" in academia and especially the sciences.[54] These were no longer trials in the formal sense. There were no prosecution or defense, no judge, no *komendant* guarding the prisoner, and no ritual of rising when the judge entered the room. Still, the core issue was the same: the ritualistic public weighing of a person's or group's conduct or ideas. A "compact collective" (as one of the agitation trial authors had once called them) in the form of either a party organization or an academic institution had to pass judgment on the individual and in the process had itself to pass through the trial intact. A moderator stated the charges; witnesses gave testimony. The subject/object of the trial/discussion was ritually separated from the rest—Kojevnikov calls this a "purgatory." After all the testimony had been heard, the individual ritually concluded his defense with a "solo performance of 'sincere self-criticism.'" He was then assigned a position as either "in" (he was acquitted) or "out" (he was exiled, as in Greek tragedy, excluded from membership in this particular cohort). The process could affect the outcome, depending on the meeting's determination of the sincerity or insincerity of the individual defendant's self-criticism. The fact that the outcome was apparently not predetermined gave the meeting a drama for all the participants. It could appear as a genuine contest, though most people must have recognized that the playing field was far from level.

Like the agitation trial, such a meeting was not difficult to manipulate. The prosecution roles could be given to the strongest orators. The sentence could be written in advance and the improvisation then directed toward that particular outcome. The higher authorities could use the meeting to discipline the members of the institute, both the leaders and the whole collective. Everyone could be chastened for insufficient criticism and self-criticism, for failing to exercise sufficient vigilance. Since there was no standard of "sufficiency," no one could ever prove conclusively that he or she was good enough.

The question is why individuals would participate in such meetings. Obviously those who were the "objects" of the discussion were probably directly coerced. But what of the others? I think the meetings may have worked for the other participants for reasons that shed light as well on the agitation and show trials. The subject matter could *appear* to be debated in a dispassionate, educational fashion when in fact all kinds of political issues were brewing beneath the surface. It is also likely that, as in the agitation trials, the subjects chosen were deliberately marginal ones, ones in which there was not a preexisting consensus but there was room for genuine debate and discussion.[55] Officials and individuals may well have submitted to such discussions (though many tried not to hold them at all) in a genuine belief that without this contest of ideas the party and academia would sink into stagnation, would cease to develop new outlooks, and could not renew themselves.[56] It is possible as well that in a political climate that permitted very little open debate, the party or institute meeting may have seemed a privilege. Only certain people were allowed to hold such discussions; only they could consider the fate of their colleagues. Thus while such *diskussii* might appear with hindsight to be rather cruel, to contemporaries they may have appeared as proof of one's elite status.

The trial as a form (whether an agitation trial, a show trial, or a party discussion) could work on all levels of society. It could attract audiences and participants in an apparently voluntary form. It could work over not only the defendant but also the whole audience and even those hearing about it who did not immediately participate. It could establish boundaries between right and wrong that were so vague that they required constant vigilance and readjudication, thus increasing the power and authority of those holding the trial/discussions. No one was innocent, so everyone could be tried and judged by the collective. Thus, the representatives of the regime could benefit from every trial performed.

Despite the hopes of some of the earlier developers of the agitation trial form that it would contribute to what they called "legal consciousness" (*pravosoznanie*), the opposite in fact occurred.[57] The agitation trial in all its many forms remained primarily a morality play. Often no legal articles were cited in the indictments. Most genuine legal safeguards (as contrasted with legal ritual) were undermined (one thinks here of habeas corpus, the right to genuine defense counsel, the impermissibility of retroactive application of new laws, the promulgation of laws so they would be well known, the right to remain silent, the right to appeal, the inadmissibility of leading questions, and so on). Even more important, the agitation trials could never have genuinely strengthened legal consciousness because of the absence of the whole apparatus of an independent legal profession, independent judges, and an independent media to monitor the actions of the courts. When the alleged truant Dmitri Timofeev Terekhin was tried on stage, the real Dmitri Timofeev Mikriukov sitting in the audience could not bring a libel suit to claim that his identity had been slandered. He had no recourse against the vicious slander of the mock trial.

From the beginning the Bolshevik regime was an example of a theatricalized state. Unfortunately for its citizens, justice and drama did not turn out to make good partners. The regime had manifestly greater power than anything the citizenry could aspire to. This was a regime that could and did manipulate war scares and grain shortages and that invented grandiose, melodramatic international conspiracies to annihilate its political enemies.

A few individuals saw the dangers of the blurring of fact and fiction that was the hallmark of the agitation and show trials. As early as the spring of 1922, David Riazanov, the Marxist scholar and party activist, speaking at the Eleventh Party Congress, opposed what he called the "dramatized trial" (*instsenirovannyi sud*) mounted against trade unionists for having the wrong understanding of their responsibilities. It was not fair, he said, to try "the unfortunate victims" for holding a now outdated view. Party policy had changed. To try people for not being able to change their opinions quickly enough to keep up with the changes in policy, in his view, went "against all laws, against all legal norms."[58] Riazanov was soon marginalized, however, and his voice in these matters silenced.[59]

On the eve of his own trial in 1938, Bukharin also rebelled against this blurring of agitation and show trials, as his biographers have shown. In his last articles he criticized the "political fiction and ideologically fraudulent decoration" of fascist regimes, and above all, the "illusion of mass participation in power."[60] Yet, as we have seen, his protests were in vain because by this time the power of the state to place anyone on trial for any reason had become too great for any individual to resist.

As one of Aleksandr Griboedov's characters says to another in his eighteenth-century play *Woe from Wit*, "I'll tell such a truth about you that it will be worse than any lie." Ultimately, the agitation trials, which were intended to reveal the truth about the new enlightened state, ended up providing a "justice" that was itself far worse than any lie.

APPENDIX

PUBLISHED AGITATION TRIAL SCENARIOS AND INSTRUCTIONS

(Note: "cop." (copies) refers to the numbers of copies printed. I include this information, where available, to give an idea of the size of the editions of the various trials.)

A., B. [Boris Andreev?]. *Sud nad "Nashei gazetoi" (instsenirovka dlia kruzhkov i krasnykh ugolkov)*. Moscow: TsK Soiuza sovtorgsluzhashchikh, 1926. (24 pp.) (3,000 cop.)

Agit-sud nad zaveduiushchim magazinom, nevypolniaiushchim ratsminimuma (minimum ratsionalizatorskikh meropriatii). Moscow: RIO MOSPO, 1930.

Agit-sud nad zaveduiushchim stolovoi (Za plokhoe obsluzhivanie potrebitelia). Moscow: RIO MOSPO, 1930.

Akkerman, A[leksandr] I[osifovich]. *Sud nad prostitutkoi. Delo gr. Zaborovoi po obvineniiu ee v zaniatii prostitutsiei i zarazhenii sifilisom kr-tsa Krest'ianova*. Moscow-Petrograd: Gos. izd-vo, 1922. (58 pp.) (3,000 cop.)

Anatema: Sud nad Anfisoi. Publitsisticheskii ocherk. Krasnoiarsk, 1913. (4 pp.)

Andreev, Boris (Petrovich). "Skhema politsuda nad negramotnym v derevne." In *Samodeiatel'nyi teatr v derevne*, 45–50. Leningrad: knizhnyi sektor GUBONO, 1924.

——. *Sud nad chitatelem*. Leningrad: knizhnyi sektor GUBONO, 1924. (44 pp.) (5,000 cop.)

——. *Sud nad komsomol'tsem ili komsomolkoi narushaiushchimi soiuznuiu distsiplinu*. Leningrad: knizhnyi sektor GUBONO, 1924. (23 pp.) (5,000 cop.)

——. *Sud nad negramotnym*. Leningrad: knizhnyi sektor GUBONO, 1924. (23 pp.) (5,000 cop.)

——. *Sud nad starym bytom. Stsenarii dlia rabochikh klubov ko dniu rabotnits 8-go marta.* Moscow-Leningrad: Doloi negramotnost', 1926 (Preface by G. Avlov) (31 pp.) (3,070 cop.)

Antonov, Maksim. *Sud nad plokhim krest'ianinom. P'esa dlia krest'ianskogo teatra v dvukh kartinakh.* Leningrad: Gos. izd-vo, 1924. (63 pp.) (10,000 cop.)

Avdeev, Vitalii. *Sheptuny i znakhari (instsenirovannyi agitsud nad znakharstvom v trekh kartinakh).* Leningrad: Priboi, 1926. (32 pp.) (8,125 cop.)

Avlov, Gr. *Sud nad khuliganami.* Moscow-Leningrad: Doloi negramotnost', 1927. (56 pp.) (4,000 cop.)

Bogomolov, Dmitrii. *Obez'iannyi sud ili 'Prestuplenie uchitelia Dzhona Klopsa'— Sovershenno neveroiatnoe no deistvitel'noe proisshestvie (komediia v 4 deistvii i 8 kartin).* Moscow: Mosk. Teatral'noe izd., 1926. (3,000 cop.)

Boichevskii, V., V. Malkis, M. Shishkevich. *Sbornik agit-sudy.* Moscow: "Novaia Moskva" (Moskovskii Gubpolitprosvet), 1926. (5,000 cop.)

Bozhinskaia, N. *Sud nad krest'iankoi-delegatkoi.* Moscow-Leningrad: Gos. izd-vo, 1926. (37 pp.) (15,000 cop.)

Brikhnichev. "Sud nad bezbozhnikom (Prestuplenie Stepana Razumskogo)." In *Massovaia rabota v klube,* edited by S. Dolinskii and S. Bergman, 75–85. Moscow: Rabotnik prosveshcheniia, 1924.

D., R. *Sud nad domashnei khoziaikoi.* Moscow-Leningrad: Gos. izd-vo, 1927. (23 pp.) (15,000 cop.)

Demidovich, E. B. *Sud nad gr. Kiselevym po obvineniiu ego v zarazhenii zheny ego gonorreei posledstviem chego bylo ee samoubiistvo.* Moscow-Petrograd: Gos. izd-vo, 1922, 1923. (At head of title: Narodnyi Komissariat Zdravookhraneniia) (54 pp.) (3,000 cop.)

——. *Sud nad polovoi raspushchennost'iu.* Edited and with introduction by Professor A. B. Zalkind. Moscow-Leningrad: Doloi negramotnost', 1927. (40 pp.) (8,000 cop.)

D'iakonova, E. A. *Sud nad golovnei: Agit-komediia s 12 risunkami.* Leningrad: Gos. izd-vo, 1925. (15,000 cop.)

Edel'shtein, A. "Neskol'ko slov o sanprosvetsudakh." Introd. to *Sud nad prostitutkoi,* by A. I. Akkerman (Moscow, 1922), and to *Sud nad gr. Kiselevym,* by E. B. Demidovich (Moscow, 1922).

Frolov, A. E. *Sud nad svin'ei (agitp'esa).* N.p., n.d. [before 1929]. (40 pp.) (1,000 cop.)

Gekhtman, I. "Sud v teatre Shatle." In *Sbornik p'es dlia gorodskikh klubov.* Moscow: Krasnaia nov', 1923. Also in *Proletarskie prazdniki v rabochikh klubakh,* 2nd ed., edited by N. K. Krupskaia, 170–75. Moscow: Krasnaia Nov', 1924.

Gekhtman-Poliakov. "Gadiuka." In *Sbornik agit-p'es dlia derevenskogo teatra,* vyp. 1. Moscow: Krasnaia Nov' (Glavpolitprosvet), 1923, 153–76.

——. "Avdot'ia Likhova (p'esa v trekh deistviiakh)." In *Agit-sbornik na bor'bu s samogonkoi,* edited by Nik. Maslenikov and M. Averbukh, 65–88. Moscow: Krasnaia nov', 1923. (12,000 cop.)

Ginzburg, B. S. *Sud nad mater'iu, podkinuvshei svoego rebenka: Delo gr. Tikhonovoi po obvineniiu v 1) prestupno-nebrezhnom otnoshenii k svoemu rebenku, povlekshem za soboi riad tiazhelykh zabolevanii, [i] 2) ostavlenii rebenka na proizvol sud'by.* Moscow: Zemlia i fabrika, 1924. (At head of title: Otdel Okhrany Materinstva i Mladenchestva NKZdrav) (Introd. by N. Semashko; preface by V. Lebedeva) (63 pp.) (100,000 cop.)

Glebova, N. *Sud nad delegatkoi: Delo po obvineniiu delegatki Tikhonovoi, ne vypolnivshei svoego proletarskogo dolga.* Moscow: Gos. izd-vo, 1924 (32 pp.); 2nd ed., 1925 (43 pp.); 3rd ed., 1926, corrected (46 pp.)

K., S. "Kto vinovat?" In *Sbornik agit-p'es dlia derevenskogo teatra,* vyp. 1, 177–93. Moscow: Krasnaia Nov' (Glavpolitprosvet), 1923.

"K instsenirovaniiu politsudov." In *Iskusstvo v rabochem klube, 96–99.* Moscow: Proletkul't, 1924.

Kalabukhov, and Semen Dolinskii. "Politsud nad fashistami." In *Massovaia rabota v klube,* edited by S. Dolinskii and S. Bergman. Moscow: Rabotnik prosveshcheniia, 1924.

Kurynikha (Sud nad znakharkoi). Leningrad: Priboi, 1925. (24 pp.)

Leizerov, M. *Instsenirovannye professional'nye sudy.* Moscow: Trud i kniga (izd. MGSPS), 1925. (55 pp.) (7,000 cop.)

L[ozhkin], Ia[kov Iakovlevich]. *Sud nad krest'ianinom, uklonivshimsia ot prizyva v Krasnuiu Armiiu.* Kharkov: izd. Voenno-Revoliutsionnogo Soveta Ukrkryma, 1922. (11 pp.) (2,000 cop.)

Malyshev, G. D. *Kak organizovat' sud nad sokhoi. Material dlia massovoi agro-propagandy.* Moscow-Leningrad: Gos. izd-vo, 1925. (32 pp.)

Materialy dlia literaturnogo suda nad Gaponom. Petrograd: izd. Politprosvet upr. P.V.O., 1921. (16 pp.) (2,000 cop.)

Materialy k prazdnovaniiu 51-oi godovshchiny Parizhskoi kommuny. Moscow: izd. Glavnoe upravlenie voenno-uchebnykh zavedenii, 1922. Rossiiskii Gosudarstvennyi Voennyi Arkhiv 9/13/92/34–47ob.

Militsyna, E. *Sud nad negramotnym.* Rostov-na-Donu: Iugo-Vostochnoe kraevoe partiinoe izd. Burevestnik, 1925. (22 pp.)

Mil'shtein, A[ron]. *Prof-sudy (Prof-propaganda).* Moscow: izd. G. F. Mirimanova, 1924. (5,000 cop.)

Mitel'man, R. M. *Sud nad gruppovodom kamenshchikom (Pokazatel'nyi sud).* Edited by S. E. Chaiko, zam. zav. sektorom massovoi kul'tprofsvetraboty TsK VSSR. Moscow: izd. TsK VSSR, 1930. (30 pp.) (3,000 cop.) (At head of title: TsK Vsesoiuznyi Profsoiuz Stroitel'nykh Rabochikh)

Nikolaev, A. *Avio-agitsud.* Moscow: Obshchestvo druzei vozdushnogo flota RSFSR, 1925. (47 pp.) (15,000 cop.)

"Organizatsiia politsuda v derevne." In *Samodeiatel'nyi teatr v derevne, 38–44* (Leningrad, 1924).

Petukhov, P. (Istomin). *Ubiistvo sel'kora (p'esa v 4 deistvii).* Edited by N. P. Goncharova. [Moscow], [1925]. (5,000 cop.)

Platonych, N. *Peremena (p'esa v 3 deistviiakh).* Moscow-Leningrad: Gos. izd-vo, 1926. (64 pp.) (35,000 cop.)

Pletnev, V. F., ed. *Sud nad Zubatovym i Gaponom.* Moscow: Vseross. Proletkul't, 1925. (99 pp.)

"Politsud nad krest'iankoi-delegatkoi. In *Mezhdunarodnyi den' rabotnits,* edited by G. S. Maliuchenko, 31–51. Rostov-na-Donu: Burevestnik, 1925.

"Professional'no-distsiplinarnyi sud nad rabochim, ne vstupivshim v chleny prof-soiuza." In *Prof-sudy (Prof-propaganda)*, by Aron Mil'shtein, 5–29. Moscow: izd. G. F. Mirimanova, 1924.

Rebel'skii, I. V. *Instsenirovannye sudy (kak ikh organizovat' i provodit')*. Moscow: Trud i kniga, 1926. (5,000 cop.)

Reinberg, L. *Instsenirovannye proizvodstvennye sudy*. Moscow: Trud i kniga 1926. (Includes a methodological article, fifteen topics for production trials, and short outlines for their production.) (66 pp.) (5,000 cop.)

Rezvushkin, Ia. *Sud nad bogom (Antireligioznyi sbornik)*. 2nd ed. Moscow-Leningrad: Gos. izd-vo, 1925. (136 pp. of materials, 31 pp. trial) (15,000 cop.)

Roman. "Politsud nad knigoubiitsei." In *Vecher knigi v klube*, edited by V. Aleksan-drov and I. Tsaregradskii, 65–76. Moscow: Novaia Moskva, 1924. (pod red. MK RKSM). (10,000 cop.)

Sigal, B. S. *Sud nad babkoi znakharkoi*. Moscow: Zhizn' i znanie, 1925. (36 pp.) (8,000 cop.)

———. *Sud nad grazhdanami Ivanom i Agaf'ei Mitrokhinymi po vine kotorykh proizoshlo zabolevanie rabochego tuberkulezom*. Moscow: Zhizn' i znanie, 1925.

———. *Sud nad grazhdaninom Fedorom Sharovym po obvineniiu v zarazhenii trip-perom*. Leningrad: Zhizn' i znanie, 1925. (5,000 cop.)

———. *Sud nad Korolevym (posledstviia p'ianstva)*. Moscow: Zhizni i znanie, 1925.

———. *Sud nad mater'iu po obvineniiu v nevezhestvennom ukhode za det'mi i nepri-vitii ospy, povlekshem za soboi smert' rebenka (Sanitarno-prosvetitel'naia ins-tsenirovka dlia derevni)*. [Omsk]: Omskii podotdel okhrany materinstva i mla-denchestva, [1925 or 1926]. (100 cop.)

———. *Sud nad mater'iu vinovnoi v rasprostranenii skarlatiny*. Moscow: Zhizn' i znanie, 1925. (5,000 cop.)

———. *Sud nad p'ianitsei*, 3rd ed. Leningrad: Leningradskaia pravda, 1930. (47 pp.) (30,000 cop.)

———. *Sud nad pionerom-kuril'shchikom i sud nad neriashlivym pionerom (dve in-stsenirovki)*. Moscow: Zhizn' i znanie, 1927. (48 pp.) (10,000 cop.)

———. *Sud nad samogonshchikami*. Moscow: Zhizn' i znanie, 1925. (8,000 cop.)

———. *Sud nad Stepanom Korolevym (posledstvie p'ianstva)*. Moscow: Zhizn' i znanie, 1926. (10,000 cop.)

Subbotin, Leonid. *Sud nad korovoi. Krest'ianskaia p'esa*. Moscow: izd. Novaia derev-nia, 1925.

Sud bespartiinykh rabochikh i krest'ian nad Krasnoi Armiei. Moscow: Krasnaia nov', 1923. Introd. by E. I. Khlebtsevich, library division, PUR. (52 pp.) (5,000 pp.)

Sud nad avariishchikami s parokhoda "Permskii pervenets." Perm': Biulleten' Proku-ratury Kamsk. basseina, 1935. (24 pp.) (1,500 cop.)

Sud nad brakodelami (Opyt organizatsii proizvodstvennogo tekhnicheskogo suda v tip. no. 7 "Iskra revoliutsii" tresta Mosoblpoligraf). Moscow: Gizlegprom, 1933. (72 pp.) (2,000 cop.)

"Sud nad chlenom fabkoma N. I. Egorovym (Instsenirovka)." In *Iskusstvo v rabochem klube*, 100–116. Moscow: Proletkul't, 1924. (5,000 cop.)

"Sud nad chlenom profsoiuza, ne plativshim chlenskii vznos." In *Prof-sudy (Prof-propaganda)*, by Aron Mil'shtein, 30–32. Moscow: izd. G. F. Mirimanova, 1924.

"Sud nad domom Romanovykh." In *Teatral'naia kul'tura. Sbornik statei,* pt. 2, 180. Kiev, 1966. (Performed by the Leningradskii Novyi Teatr in Kiev in the circus building, April 1926.)

"Sud nad fashizmom (Instsenirovka)." In *Iskusstvo v rabochem klube,* 117–39. Moscow: Vseross. Proletkul't, 1924. (5,000 cop.)

Sud nad Ivanom Temnym. Moscow-Leningrad: Doloi Negramotnost', 1927. (Kollektivnyi trud 4-i gruppy B 7-i Voronezhskoi shkoly vtoroi stepeni) (Introd. by M. S. Epshtein) (31 pp.) (5,000 cop.)

Sud nad K. Libknekhtom. Materialy. Petrograd, 1918. (26 pp.)

"Sud nad kaveleristom." In *Klub! Pomogi politruku! Materialy dlia instsenirovok* (prilozhenie k "Krasnoi Rote" no. 12). Kharkov, izd. Voenno-Redaktsionnogo Soveta UVO, 1922. Rossiiskii Gosudarstvennyi Voennyi Arkhiv 9/13/112/58.

"Sud nad kavaleristom, zarazivshim chesotkoi svoiu loshad' i loshad' svoego tovarishcha." N.d., n.p. Rossiiskii Gosudarstvennyi Voennyi Arkhiv 9/13/108/23–26ob. (printed, 10 pp.)

Sud nad komarom (Instsenirovka). N.p., 1926. (29 pp.)

"Sud nad krasnoarmeitsem, ne pozhelavshim obuchat'sia voennomu iskusstvu." In *Sbornik. No. Pervyi. Vecher voennoi propagandy (Materialy dlia kluba).* Nikolaev: Podiv 15, 1922. Rossiiskii Gosudarstvennyi Voennyi Arkhiv 9/13/108/32–37.

"Sud nad krasnoarmeitsem za narushenie prisiagi." In *Klub! Pomogi komandiru i politruku!* Kharkov, izd. Voenno-Redaktsionnogo Soveta UVO, 1923 (prilozhenie k "Krasnoi Rote" no. 17). Rossiiskii Gosudarstvennyi Voennyi Arkhiv 9/13/112/ 241–51.

Sud nad krest'ianinom Medvedevym, sorvavshim vybory kandidatki ot zhenshchin v sel'sovet. Leningrad: Priboi, 1925. (At head of title: Sektor "Rabotnitsa i krest'ianka") (30 pp.) (10,000 cop.)

Sud nad lavochnei komissiei. Moscow: RIO MOSPO, 1930. (At head of title: Moskovskii Oblastnoi Soiuz Potrebitel'skykh Obshchestv) (2,000 cop.)

Sud nad mestnoi korovoi (Agropropaganda po voprosu prigodnosti skota dlia razvedeniia). Moscow: Novaia derevnia, 1923. (8 pp.)

Sud nad narushiteliami truddistsipliny po materialam kinofil'my. Iz opyta kul'traboty Metrostroia. Moscow: Profizdat, 1933.

Sud nad negramotnymi. Tashkent: Turk. Glavpolitprosvet, 1923. (At end of text: Turkestansk. chrezv. kom. po likvidatsii negramotnosti) (9 pp.)

Sud nad nemetskimi merzavtsami. Sudebnyi prosess po delu o zverstvakh nem.-fashist. zakhvatchikov i ikh posobnikov na territorii gor. Krasnodara i Krasnodarskogo kraia v period ikh vremennoi okkupatsii. Sbornik materialov. N.p.: Krasnyi Krym, 1943. (63 pp.)

Sud nad Neriashkinym. [Kiev]: izd. Kievskogo Voennogo okruga, 1921. (28 pp.) (2,000 cop.)

Sud nad pornografiei v literature (Diskussiia, ustroennaia mestkomom pisatelei 17 noiabria 1925 goda v Dome Pechati nad proizvedeniem A. Volzhskogo "Druz'ia po Volge"). Moscow: Vseross. soiuz krest'ianskikh pisatelei, 1926. (47 pp.) (5,000 cop.)

"Sud nad vodkoi," St. Petersburg: Aleksandro-Nevskoe obshchestvo trezvosti pri Voskresenskoi tserkvi "Obshchestva rasprostraneniia religiozno-nravstvennago prosveshcheniia v dukhe Pravoslavnoi Tserkvi," 1904. (4 pp.)

Trukhin, *Sud nad klassom*. N.p., n.d.

Vasilevskie, L. A., and L. M. *Sud nad akusherkoi Lopukhinoi sovershivshei opera-tsiiu aborta, sledstviem chego iavilas' smert' zhenshchiny.* [Moscow]: Oktiabr', 1923. (64 pp.) (3,000 cop.)

——. *Sud nad samogonshchikami. Delo Karpova Tikhona i ego zheny Agaf'i po ob-vineniiu v izgotovlenii i tainoi torgovle samogonkoi.* [Moscow]: Oktiabr', 1923. (52 pp.) (5,000 cop.)

Vedernikov, P. M. *Obshchestvennye sudy v postanovke na osnove kollektivizma tvorchestva kak put' k motivirovaniiu samodeiatel'nosti mass.* (Leningrad-Mos-cow: "Kniga," 1925.

——. *San-sudy v postanovke na osnove kollektivizma tvorchestva, kak put' k ak-tivirovaniiu samodeiatel'nosti mass (Po sledstvennym materialam).* N.p.: izd. Dor-profsozha Riaz.-Ural. zh.d., 1924. (At head of title: Otdel Zdravookhraneniia Riaz.-Ur. zh.d.) (500 cop.)

Vetrov, B., and L. Petrov, *Agitsud i zhivaia gazeta v derevne*, 3–50. Moscow-Leningrad: Gos. izd-vo, 1926. (15,000 cop.)

Vinogradov, V. *Sud nad muzykal'noi khalturoi.* Moscow: Gos. muz. izd., 1931. (45 pp.) (5,000 cop.)

Vsesoiuznyi tekhnicheskii sud nad sbornym zhelezobetonom (27, 28, i 30 marta 1933 g. v Moskve). Moscow: 1933. (At head of title: Postoianoe soveshchanie po sbornym konstruktsiiam Glavstroiproma NKTP SSSR.)

Zamoskvoretskii, V. *Klub rabochei molodezhi.* Moscow: Novaia Moskva, 1924.

UNPUBLISHED AGITATION TRIAL TEXTS AND TRIALS IN PERIODICALS

A. Abramov. "Kak my 'sdelali' sud (Klub Mytishchenskoi gruppy kirpichnykh za-vodov Mossilikata)." *Rabochii zritel'* 22 (1924): 22.

Abserman, "Agitsudy, disputy, i ustgazety" (report at a meeting of the club section of the conference of political education workers in the Tenth Rifle Division, Octo-ber 2, 1923). Rossiiskii Gosudarstvennyi Voennyi Arkhiv 9/13/111/226.

"Agitatsionnye sudy" (Politicheskii otdel 42 str. div.). Printed, n.p., ca. 1921. Rossi-iskii Gosudarstvennyi Voennyi Arkhiv 192/2/559/80.

"Agitsud nad kaptenarmusom-vorom." 1923. Rossiiskii Gosudarstvennyi Voennyi Arkhiv 9/13/113/11.

"Agitsud nad Koalitsionnym Pravitel'stvom." Privo, 1923. Rossiiskii Gosudarstven-nyi Voennyi Arkhiv 9/13/112/182–183; review in 9/13/97/180–180ob. and 9/13/112/265–266ob.

"Agitsud nad konstitutsiei RSFSR" (PU Zapsib). Review in Rossiiskii Gosudarst-vennyi Voennyi Arkhiv 9/13/258/270.

"Agitsud nad mezhdunarodnym imperializmom (izd. PUSKVO)." Rossiiskii Gosudarst-vennyi Voennyi Arkhiv 9/13/112/252–64; review in 09/13/97/214; 09/13/112/361.

"Agitsud nad RSFSR." Reference in Rossiiskii Gosudarstvennyi Voennyi Arkhiv 9/13/111/11–14.

"Agitsud nad samostrelom." Rossiiskii Gosudarstvennyi Voennyi Arkhiv 9/13/108/ 72–73.

"Agitsud nad terarmeitsem, ne iavivshemsia na uchebnye sbory." Rossiiskii Gosudarstvennyi Voennyi Arkhiv 9/13/113/216–17.

Aleko. "Obzor faktov." *Vestnik teatra* 67 (September 7, 1920). (Re: "Sud nad panskoi Pol'shei").

Alotin-Elota, L. "Ekspromptnye sansudy." Typescript, 1926. Gosudarstvennyi Arkhiv Rossiiskoi Federatsii 9636/5/125/1–7.

Berner, N. "Sud nad Saninym." *Entrakt* 3 (1923): 15.

Bogoslovskii, A. A. "Sami kolkhozniki daiut otpor ukloneniiam ot privivok." Typescript, 1933. Gosudarstvennyi Arkhiv Rossiiskoi Federatsii 9636/5/126/1–3.

Borodin A., and D. Dolev, "Kak rabotat' nad malymi formami: V pomoshch' derevenskomu avtoru. Instsenirovannyi sud." *Derevenskii teatr* 12 (1930): 22–24.

G., K. "Sud nad Dantesom." *Krasnaia gazeta,* July 8, 1924, 4.

Gard, Z. "Abort na skam'e podsudimykh." *Krasnaia gazeta,* September 11, 1924, 3.

Garin, Artemii. "Instsenirovka suda." *Pravda,* February 26, 1921.

Iakhnin. "Agitsud, kak forma bor'by s progulami." *Rabochii klub* 1 (1928): 67–69.

"Instruktsiia k postanovke instsenirovannykh sudov." Kharkov: Voenno-Revoliutsionnyi Sovet Ukrkryma, 1922. Rossiiskii Gosudarstvennyi Voennyi Arkhiv 9/13/ 108/15–21. (11 pp.) (1,000 copies)

"Instsenirovannyi sud nad Makhno." *Pravda,* January 6, 1921.

Ioff, L. S. "Obshchestvennyi sud nad bol'nym tripperom, zarodivshem zhenu i rebenka." Typescript, 1930. Gosudarstvennyi Arkhiv Rossiiskoi Federatsii 9636/ 5/127/20–52.

K., E. "Sud pod suflera (Novyi sposob khaltury)." *Krasnaia gazeta,* November 17, 1921, 4.

K., F. "Privet novomu godu." *Pravda,* January 5, 1921.

"Kak postavit' sud nad negramotnym." Typescript, PUKVO, 1922. Rossiiskii Gosudarstvennyi Voennyi Arkhiv 9/13/51/224–25.

Karachunskaia, E. "Sud nad khuliganom." *Rabochii klub* 12 (1926): 37–38.

Kokin. "Sud nad sorokovkoi" (newspaper article). Rossiiskii Gosudarstvennyi Voennyi Arkhiv 34/1/9/76.

"Kommuna 1871 goda (Stsenarii dlia samodeiatel'nogo tvorchestva)." Typescript, OKA, 1922. Rossiiskii Gosudarstvennyi Voennyi Arkhiv 9/13/51/66–68ob.

"Kommunary pered sudom." In *Materialy k prazdnovaniiu 51–oi godovshchiny Parizhskoi kommuny.* Moscow: izd. Glavnoe upravlenie voenno-uchebnykh zavedenii, 1922. Rossiiskii Gosudarstvennyi Voennyi Arkhiv 9/13/92/40–41.

"Konspekt politsuda nad kulakom, zakliuchivshim kabal'nuiu sdelku." *Sputnik politruka* 3 (1922): 37–44. Rossiiskii Gosudarstvennyi Voennyi Arkhiv 9/13/112/ 210–214.

Lebedev, M. "Sud nad karaulom, dopustivshim sozzhenie ssypnogo punkta prodnaloga." Kiev: izd. Politupravlenie Kievskogo Voennogo Okruga, 1921. Rossiiskii Gosudarstvennyi Voennyi Arkhiv 9/13/108/27–30ob. (Preface by the Biuro Voennoi Propagandy K.V.O.) (8 pp.) (1,000 cop.)

Leonov, N. "Agro-sudy." *Derevenskii teatr* 2 (1925): 24–25.

"Neobyknovennoe sobytie v zhizni. Otets Evlampiia." (P'esa-sud v 3-kh kartinakh s prologom) (By the collective labor of the literature kruzhok of the Karl Marx Club in Tbilisi, May 1922). Rossiiskii Gosudarstvennyi Voennyi Arkhiv 9/13/93/101–113; also reference in RGVA 9/13/97/127, 9/13/112/113–113ob.

"Novaia forma agitatsii." *Pravda,* November 21, 1920.

"Obraztsovyi litsud." *Rabochii klub* 5 (1926): 58–59.

"Obzor agitatsionnogo materiala: Instsenirovka agitatsionnykh sudov." *Vestnik agitatsii i propagandy,* November 25, 1920, 25–26.

Peniaev, D. "Sud nad pravleniem kluba (Stalingradskii rudkom, Donbass)." *Klub* 11 (1927): 68–69.

"Pokazatel'nyi sud nad belozelennymi." Mentioned in Rossiiskii Gosudarstvennyi Voennyi Arkhiv 192/1/138/26 (probably not scripted).

Polin, M. "Rabotnitsa ne poseshchaiushchaia obshchikh sobranii (Instsenirovannyi sud)." *Rabochii klub* 8–9 (1925): 20–28.

"Politsud (Instruktsiia)." [1922]. Rossiiski Gosudarstvennyi Voennyi Arkhiv 9/13/51/215–18.

"Politsud nad barakhol'shchikami." SKVO, 1922. RGVA 9/13/51/199–199ob.

"Politsud nad krasnoarmeitsem ne poseshchavshim blagodaria svoei leni i podstrekaniiam zlonamerennykh elementov, zaniatii kruzhka, i vernulsia domoi nichemu ne nauchivshis'." Rossiiskii Gosudarstvennyi Voennyi Arkhiv 9/13/93/207–8ob.

"Politsud nad krest'ianinom, uklonivshemsia ot vneseniia podvornogo naloga." [1922] Rossiiskii Gosudarstvennyi Voennyi Arkhiv 9/13/51/228–231.

"Politsud nad popom Obiralovym." July 1922. Rossiiskii Gosudarstvennyi Voennyi Arkhiv 9/13/51/183–96.

"Politsud nad Pil'sudskim." Rossiiskii Gosudarstvennyi Voennyi Arkhiv 9/13/51/135–137ob.

"Politsud nad voenno-sluzhashchim, vydavshim voennuiu tainu." SKVO, 1922. Rossiiskii Gosudarstvennyi Voennyi Arkhiv 9/13/51/200.

Popov, A. "Sud nad progul'shchikom." *Rabochii klub* 11 (1927): 57–58.

"Primernyi instsenirovannyi politsud nad frantsuzskim ministrom truda Al'bertom Toma." *Politvestnik* 8 (1922): 41–43.

"Primernyi politicheskii sud nad tserkov'iu." Rossiiskii Gosudarstvennyi Voennyi Arkhiv 9/13/51/86–92.

Priokskii. "Sud nad khuliganstvom i izbienniem stenkora," *Rabochii klub* 11 (1925): 80.

"Protokol instsenirovki Politsansuda nad neriashlivym i neradivym krasnoarmeitsem sostoiavsheisia v Krasnodarskom Voennom Gospitale 28 dekabria 1923 goda." Rossiiskii Gosudarstvennyi Voennyi Arkhiv 34/1/8/215–16.

"Put' na skam'iu prestupnikov." 1922. Rossiiskii Gosudarstvennyi Voennyi Arkhiv 9/13/51/94–106.

Rebel'skii, I. V. "Agit-sud po likvidatsii negramotnosti." *Prosveshchenie na transporte* 9–10 (1923): 34–38.

——. "Instsenirovannye sudy (Metodicheskie zametki)." *Kul'turnyi front* 2 (May-June) (1924): 33–38.

Safarov, G. "Sud nad zheltym 'Internatsionalom.'" *Pravda,* July 30, 1920.

"Sanitarnyi sud nad sifilitikom." Razrabotannyi Sanprosvetotdelom Tsentral'nogo

Kommunisticheskogo Kluba Oktiabr'skoi Revoliutsii. [1923] Rossiiskii Gosudarstvennyi Voennyi Arkhiv 9/13/108/2–12.

"Sansud nad rabochim Pavlovym I.S." Typescript, ca. 1934. Gosudarstvennyi Arkhiv Rossiiskoi Federatsii 9636/5/127/90–98.

Shirin, D. "Sud nad negramotnym chasovym." *Krasnaia Armiia* (organ PU Ukrkrym) 399 (July 23, 1922). Rossiiskii Gosudarstvennyi Voennyi Arkhiv 9/13/51/227.

"Skhema part. i politraboty (Rukovodstvo komiacheikam chastei KVO." June 15, 1921. *Listok politrabotnika* 7–8 (June 27, 1921): 110–15.

Sladkovich, S.E. "Skhema suda nad chlenami pravleniia zhiltovarishchestva No. 56300 grazhdanami Primazkinym, Nedozrelovym i Pivovarom po obvineniiu ikh v sposobstvovanii razvitiiu tuberkuleza v sem'e rabochego Chakhotina (Instsenirovka san. suda)." Typescript, n.d. Gosudarstvennyi Arkhiv Rossiiskoi Federatsii 9636/5/127/54–88.

"Stsenarii Agitsuda 'nad T'erom.' " In *Materialy k prazdnovaniiu 51-oi godovshchiny Parizhskoi kommuny.* Moscow: izd. Glavnoe upravlenie voenno-uchebnykh zavedenii, 1922. Rossiiskii Gosudarstvennyi Voennyi Arkhiv 9/13/92/45–47.

"Sud nad Gaponom (Instsenirovka v Gubsude)." *Krasnaia gazeta* January 24, 1924, 4.

"Sud nad klubom." *Rabochii klub* 2 (1924): 30.

"Sud nad komandirom." Rossiiskii Gosudarstvennyi Voennyi Arkhiv 9/13/113/196–99.

"Sud nad krasnoarmeitsem, narushivshim prisiagu." *Klub, pomogi komandiru i politruku,* izd. VRS UVO. Review in Rossiiskii Gosudarstvennyi Voennyi Arkhiv 9/13/112/207.

"Sud nad kulakom, zakliuchivshim kabal'nuiu sdelku." *Sputnik politruka,* izd. MVO. Review in Rossiiskii Gosudarstvennyi Voennyi Arkhiv 9/13/112/207.

"Sud nad Leninym." *Pravda,* April 22, 1920.

"Sud nad Leninym i Trotskim." *Pravda,* February 15, 1921.

"Sud nad negramotnym (Instsenirovka v sviazi s kampaniei po likbezgramote)." Prilozhenie k *Krasnoi Rote,* no. 11. Kharkov, 1922, Voenno-Redaktsionogo Soveta UVO. Rossiiskii Gosudarstvennyi Voennyi Arkhiv 9/13/112/43ob.–46. (1,500 cop.)

"Sud nad neplatel'shchikami chlenskikh vznosov." *Rabotnik prosveshcheniia* 1 (January 1926): 60–63.

"Sud nad novoi zhenshchinoi." *Pravda,* February 20, 1921.

"Sud nad okkupantami Rurskogo basseina." Typescript, 1923, OKA. Rossiiskii Gosudarstvennyi Voennyi Arkhiv 9/13/112/109–110; reviews in ll. 113–113ob. and 9/13/97/127.

"Sud nad Oktiabr'skim perevorotom 1917 goda" (kollektivnyi trud litkruzhka kluba im. "Karla Marksa" rukovoditelia kruzhka Bova i chlena Aleksandrova). Typescript, [1922]. Rossiiskii Gosudarstvennyi Voennyi Arkhiv 9/13/93/143–44.

"Sud nad panskoi Pol'shei." *Pravda,* July 1, 1920.

"Sud nad Parizhskoi kommuny." *Rabochii zritel'* 5 (February 5–12, 1924): 9.

"Sud nad Parizhskoi kommuny." In *Materialy k prazdnovaniiu 51-oi godovshchiny Parizhskoi kommuny.* Moscow: izd. Glavnoe upravlenie voenno-uchebnykh zavedenii, 1922. Rossiiskii Gosudarstvennyi Voennyi Arkhiv 9/13/92/38ob.–40.

"Sud nad p'esami." *Vestnik teatra* 85–86 (March 15, 1921): 4.

"Sud nad politicheskim negramotnym." 1923. Rossiiskii Gosudarstvennyi Voennyi Arkhiv 9/13/108/36–37.

"Sud nad R.K.P." *Pravda,* February 18, 1921.

"Sud nad S. Petliuroi," Kiev military okrug, [1922]. Typescript in Ukrainian. Rossiiskii Gosudarstvennyi Voennyi Arkhiv 9/13/51/69–81. (12 pp.)

"Sud nad samogonshchikom." *Rabochii zritel'* 5 (February 5–12, 1924): 9.

"Sud nad shest'iu rabochimi zavoda 'Krasnyi Oktiabr' vedushchimi agitatsiiu protiv kluba." *Rabochii klub* 2 (1924): 30–32.

"Sud nad Sovetskoi vlast'iu." *Pravda,* December 21, 1920.

"Sud nad starym teatrom." *Vestnik teatra* 89–90 (May 1, 1921): 6.

"Sud nad vinovnikami goloda (ukazaniia dlia instsenirovki)." Kiev VO, 1922. Rossiiskii Gosudarstvennyi Voennyi Arkhiv 9/13/51/219–23.

"Sud nad Vrangelem." *Vestnik teatra* 72–73 (November 1920): 16–17.

"Sud nad zhenshchinami, otkazavshimisia ot pomoshchi golodaiushchemu Povolzhiu." [1921]. Rossiiskii Gosudarstvennyi Arkhiv Sotsial'noi i Politicheskoi Istorii 17/10/76/231–34.

"Sud v Groznom." *Rabochii klub* 3–4 (1924): 85

"Sudebnyi otdel: Bor'ba s prostitutsiei." *Pravda,* August 14, 1921.

"Tekhnika organizatsii primernykh sudov (politicheskikh, istoricheskikh, sanitarnykh i dr.)" PUKVO, [1922]. Rossiiskii Gosudarstvennyi Voennyi Arkhiv 9/13/51/211–14.

Van'ian, G. D. "Agitsud nad gr. Malkinym, Timokhinoi i Baikhovoi, po obvineniiu ikh v narushenii dekreta Sovnarkoma ob obiazatael'nom ospoprivivanii." Typescript, [1933]. Gosudarstvennyi Arkhiv Rossiiskoi Federatsii 9636/5/127/1–19.

"Vinovny li? (Primernyi agitsud nad krest'ianskim komitetom vzaimopomoshchi, v dvukh kartinakh)." *Rabochii klub* 7 (July 1924): 23–31. (3,000 cop.)

"Voenno-politicheskii sud nad Baronom Vrangelem." Typescript, 1922. Rossiiskii Gosudarstvennyi Voennyi Arkhiv 9/13/51/82–84.

"Voenno-politicheskii sud nad neriashlivym krasnoarmeitsem." Printed [Odessa, 1923]. Rossiiskii Gosudarstvennyi Voennyi Arkhiv 9/13/258/77–82. (5 pp.) (700 cop.)

Vokukin, Vlad. "Kak organizovat' sud nad stennoi gazetoi." *Raboche-Krest'ianskii Korrespondent* 4 (February 28, 1927): 8–10.

Zhemchuzhnyi, V., Roman, and Veprinskii. "Politsud nad vinovnikami Imperialisticheskoi voiny." *Pamiatka agitatora* 5 (June–Aug. 1924): 81–125.

"Zhenskii samosud." *Pravda,* November 21, 1921.

ARCHIVES CONSULTED

MOSCOW

Gosudarstvennyi Arkhiv Rossiiskoi Federatsii (GARF, formerly TsGAOR)
    f. 2306, op. 24, dd. 2, 344, 530, 545, 546
    f. 2313, op. 6, d. 87; op. 7, d. 14
    f. 5451, op. 4, dd. 308-310; op. 5, dd. 568, 634

Gosudarstvennyi Tsentral'nyi Teatral'nyi Muzei im. A. A. Bakhrushina (GTsTM)
    f. 150, N. I. Lvov (lichnyi fond)

Politekhnicheskii muzei
    f. 3: records of lectures and performances

Rossiiskii Gosudarstvennyi Arkhiv Ekonomiki (RGAE, formerly Tsentral'nyi Gosudarstvennyi Arkhiv Narodnogo Khoziaistva, TsGANKh)
    f. 1884, op. 3, dd. 56, 63, 85, 153-5; op.70, d. 7
    f. 9474, op. 7, dd. 183-184

Rossiiskii Gosudarstvennyi Arkhiv Literatury i Iskusstva (RGALI)
    f. 998, op. 1, d. 814
    f. 1708, op. 1, dd. 1, 13, 17, 24, 44-45, N. Karzhanskii (lichnyi fond)

Rossiiskii Gosudarstvennyi Arkhiv Nauchno-Tekhnicheskoi Dokumentatsii (RGANTD, formerly part of GARF)
    f. 9636, op. 5, dd. 1-10, 22, 80-89, 111, 113, 117-18, 124-27; op. 7, dd. 1, 13-31

Rossiiskii Gosudarstvennyi Arkhiv Sotsial'noi i Politicheskoi Istorii (RGASPI, formerly Tsentr Khraneniia i Izucheniia Dokumentov Noveishei Istorii, RTsKhIDNI, formerly TsPA)
    f. 17, op. 3, d. 804; op. 60, dd. 1-4, 6, 9, 12, 15, 18-20, 29, 48, 82, 752-53; op.

84, dd. 128-29, 135, 151-52, 263, 265, 309, 420, 421, 443-45, 633, 685-87, 689, 1012
f. 111, op. 22, dd. 70, 101, 152

Rossiiskii Gosudarstvennyi Voennyi Arkhiv (RGVA, formerly TsGASA)
  f. 9, op. 11, d. 13; op. 12, dd. 45, 53; op. 13, dd. 15, 51, 91-93, 97, 108-113, 258
  f. 34, op. 1, dd. 1, 3-5, 7-10; op. 2, d. 44
  f. 90, op. 970, lichnoe delo: A. Shimanko
  f. 192, op. 1, dd. 138-140, 144; op. 2, dd. 506, 537-538, 558-559
  f. 246, op. 2, d. 12, 29, 32, 54, 57, 65, 102, 105, 107-8, 111, 114-16, 120
  f. 37976, op. 1, d. 12101, lichnoe delo: I. V. Korobochkin

Tsentral'nyi Gosudarstvennyi Arkhiv Moskovskoi oblasti (TsGAMO)
  f. 180, op. 1, dd. 262-63, 606
  f. 880, op. 1, dd. 4-7, 17-18, 25-27, 34-35, 39-40, 42, 45, 47, 50, 54, 58, 60, 61, 67, 70-74, 76, 93, 262-63, 606

ST. PETERSBURG

Tsentral'nyi Gosudarstvennyi Arkhiv Oktiabr'skoi Revoliutsii i Sovetskogo Stroitel'stva goroda Leningrada (TsGAORL)
  f. 2552, op. 1, dd. 897-99, 1110-11, 2169, 2497
  f. 4301, op. 1, dd. 798, 801, 1258-59, 1704-6, 1991
  f. 6276, op. 10, dd. 65, 88; op. 11, dd. 473-75, 477; op. 12, dd. 164, 469, 473-74, 573, 636; op. 13, d. 373-78, 413, 420
  f. 6983, op. 1, d. 9

NEW YORK

Bakhmeteff Archives, Columbia University
  Papers of N. A. Gorchakov and G. A. Aleksinskii

The following system of abbreviation is used in Russian archival citations: fond/opis'/delo/list. In other words, the citation RGVA 9/13/51/215–18 would mean fond 9, opis' 13, delo 51, listia 215–18.

The standard Library of Congress transliteration has been used with the exception of names that are customarily used in other forms (for example, Meyerhold instead of Meierkhol'd).

Variations in the spellings of authors and titles have been kept as they appeared in the original publication or archival citation.

All translations, unless otherwise noted, are the author's.

NOTES

Introduction

1. "Plany stat'i 'Ocherednye zadachi sovetskoi vlasti,'" in V. I. Lenin, *Polnoe Sobranie Sochinenii (PSS)* (Moscow, 1958–1965), 36:547.

2. Robert C. Tucker, *Political Culture and Leadership in Soviet Russia* (New York, 1987); also Abbott Gleason, Peter Kenez, and Richard Stites, eds., *Bolshevik Culture* (Bloomington, 1985); Nina Tumarkin, *Lenin Lives! The Lenin Cult in Soviet Russia* (Cambridge, Mass., 1983); Jeffrey Brooks, *When Russia Learned to Read: Literacy and Popular Literature, 1861–1917* (Princeton, 1985); Laura Engelstein, *The Keys to Happiness: Sex and the Search for Modernity in Fin-de-Siècle Russia* (Ithaca, 1992); Mark D. Steinberg, *Moral Communities: The Culture of Class Relations in the Russian Printing Industry, 1867–1907* (Berkeley, 1992); Stephen P. Frank and Mark D. Steinberg, eds., *Cultures in Flux: Lower-Class Values, Practices, and Resistance in Late Imperial Russia* (Princeton, 1994); Joan Neuberger, *Hooliganism: Crime, Culture, and Power in St. Petersburg, 1900–1914* (Berkeley, 1993); Orlando Figes and Boris Kolonitskii, *Interpreting the Russian Revolution: The Language and Symbols of 1917* (New Haven, 1999); Frederick Charles Corney, *Telling October: Memory and the Making of the Bolshevik Revolution* (Ithaca, 2004); Eric Naiman, *Sex in Public: The Incarnation of Early Soviet Ideology* (Princeton, 1997); Michael Gorham, "Tongue-tied Writers: The *Rabsel'kor* Movement and the Voice of the 'New Intelligentsia' in Early Soviet Russia," *Russian Review* 55, no. 3 (1996): 412–29. Several pioneering studies address the agitation trials themselves. Julie A. Cassiday, *The Enemy on Trial: Early Soviet Courts on Stage and Screen* (DeKalb, 2000); Lynn Mally, *Revolutionary Acts: Amateur Theater and the Soviet State, 1917–1938* (Ithaca, 2000); Richard Stites, "Trial as Theatre in the Russian Revolution," *Theatre Research International* 23, no. 1 (1999): 7–13; Claudine Amiard-Chevrel, "Methodes et Formes Specifiques," in *Le Theatre d'Agit-Prop de 1917 a 1932* (Lausanne: La Cite- L'Age d'Homme, 1977), vol. 1, *L'URSS—Recherches*, 52–54.

3. In Russian the relevant terms are *obshchestvennye sudy, primernye sudy, diskussionnye sudy, instsenirovannye sudy,* and *pokazatel'nye sudy* (which also means "show trial"). The diversity of these terms suggests the heterogeneity of the agitation trials' origins. They were not merely "imposed from above" but developed in a rather unorganized fashion. The terms also suggest the degree to which many members of the intelligentsia were thinking of them as a "civic" project (hence the phrases "public trials" and "discussion trials"). Obviously the show trials of living individuals (as opposed to fictional ones) were quite different from agitation trials, a topic to which I will return below.

4. "Sud nad Vrangelem," *Vestnik teatra* 72–73 (November 1920): 16–17; "Obzor agitatsionnogo materiala: Instsenirovka agitatsionnykh sudov," *Vestnik agitatsii i propagandy* 3 (November 25, 1920): 25–26; "Voenno-politicheskii sud nad Baronom Vrangelem" (1922) (typescript); Rossiiskii Gosudarstvennyi Voennyi Arkhiv (RGVA) 9/13/51/82–84. "Agitation" in the 1920s, as in the prerevolutionary period, meant trying to reach and influence the mood of a broad audience by concentrating on one immediate issue. "Propaganda," by contrast, was designed to foster a broader intellectual and organizational understanding of a number of issues. On motivating the masses' activism through trials, see P. M. Vedernikov, *Obshchestvennye sudy v postanovke na osnove kollektivizma tvorchestva kak put' k motivirovaniiu samodeiatel'nosti mass* (Leningrad-Moscow, 1925).

5. A complete list of the agitation trials examined is included in the appendix to this book.

6. Gosudarstvennyi Arkhiv Rossiiskoi Federatsii g. Leningrada 6276/11/474/54.

7. In picking the two lay assessors who were to sit at the bench, the judge in some cases was instructed to tell the audience to choose a woman for one of the two spots. L. A. and L. M. Vasilevskie, *Sud nad samogonshchikami* (Moscow, 1923), v.

8. The issue of telling the truth "without regard for kinship or friendship" is important because it symbolically establishes the hegemony of the state and the court over the ties of the village and family, an issue that will be raised in chapter 4. For discussion of the transition from kinship ties to state hegemony, see Linda J. Nicholson, *Gender and History: The Limits of Social Theory in the Age of the Family* (New York, 1986).

9. "Tekhnika organizatsii primernykh sudov (politicheskikh, istoricheskikh, sanitarnykh i dr.) [1922]," RGVA 9/13/51/212. The normal judicial procedures for court trials were set out in "Polozhenie o sudoustroistve RSFSR," in *Sobranie uzakonenii (SU)* (1922), 69–902; "Grazhdanskii-Protsessual'nyi Kodeks," in *SU* (1923), 46/47–478; and "Ugolovno-Protsessual'nyi Kodeks," in *SU* (1923), 7–106, reprinted in *Sobranie kodeksov R.S.F.S.R.,* 3rd ed. (Moscow, 1925), 617–44, 681–722, 726–99; these are described in John Hazard, *Settling Disputes in Soviet Society* (New York, 1978), 321–27.

10. A. Edel'shtein, "Neskol'ko slov o sanprosvetsudakh," introduction to A. I. Akkerman, *Sud nad prostitutkoi. Delo gr. Zaborovoi po obvineniiu ee v zaniatii prostitutsiei i zarazhenii sifilisom kr-tsa Krest'ianova* (Moscow–Petrograd, 1922), 4.

11. *Klubnaia rabota: Prakticheskaia entsiklopediia dlia podgotovki klubnykh rabotnikov* (Moscow, [1926]), v. 6, 13–18.

12. Vitalii Avdeev, "Poiasneniia k postanovke suda," in *Sheptuny i znakhari (Instsenirovannyi agitsud)* (Leningrad, 1926), 4.

13. "Politsud (Instruktsiia)," RGVA 9/13/51/215–18; P. M. Vedernikov, "Sansudy i ikh postanovka na osnove kollektivizma ispolnitelei," *Krasnyi put'* 19 (November 1924): 97–122; L. Reinberg, *Instsenirovannye proizvodstvennye sudy* (Moscow, 1926), 10.

14. Julia Kristeva, *Powers of Horror: An Essay on Abjection,* trans. Leon S. Roudiez (New York, 1982); also Mary Douglas, *Purity and Danger: An Analysis of Concepts of Pollution and Taboo* (New York, 1966); on "prereflective" views that tend to include "taken-for-granted consensus about values and ends," Nancy Fraser, "What's Critical about Critical Theory? The Case of Habermas and Gender," in her *Unruly Practices: Power, Discourse, and Gender in Contemporary Social Theory* (Minneapolis, 1989), 120, 139–40n. Theater historian Bruce A. McConachie notes that one means authorities have of fostering cooperation is by creating what he calls a "hegemonic we," in which audiences are asked to identify with certain dramatic characters on the basis of certain shared and "taken-for-granted" values. Bruce A. McConachie, "Using the Concept of Cultural Hegemony to Write Theatre History," in *Interpreting the Theatrical Past: Essays in the Historiography of Performance,* ed. Thomas Postlewait and Bruce A. McConachie (Iowa City, 1989), 47.

15. There is an enormous literature on the prerevolutionary intelligentsia's determination to "enlighten" the dark masses, including Stephen P. Frank, "Confronting the Domestic Other: Rural Popular Culture and Its Enemies in Fin-de-Siècle Russia," in *Cultures in Flux,* ed. Stephen P. Frank and Mark D. Steinberg (Princeton, 1994), 74–107; Jeffrey Brooks, *When Russia Learned to Read: Literacy and Popular Literature, 1861–1917* (Princeton, 1985); Reginald E. Zelnik, *Labor and Society in Tsarist Russia: The Factory Workers of St. Petersburg, 1855–1870* (Stanford, 1971); Nancy Mandelker Frieden, *Russian Physicians in an Era of Reform and Revolution, 1856–1905* (Princeton, 1981), and "Child Care: Medical Reform in a Traditionalist

Culture," in *The Family in Imperial Russia,* ed. David L. Ransel (Urbana, 1978), 236–59; John F. Hutchinson, *Politics and Public Health in Revolutionary Russia, 1890–1918* (Baltimore, 1990).

16. Stephen Kotkin, *Magnetic Mountain: Stalinism as a Civilization* (Berkeley, 1995), esp. 198–237.

17. *Selections from the Prison Notebooks of Antonio Gramsci,* ed. Quintin Hoare and Geoffrey Nowell Smith (New York, 1971), esp. 12–13, 52–59, 104, 130–33, 165, 168, 170–71, 181–82, 202–5, 206–9, 238–39, 247, 258–65, 267–68, 365–67, 403.

18. Ibid., 258, 247, 350.

19. Clifford Geertz, *Negara: The Theater State in Nineteenth-Century Bali* (Princeton, 1980); see also Geertz, "Centers, Kings, and Charisma: Reflections on the Symbolics of Power," in his *Local Knowledge: Further Essays in Interpretive Anthropology* (New York, 1983), 121–46. In the latter essay Geertz develops the useful notion of a "cultural frame" (143) in which all political authority must operate. In the Russian context the great scholars of theatricality as it relates to both everyday life and politics are Yuri Lotman and Boris Uspensky, whose oeuvre is enormous. More recently some preliminary work on the interconnections between theater, ritual, politics, and culture has been done in Cassiday, *Enemy on Trial;* James von Geldern, *Bolshevik Festivals, 1917–1920* (Berkeley, 1993); Harriet Murav, *Russia's Legal Fictions* (Ann Arbor, 1998); Katerina Clark, *Petersburg, Crucible of Cultural Revolution* (Cambridge, Mass., 1995); A. Antonov-Ovseenko, *Teatr Iosifa Stalina* (Moscow, 1995); Mark Von Hagen, *Soldiers of the Proletarian Dictatorship: The Red Army and the Soviet Socialist State, 1917–1930* (Ithaca, 1990); Andrei Sinyavsky, *Soviet Civilization: A Cultural History,* trans. Joanne Turnbull (New York, 1990); Svetlana Boym, *Common Places: Mythologies of Everyday Life in Russia* (Cambridge, Mass., 1994); Sheila Fitzpatrick, *The Cultural Front: Power and Culture in Revolutionary Russia* (Ithaca, 1992); Spencer Golub, *The Recurrence of Fate: Studies in Theatre History and Culture* (Iowa City, 1994). See also the important essays in the special issue on "Language and Meaning in Russian History," *Russian Review* 55, no. 3 (1996): Mark Steinberg, "Stories and Voices: History and Theory," 347–54; Caryl Emerson, "New Words, New Epochs, Old Thoughts," 355–64; and the articles by James von Geldern, Diane P. Koenker, and Michael Gorham.

20. Victor Turner, "Are There Universals of Performance in Myth, Ritual, and Drama?" in *By Means of Performance: Intercultural Studies of Theatre and Ritual,* ed. Richard Schechner and Willa Appel (Cambridge, 1990), 8; also Turner, *The Anthropology of Performance* (New York, 1987).

21. Lenin, "O kharaktere nashikh gazet," in *Sochineniia,* 4th ed. (Moscow, 1942), 78–80.

22. Leon Trotsky, "The Newspaper and Its Readers" (first published in *Pravda,* July 1, 1923), in *Problems of Everyday Life* (New York, 1973), 126–27.

23. Lenin, *PSS,* 4:407–8, cited in Yuri Feofanov and Donald D. Barry, *Politics and Justice in Russia: Major Trials of the Post-Stalin Era* (Armonk, N.Y., 1996), 314.

24. "Plany stat'i 'Ocherednye zadachi sovetskoi vlasti'" (March 1918), in *PSS,* 36:547.

Chapter 1. A Question of Origins

1. "Sud nad vodkoi" (St. Petersburg: Aleksandro-Nevskoe obshchestvo trezvosti, 1904).

2. Anatema (pseud.), *Sud nad Anfisoi. Publitsisticheskii ocherk* (Krasnoiarsk, 1913). The original play of *Anfisa* was published in *Literaturno-khudozhestvennye al'manakhi izdatel'stva "Shipovnik,"* kn. 11 (St. Petersburg, 1909), and performed in 1910 by the Nezlobin Theater in Moscow. See *Teatral'naia entsiklopediia* (Moscow, 1967), 1:204–5. Trials of Anfisa seem also to have been staged in Taganrog (December 1909), in Tbilisi (January 1910), and in Kutaisi (Georgia, February 1910): "Sud nad Anfisoi," *Priazovskaia rech'* Taganrog, December 9, 1909, and "Sud nad Anfisoi," *Taganrogskii vestnik,* December 9, 1909, listed in *Leonid Nikolaevich Andreev: Bibliografiia,* ed. V. N. Chuvakov (Moscow, 1998), 563; Zritel', "Sud nad Anfisoi," *Zakavkaz'e* 37 (1910), cited in L. A. Saribekova, "Leonid Andreev i Gruziia (1900–1919 gg.)," in *Leonid Andreev: Materialy i issledovaniia* (Moscow, 2000), 332–33. A literary circle in Kharkov also put on a trial of Ekaterina Ivanovna, another title character of Andreev's, in February 1913, declaring her insane. See *Utro,* February 16, 1913, mentioned in Leonid Andreev,

Sobranie Sochinenii (Moscow, 1994), 4:628. These trials by the public of his main characters (Anfisa and Ekaterina Ivanovna) apparently pleased Andreev. See V. Beklemisheva, in *Rekviem: Sbornik pamiati Leonida Andreeva* (Moscow, 1930), 242, cited in Andreev, *Sobranie Sochinenii*, 4:628–29). My thanks to Richard Davies for these references. Andreev himself had begun life as a chronicler of court cases. See *Leonid Nikolaevich Andreev: Bibliografiia*, vyp. 1, 210–13.

3. "Anathema" is the title character in another Andreev play.

4. Anatema (pseud.), *Sud nad Anfisoi*, 6.

5. Ibid., 8.

6. *Ocherednye zadachi politprosvetitel'noi raboty Glavpolitprosveta* (Kharkov: izd. Politupravleniia vsekh vooruzhennykh sil Ukrainy i v Krymu, 1921), 2–3; Ia. V. Ratner, "Iz istorii Sovetskogo teatra (1917–1919 gg.)," *Istoriia SSSR* 6 (November–December 1962): 115–25.

7. "Sud nad Vrangelem," *Vestnik teatra* 72–73 (November 1920): 16–17; B. El'tsin, "Ocherednye zadachi, formy i metody agitatsii (tezisy) [ca. Oct. 1921]," Rossiiskii Gosudarstvennyi Arkhiv Sotsial'noi i Politicheskoi Istorii (RGASPI) 17/84/151/70–71.

8. D. El'kina, "Predislovie" in V. A. Nevskii, *Massovaia politiko-prosvetitel'naia rabota revoliutsionnykh let. Kriticheskii obzor vazhneishikh form agitatsii i propagandy* (Moscow-Leningrad: izd. Ts.K.Zh.D. "Gudok," 1925), 3. This was echoed in later studies: "We would look for the originator in vain. The form of the trial . . . was born spontaneously; it arose somewhere in the depths of popular amateur theater [*samodeiatel'nost'*]. A. Makarov, "Ob etom sbornike," in Vsevolod Vishnevskii, *Stat'i, dnevniki, pis'ma* (Moscow, 1961), 16.

9. I. V. Rebel'skii, "Agit-sud po likvidatsii negramotnosti," *Prosveshchenie na transporte* 9–10 (1923): 34–38; *Klubnaia rabota. Prakticheskaia entsiklopediia dlia podgotovki klubnykh rabotnikov* (Moscow: Proletkul't, [1926]), 6:13.

10. E. N. Medynskii, *Entsiklopediia vneshkol'nogo obrazovaniia. Lektsii, chitannye na pedagogicheskikh fakul'tetakh Ural'skogo universiteta v 1920–1922 gg. i vtorogo Moskovskogo universiteta v 1922–1924 gg.*, vol. 2, *Otdel'nye vidy sodeistviia vneshkol'nomu obrazovaniiu* 2nd ed. (revised) (Moscow-Leningrad: Gos. izd-vo, 1925), 161–62.

11. V. N. Vsevolodskii-Gerngross, *Istoriia russkogo teatra* (Leningrad-Moscow: Teakinopechat', 1929), 397; P. M. Vedernikov, *Obshchestvennye sudy* (Leningrad-Moscow: Kniga, 1925), 5.

12. I. V. Rebel'skii, *Instsenirovannye sudy (kak ikh organizovat' i provodit')* (Moscow: Trud i kniga, 1926), 10–13. In the Soviet era Rebel'skii worked for Tsentragit, for the party's agitprop section, and for Glavpolitprosvet. *Pravda*, April 22, 1920; RGASPI 17/60/18/30; 17/84/151.

13. Nevskii, *Massovaia politiko-prosvetitel'naia rabota*, 45.

14. Although the plays were supposed to combat Jesuit influence, in fact, they often borrowed heavily from the Jesuits, who also had judgment and trial scenes in their plays.

15. P. O. Morozov, *Istoriia russkogo teatra do poloviny XVIII stoletiia* (St. Petersburg, 1889); V. I. Rezanov, *Iz istorii russkoi dramy. Shkol'nyia deistva XVII–XVIII vv. i teatr iezuitov* (Moscow: izd. Imperatorskago obshchestva Istorii i Drevnostei Rossiiskikh pri Moskovskom Universitete, 1910); A. Beletskii, *Starinnyi teatr v Rossii* (Moscow: T-va V. V. Dumnov, nasl. br. Salaevykh, 1923). Berlin director Max Reinhardt was also interested in medieval mystery plays in this period, and Russian directors were much influenced by him. See James von Geldern, *Bolshevik Festivals, 1917–1920* (Berkeley 1993), 23–25.

16. This scene served as a prologue in many Western European mysteries as well as in Jesuit morality plays. See I. M. Badalich and V. D. Kuz'mina, *Pamiatniki russkoi shkol'noi dramy XVIII veka (po Zagrebskim spiskam)* (Moscow, 1968), 11.

17. "Rozmova vo kratse o dushe greshnoi, sud priniavshei ot sudii spravedlivago Khrista Spasitelia," in Morozov, *Istoriia russkogo teatra*, 112–13.

18. Ts. G. Neiman, "Sud bozhii nad dushoi greshnika, iuno-russkaia religioznaia drama kontsa XVII st.," *Kievskaia starina* 6 (June 1884): 289–305.

19. Notes of I. A. Dmitrievskii, in O. A. Derzhavina, A. S. Demin, "Dmitrii Rostovskii, *Kaiushchiisia greshnik*," in *Russkaia dramaturgiia poslednei chetverti XVII i nachala XVIII v.*, ed. O. A. Derzhavina (Moscow, 1972), 202–19, 335–37. A. N. Veselovskii published the play in *Stariinyi teatr v Evrope* (Moscow, 1870).

20. Badalich and Kuz'mina, *Pamiatniki*, 12–13. Icons of the Last Judgment and the weighing of sins would have been known to every Russian, both in churches and also in popular images placed in the Red Corner of the house, as well as in texts of the Saints' Lives. See ibid., 28; Jeffrey Brooks, *When Russia Learned to Read: Literacy and Popular Literature, 1861–1917* (Princeton, 1985), 22–27.

21. V. Dubovskii, *Sud nad greshnoi dushoi* (Biblioteka bezbozhnika, no. 3) (Moscow, [1924]). This, of course, was intended for atheistic rather than religious purposes.

22. Speaking names obviously carried over from eighteenth-century secular drama as well. For more on this, see David J. Welsh, *Russian Comedy, 1765–1823* (The Hague, 1966), 62–66, 18–19, 42–49; Elise Kimerling Wirtschafter, *The Play of Ideas in Russian Enlightenment Theater* (DeKalb, Ill., 2003). On the general subject of *oblichenie* and *raskaianie*, see Oleg Kharkhordin, *The Collective and the Individual in Russia: A Study of Practices* (Berkeley, 1999). Kharkhordin's work makes a great leap from the medieval practices of the Russian Orthodox Church to the Soviet era, without (to my mind) adequately explaining the possible reasons for his comparisons between the two types of practices. It is entirely possible that the political instructors in the early Soviet era, in choosing to try out agitation trials as a method of instruction, imbibed not only the forms of the medieval church but also much of its mentality. Thus the decision to revive the trial as a didactic form of dramaturgy may well have brought with it much of the *mental content* of that form, with its emphasis on sins (*grekhi* and *greshki*), public denunciation of those sins (*oblichenie*), repentance (*raskaianie*), and public admonition (*poritsanie*).

23. *The Hasidic Anthology: Tales and Teachings of the Hasidim,* ed. Louis I. Newman (New York, 1934), 5, 56–59, 167–70, 401; "Sud nad Bogom," in *Evreiskie narodnye skazki: predaniia, bylichki, rasskazy, anekdoty,* originally collected by E. S. Raize; reedited with introduction and commentary by Valerii Dymshits (St. Petersburg, 1999), 150–54, 441–43; Anson Laytner, *Arguing with God: A Jewish Tradition* (Northvale, N. J., 1990), xiv–xxi. Elie Wiesel has also written a brilliant play, *The Trial of God (As It Was Held on February 25, 1649 in Shamgorod),* trans. Marion Wiesel (New York, 1979).

24. Zvi Y. Gitelman, *Jewish Nationality and Soviet Politics: The Jewish Sections of the CPSU, 1917–1930* (Princeton, 1972), 300–1; Gitelman, *A Century of Ambivalence* (New York, 1988), 118.

25. Publicly organized debates over religion were frequently reported in the early Soviet press: "Neobychainyi miting," *Pravda,* October 27, 1920; "Sud nad dukhovenstvom," *Pravda,* November 5, 1920; "Disput," *Pravda,* November 10, 1920; "V Klube im. Maksima Gor'kogo (Rogozhsko-Simon. raion)," *Pravda,* February 11, 1921; "Disputy po religii," *Pravda,* September 15, 1921. For more on debates over religion, see Richard Stites, *Revolutionary Dreams: Utopian Vision and Experimental Life in the Russian Revolution* (New York, 1989), 107, 110; Glennys Young, *Power and the Sacred in Revolutionary Russia: Religious Activists in the Village* (University Park, Pa., 1997); William B. Husband, *"Godless Communists": Atheism and Society in Soviet Russia, 1917–1932* (Dekalb, Ill., 2000).

26. Ia. Rezvushkin, *Sud nad bogom (Antireligioznyi sbornik),* 2nd ed. (Moscow-Leningrad: Gos. izd-vo, 1925); *Komsomolskaia Paskha* (Moscow: Novaia Moskva, 1924).

27. The leading sources on jury trials include Alexander K. Afanas'ev, "Jurors and Jury Trials in Imperial Russia, 1866–1885," in *Russia's Great Reforms, 1855–1881,* ed. Ben Eklof, John Bushnell, and Larissa Zakharova (Bloomington, Ind., 1994), 214–30; Jörg Baberowski, *Autokratie und Justiz: zum Verhältnis von Rechtsstaatlichkeit und Rückständigkeit im ausgehenden Zarenreich 1864–1914* (Frankfurt am Main, 1996); Richard S. Wortman, *The Development of a Russian Legal Consciousness* (Chicago, 1976); Eugene Huskey, *Russian Lawyers and the Soviet State: The Origins and Development of the Soviet Bar, 1917–1939* (Princeton, 1986); Samuel Kucherov, *Courts, Lawyers, and Trials under the Last Three Tsars* (Westport, 1974). For discussion of the fascination with jury trials and the connection between law and literature, see Harriet Murav, *Russia's Legal Fictions* (Ann Arbor, Mich., 1998).

28. Huskey, *Russian Lawyers,* 107–12; N. A. Troitskii, *Tsarizm pod sudom progressivnoi obshchestvennosti, 1866–1895* (Moscow, 1979), 183.

29. V. Dal', *Tolkovyi slovar' zhivago velikorusskago iazyka* (St. Petersburg-Moscow,

1882), 4:355n.; Alexander Solzhenitsyn, *The Gulag Archipelago* (New York, 1973), 287. The one positive proverb (probably dating from after 1864) was "Now all are equal before the courts as they are before God."

30. Dal', *Tolkovyi slovar',* 4:355–56; V. Dal', *Poslovitsy russkago naroda: Sbornik* (Moscow, 1862), 169–75.

31. *Sud Shemiakin s izobrazheniem deistvuiushchikh lits i s priobshcheniem nravouchitel'nykh basen* (Moscow, 1794). The story can be found in Serge A. Zenkovsky, ed., *Medieval Russia's Epics, Chronicles and Tales* (New York, 1963, 1974), 449–52; *Russian Fairy Tales,* ed. Aleksandr Afanas'ev (New York, 1945), 625–27.

32. E. V. Lavrova and N. A. Popov, eds., *Narodnyi teatr* (Moscow, 1896), 23, 176–184. "Shemiakin sud" continued to be performed and recommended throughout the 1920s. See V. Smyshliaev, "Doklad v Teatral'noi sektsii Vtoroi Obshchegorodskoi konferentsii Kul'turno-Prosvetitel'nykh organizatsii," in *Gorn* (Moscow: Mosk. Proletkul't, 1920), 5:84; Glavnyi politiko-prosvetitel'nyi komitet, khudozhestvennyi otdel, *Repertuarnyi ukazatel'* (Moscow: Mosk. Teatral'noe izd. 1925), 121–22.

33. Other pre-Reform writers who commented on the iniquities of the courts included Radishchev, Krylov, Pushkin, Gogol, Nekrasov, Herzen, Dobroliubov, Ostrovskii, Saltykov-Shchedrin, and Sukhovo-Kobylin. See I. T. Goliakov, *Sud i zakonnost' v khudozhestvennoi literature* (Moscow, 1959), 81–183; Murav, "The Theater of Sukhovo-Kobylin," in *Russia's Legal Fictions.*

34. *Prisutstvennyi den' ugolovnoi palaty. Sudebnye stseny iz zapisok chinovnika ochevidtsa* (Leipzig: E. I. Kasprowicz, 1874) (preface, 1853); Huskey, *Russian Lawyers,* 14. The archives contain an early Soviet dramatization based on Aksakov's work: M. S. Narokov, "Ugolovnaia palata" (typescript, n.d.), Rossiiskii Gosudarstvennyi Arkhiv Literatury i Iskusstva (RGALI) 2016/3/142.

35. Alexander Herzen, the famous revolutionary thinker, told Aksakov in 1857 that he considered the play a "work of genius." After much discussion he persuaded Aksakov to let him publish it in his *Poliarnaia zvezda (The Northern Star)* in 1858. See I. V. Porokh and Vl. I. Porokh, "Gertsen i I. Aksakov na rubezhe 50–60kh godov XIX v.," in *Revoliutsionnaia situatsiia v Rossii v seredine XIX veka: deiateli i istoriki,* ed. M. V. Nechkina (Moscow, 1986), 9:85–102.

36. Wortman, *Development,* 260; Rebel'skii, *Instsenirovannye sudy,* 11; on the practice of moot courts among students, Huskey, *Russian Lawyers,* 138; on the popularity of the *mirovoi sud* and jurists' hopes that it would teach people the law, Joan Neuberger, "Popular Legal Cultures: The St. Petersburg *Mirovoi Sud,*" in *Russia's Great Reforms,* ed. Ekloff et al., 231–46.

37. Troitskii, *Tsarism pod sudom,* 223; Huskey, *Russian Lawyers,* 212–14; V. R. Leikina-Svirskaia, *Russkaia intelligentsiia v 1900–1917 godakh* (Moscow, 1981), 78–85; cf. Murav, *Russia's Legal Fictions,* 78–79 (on the otherwise negative view of lawyers).

38. Some of the most famous trials of revolutionaries continued to be cited as materials for agitation trials in the 1920s—for example, "Sud nad Veroi Zasulich," in "Otzyv o materialakh k instsenirovannym sudam [1923]," Rossiiskii Gosudarstvennyi Voennyi Arkhiv (RGVA) 9/13/97/109. Speeches of famous trial defendants (including Karl Marx and Vera Zasulich) continued to be published in the Soviet era; see, for example, A. V. Tolmachev, ed., *Podsudimye obviniaiut* (Moscow, 1962).

39. Leikina-Svirskaia, *Russkaia intelligentsiia,* 80.

40. Franco Venturi, *Roots of Revolution: A History of the Populist and Socialist Movements in Nineteenth-Century Russia* (Chicago, 1960); Murav, *Russia's Legal Fictions,* 57–58; Troitskii, *Tsarizm pod sudom,* 292–335; Troitskii, *Tsarskie sudy protiv revoliutsionnoi Rossii* (Saratov, 1976); M. Lemke, *Politicheskie protsessy v Rossii 1860–kh gg.* (Moscow-Leningrad, 1923); M. N. Kovalenskii, *Russkaia revoliutsiia v sudebnykh protsessakh i memuarakh* (Moscow, 1924). For examples of famous speeches, A. G. Timofeev, *Ocherki po istorii krasnorechiia* (St. Petersburg, 1899); Lutskii, *Sudebnoe krasnorechie* (St. Petersburg, 1913); *Sudebnoe krasnorechie v Rossii: kriticheskie ocherki* (St. Petersburg, 1900); *Molodaia advokatura,* vol. 1 of *Sbornik rechei po politicheskim protsessam A. M. Aleksandrova, V. V. Berenshtama, F. A. Vol'kenshteina i dr.* (St. Petersburg, [1909]).

41. M. Kovalenskii, *Russkaia revoliutsiia v sudebnykh protsessakh i memuarakh* (Moscow: Mir, 1923).

42. G. V. Plekhanov, "To Russian Society [1879]," cited in Venturi, *Roots of Revolution*, 607.

43. Cited in Huskey, *Russian Lawyers*, 36.

44. V. I. Lenin, "Katorzhnye pravila i katorzhnyi prigovor" (1901), in *Polnoe sobranie sochinenii (PSS)*, 5th ed. (Moscow, 1960–65), 5:294.

45. Lenin, letter to E. D. Stasova (January 1, 1905), *PSS*, 9:169–72. He also urged the Bolshevik deputies to the Fourth State Duma who were on trial in 1914 "to use the open doors of the courtroom to lay out directly the views of the social democratic movement." See Lenin, "Chto dokazal sud nad RSDR fraktsiei?" *Sochineniia* 4th ed. (Moscow, 1941), 21:150.

46. Murav, "Dostoevsky's *Diary:* A Child Is Being Beaten," in *Russia's Legal Fictions*; Fedor Dostoevskii, "Dnevnik pisatelia," in *Polnoe sobranie sochinenii v tridtsati tomakh* (Leningrad, 1972–1990), vols. 22–25; Goliakov, *Sud i zakonnost'*, 210–30. Court scenes appear in Dostoevsky's novels *Crime and Punishment, The Brothers Karamazov,* and *The Idiot.*

47. Mikhail Bakhtin wrote extensively about the court in Tolstoy's *Resurrection* in "Ideologicheskii roman L. N. Tolstogo," in M. M. Bakhtin, *Sobranie sochinenii* (Moscow, 2000), 2:185–204, especially the ways in which the whole novel is constructed as "a social trial" (*sotsial'nyi sud*).

48. M. Gorky, *Sobranie sochinenii v vosemnadtsati tomakh* (Moscow, 1960–63), v. 4.

49. *Sudebnye Dramy: zhurnal s illiustratsiiami* (monthly, from 1898).

50. Interestingly, Andreev (1871–1919) himself had begun his university studies as a law student but quit before graduating. Leonid Andreev, *King Hunger,* trans. Eugene M. Kayden (Sewanee, Tenn., 1973). Andreev's play *Seven Who Were Hanged* also contains a trial scene. On July 23, 1920, theater historian and activist Nikolai L'vov staged *King Hunger* and its third act, "The Trial of the Hungry," in the club of the Aleksandrovskaia Railway in Moscow (GTsTM 150/1/5/8), so it evidently still had resonance in the Soviet period.

51. Gabriella Safran, "Revolutionary Rabbis: S. An-sky, Hasidic Legend, and the Hero of Words after 1905" (unpublished manuscript); many thanks to the author for sharing her work and her thoughts.

52. S. Ansky, *The Dybbuk and Other Writings* (New York, 1992), xxvi, 212n. An-sky was also friends with I. L. Peretz, a Jewish writer who published *The Trial of the Wind* based on a Midrashic legend. For a modern adaptation see Samuel J. Citron, *A Peretz Trio: Three Plays* (New York, 1964), and "Bontse Shvayg" (the story of a poor mortal who has to appear before the Heavenly Tribunal), in *The I. L. Peretz Reader,* ed. Ruth R. Wisse (New Haven, 2002, 146–52). Like Andreev and An-sky, Peretz had trained as a lawyer, and even worked as one until the tsarist government disbarred him in response to an anonymous denunciation.

53. *Sud nad "Saninym" v Germanii* (St. Petersburg: izd. V. I. Rotenshterna, 1909).

54. Of course, as in all of Europe, Russians were deeply disturbed by the trials of Dreyfus (1894 and 1899), Wilde (1895), and Beilis (1911). On the Beilis trial, see Laura Engelstein, *The Keys to Happiness: Sex and the Search for Modernity in Fin-de-Siècle Russia* (Ithaca, 1992), 300–301, 324–26, 334; Hans Rogger, *Jewish Policies and Right-Wing Politics in Imperial Russia* (Berkeley, 1986), 40–55; *Delo Beilisa: Stenograficheskii otchet* (Kiev, 1913).

55. The Soviet authorities created an "Extracurricular Department" (*Vneshkol'nyi otdel*) almost immediately after coming to power. See T. A. Remizova, *Kul'turno-prosvetitel'naia rabota v RSFSR, 1921–1925 gg.* (Moscow, 1962), 4; T. A. Remizova, ed. *Kul'turno-prosvetitel'naia rabota v SSSR* (Moscow, 1974), 45. The fact that this department was organized so quickly after the seizure of power suggests both its importance to the early government and also perhaps the leaders' confidence that this was one area where they had some prior experience.

56. Scott J. Seregny, "Zemstvos, Peasants, and Citizenship: The Russian Adult Education Movement and World War I," *Slavic Review* 59, no. 2 (2000): 290–316; Susan Bronson, "Enlightening the Urban Poor: Adult Education in late Imperial Russia, 1859–1914" (Ph.D. diss., University of Michigan, 1995), and Bronson, "Enlightening the Urban Poor: The Adult Education Movement and the Conference of 1908," *East/West Education* 13, no. 2 (1992), 89–107; Gary Thurston, *The Popular Theatre Movement in Russia, 1862–1919* (Evanston, Ill.,

1998); E. N. Medynskii, *Vneshkol'noe obrazovanie. Ego znachenie, organizatsiia i tekhnika*, 2nd rev. ed. (Moscow: Nauka, 1916); V. A. Zelenko, *Praktika vneshkol'nogo obrazovaniia v Rossii*, 3rd rev. ed. (Moscow-Leningrad: Gos. izd-vo, 1923).

57. S. An-sky, who wrote various versions of the *Trial of God*, also wrote a long treatise, *Narod i kniga: Opyt kharakteristiki narodnago chitatelia* (Moscow: Universal'noe knigoizda-tel'stvo L. A. Stoliar, 1914). In this work An-sky points out that peasants particularly liked literature that had a moral to it *(pouchitel'naia)*,while workers liked stories that were realistic (71, 76, 88). Both peasant and worker audiences tended to interact with characters as if they were real people, often asking what happened to a particular character after the story was over (79–81). In the Soviet era the term "extracurricular education" continued to be used until the middle of 1920 when it was renamed "political-educational work" *(politichesko-prosvetitel'naia rabota)*. Zelenko, *Praktika vneshkol'nogo*, 11.

58. Esther Kingston-Mann, *In Search of the True West: Culture, Economics, and Problems of Russian Development* (Princeton, 1999).

59. *Trudy Pervago Vserossiiskago s"ezda deiatelei obshchestv narodnykh universitetov i drugikh prosvetitel'nykh uchrezhdenii chastnoi initsiativy* (1908), quoted in Thurston, *Popular Theatre*, 236.

60. On the complex turmoil of the late nineteenth and early twentieth centuries, see especially Brooks, *When Russia Learned to Read*; Engelstein, *Keys to Happiness*; Stephen P. Frank and Mark D. Steinberg, eds., *Cultures in Flux* (Princeton, 1994).

61. On extracurricular education as a protest against traditional education, see Anita B. Baker, "Rural Education in Russia: *Vneshkol'noe obrazovanie* and the Cooperatives," *Slavic and European Education Review* 1 (1977): 10–21; Ronald Hideo Hayashida, "The Pedagogy of Protest: Russian Progressive Education on the Eve of Revolution," *Slavic and European Education Review* 2 (1978): 11–30.

62. One Soviet author has argued that in the period 1905–1917 the Kharkov Society influenced the extracurricular work of the whole country (Remizova, ed. *Kul'turno-prosvetitel'naia rabota*, 27–28). This has important bearing on the history of the agitation trials since a large number of the very earliest trials in the Red Army came from Kharkov and, to a lesser but still significant extent, Kiev. The Moscow and Petersburg Literacy Committees were both closed by the tsarist government in 1895; only the Kharkov Society lasted until 1917 (Zelenko, *Praktika vneshkol'nogo*, 33–34).

63. Victoria E. Bonnell, *Roots of Rebellion: Workers' Politics and Organizations in St. Petersburg and Moscow, 1900–1914* (Berkeley, 1983), 328–34, 402–4.

64. G. A. Khaichenko, *Russkii narodnyi teatr kontsa XI–nachala XX veka* (Moscow, 1975), 255. On the role of the intelligentsia in these years, Leikina-Svirskaia, *Russkaia intelligentsiia*. This Congress particularly recommended the use of art (including the performing arts) as a method for social development (Zelenko, *Praktika vneshkol'nogo*, 52).

65. The Soviet historiographical insistence that prerevolutionary political movements and clubs were strictly segregated into bourgeois, conservative, and radical in this period appears to be false. Future research will undoubtedly show the degree to which, in addition to learning about mock trials, the Bolsheviks were learning a wide range of techniques from movements across the political spectrum.

66. One author in 1918 criticized this "unfortunate term" ("vneshkol'nik") on the grounds that it came into use in 1914 primarily among zemstvo staff members. (The zemstva were regional organizations of self-government introduced in Russia in 1864; the Bolsheviks disdained them on the grounds that they tended to be philanthropists and liberals rather than revolutionaries.) E. A. Zviagintsev, *Slovar' vneshkol'nago obrazovaniia* (Moscow: izd. Narodnyi uchitel'*, 1918), 18.

67. Vladimir Antonov-Ovseenko (1884–1939), a leading Bolshevik who had served initially in the tsarist army, organized a Club for Rational Recreation (*Klub razumnykh razvlechenii*) in 1910. In the Soviet era Antonov-Ovseenko went on to become an organizer of the Red Army in Ukraine and southern Russia in 1917–19, and the head of the Political Administration of the Red Army (PUR) from August 1922 to January 1924. Soviet authorities were still using the term "rational recreation" in 1920 and 1921; "Primernyi ustav Rabochago [*sic*]

Kluba" (1920), Gosudarstvennyi Arkhiv Rossiisskoi Federatsi (GARF) 5451/4/308/50–51. For an overview of the different clubs and especially the "Obshchestvo sodeistviia ustroistvu obshcheobrazovatel'nykh razumnykh razvlechenii," see *Klubnaia rabota. Prakticheskaia entsiklopediia,* 2:1–5. One defendant in an agitation trial in 1924, a certain Mr. Bezchestnov (meaning "dishonorable" or "dishonest"), was sentenced to provide the equipment for a "rational cinema" *(razumnogo kino)* in the village he had allegedly corrupted with his drunkenness (GARF 9636/5/124/107).

68. N. Timkovskii, "O repertuare narodnogo teatra," *Zhurnal dlia vsekh* 4 (1898), 441. The best overviews of the nineteenth-century popular theater movement can be found in E. Anthony Swift, *Popular Theater and Society in Tsarist Russia* (Berkeley, 2002); Thurston, *Popular Theatre;* Khaichenko, *Russkii narodnyi teatr.*

69. One Proletkult activist, B. Arbatov, referred to the theater as "the factory of the skilled person." "Voennye shkoly. Teatral'naia rabota v voennykh uchebnykh zavedeniiakh, 1920–1924," GTsTM 150/1/5. Lidiia Armand, an activist involved in theater by and for the cooperatives, also advocated using the theater to spread particular ideas (such as those of the cooperatives), to reform those inclined toward drink and gambling, and to draw in those with high ideals who could further the cause even if they were not interested in the economics of cooperatives. See "Narodnyi teatr i kooperatsiia," in L. Armand and A. Evdokimov, *Narodnyi teatr i kooperatsiia (Doklady teatral'nomu s"ezdu v Moskve)* (Moscow, 1916), 3–14.

70. Konstantin Rudnitsky, *Russian and Soviet Theater, 1905–1932* (New York, 1988), 41. As Anthony Swift points out in *Popular Theater,* popular theater was often the site of conflicts among many different groups in society.

71. V. V. Tikhonovich, *Narodnyi teatr. Posobie dlia rezhisserov, instruktorov i rukovoditelei narodnykh teatral'nykh kursov,* vyp. 1, *Sushchnost' i znachenie narodnago teatra* (Moscow: izd. Teatral'nogo knizhnago sklada V. Magnussen, 1918), 18.

72. Swift, *Popular Theater,* 131–80; Patricia Herlihy, *The Alcoholic Empire: Vodka and Politics in Late Imperial Russia* (Oxford, 2002); Stephen P. Frank, "Confronting the Domestic Other: Rural Popular Culture and Its Enemies in Fin-de-Siècle Russia," in *Cultures in Flux,* ed. Frank and Steinberg; S. Varb, "Obshchestvenno-pedagogicheskoe znachenie deiatel'nosti popechitel'stv o narodnoi trezvosti," *Vestnik vospitaniia* 8 (1898); V. Ivanovich, "God deiatel'nosti popechitel'stva narodnoi trezvosti," *Vestnik vospitaniia* 8 (1904): 51–58; "Ustav Nevskago Obshchestva ustroistva narodnykh razvlechenii," *Narodnyi teatr. Sbornik* ([ca. 1896]), 31–42. The theater work of the temperance societies also had many critics, including Ivan Shcheglov, *V zashchitu narodnago teatra (Zametki i vpechatleniia)* (St. Petersburg: tipografiia V. Kirshbauma, 1903).

73. Vrach Putilov, "Razbor p'es, odobrennykh dlia narodnykh i soldatskikh teatrov," *Deiatel'* 11 (1898): 507–30. Enlightenment activists were very concerned about soldiers' theater in general: Ivan Shcheglov, "Po povodu detskikh i soldatskikh teatrov (Sluchainaia zametka)," in *Narodnyi teatr,* ed. Lavrova and Popov, 69–85; also a listing of plays for soldiers ibid., xxiii–xxiv.

74. Ivanovich, "God deiatel'nosti"; Swift (*Popular Theater,* 69–70) notes that between 1899 and 1909 the Guardianships spent roughly 8,600,000 rubles on 47,000 theater performances with 18 million viewers. Other sources on the Guardianship of Popular Temperance include Herlihy, *Alcoholic Empire,* 7, 14–35; Swift, *Popular Theater,* 134, 153–57; Gary Thurston, "The Impact of Russian Popular Theatre, 1886–1915," *Journal of Modern History* 55 (June 1983): 238; Medynskii, *Entsiklopediia vneshkol'nogo obrazovaniia,* 288–89.

75. Ivan Shcheglov, *Narod i teatr. Ocherki i izsledovaniia sovremennago narodnago teatra* (St. Petersburg: izd. P. P. Soikina, [1911? or 1914?]), 106. One Red Army officer, a certain Kin, commented at a meeting of heads of agitprop sections on October 23, 1921, that the tsarist army ("the old army," as he called it) had in fact experimented with different games and riddles as a way of interesting soldiers. RGVA 9/13/15/122ob.; also "Vneshkol'noe obrazovanie," *Bol'shaia Sovetskaia Entsiklopedia* (BSE)(Moscow, 1930), 11:680.

76. *Klubnaia rabota. Prakticheskaia entsiklopediia,* 2:1–9.

77. N. K. Krupskaia, "Narodnyi dom" (1919), in *Pedagogicheskie sochineniia* (Moscow, 1957), 8:24.

78. Ibid.; Lenin, *PSS,* 36:535–36; Maksim Gorkii, "O p'esakh" (1933), in *Sovetskie dramaturgi o svoem tvorchestve. Sbornik statei* (Moscow, 1967), 16.

79. One cannot help remembering viewers' shocked reactions in the early glasnost years (1986–91) to the first plays and films that dealt with prostitution and family dramas, especially "The House under the Starry Sky" and "Little Vera."

80. B. Bentovin, "Prostitutki v osveshchenii sovremennoi russkoi stseny," in Filos', *Stsena i prostitutsiia,* trans. from German (St. Petersburg: tip. L. D. Saper', 1910), 57–101. The nine plays he discussed included Gorkii, *Na dne;* V. Trakhtenberg, *Fimka;* S. Naidenov, *Steny;* S. Iushkevich, *V gorode;* I. Platon, *Liudi;* Sh. Ash, *Bog Mesti;* K. Folomeev, *Zlaia iama;* V. Protopopov, *Padshiia;* and L. Andreev, *Dni nashei zhizni.* For discussion of Bentovin (1865–1929) and his role in the prostitution debates before and after 1905, see Engelstein, *Keys to Happiness,* esp. 289–90; also 160–61, 293–97.

81. Jane Addams, *Twenty Years at Hull-House* (New York: Macmillan, 1910). For a discussion of the close friendship and collegial relations between Addams and educator John Dewey, see Louis Menard, *The Metaphysical Club: A Story of Ideas in America* (New York, 2001), 307–30.

82. William W. Brickman, ed., *John Dewey's Impressions of Soviet Russia and the Revolutionary World* (New York, 1964), 16. Dewey himself claimed (ibid., 98) that the idea for what he called "auto-organization" arose first in the American schools and then served to stimulate Russian development. This term was undoubtedly translated into Russian as *samodeiatel'nost',* which is usually translated as "amateur theater" but which refers more generally to any kind of independent learning and activity.

83. Ibid., 16, 75; Thomas Woody, *New Minds: New Men? The Emergence of the Soviet Citizen* (New York: Macmillan, 1932), 46–47; Bronson, "Enlightening the Urban Poor."

84. William W. Brickman, "Soviet Attitudes toward John Dewey as an Educator," in *John Dewey and the World View,* ed. Douglas E. Lawson and Arthur E. Leon (Carbondale, Ill., 1964), 64–136; *Internatsional'nye problemy sotsial'noi pedagogiki,* ed. S. A. Levitin (Moscow: Gos. izd-vo, 1920), sbornik II-i, for examples of "the newest tendencies in the theory and practice of international pedagogy" being published in the rival journal *Russkaia shkola* from 1914 to 1917.

85. Krupskaia, "Narodnoe obrazovanie i demokratiia" (1916), *Pedagogicheskie sochineniia,* 1:249–350.

86. Cited in Richard Courtney, *Play, Drama and Thought: The Intellectual Background to Drama in Education* (New York, 1968), 42.

87. The American Institute of Child Life, *The Dramatic Instinct in Children* (Philadelphia: American Institute of Child Life [ca. 1913]); Percival Chubb, *Festivals and Plays in Schools and Elsewhere* (New York and London: Harper & Brothers, 1912); Emma Viola (Sheridan) Fry, *Educational Dramatics; A Handbook on the Educational Player Method* (New York: Moffat, Yard and Company, 1913); Elnora W. Curtis, *The Dramatic Instinct in Education* (Boston: Houghton Mifflin Co., 1914); Elizabeth Erwin Miller, *The Dramatization of Bible Stories; An Experiment in the Religious Education of Children* (Chicago, Ill.: The University of Chicago Press [ca. 1918]); see also Rachel Fordyce, *Children's Theatre and Creative Dramatics: An Annotated Bibliography of Critical Works* (Boston: G. K. Hall, [1975]); Addams, *Twenty Years,* 162–90; Menard, *Metaphysical Club,* 308. For a list of thirteen articles and books published on this subject in Russia between 1911 and 1916, see *Ukazatel' literatury po voprosam vneshkol'nogo obrazovaniia i kooperativnogo prosveshcheniia vzroslykh, podrostkov i detei* (Moscow: tip. N. A. Sazonova, 1919), 59–60.

88. Evelyne Hilliard, Theodora McCormick, and Kate Oglebay, *Amateur and Educational Dramatics* (New York: Macmillan, 1917); Percy MacKaye, *The Civic Theatre* (New York: Mitchell Kennerly, 1912); George A. McPheters, *Citizenship Dramatized: A Bit of Brightening for the Study of Civil Government* (New York: H. Holt, 1921). Of the Russian authors writing about dramatization in schools and clubs, the most prominent is P. M. Kerzhentsev, *Tvorcheskii teatr,* 4th ed. (Petrograd: Gos. izd-vo, 1920), 126–33. As von Geldern has noted, both Kerzhentsev and A. A. Gvozdev, another writer on festivals, were much influenced by MacKaye's work. A. A. Gvozdev, "Massovye prazdnestva na zapade," in Gvozdev, ed., *Massovye*

prazdnestva na zapade (Peterhof, 1926), 48–50; von Geldern, *Bolshevik Festivals,* 27–28. Also V. Popov, "Dramatizatsiia kak metod politicheskogo vospitaniia," in *Na tret'em fronte* (Perm', 1923), 2–3, on school dramatizations of current events in the early 1920s.

89. Kh. Finlei Dzhonson (Finlay-Johnson), "Dramatizatsiia, kak metod prepodovaniia," *Svobodnoe vospitanie* 6 (1914–15), 37–44; 7 (1914–15), 67–88; 9 (1914–15), 71–84. In England her work was published as *The Dramatic Method of Teaching* ([S.I.]: Nisbet, n.d.). Krupskaia also published in *Svobodnoe vospitanie,* so she would almost certainly have read this article. It was also included in later Soviet-era bibliographies (e.g., *Ukazatel' literatury po voprosam vneshkol'nogo obrazovaniia,* 59).

90. Finlei Dzhonson [Finlay-Johnson], "Dramatizatsiia," 9, 79.

91. For rich descriptions of the Russian people's "love affair" with the theater, their hunger to be involved as amateur actors and as passionate audiences, see N. A. Gorchakov, *Istoriia sovetskogo teatra* (New York, 1956), 59–63; Victor Shklovskii, *Khod konia* (Moscow-Berlin, 1923), 59; Rudnitsky, *Russian and Soviet Theater,* 41–46.

92. V. A. Zelenko, *Kak ustroit' politicheskii klub* (Moscow: Kniga i zhizn', 1917), 7, 12. In the Soviet era V. A. Zelenko served as rector of the Institute of Extracurricular Education in Petrograd. On the connection between Russian political clubs and the French Revolution, see also E. Khersonskaia (starshaia), *Diskussii i disputy v klubakh* (Moscow: Krasnaia nov', 1924), 4; "Rabochie kluby i zadachi klubnoi sektsii," *Vneshkol'noe obrazovanie,* 1 (1918): 23; S. S. Komissarenko, *Klub kak sotsial'no-kul'turnoe iavlenie: Istoricheskie aspekty razvitiia* (St. Petersburg, 1997), 139–40. On clubs in England as a model, see V. A. Nevskii, "Prakticheskie zaniatiia so vzroslymi po obshchestvennym naukam," in Zelenko, *Vtoroi sbornik statei po Vneshkol'nomu Obrazovaniiu,* 2nd ed. (Kazan': Gos. izd-vo Kazanskoe otdelenie, 1921), 35–55; and in New York City, V. Buk, "Samoupravliaiushchiesia kluby mal'chikov v N'iu-Iorke," *Svobodnoe vospitanie* 11–12 (1908–9).

93. Borovich, *Detskii klub (Istoriia odnogo opyta)* (Kharkov: Kul'turno-Prosvetitel'naia Organizatsiia "Trud," 1919), 5.

94. One of the prerevolutionary educators most indebted to Tolstoy by her own admission was Krupskaia: "Lev Tolstoi v otsenke frantsuzskogo pedagoga" (1912), in *Pedagogicheskie sochineniia,* 1:196–200; Robert H. McNeal, *Bride of the Revolution: Krupskaya and Lenin* (Ann Arbor, 1972), 21–25. Pavel Gaideburov (1877–1960), an activist in the popular theater movement, also wrote about the value of teaching through improvisation. "Tvorcheskaia igra. Improvizatsionnyi metod N. F. Skarskoi," *Vneshkol'noe obrazovania* 6–8 (1919): 38–40. He later played an important role in the Petrograd division of extracurricular education, where he trained many of the amateur theater activists of the early Soviet era. Von Geldern, *Bolshevik Festivals,* 119–22; Lynn Mally, *Revolutionary Acts: Amateur Theater and the Soviet State, 1917–1938* (Ithaca, 2000), 33–34.

95. For an excellent overview, see Mary Stuart, "'The Ennobling Illusion': The Public Library Movement in Late Imperial Russia," *The Slavonic and East European Review* 76, no. 3 (1998): 401–40.

96. According to information compiled by the librarians of the Russian State Library in St. Petersburg, Borovich was actually the pseudonym of Boris Osipovich Finkel'shtein. Borovich remained in library work throughout his life.

97. Borovich, *Detskii klub,* 5. In addition to these values, the organizers spoke often of conveying the values of "civic habits [*grazhdanskie navyki*] and a comradely spirit." Ibid., 10, 7, 16; Borovich, "Grazhdanskoe vospitanie detei," in *Sputnik lektora. Plany, tezisy, literatura,* ed. Borovich, Sbornik 1 (Kharkov: Kul'turno-Prosvetitel'naia Organizatsiia "Trud," 1919), 55–62.

98. Borovich, *Detskii klub,* 91–94. Borovich states in his preface that the book was originally written in 1914. Parts of it were published in B. Borovich, "Bor'ba s ulitsei," *Psikhologiia i deti,* 6–8 (1917).

99. Borovich, *Detskii klub,* 109.

100. Borovich later went on to author one of the earliest pamphlets on dramatizing trials in the Soviet era: *Instsenirovki kak metod prosvetitel'noi raboty* (Kharkov: Kul'turno-Prosvetitel'naia Organizatsiia "Trud," 1923).

101. Nevskii, "Prakticheskie zaniatiia," 40. Nevskii knew all this from personal experience since he had worked among railroad employees and textile workers in Kostroma province before 1917, as well as organizing soldiers' committees and teaching courses for agitators from the February Revolution (1917) on. As head of the provincial literacy organization (*gubono*) in Kostroma after October 1917, he developed lists of books, brochures, and methodologies to help librarians, reading hut organizers, and agitators in the Red Army. Iu. S. Pertsovich, "Vladimir Aleksandrovich Nevskii," *Sovetskaia bibliografiia* 6 (1978): 49–50.

102. Nevskii, "Prakticheskie zaniatiia," 42; Nevskii also cites P. A. Bliakhin, "O politicheskikh instsenirovkakh," *Sbornik Kostromskogo Proletkul'ta* 2 (1919), 53–54. In the postrevolutionary period Borovich also recommended staging public meetings as a way of interesting the audience (*Instsenirovki kak metod,* 13).

103. Russia under Peter the Great had also known such disputations and school plays. The latter, very much like the agitation trials in the Soviet era, focused on demonstrating the contrast between the bad old days (*prezhde*) and the glorious new ones (*nyne*). See Richard Wortman, *Scenarios of Power: Myth and Ceremony in Russian Monarchy* (Princeton, 1995), 1:48, 64–65, 69; V. Vsevolodskii (Gerngross), *Istoriia teatral'nogo obrazovaniia v Rossii* ([St. Petersburg?]: izd. Direktsii imperatorskikh teatrov, 1913), 17.

104. Nevskii took his information from several articles in the liberal journals, including I. Ozerov, "Rabochie kluby v Anglii," *Russkaia mysl'* 4, 2 (1898): 1–20. For more on the practice of mock Parliaments in clubs in England, see also V. A. Zelenko, *Kak ustroit',* 21–22, and "Vneshkol'noe obrazovanie," in *BSE,* 11:692–94.

105. Nevskii, "Prakticheskie zaniatiia," 45.

106. Nevskii, of course, was absolutely correct in asserting that liberals blamed many of Russia's woes on villagers' communal ownership of property and collective responsibility. For fascinating discussion of this subject see Horace W. Dewey and Ann M. Kleimola, "Suretyship and Collective Responsibility in Pre-Petrine Russia," *Jahrbucher fur Geschichte Osteuropas* 18 (1970): 337–54. For some of the nineteenth-century debates see Esther Kingston-Mann, "Peasant Communes and Economic Innovation: A Preliminary Inquiry," in *Peasant Economy, Culture, and Politics of European Russia, 1800–1921,* ed. Esther Kingston-Mann and Timothy Mixter (Princeton, 1991), 23–51; see also Moshe Lewin, "Customary Law and Russian Rural Society in the Post-Reform Era," *Russian Review* 44, no. 1 (1985): 1–19, and the commentaries by Christine Worobec, George Yaney, and Michael Confino, *Slavic Review* 44, no. 1 (1985): 21–43; Boris Mironov, "The Russian Peasant Commune after the Reforms of the 1860s," *Slavic Review* 44, no. 3 (1985): 438–67; Stephen P. Frank, "Popular Justice, Community, and Culture among the Russian Peasantry, 1870–1900," *Russian Review* 46, no. 3 (1987): 239–65.

107. Rolland's study *Le theatre du peuple* was translated into Russian as *Narodnyi teatr* in 1910.

108. Romain Rolland, "Narodnyi teatr" in *Sobranie sochinenii* (Moscow, 1958), 14:254.

109. Lunacharskii, "O massovykh prazdnestvakh," *Vestnik Teatra* 62 (April 27–May 2, 1920): 4–5. Of course, it was not Robespierre who originally made this comment, but rather Rousseau in his "Letter to D'Alembert" (1758).

110. Lynn Mally notes this as well in her work on "small forms" in the theater, *Revolutionary Acts.*

111. Although I have found no evidence directly linking these directors and the agitation trials, it is interesting that Meyerhold was the first to receive a letter in fall 1920 describing *The Trial of Wrangel* in the Kuban, a region he himself had only just left. See chapter 2 for more on this. In 1924 V. Ardov wrote a newspaper article containing a fantasy of a trial of Meyerhold's production of an Ostrovsky play (discussed in chapter 9). Sergei Eisenstein, the great film director, was also nearby. He was serving on the Western front in the region around Smolensk at just the time that a young theater director named Nikolai Karzhanskii was staging agitation trials with his local acting troupe. SeeAndrei Nikitin, *Moskovskii debiut Sergeia Eizenshteina: Issledovanie i publikatsii* (Moscow, 1996), 19, 194n.; A. Fevral'skii, *Moskovskie vstrechi* (Moscow, 1982), 72; N. Karzhanskii, *Kollektivnaia dramaturgiia. Material dlia rabot dramaticheskikh studiei i kruzhkov* (Moscow, 1922); for Karzhanskii's biography, RGALI, 1708/1/1.

112. For an overview of some of these ideas see von Geldern, *Bolshevik Festivals,* 15–71;

Spencer Golub, *Evreinov: The Theater of Paradox and Transformation* (Ann Arbor, 1984) and Golub, *The Recurrence of Fate: Studies in Theatre History and Culture* (Iowa City, 1994); Katerina Clark, *Petersburg, Crucible of Cultural Revolution* (Cambridge, Mass., 1995), 77–80; Betsy F. Moeller-Sally, "The Theater as Will and Representation: Artists and Audience in Russian Modernist Theater, 1904–1909," *Slavic Review* 57, no. 2 (1998): 350–71. Karzhanskii, *Kollektivnaia* (7–12) claimed that the theaters tried to revive Commedia dell'arte in the years 1913–15 with only minimal success. On the other hand, local groups at the popular level often improvised melodramas on holidays, such as Christmas (*sviatki*) and Shrovetide (the traditional Carnival time) (*maslennitsa*), especially the "farewell to winter" (*proshchanie s zimoi*). This last may have had an important influence on *The Trial of 1920* (see chapter 3).

113. Evreinov also created a Starinnyi teatr, which played for two seasons (1907–8 and 1911–12). In the first season they put on two medieval plays, one a miracle play (*Deistvo o Teofile*) and the other a morality play (*Nyneshnie brat'ia*). *Teatral'naia entsiklopediia*, 4:1081.

114. Zhiul'en T'erso [Julienne Tiersot], *Prazdnestva i pesni frantsuzskoi revoliutsii,* trans. K. Zhikharevoi (P[etrograd]: izd. "Parus," 1917).

115. Nietzsche's *Birth of Tragedy* was published in Russian in 1903; Wagner's *Art and Revolution* in 1906. Golub, *Recurrence of Fate,* 12; Claudine Amiard-Chevrel, *Les symbolistes russes et le theatre* (Lausanne, 1994).

116. N. A. Gorchakov, "Evreinov" and "Research Notes on Nikolai Evreinov" in the Bakhmeteff archive, "N. A. Gorchakov," box 7, 103–11 and box 8, folder 16. For secondary sources see Sharon Marie Carnicke, *The Theatrical Instinct: Nikolai Evreinov and the Russian Theater of the Early Twentieth Century* (New York, 1989); Golub, *Evreinov;* Julie A. Cassiday, *The Enemy on Trial: Early Soviet Courts on Stage and Screen* (DeKalb, Ill., 2000), 10, 13–19.

117. Ivan Shcheglov, "Po povodu detskikh i soldatskikh teatrov (Sluchainaia zametka)," in *Narodnyi teatr,* ed. Lavrova and Popov, 69; Nikolai Popov, "O repertuare narodnago teatra (Zametki)," in *ibid.,* 237.

118. *Vneshkol'noe obrazovanie,* 2–3 (1919): 170, cited in Nikolai A. Gorchakov, *The Theater in Soviet Russia* (New York, 1957), 418; *Vestnik teatra* 23 (1919): 3, cited in Rudnitsky, *Russian and Soviet Theater,* 54.

119. "Kakoi teatr nam nuzhen?" *Komsomol'skaia pravda,* August 12, 1925, cited in Rudnitsky, *Russian and Soviet Theater,* 117.

120. V. Belousov, *Sergei Esenin, Literaturnaia khronika* (Moscow, 1969), 1:170–74, 279 (my thanks to Ulrich Schmid for this reference); Matvei Roizman, *Vse, chto pomniu o Esenine* (Moscow, 1973), 102–7.

121. Roizman, *Vse, chto pomniu,* 107.

122. Quoted in E. Naumov, *Sergei Esenin: Zhizn' i tvorchestvo* (Leningrad, 1960), 96.

123. Ibid.

124. Since Esenin and the Imaginists in this period adamantly opposed political interference in the arts, it is possible that they chose this form in part to protest the one-sidedness of official Soviet control. Ibid., 91–96.

125. Also, as von Geldern has shown, many of the popular theater activists who had pioneered methods that would influence Soviet festivals and theater fell afoul of the Soviet authorities almost as soon as the latter came to power (*Bolshevik Festivals,* 122–23 and notes).

126. Attacks on Dewey became particularly virulent after his decision to side with Trotsky in criticizing the Moscow Show Trials of 1936–38.

127. Richard Pipes, *Russia under the Bolshevik Regime* (New York, 1994), 305, 353; L. Tamashin, *Sovetskaia dramaturgiia v gody grazhdanskoi voiny* (Moscow, 1961); N. A. Gorchakov, *Istoriia sovetskogo teatra* (New York, 1956).

128. E. A. Zviagintsev, *Slovar' vneshkol'nago obrazovaniia* (Moscow: izd. Narodnyi uchitel', 1918); Kerzhentsev, *Tvorcheskii teatr,* 35–36, 43, 83. In the Soviet era, Krupskaia, for example, refers to these same principles when suggesting that reading huts should occasionally dramatize trials for local audiences. "Kak dolzhna vesti izba-chital'nia propagandu sel'skokhoziaistvennykh znanii" (1922), in *Pedagogicheskie sochineniia,* 8:64–65. Krupskaia herself acknowledged that she had gained the skills needed for later political education work

through her work in extracurricular education before 1917. "Piat' let raboty v vechernykh Smolenskikh klassakh" (1929), ibid., 1, 55; "Vystuplenie na pervom s"ezde klubnykh rabotnikov" (1924), ibid., 8:102–11.

129. Khersonskaia, *Diskussii i disputy*, 8, 12. On Capri in 1909–10 the Russian Social Democratic Labor Party in exile also had students work on debates with representatives from other parties in order to practice their rhetorical and polemical skills. Michael David-Fox, *Revolution of the Mind: Higher Learning among the Bolsheviks, 1918–1929* (Ithaca, 1997), 33.

130. N. G. Vinogradov-Mamont, *Krasnoarmeiskoe chudo* (Leningrad, 1972).

131. Krupskaia, "K voprosu o shkol'nykh sudakh" (1911), in *Pedagogicheskie sochineniia*, 1:130–34.

132. She made this comment in a letter accompanying the article that she sent from Paris to the editor of the journal *Svobodnoe vospitanie* on June 3, 1911. Ibid., 485n.

133. This, of course, was the dilemma over "victor's justice" at the Nuremberg Trials in 1945. Harriet Murav, in *Russia's Legal Fictions*, 78–84, also quotes the famous jurist A. F. Koni and others on the danger of jury trials' turning into spectacles. As will become evident in later chapters, their concern that everyone in a public trial could be subject to abuse and denigration correctly foresaw just what would happen in the Soviet era.

134. Krupskaia, "K voprosu." Krupskaia was rather ambivalent about school self-government in general. She ended one article on the subject with an expression of pity for the "poor school children—they [the schools] work over their souls so." "O shkol'nom samoupravlenii," *Svobodnoe vospitanie* 12 (1914–15): 19–30.

Chapter 2. Experimental Trials in the Red Army, 1919–20

1. "Literaturnyi sud 'Mest' sudby,'" *Revolutsionnyi front* 1 (February 15, 1920): 28–29, reprinted in *Russkii sovetskii teatr, 1917–1921: Dokumenty i materialy,* ed. A. Z. Iufit (Leningrad, 1968), 317.

2. G. Shubin, "Rabota klubov v Zapchasti" *Politrabotnik* 10 (November 1920): 4–7; A. I. Fuks, "K voprosu o metodakh proizvodstvennoi propagandy," *Pravda,* January 15, 1921; "Novye formy i metody agitpropagandy," *Pravda,* March 16, 1921; "Obzor agitatsionnogo materiala: Instsenirovka agitatsionnykh sudov," *Vestnik agitatsii i propagandy* 3 (November 25, 1920): 25; "Sud nad Vrangelem," *Vestnik teatra* 72–73 (October–November 1920): 16; V. A. Nevskii, *Massovaia politiko-prosvetitel'naia rabota revoliutsionnykh let* (Moscow-Leningrad, 1925), 45.

3. This use of the passive voice makes the historian's work extremely complicated because it obscures who the actual initiators and authors were. *Ocherednye zadachi polit-prosvetitel'noi raboty Glavpolitprosveta* (Kharkov: izd. Politupravleniia vsekh vooruzhennykh sil Ukrainy i v Krymu, 1921), 2; B. El'tsin, "Ocherenye zadachi, formy i metody agitatsii (tezisy)" (n.d.), Rossiiskii Gosudarstvennyi Arkhiv Sotsial'noi i Politicheskoi Istorii (RGASPI) 17/84/151/68–72; "Agitatsionnye sudy" [January–March 1921], Rossiiskii Gosudarstvennyi Voennyi Arkhiv (RGVA) 192/2/559/80.

4. One Soviet historian writing about the earliest work of playwright Vsevolod Vishnevksii (to whom we shall return later) has argued: "The form of trials, which developed in the 1920s into trials of literary heroes of the past, was born spontaneously. It arose somewhere in the heart of popular amateur acting [*narodnoi samodeiatel'nosti*]. We would search in vain to find its discoverers. People from the depths of the masses were the creators of such spectacles." Vishnevskii belonged to that group in those years." A. Makarov, "Ob etom sbornike," introduction to Vsevolod Vishnevskii, *Stat'i, dnevniki, pis'ma* (Moscow, 1961), 16.

5. The best in-depth study of this work in the Red Army is Mark von Hagen, *Soldiers in the Proletarian Dictatorship: The Red Army and the Soviet Socialist State, 1917–1930* (Ithaca, 1990).

6. *Organizatsionnye kursy po kul'turno-prosvetitel'nomu delu na zheleznykh dorogakh,* ed. N. S. Zaichenko (Moscow: izd. Tsentral'nogo Sovetskogo Kul't-prosvetitel'nogo zheleznogo dorozhnogo uchrezhdeniia [Tsekul't], 1918); "Skhema organizatsii kul'turno-prosvetitel'nogo dela v krasnoarmeiskikh chastiakh, nakhodiashchikhsia na fronte," reprinted in *Partiino-*

politicheskaia rabota v Krasnoi Armii (aprel' 1918–fevral' 1919): Dokumenty (Moscow, 1961) (*PPRI*), 93–96.

7. N. K. Krupskaia, "Politiko-prosvetitel'naia rabota," *Bol'shaia Sovetskaia Entsiklopediia*, 1st ed. (Moscow, 1940), 46:71; T. A. Remizova, *Kul'turno-prosvetitel'naia rabota v RSFSR (1921–1925 gg.)* (Moscow, 1962), 4.

8. Katerina Clark also suggests the importance of this younger generation for understanding some of the "soviet" qualities of literary culture in the 1920s. "The 'Quiet Revolution' in Soviet Intellectual Life," in *Russia in the Era of NEP*, ed. Sheila Fitzpatrick et al. (Bloomington, Ind., 1991), 223–25.

9. D. Furmanov, "Formy agitatsii i propagandy," *Krasnoe znamia*, October 28, 1920, 2; Leman, "Iskusstvo v Krasnoi Armii i Khudozhestvennom Biuro voennoi sektsii," *Politrabotnik* 14 (1921): 60–61; "Agitatsionnye sudy" [January–March 1921], RGVA 192/2/559/80; Gr. Port-Ianskii, "Prosveshchenie krasnoarmeitsev," *Krasnaia gazeta*, April 27, 1921, 4. On February 7, 1920, Dmitrii Furmanov, the budding writer, confided in his diary that he, too, had grown tired of the endless rallies. He admitted that he went to them primarily out of a sense of party discipline but wished there would be less empty talk and more action. D. Furmanov, *Sobranie sochinenii* (Moscow, 1961), 221–22.

10. O. Popova, "Koe-chto o metodakh ustnoi agitatsii," *Politrabotnik* 14 (1921): 62–63.

11. "Ob ozhivlenii agitatsionnoi raboty," *Vestnik agitatsii i propagandy* 19 (September 15, 1921): 45–46.

12. Ibid.

13. "Prosveshchenie na fronte (Zametki lektora)," *Politrabotnik* 10 (November 1920): 5.

14. N. Krupskaia, undated letter to the Politburo (ca. 1922), RGASPI 17/84/421/39–44.

15. "Instruktsiia partiinym iacheikam chastei XI otdel'noi armii o partiino-politicheskoi rabote" (June 12, 1919), in *Partiino-politicheskaia rabota v Krasnoi Armii (mart 1919–1920 gg.): Dokumenty* (Moscow, 1964) (*PPRII*), 298.

16. "Iz doklada zaveduiushchego politodelom Pervoi Konnoi Armii o partiino-politicheskoi i kul'turno-prosvetitel'noi rabote v armii po sostoianiiu na 15 ianvaria 1920 g.," in *PPRII*, 348–50; "Tsirkuliarnoe rasporiazhenie Politupravleniia Respubliki politotdelam armii i gubvoenkomatam" (April 16, 1920), ibid., 88; "Dokladnaia zapiska Vrid. nach. politotdela zapadnogo fronta A. F. Miasnikova v Revvoensovet respubliki o nedostatke politrabotnikov na fronte" (June 27, 1920), ibid., 374–75; A. S., "Kluby Krasnoi Armii," *Politrabotnik* 14 (1921): 57–58; Leman, "Iskusstvo v Krasnoi Armii," 60–61; *Kratkii ocherk kul'turno-politicheskoi raboty v Krasnoi Armii za 1918 god* (Moscow, 1919), 140; also *PPRII*, 57, 284, 310, 337, 449–50, 459, 477, 495.

17. Preobrazhenskii, "O soderzhanii, metodakh i formakh agit-prop. raboty partii v tekushchii moment," *Vestnik agitatsii i propagandy* 16–17 (August 10, 1921): 24–27.

18. Oliver Radkey comments on the dangers posed by the ending of the Civil War because the peasants could no longer be terrified into submission with threats of "Denikin!" *The Unknown Civil War in Soviet Russia* (Stanford, 1976), 32–33.

19. "Ob ocherednykh zadachakh partiinogo stroitel'stva," in *Deviataia konferentsiia RKP(b), sentiabr' 1920* (Moscow, 1972), 278; A. V. Tolmachev, "Formy i metody rukovodstva agitatsionno-propagandistskoi rabotoi v gody grazhdanskoi voiny," *Voprosy istorii KPSS* 8 (1970): 71.

20. A. V. Lunacharskii, "Vseross. soveshchanie politprosvetov," *Pravda*, November 3, 1920; V. I. Lenin, "Rech' na Vserossiiskom soveshchanii politprosvetov gubernskikh i uezdnykh otdelov narodnogo obrazovaniia" (November 3, 1920), in *Polnoe sobranie sochinenii* (*PSS*) (Moscow, 1960–65), 41: 398–408.

21. "Prikaz (No. 1694) Revvoensoveta Respubliki o vvedenii dolzhnosti politicheskogo rukovoditelia" (October 14, 1919), in *PPRII*, 50–52, 52–54; V. G. Kolychev, *Partiino-politicheskaia rabota v Krasnoi Armii v gody grazhdanskoi voiny, 1918–1920 gg.* (Moscow, 1979), 99; "Iz otcheta politotdela 16-i armii o deiatel'nosti za 1919 g." in *Iz istorii grazhdanskoi voiny v SSSR* (Moscow, 1961), 2:704; von Hagen, *Soldiers*, 99–114.

22. "Ot redaktsii," *Politrabotnik* 1 (February 1920): 1–2.

23. Cited in N. I. Shatagin, *Organizatsiia i stroitel'stvo Sovetskoi armii v period inostran-*

noi voennoi interventsii i grazhdanskoi voiny (1918–1920 gg.) (Moscow, 1954), 231; "Instruktsiia politrukam," in *PPRII*, 512n. An instruction on the regimental commissar also referred to the political instructor as the "father and spirit of his regiment." "Instruktsiia dlia komissara polka v deistvuiushchikh chastiakh" (izd. PO Iuzhfronta, 1919), 4, cited in Shatagin, 230.

24. RGVA 34/1/10/49. Soldiers also reproached the political instructors for making them spend time studying the "ABC of communism" as if it were Gospel readings and the Soviet version of the "Law of God" (*zakon bozhii*). See V. Girov, "O politicheskom ustave," *Krasnyi strelok* 2 (1922): 32.

25. "Vsem politrukam i komissaram" (February 23, 1921), RGASPI 17/60/48/16ob.

26. "Protokol no. 6 zasedaniia rabochego iadra religioznoi komissii pri Agitotdele MK RKP" (July 19, 1921), RGASPI 17/60/29/40.

27. "Iz doklada zaveduiushchego," in *PPRII*, 348–50.

28. See chapter 4 for more on the tension over voluntary versus obligatory work with the soldiers.

29. Bor. Vaks, "Tezisy-doklad po voprosu o politprosvetrabote v Krasnoi Armii. K Vserossiiskomu S"ezdu Glavpolitprosveta" (September 15, 1921), RGASPI 17/84/151/59–67.

30. Ibid.; *Vos'moi s"ezd RKP(b)*, mart 1919 g. (Moscow, 1959), 415.

31. *KPSS v rezoliutsiiakh i resheniiakh*, 7th ed. (Moscow, 1954), chast' 2, 112; Kolychev, *Partiino-politicheskaia rabota*, 214–15.

32. The total budget for PUR in the second half of 1919, according to PUR deputy director Rakovskii, was approximately 664 million rubles, of which 215 million (32 percent) were sent to the political departments of the fronts; 106 million (16 percent) to the politotdely of the military districts; 48 million (7 percent) to agitation and political work; another 48 million to education work (for existing and new schools); 6 million (1 percent) for traveling theater troupes for the front; 159 million (24 percent) for agitation literature for the armies and the population just behind the front lines; plus 19 million (3 percent) for the maintenance of the central apparatus (of which 11 million was designated for the staff, for contract agitators, and for courses in extracurricular education); and the rest (65 million, 10 percent), for secretarial and business expenses. "Rech' tov. Rakovskogo," *Politrabotnik* 1 (February 1920): 9–10.

33. Ibid.," 12. Rakovskii commented in this article that only now (in February 1920) was cultural-educational work in the army becoming developed on a large scale.

34. "Otchet o deiatel'nosti politupravleniia respubliki za 1920," *PPRII*, 108.

35. N. K. Krupskaia, "Ocherednoi (Tretii) Vserossiiskii s"ezd politprosvetov," *Pedagogicheskie sochinenii* (Moscow, 1947), 7:164. The numbers of political instructors were increasing so rapidly that many of the new political education staffs would have learned everything they knew from hastily created political education courses in the military, and, after 1921, in the civilian world. By late 1922, however, because of the cutbacks associated with the New Economic Policy, the numbers of political workers had dropped to 10,000 staff people instead of 475,000. Cutbacks by up to 75 percent took place all over the Russian Republic. Ibid. This shows not only the rapid expansion but also the volatility and insecurity of the position of the political instructors.

36. "Rezoliutsiia I S"ezd Politrabotnikov Krasnoi Armii o printsipakh politiko-prosvetitel'noi raboty v armii" (December 11–15, 1919), in *PPRII*, 55.

37. Vorob'ev, "Organizatsiia klubov" (Protokol Pervoi armeiskoi kul'turno-prosvetitel'noi konferentsii [9th Army]), RGVA 192/2/538/56. At the end of 1920 the political authorities on the Western front created a special leaflet for Red Army soldiers leaving the army, enjoining them to be prepared to come back into the army at any time, to work hard at home, to watch out for labor deserters and wolves in sheep's clothing. "The most fearsome enemy of the toilers is ignorance," they were told. To fight that enemy, the returning soldier was to transmit all his accumulated knowledge to the villagers and factory workers at home. "Pamiatka Politupravleniia Zapadnogo Fronta dlia krasnoarmeitsa-otpusknika," in *PPRII*, 452–53. Also, Vaks, "Doklad po voprosu"; Preobrazhenskii, "Vsem gubkomam RKP," *Pravda*, January 21, 1921; "Ko vsem kommunistam, uvol'niaemym v bessrochnyi otpusk iz Krasnoi Armii," *Pravda*,

April 28, 1921; "Iz rezoliutsii Vserossiiskogo soveshchaniia po agitproprabote v Krasnoi Armii i Flote" (September 1–6, 1922), in *Partiino-politicheskaia rabota v Krasnoi Armii (1921–1929 gg.): Dokumenty* (Moscow, 1981) (*PPRIII*), 79.

38. "Vnimanie k demobilizuemym tovarishcham-krasnoarmeitsam," *Pravda*, February 18, 1921.

39. "Vtoraia armeiskaia kul'turno-prosvetitel'naia konferentsiia," *Krasnoe znamia*, October 27, 1920, 4. The political instructors were also finally being allowed to stay in one unit. During the height of the Civil War they had been sent from unit to unit, from front to front. Report from I. V. Korobochkin, Nachal'nik prosvetchasti politotdela, to the Nach. politotdela 2 Ko-narmii (November 11, 1920), RGVA 246/2/115/70.

40. A. Furmanova, "V Chapaevskoi divizii," in *Furmanov v vospominaniiakh sovremennikov* (Moscow, 1959), 33–46; for a fictionalized account, see Dmitry Furmanov, *Chapaev* (Moscow, 1955), 288–95. For other accounts of soldiers' love of the theater, see "Iz otcheta o deiatel'nosti voennogo komissariata g. Petrograda i Petrogradskoi gubernii so dnia osnovaniia po oktiabr' 1919 g." (October 1919), in *PPRII*, 476–77; F. Tartakovskaia, zav. politotdelom divizii, *Pravda*, July 10, 1919, cited in Kolychev, *Partiino-politicheskaia rabota*, 146.

41. *Politrabotnik* 7 (August 1920): 15; *Politrabotnik* 8 (September 1920): 3; "Politprosvetitel'naia rabota v Krasnoi Armii (tezisy doklada t. Anuchina)" *Politrabotnik* 9 (October 1920): 4–8; Nevskii, *Massovaia*, 49–50; I. Korobochkin and V. Kurdiumov, "Otzyv ob agitsude nad mezhdunarodnym imperializmom (izd. PUSKVO) (May 29, 1923)," RGVA 9/13/97/214. For rich descriptions of new forms during the Civil War, see James von Geldern, *Bolshevik Festivals, 1917–1920* (Berkeley, 1990), esp. 103–33; Lynn Mally, *Revolutionary Acts* (Ithaca, 2000); N. A. Gorchakov, *Istoriia sovetskogo teatra* (New York, 1956), 87–92; Catriona Kelly, "Petrushka and the Pioneers: The Russian Carnival Puppet Theatre after the Revolution," in *Discontinuous Discourses in Modern Russian Literature*, ed. Catriona Kelly, Michael Makin, and David Shepherd (New York, 1989), 73–111.

42. "Pervyi Vserossiiskii s"ezd bibliotechnikh rabotnikov Krasnoi Armii," *Politrabotnik* 10 (November 1920): 16; Vaks, "Doklad po voprosu."

43. Mikh. Luzgin, "Ot kommunistov po instinktu k kommunistam po soznaniiu," *Politrabotnik* 10 (November 1920): 9–10.

44. Shubin, "Rabota klubov v Zapchasti," 5.

45. Krupskaia, *Pedagogicheskie sochinenii*, 7:196, cited in K. M. Temirbaev and V. V. Ukraintsev, *Ocherki istorii sovetskoi kul'tury* (Moscow, 1980), 78–79; *Kratkii ocherk kul'turno-politicheskoi raboty v Krasnoi Armii za 1918 god* (Moscow, 1919), 69–70, 141; von Hagen, *Soldiers*, 104–7; "Nuzhna operatsiia," *Krasnaia gazeta*, May 9, 1920, 4 (on the working masses' thirst for enlightenment and particularly for opportunities to visit the theater); Gr. Port-Ianskii, "Prosveshchenie krasnoarmeitsev," *Krasnaia gazeta*, April 27, 1921, 4. On the workers' desires to read and study, see Richard Pipes, *Social Democracy and the St. Petersburg Labor Movement, 1885–1897* (Cambridge, Mass., 1963); Reginald E. Zelnik, *Labor and Society in Tsarist Russia: The Factory Workers of St. Petersburg, 1855–1870* (Stanford, 1971); Laura Engelstein, *Moscow, 1905: Working-Class Organization and Political Conflict* (Stanford, 1982); Victoria E. Bonnell, *Roots of Rebellion: Workers' Politics and Organizations in St. Petersburg and Moscow, 1900–1914* (Berkeley, 1983); Diane Koenker, *Moscow Workers and the 1917 Revolution* (Princeton, 1981).

46. L. Trotsky, "Prikaz No. 254" (August 5, 1921) in *Kak vooruzhalas' revoliutsiia* (Moscow, 1924), v. 3, pt. 1, 154–56.

47. Vaks, "Doklad po voprosu"; El'tsin, "Ocherednye zadachi"; Popova, "Koe-chto o metodakh," 62–63.

48. "Rezoliutsiia I S"ezda Politrabotnikov Krasnoi Armii," 56–57.

49. Shubin, "Rabota klubov v Zapchasti," 4–5.

50. V. Astrov, "Teatr proizvodstvennoi propagandy," *Pravda*, January 26, 1921.

51. P. Markov, *Noveishie teatral'nye techeniia (1898–1923)* (Moscow, 1924).

52. A. Serafimovich, "Svoei sobstvennoi rukoi," *Petrogradskaia Pravda*, April 18, 1920.

On peasant isolation, see Leopold H. Haimson, "The Problem of Social Identities in Early Twentieth Century Russia," *Slavic Review* 47, no. 1 (1988): 1–20.

53. M. Boguslovskii, "Kul'turnichestvo ili politicheskoe prosveshchenie," *Pravda*, October 31, 1920.

54. The first formal endorsement of the agitation trial form that I have been able to find in any periodical is "Polit-prosvetitel'naia rabota v Krasnoi Armii (tezisy doklada t. Anuchina)" *Politrabotnik* 9 (October 1920): 4–8; also reprinted in *PPRII*, 95–101. Sergei A. Anuchin gave this report at a meeting of military representatives to the Ninth Party Conference. At the time he was head of the political division of the Ninth Army, which was stationed in the Kuban region in southern Russia and which played a central role in pioneering the agitation trials. Dmitrii Furmanov was his coworker. Anuchin recommended "literary trials" as one form among many. Others he mentioned included readings of the newspaper out loud with explanations, the organization of debates and literary commissions, and amateur theater in the clubs. In the very next issue of *Politrabotnik*, G. Shubin reported that the trials were a completely new form being explored and developed in the outlying areas (i.e., not in the capital cities) and that there were as yet no instructions on how to stage them. "It is not the center that has dictated them from above, but the local areas that have given a push to the center in popularizing this work," he insisted ("Rabota klubov v Zapchasti," 6).

55. "Sud nad sovetskoi vlast'iu," *Pravda*, December 21, 1920. G. Sh., "O tea-rabote v krskikh chastiakh," *Politrabotnik* 10 (November 1920): 7–9; I. Korobochkin, "Klub na puti k sisteme" (n.d.), in RGVA 9/13/97/294–300.

56. A. F., "Dorprofsozh Aleks. zh.d. i masterskaia Kommunisticheskoi dramaturgii," *Pravda*, January 14, 1921.

57. Elena Iur'evna Strel'tsova, "Razvitie teorii i praktiki klubnogo publitsisticheskogo teatra, 1917–1930 gg." (Kand. diss., Mosk. gos. institut kul'tury, 1993), 80.

58. G. Sh., "O tea-rabote," 7–9; Tsentral'nyi Gosudarstvennyi Arkhiv Moskovskoi Oblasti [TsGAMO] 880/1/17/16; Korobochkin, "Klub na puti k sisteme," RGVA 9/13/97/294.

59. G. Sh., "O tea-rabote," 7.

60. Borovich, *Instsenirovki kak metod prosvetitel'noi raboty* (Kharkov, 1923), 15–19.

61. Ibid., 24–25.

62. Ibid., 25.

63. Maria Konopnicka, *Mendil Dantsiger,* translated originally into Russian as Mariia Konopnitskaia, *Mendel' Idanskii* (Rostov-na-Donu, 1906). Borovich comments that the book was published in a shortened version as "Zhid" (M. N. Sleptsova, n.d.), then as "The Old Bookbinder and his Grandson" (*Staryi perepletchik i ego vnuk*) (Moscow: Gos. izd-vo, 1921).

64. This term, "show exercise," exemplifies the way that the early Soviet regime staged many events as a means to "show" others how they should be done. From show exercises it was not a far step to show trials and agitation trials. Elsewhere Borovich had commented on the holding of "pokazatel'nye sudy" in law divisions of higher education schools; by this he evidently meant moot courts used to teach law students, especially in the years after the legal reforms of the 1860s (*Instsenirovki kak metod*, 8).

65. Unfortunately, Borovich never states exactly how many people were in the audience. In December 1920 another army instructor, I. Bliumin, argued that literary trials of Jews (*literaturnye sudy nad evreiami*) could serve as a way of "paralyzing" anti-Semitic influence. "Ser'eznyi vopros (O bor'be s antisemitizmom)," *Politrabotnik* 11 (December 1920): 6. Lunacharsky at several points insisted that one of the principal purposes of the new theater was to fight against old prejudices (e.g., *Kul'tura teatra,* 4 [1921], 2).

66. Borovich, *Instsenirovki,* 35–36.

67. Ibid., 15.

68. "Prikaz po Politicheskomu Upravleniiu Revvoensoveta respubliki i instruktsii o prazdnovanii Oktiabr'skoi godovshchiny" *Politrabotnik* 9 (October 1920): 21–24; E. Medynskii, *Entsiklopediia vneshkol'nogo obrazovaniia,* vol. 2, *Otdel'nye vidy sodeistviia vneshkol'nomu obrazovaniiu,* 2nd ed. (Moscow-Leningrad: Gos. izd-vo, 1925), 164; A. Rozinskii, "K voprosu o formakh politprosvetraboty," *Put' politrabotnika* 8 (1921): 50–52; Nevskii, *Massovaia,* 45;

Konspekt rukovodstva po shkol'noi rabote v Krasnoi Armii (Kharkov: izd. Politupravleniia vsekh vooruzhennykh sil na Ukraine, 1921), 15; I. V. Rebel'skii, *Instsenirovannye sudy* (Moscow: Trud i kniga, 1926), 16.

69. Rebel'skii, *Instsenirovannye sudy,* 15–16.

70. Katerina Clark and Michael Holquist, *Mikhail Bakhtin* (Cambridge, Mass., 1984), 50.

71. V. Belousov, *Sergei Esenin. Literaturnaia khronika* (Moscow, 1969), 170–74, 279; my thanks to Ulrich Schmid for this reference.

72. "Sud pod suflera (Novyi sposob khaltury)," *Krasnaia Gazeta,* November 17, 1921; other such performances were also reported in "Sud nad Dantesom," *Krasnaia gazeta,* July 8, 1924; N. Berner, "Sud nad Saninym," *Entrakt* 3 (1923): 15 (professor Gurevich, an eminent lawyer, played the prosecutor).

73. "Sud nad p'esami," *Vestnik teatra* 85–86 (March 15, 1921); "Instruktsiia po rabote vokrug spektaklia (kontserta)" (February 16, 1922), RGVA 9/1/76a/19ob. In 1925 the writers' trade union committee held a "Trial of Pornography in Literature" in which they criticized a story by A. Volzhskii, "Friends on the Volga." *Sud nad pornografiei v literature* (Moscow, 1926).

74. V. A. Nevskii, "Prakticheskie zaniatiia so vzroslymi po obshchestvennym naukam," in *Vtoroi sbornik statei po Vneshkol'nomu Obrazovaniiu,* 2nd ed., ed. V. A. Nevskii (Kazan: Gos. izd-vo, 1921), 54. Nevskii describes the dramatizing of a wide range of new Soviet institutions, including the new courts. On collective creativity and "ritual drama" *(obriadovaia drama),* A. I. Piotrovskii, "Prazdnestva 1920 goda" (March 1922) in Piotrovskii, *Za sovetskii teatr* (Leningrad, 1925), 9–17. Other sources on collective creation include P. M. Kerzhentsev, *Tvorcheskii teatr,* 5th ed. (Moscow-Petrograd: Gos. izd-vo, 1923); speeches by Kerzhentsev and E. M. Bagdateva in *Protokoly pervoi Vserossiiskoi konferentsii proletarskikh kul'turnoprosvetitel'nykh organizatsii, 15–20 sent. 1920* (Moscow: 1918), 121–125, and P. Kogan, "Socialist Theater in the Years of the Revolution," *Vestnik teatra* 40 (November 4–9, 1919), translated in William G. Rosenberg, *Bolshevik Visions* (Ann Arbor, 1984), 428, 431, 440; Kerzhentsev, *K novoi kul'tury,* 54–57, discussed in Zenovia A. Sochor, *Revolution and Culture* (Ithaca, 1988), 136–37.

75. Nevskii, "Prakticheskie zaniatiia," 54; P. M. Kerzhentsev, *Tvorcheskii teatr* (1920), 130. Pavel Andreevich Bliakhin (1886–1961), a party member from 1903, wrote many later stories as well. At this time, according to Nevskii, he was a local soviet worker. He also authored a booklet called *O novykh metodakh mestnoi agitatsii* (Baku, 1922). Nevskii claims that Bliakhin published his results on the dramatizations in *Vtoroi Sbornik Kostromskogo Proletkul'ta.*

76. Nevskii, "Prakticheskie zaniatiia," 55.

77. Ibid., 40–42.

78. N. Karzhanskii, *Kollektivnaia dramaturgiia. Material dlia rabot dramaticheskikh studii i kruzhkov* (Moscow, 1922), 3. Karzhanskii, like Borovich, had at one time chosen a revolutionary pseudonym; his given family name was Zeziulinskii. His father had been a teacher who later became a priest. In addition to carrying out agitation among the peasants of Smolensk province, Karzhanskii completed law school and also wrote many plays. In 1907–8 he lived abroad in Paris, where he helped Lenin edit the notes from the Fifth (London) Party Congress. He was close friends with N. I. Podvoiskii, who was to become head of the military reserves (Vsevobuch) and who was himself a close friend of Meyerhold. Rossiiskii Gosudarstvennyi Arkhiv Literatury i Iskusstva (RGALI) 1708/1/1/13, 44–45.

79. Karzhanskii, *Kollektivnaia dramaturgiia,* 7–12. The lack of revolutionary plays was constantly lamented by contemporaries: "Repertuar geroicheskogo, bodrogo, iarkogo," *Vestnik teatra* 14 (1919): 3; Seniushkin, "Metodicheskie materialy po proizvodstvennoi propagande," GARF 5451/5/634/22; Markov, *Noveishie teatral'nye techeniia,* 39–43; *Protokoly pervoi Vserossiiskoi konferentsii proletarskikh,* 122 (Kerzhentsev), 431 (E. M. Bagdateva).

80. Karzhanskii, *Kollektivnaia dramaturgiia,* 12.

81. Ibid., 66–69.

82. *Vos'moi s"ezd RKP(b),* 422; "Iz istoricheskogo ocherka organizatsii i deiatel'nosti politotdela Chernomorskogo i Azovskogo flotov v 1920 g." (June 2, 1923), in *PPRII;* Kolychev,

Partiino-politicheskaia rabota, 247–54; Orlando Figes, "The Red Army and Mass Mobilization during the Russian Civil War 1918–1920," *Past and Present*, 129 (November, 1990): 168–211.

83. RGVA 4/10/569/34, cited in Kolychev, *Partiino-politicheskaia rabota*, 259.

84. RGVA 4/10/572, 577, ibid. Proletkul't, the proletarian cultural organization, organized a number of such "military play-rallies" (*boevye spektakli-mitingi*) from 1919 onward. L. Tamashin, *Sovetskaia dramaturgiia v gody grazhdanskoi voiny* (Moscow, 1961), 108–9. Von Hagen, *Soldiers*, 76n., also cites the confession of a deserter published in *Bednota* for agitation purposes in August 1920.

85. RGVA 4/10/543/3, cited in Kolychev, *Partiino-politicheskaia rabota*, 257–58.

86. "Prikaz PURa o merakh po usileniiu bor'by s dezertirstvom" (May 29, 1920), in *PPRII*, 88–89. On April 22, 1920, for example, the Ninth Army (an important player in the development of the agitation trials) passed a conference resolution that any cultural education commissions that did not fulfill their obligations could be "brought to court for nonfulfillment of their military assignments." "Polozhenie o kul'turno-prosvetitel'noi rabote v armii," RGVA 192/2/537/140.

87. Politupravlenie Iuzhnogo fronta, "Direktiva vsem kommunistam armii iuzhfronta" (Kharkov, September 30, 1920) in *M. V. Frunze na frontakh grazhdanskoi voiny. Sbornik dokumentov* (Moscow, 1941), 338–40.

88. *Kul'turno-prosvetitel'naia rabota v SSSR*, ed. T. A. Remizova (Moscow, 1974), 56–57.

89. "Instsenirovka suda nad dezertirom," *Rabochii put'* (Smolensk newspaper), December 1920, quoted at length in Karzhanskii, *Kollektivnaia dramaturgiia*, 13. Karzhanskii may well have been involved in this mock trial since he was in Smolensk at this time.

90. "Nedel'naia armeiskaia politsvodka za pervuiu nedeliu dekabria 1920 g." (signed Nach. Polit. otdela IX Kubarmii and Nach. Osvedomitel'noi chasti Poarma IX), in RGVA 192/1/138/26; "Mesiachnyi plan agitatsionno-prosvetitel'noi raboty (s 10 aprelia po 10e maia [1921]). Vsem iacheikam, politrukam, i kul'turnikam 22 str. divizii," in RGVA 192/2/559/75ob.

91. P. Kolmakova, "Literaturnye sudy" in *V pomoshch' bibliotekariu*, quoted in Nevskii, *Massovaia*, 45.

92. "Sud nad panskoi Pol'shei," *Pravda*, July 1, 1920; Aleko [*sic*], "Obzor faktov," *Vestnik teatra* 67 (September 7, 1920): 3.

93. Karzhanskii, *Kollektivnaia dramaturgiia*, 66–69.

94. "Sud nad Vrangelem," 16; "Obzor agitatsionnogo materiala," 25–26. Such mass agitation trials were rare.

95. "Sud nad Vrangelem," 16–17. The article named comrade Bakulin as the author of the letter. Meyerhold and the Ninth Army had other connections as well. Four months later, on February 12, 1921, Bakulin's boss, M. A. Aleksinskii, head of cultural education in the Ninth Army, wrote to Meyerhold asking him to send more literature since in their army, theater work was "boiling over" and their theater wanted to put on something fresh (RGALI 998/1/1050). Meyerhold had already produced several mass performances in the capital cities in 1919–20. Most important, Meyerhold had been living in Novorossiisk in 1919–20, under the Reds, then the Whites (who imprisoned him), and then again under the Reds. Though he himself worked with the Tenth Army, he would have had opportunities to meet some of the staff of the Ninth Army. Iurii Elagin, *Temnyi genii (Vsevolod Meierkhol'd)* (London, 1955, 1982); Edward Braun, *Meyerhold: A Revolution in Theatre* (Iowa City, 1995); Konstantin Rudnitsky, *Meyerhold: The Director* (Ann Arbor, 1981).

96. This was not the final defeat of Wrangel (which would take place a month later in the Crimea itself) but was nonetheless an important milestone.

97. "Sud nad Vrangelem," 16; "Obzor agitatsionnogo materiala," 26.

98. Furmanov, "Formy agitatsii," 2–3; "Obzor agitatsionnogo materiala"; "Sud nad Vrangelem."

99. For a recent discussion of Furmanov's *Chapaev*, see Ronald Vroon, "Dmitrii Furmanov's *Chapaev* and the Aesthetics of the Russian Avant-Garde," in *The Russian Avant-Garde and Cultural Experiment*, ed. John E. Bowlt and Olga Matich (Stanford, 1997), 219–34. For

materials on Furmanov and Vishnevskii in this period, see D. A. *Furmanov: Letopis' zhizni i deiatel'nost'i, bibliografiia materialy* (Ivanovo, 1963); Vsevolod Vishnevskii, "Dvadtsatiletie sovetskoi dramaturgii," *Sovetskie dramaturgi o svoem tvorchestve: Sbornik statei* (Moscow, 1967), 140–52; Boris M. Filippov, *Muzy na fronte: Ocherki, dnevniki, pis'ma* (Moscow, 1975).

100. Furmanova, "V Chapaevskoi divizii," 33–51. The precise authorship of the *Trial of Wrangel* has never been determined. Still, it is striking that the political division of the Ninth Army where it was performed had a number of young rising stars in the new Soviet intelligentsia, all of whom were connected with agitation trials in one way or another. In addition to Dmitrii and Anna Furmanov, other key players in the Ninth Army political section included: Sergei A. Anuchin, already a senior member of PUR, as well as head of the political section in the Ninth Army, who gave the first official report on agitation trials at a meeting of military representatives to the Ninth Party Conference (September 1920); Moisei Solomonovich Epshtein (1890–?), who had worked his way up in the Red Army after extensive prerevolutionary engagement in the Bund and who went on to become the first president of the End to Illiteracy Society (Obshchestvo Doloi Negramotnosti) as well as deputy commissar of education in the Russian Repdublic; M. A. Aleksinskii, later deputy director of the agitprop section of PUR. One of Vishnevskii's biographers claims that he (Vishnevskii) was the "coauthor" of the *Trial of Wrangel*. M. Savchenko, *Oni byli na Kubani* (Krasnodar, 1974), 100.

101. Furmanov, "Formy agitatsii," 2–3; this article originated as a report he gave at a conference of division-level political department heads and division political commissars in the Ninth Army from October 12 to 15, 1920.

102. Speech to the Union of Soviet Writers, November 4, 1937, in V. Vishnevskii, *Sobranie Sochinenii* (Moscow, 1961), 6:52. It seems curious that Vishnevskii spoke of this in late 1937 when two major show trials had already taken place in Moscow and a third was being prepared. It is also curious that he wrote about the play as if he had helped to stage it. He was in the region but not in the Ninth Army, which put it on.

103. Evan Mawdsley, *The Russian Civil War* (Boston, 1987), 264; Peter Kenez, *Civil War in South Russia, 1919–1920* (Berkeley, 1977), 259–67; William Henry Chamberlin, *The Russian Revolution,* (New York, 1935): 134–49, 318–35; Peter Holquist, "A Russian Vendee: The Practice of Revolutionary Politics in the Don Countryside" (Ph.D. diss., Columbia University, 1995).

104. Telegrams of February 17; June 2; August 2, 3, 5, 19, 20; September 2, 9, 1920, in *Direktivy glavnogo komandovaniia Krasnoi Armii (1917–1920): Sbornik dokumentov* (Moscow, 1969), 731, and Lenin, in *PSS,* 51:205, 247–49, 265, 277, 349.

105. "Telegrama Kavkazskogo biuro TsK RKP(b)" (August 1, 1920), in *Iz istorii grazhdanskoi voiny,* 3:383; "Direktiva komandovaniiu 9–oi armii ob usilenii bor'by s ostatkami belogvardeiskikh band na Severnom Kavkaze" (July 3, 1920), in *Direktivy komandovaniia frontov Krasnoi Armii (1917–1922): Sbornik dokumentov* (Moscow, 1974), 3:328–29.

106. "F. E. Dzerzhinskomu" (Aug. 28, 1920), in *PSS,* 51:271.

107. Trotsky in *Deviataia konferentsiia RKP(b),* 24–25; Trotsky "Kuban' ne podnialas'," *V puti* (Rostov), August 28, 1920, reprinted in *Kak vooruzhalas' revoliutsiia,* 199–200.

108. "Tsirkuliarnoe pis'mo TsK gubernskim komitetam partii o novoi mobilizatsii kommunistov na Vrangelevskii front" (August 1920), in *Iz istorii grazhdanskoi voiny v SSSR,* 3:228; "Na barona Vrangelia!" *Izvestiia TsK RKP(b),* July 17, 1920, in *PPRII,* 392–93; Radkey, *Unknown Civil War,* 34, 120; Holquist, "A Russian Vendee," 795–804, 817.

109. Kenez, *Civil War,* 265, 278–88; Holquist, "A Russian Vendee."

110. Furmanov, "Formy agitatsii," 3.

111. Cited in Iu. Osnos, *V mire dramy* (Moscow, 1971), 62; a similar account is contained in *Russkaia literatura* 1 (1959): 155, cited in N. S. Sharapkov, *Vsevolod Vishnevskii: Kritiko-biograficheskii ocherk* (Kishinev, 1965), 13. The performance of the trial itself was reported in "Instsenirovannyi sud nad Kronshtadtskimi miatezhnikami," *Pravda,* April 14, 1921. The article commented only that the trial had been staged by the political department of the sailors in Novorossiisk, that more than a thousand people had been in the audience, that it had been a great success, and that a second dramatized trial, this time of the communists, had been held on April 7. (It is possible that this latter date is a typo and the "later" date was April 17, which

would be both later than April 14 and the anniversary of the "Trial of Lenin" from the year before.)

112. *Sobranie sochinenii,* 6:355.

113. V. Vishnevskii, "Grazhdanskaia voina (1917–1921 gg.)," in *Sobranie sochinenii,* 2:764, 774–75, 799; Vishnevskii, "Avtobiografiia" (1939), quoted in Sharapkov, *Vishnevskii,* 8–9; P. Vershigora, "Vsevolod Vishnevskii" in Vishnevskii, *Sobranie sochinenii,* 1:15–17; M. Savchenko, *Oni byli na Kubani* (Krasnodar, 1974), 101.

114. Vishnevskii, cited in Osnos, *V mire dramy,* 62.

115. Cited in Sharapkov, *Vsevolod Vishnesvkii,* 13.

116. Savchenko, *Oni byli,* 102; Osnos, *V mire dramy,* 63.

Chapter 3. The Trial of Lenin

1. "Sud nad Leninym," *Pravda,* April 22, 1920.

2. N. Karzhanskii, *Kollektivnaia dramaturgiia. Material dlia rabot dramaticheskikh studii i kruzhkov* (Moscow, 1922), 12, 66.

3. "Paskhal'nyi voskresnik v Basmannom raione," *Pravda,* April 16, 1920; "Segodnia godovshchina lenskogo rasstrela rabochikh oprichnikami kaznennogo narodom tsaria," *Pravda,* April 17, 1920.

4. Occasionally historians give April 23 as Lenin's birthday rather than the twenty-second. The reason for the discrepancy is that Lenin's birthday was April 10, 1870, in the Old Style calendar used in the Russian Empire at that time. This calendar differed from the European and later Soviet calendars by twelve days in the nineteenth century and thirteen in the twentieth. Thus, in the nineteenth century the New Style date would have been the twenty-second; this is the date that was commonly used in 1920.

5. Richard Wortman, *Scenarios of Power: Myth and Ceremony in Russian Monarchy,* 2 vols. (Princeton, 1995, 2000); also see Robert O. Crummey, "Court Spectacles in Seventeenth-Century Russia: Illusion and Reality," in *Essays in Honor of A. A. Zimin,* ed. Daniel Clarke Waugh (Columbus, Ohio, 1985); Nancy Shields Kollmann, "Ritual and Social Drama at the Muscovite Court," *Slavic Review* 45, no. 3 (1986): 486–502.

6. James Von Geldern, *Bolshevik Festivals, 1917–1920* (Berkeley, 1993); Richard Stites, *Revolutionary Dreams: Utopian Vision and Experimental Life in the Russian Revolution* (New York, 1989); *Agitatsionno-massovoe iskusstvo pervykh let Oktiabria: materialy i issledovaniia,* ed. E. A. Speranskaia (Moscow, 1971); Katerina Clark, *Petersburg, Crucible of Cultural Revolution* (Cambridge, Mass., 1995); Frederick C. Corney, *Telling October: Memory and the Making of the Bolshevik Revolution* (Ithaca, 2004).

7. As Lenin noted in November 1920, "the bourgeoisie is slandering us tirelessly with its whole apparatus of propaganda and agitation," "Rech' na Vserossiiskom soveshchanii polit-prosvetov," in *Polnoe Sobranie Sochinenii,* 5th ed. (Moscow, 1960–65), 41:406–7.

8. "Novaia forma agitatsii," *Pravda,* November 21, 1920; "Sud nad R.K.P.," *Pravda,* February 18, 1921; "Sud nad Oktiabr'skim perevorotom 1917 goda" (typescript, 1922), Rossiiskii Gosudarstvennyi Voennyi Arkhiv (RGVA) 9/13/93/143–44.

9. "Sud nad R.K.P."

10. "Sud nad Sovetskoi vlast'iu," *Pravda,* December 21, 1920.

11. "Sud nad novoi zhenshchinoi," *Pravda,* February 20, 1921; see also Elizabeth A. Wood, "The Trial of the New Woman: Citizens-in-Training in the New Soviet Republic," *Gender and History* 13, no. 3 (2001): 524–45.

12. F. K., "Privet novomu godu," *Pravda,* January 5, 1921.

13. "Instruktsii otdelam rabotnits po provedeniiu 'nedeli front,' . . . , po organizatsii 'suda nad RKP'" (1920), Tsentral'nyi Gosudarstvennyi Arkhiv Istoriko-Politicheskikh Dokukmentov g. Sankt-Peterburga, 1/1/924.

14. M. Antonov, "O kul'tprosvetakh," *Pravda,* March 16, 1921.

15. "Sud nad panskoi Pol'shei," *Pravda,* July 1, 1920.

16. "Sud nad Leninym i Trotskim," *Pravda,* February 15, 1921; "Amnistiia 400 krest'ian"; and "Bespartiinye krest'ianskie konferentsii," *Pravda,* February 15, 1921.

17. "Sud nad Leninym"; "Politicheskii otdel 1–go raiona Moskovsko-Vindavsko-Rybinskoi zheleznoi dorogi Moskovskoi seti, 26/IV [1920]," Rossiiskii Gosudarstvennyi Arkhiv Sotsial'noi i Politicheskoi Istorii (RGASPI) 111/22/153/18; Sof'ia Vinogradskaia, "Pervye gody. Rasskazy," *Novyi mir* 10 (1957): 46–48.

18. "Politicheskii otdel 1–go raiona Moskovsko-Vindavsko-Rybinskoi zheleznoi dorogi," l. 18.

19. Ibid.

20. In addition to the article in *Novyi mir*, Vinogradskaia also published a book, *Rasskazy o Lenine* (Moscow, 1965), 106–7, which tells substantially the same story. Her sister, Polina Semenovna Vinogradskaia, also published two volumes of memoir materials, *Pamiatnye vstrechi* (Moscow, 1972), and *Sobytiia i pamiatnye vstrechi* (Moscow, 1968). A whole study could be written on the myths of Lenin in the Khrushchev years, the renewed attempts to make him seem more human and thus free of Stalin's "cult of personality."

21. "Doklad agitatsionno-prosvetitel'nogo podotdela Dorpolita Moskovsko-Vindavsko-Rybinsk zheleznoi dorogi s 1/III po 1/IV/1920 god" (April 20, 1920), RGASPI 111/22/153/14.

22. Ibid. Even in June 1920, though, the whole Vindava line had only an acting head of its political department. "Shtaty dorpolita M-V-R zh.d." (June 18, 1920), RGASPI 111/22/880/60.

23. "Biulleten' no. 12 informatsionnogo-instruktorskogo otdela Glavnogo Politicheskogo Upravleniia NKPS, 26 aprelia 1920 g.," in RGASPI 17/60/19/145.

24. Npolkom Umrikhin, "Pamiatka dlia komissarov sluzhb chastei i uchastkov" (February 12, 1920), Rossiiskii Gosudarstvennyi Arkhiv Ekonomiki (RGAE) 1884/3/154/6 ob.

25. RGASPI 111/22/378/73–75. On January 12, 1920 the Orgbiuro of the Central Committee of the party resolved officially to mobilize experienced political workers from the Red Army to the railroads as quickly as possible. About eight hundred were transferred. This was followed by a general transfer of communists from other areas to the railroads. "Doklad" (August 8, 1920), RGASPI 17/60/19/20. Two months later, the Ninth Party Congress (March–April 1920) considered the matter of the railroads so important that it passed a special resolution ordering Glavpolitput "urgently to improve transport through the organized influence of experienced communists." *VKP v rezoliutsiiakh* (Moscow, 1941), 1:335, cited in E. H. Carr, *The Bolshevik Revolution* (New York, 1950–1953), 2:220. On the general struggle over the relations between Glavpolitput and the railroad workers' union, see Leonard Schapiro, *The Origin of the Communist Autocracy* (Cambridge, Mass., 1977), 253–61; James Bunyan, *The Origin of Forced Labor in the Soviet State, 1917–1921* (Baltimore, 1967), 181–212; William G. Rosenberg, "The Social Background to Tsektran," in *Party, State, and Society in the Russian Civil War,* ed. Diane P. Koenker et al. (Bloomington, Ind., 1989), 349–73; Robert Thomas Argenbright, "The Russian Railroad System and the Founding of the Communist State, 1917–1922" (Ph.D. diss., University of California, 1990).

26. Bunyan, *Origin,* 183–84. Argenbright, "Russian Railroad System," 358, discusses the "demonstration effect" of the railroad tribunals. They were held in public and "their purpose was to inculcate ideals, not just punish."

27. Umrikhin, "Pamiatka," RGAE 1884/3/154/6ob.

28. "Doklad agitatsionno-prosvetitel'nogo podotdela Dorpolita Moskovsko-Vindavsko-Rybinskoi zheleznoi dorogi s 1/IV po 1/V 1920 g.," RGASPI 111/22/874.

29. Orlando Figes and Boris Kolonitskii, *Interpreting the Russian Revolution: The Language and Symbols of 1917* (New Haven, 1999); B. Kolonitskii, "Antibourgeois Propaganda and Anti-'Burzhui' Consciousness in 1917," *Russian Review* 53, no. 2 (1994): 183–96.

30. V. I. Lenin, "Reply to the discussion on the report of the Central Committee" (March 30, 1920), *Collected Works* (Moscow, 1960–72), 30:469.

31. Ibid., 472.

32. Karzhanskii, *Kollektivnaia,* 66–67.

33. "Sud nad Leninym."

34. L. A. and L. M. Vasilevskie, *Sud nad samogonshchikami. Delo Karpova Tikhona i ego*

zheny Agaf'i po obvineniiu v izgotovlenii i tainoi torgovle samogonkoi ([Moscow]: Oktiabr', 1923), ii; Predislovie, *Sud bespartiinykh rabochikh i krest'ian nad Krasnoi Armiei* (Moscow: Krasnaia nov', 1923).

35. "Politsud: Instruktsiia k postanovke instsenirovannykh sudov" (Kharkov, 1922), RGVA 9/13/108/16; draft version, RGVA 9/13/51/215–18. Gr. Avlov, *Klubnyi samodeiatel'nyi teatr: Evoliutsiia metodov i form* (intr. A. Piotrovskii) (Leningrad-Moscow: Teakinopechat', 1930), 92–93.

36. "Otzyv o materialakh PRIVO: Terarmeets—dezertir. Agitsud nad terameitsem" (December 20, 1923), RGVA 9/13/97/459.

37. "Sud nad Leninym."

38. "Novaia forma agitatsii," 3; also B. D. Sverdlov, *Sovetskaia propaganda v 20–e gody* (Moscow, 1990), 40.

39. P. M. Kerzhentsev, *Tvorcheskii teatr,* 5th ed. (Moscow-Petrograd: Gos. izd-vo, 1923); V. N. Vsevolodskii-Gerngross, *Istoriia russkogo teatra,* 2 vols. (Leningrad-Moscow: Teakinopechat', 1929), 302.

40. "Politsud: Instruktsiia"; Vsevolodskii-Gerngross, *Istoriia,* 397; A. Rozinskii, "K voprosu o formakh politprosvetraboty," *Put' politrabotnika* 8 (1921): 50.

41. In one trial, for example, the judges were played by two students, one employee, and two army stable workers ("Sud nad Sovetskoi vlast'iu").

42. In a similar vein some observers of the show trials of the 1930s believed that they were real because of this very appearance (obviously illusory) of free speech. As A. J. Cummings, a British observer, noted in conjunction with the Metro-Vickers trial: "The narrative method is effective and impressive; for the prisoners are allowed virtually to tell the story themselves. We are permitted to know nearly everything relevant to the accusations they say to their interrogators. All that we are not permitted to know is what the interrogators say to them." A. J. Cummings, *The Moscow Trial* (London, 1933), cited in Friedrich Adler, "The Witchcraft Trial in Moscow," in *The Opposition: At Home and Abroad* (Nendeln, Lichtenstein, 1975), 20n.

43. "Otzyv o materialakh k instsenirovannym sudam (izd. U.V.O.)," RGVA 9/13/97/109–10.

44. "Organizatsiia proletarskikh prazdnikov" in *Proletarskie prazdniki v rabochikh klubakh,* 2nd ed., ed. N. K. Krupskaia (Moscow: Krasnaia Nov', 1924). M. Shishkevich, "Metodika agit-sudov," in *Sbornik agit-sudy,* ed. V. Boichevskii, V. Malkis, and M. Shishkevich (Moscow: "Novaia Moskva" [Moskovskii Gubpolitprosvet], 1926), 5.

45. Stites, *Revolutionary Dreams,* 80–83.

46. Leon Trotsky, "Dnevnik," Trotsky Archive, Houghton Library, Harvard University, bMS/Russ 13, T3731, 110, also translated in *Trotsky's Diary in Exile 1935* (Cambridge, Mass., 1958), 80; discussion in Mark D. Steinberg and Vladimir M. Khrustalev, *The Fall of the Romanovs* (New Haven, 1995), 182, 223, 224–25, 233, 287–88.

47. N. Antonov, *Karl I-Liudovik XVI-Nikolai II* (Moscow: izd. Vseross. Tsentral'nogo Ispolnitel'nago Komiteta Sovetov R. S. K. i K. [sic] Deputatov, 1918); K. N. Berkova, *Protsess Liudovika XVI* (Moscow: Gos. izd-vo, 1920); *Protsess Zhirondistov (Iz istorii Velikoi Frantsuzskoi Revoliutsii)* (Petrograd: izd. sov. rab. i krest. dep., 1919; Gos. izd-vo, 1920); P. A. Kropotkin, *Velikaia frantsuzskaia revoliutsiia* (Moscow: Gos. izd-vo, 1917, 1919, 1922).

48. Antonov, *Karl I,* 14.

49. Von Geldern, esp. ch. 6, "Marking the Center," 175–207.

50. Corney, *Telling October.*

51. "Agitsudy, disputy i ustgazety (dokladchik tov. Abserman)," Protokol utrennego zasedaniia Klubnoi sektsii Konferentsii politprosvetrabotnikov X-i str. div. (October 2, 1923), RGVA 9/13/111/226.

52. A. Sipachev, "Massovaia rabota, kak rezul'tat organizatsionnoi samodeiatel'nosti iacheek kluba," *Politrabotnik* 1 (1922): 75–80.

53. The classic works on separation, liminality, and reabsorption into the community are Arnold van Gennep, *The Rites of Passage* (Chicago, 1960), and Victor W. Turner, *The Ritual Process: Structure and Anti-Structure* (Chicago, 1969); also Victor Turner, *Dramas, Fields, and Metaphors: Symbolic Action in Human Society* (Ithaca, 1974).

54. *Spisok materialov dlia raboty dramkruzhkov v klubakh,* ed. A. K. Mavrogan (Moscow: Mosk. Teatral'noe izd., 1925), 3.

55. Fainblit, S., "O formakh politraboty," *Put' politrabotnika* 6 (1921): 5; see also Stephen P. Frank, "Popular Justice, Community, and Culture among the Russian Peasantry, 1870–1900," *Russian Review* 46, no. 3 (1987): 239–65. As we saw in chapter 1, a popular play at the turn of the twentieth century was "Shemiakin sud," which satirized the corruption and venality of the courts.

56. N. A. Troitskii, *Tsarizm pod sudom progressivnoi obshchestvennosti, 1866–1895 gg.* (Moscow, 1979).

57. F. N. Samoilov at the trial of the Bolshevik deputies to the Fourth Duma (1914–1915), in *Podsudimye obviniaiut,* ed. A. V. Tolmachev (Moscow, 1962), 247.

58. Eugene Huskey, *Russian Lawyers and the Soviet State: The Origins and Development of the Soviet Bar, 1917–1939* (Princeton, 1986), 119n. It is even possible to view these trials of Lenin and the Communist Party as a transmogrified and secularized version of the kenotic (Christlike) ideals of medieval Russia. See Michael Cherniavsky, *Tsar and People: Studies in Russian Myths* (New York, 1961); Gregory Freidin, "By the Walls of Church and State: Literature's Authority in Russia's Modern Tradition," *Russian Review* 52, no. 2 (1993): 149–65. As in the ideal medieval world, one can see in the Soviet political realm a longing for union between ruler and ruled. The mock trial in this early period was the one place where the ruler appeared to submit to the will of the people. Not surprisingly, these heroic versions of the agitation trials died out almost entirely once Stalin came to power following Lenin's death.

59. For a brief discussion of one last heroic trial in 1933, see chapter 10 .

60. "Novaia forma agitatsii"; Degtiarev, "O novykh formakh politraboty," *Put' politrabotnika* 8 (1921): 44–45; M. Gekker, "Istoricheskie otdeleniia i politrabota v Krasnoi armii," *Put' politrabotnika* 8 (1921): 52; Karzhanskii, *Kollektivnaia,* 11–12.

61. It may even in fact be significant that Lenin had never been publicly tried while Trotsky had. Lenin's only day in court had been a closed party tribunal in 1907 when he was accused of splintering the party. Trotsky by contrast had been publicly tried by the Tsarist regime in 1906 for his role in organizing the Petersburg Soviet.

Chapter 4. Teaching Politics through Trials, 1921–23

1. V. I. Lenin (February 1921), in *Polnoe sobranie sochinenii* (Moscow, 1958–65) (*PSS*), 42:364.

2. V. I. Lenin, "Communism and the New Economic Policy" (March 1922), in *The Lenin Anthology,* ed. Robert C. Tucker (New York, 1975), 522.

3. Lenin, *PSS* 44:174; 41:315; 45:372. For a general discussion of Soviet policies on illiteracy and the importance of its elimination, see Peter Kenez, *The Birth of the Propaganda State* (Cambridge, 1985), 70–83, 145–66.

4. N. Krupskaia, "Nuzhno sushchestvovat' politprosvetam?" (1921), in *Pedagogicheskie sochineniia* (Moscow, 1957), 7:103.

5. M. A. Aleksinskii in "Protokol zasedaniia 1-i armeiskoi kul'truno-prosvetitel'noi konferentsii 27 maia 1920 g.," RGVA 192/2/538/57.

6. The principal articles in *Pravda* include: "Novaia forma agitatsii," November 21, 1920; "Sud nad Sovetskoi vlast'iu," December 21, 1920; F. K., "Privet novomu godu," January 5, 1921; "Instsenirovannyi sud nad Makhno," January 6, 1921; "Sud nad Leninym i Trotskim," February 15, 1921; "Sud nad R.K.P.," February 18, 1921; "Sud nad novoi zhenshchinoi," February 20, 1921; Artemii Garin, "Instsenirovka suda," February 26, 1921. Most of these are discussed in the previous chapter. A thorough search of *Pravda* revealed no agitation trials before *The Trial of Lenin* in April 1920; there were also two trials in the summer (one of "upper-crust Poland" and one of the Third International, the latter probably more of a discussion than a trial performance). The theater journal edited by Meyerhold, *Vestnik teatra,* also carried two articles on agitation trials in September and November 1920 (duplicate versions of *The Trial of Upper-Crust Poland* and *The Trial of Wrangel*).

7. Garin, "Instsenirovka suda."

8. Sheila Fitzpatrick, *Everyday Stalinism: Ordinary Life in Extraordinary Times. Soviet Russia in the 1930s* (New York, 1999), 24–28; Fitzpatrick, "How the Mice Buried the Cat: Scenes from the Great Purges of 1937 in the Russian Provinces," *Russian Review* 52, no. 3 (1993): 299–320; Fitzpatrick, "Signals from Below: Soviet Letters of Denunciation of the 1930s," *Journal of Modern History* 68, no. 4 (December 1996): 831–66.

9. "Vesti s mest," *Pravda*, April 12, 1921.

10. V. Mikhailov and A. Kollontai, "Ob Oktiabr'skikh torzhestvakh. Vsem gubzhenotde-lam" (October 12, 1921), Rossiiskii Gosudarstvennyi Arkhiv Sotsial'noi i Politicheskoi Istorii (RGASPI) 17/84/151/18; also *Izvestiia TsK*, November 15, 1921, 17. I will return to the topic of trials in the women's section in chapter 7.

11. "Instruktsiia k postanovke instsenirovannykh sudov" (Kharkov: Voenno-Revoliutsion-nyi Sovet Ukrkryma, 1922) (1,000 copies), Rossiiskii Gosudarstvennyi Voennyi Arkhiv (RGVA) 9/13/108/15–21; "Politsud (Instruktsiia)" (dated July 26, 1922, but with a note by Kamskii, head of the club division, that it dates from the previous year), RGVA 9/13/51/215–18; "Tekhnika organizatsii primernykh sudov (Politicheskikh, istoricheskikh, sanitarnykh i dr.)" [1922], RGVA 9/13/51/211–14.

12. Head of the agit-prop section and the head of the club division of the Politupravlenie Ukrkrym, letter to the Military Section of Glavpolitprosvet (August 2, 1922), RGVA 9/13/51/210.

13. "Ustav Klubov Krasnoi Armii i Krasnogo Flota" (April 4, 1923), *Partiino-politiches-kaia rabota v Krasnoi Armii (1921–1929 gg.): Dokumenty* (Moscow, 1981) (*PPRIII*), 135; also RGVA 9/13/97/13–19, 184–185ob.

14. "Instruktsiia k postanovke instsenirovannykh sudov"; "Politsud (Instruktsiia)"; "Tekhnika organizatsii primernykh sudov."

15. Mikhail Landa and M. Rafes, Letter to the head of the Politupravlenie Otdel'noi Kavkazskoi Armii (OKA) (July 19, 1922), RGVA 9/13/93/20–20ob.; Abserman, "Agitsudy, disputy, i ustgazety" (October 2, 1923), RGVA 9/13/111/226; S. Sosnovskii, "Klubnaia rabota v voennoe vremia" (1923), RGVA 9/13/87/358–59.

16. N. Dmitriev, "Kruzhki voennykh znanii v klubakh" (1923), RGVA 9/13/97/52–57.

17. "Instruktsiia raboty kluba" [*sic*] (Oct. 1922), *Politrabotnik* (prilozhenie k *Krasno-armeiskoi zvezde*), in RGVA 9/13/111/56ob.

18. Mikhail Landa, M. Rafes, and I. Korobochkin, letter to the head of the Political Ad-ministration of the Ukrainian Military District (December 30, 1922), RGVA 9/13/97/8; I. Ko-robochkin, "Ocherednye zadachi klubnoi raboty" (January 12, 1923), RGVA 9/13/97/9; "Blizhaishie zadachi klubnoi raboty v Otdel'noi Kavkasskoi Armii (po dokladu t. Koroboch-kina)" [1922], RGVA 9/13/93/146–47; "Iz rezoliutsii Vserossiiskogo soveshchaniia po agit-proprabote v Krasnoi Armii i Flote" (September 1–6, 1922), in *PPRIII*, 77–93. A requirement that soldiers in the reserve units attend daily lessons in political literacy seems to have been in-troduced as early as November 1920. *Politrabotnik* 11 (1920): 16, cited in V. G. Kolychev, *Par-tiino-politicheskaia rabota v Krasnoi Armii v gody grazhdanskoi voiny, 1918–1920 gg.* (Moscow, 1979), 140–41. By 1922 this had become known as the *politchas*. "Polozhenie o politchase" (May 25, 1922), RGVA 9/13/51/145–46; von Hagen, *Soldiers of the Proletarian Dictatorship* (Ithaca, 1990), 168–69.

19. M. Rafes and I. Korobochkin, "Instruktsiia o provedenii vneshkol'nykh voennykh za-niatii letom 1923 goda," RGVA 9/13/97/259, 147.

20. N. Dmitriev, "Kruzhki voennykh znanii v klubakh," RGVA 9/13/97/54; N. Dmitriev, "Voennye instsenirovki v klube," *Politrabotnik* 5 (1923): 54–56.

21. Vrid. Nachagitprop Puokra Z.S.V.O. and NachKlubotd. Semkov, "Dopolnenie k in-struktsii o rabote krasnykh ugolkov" [1923], RGVA 9/13/111/65–72.

22. Ibid., l. 92ob.

23. I. Korobochkin, "Primernaia programma vneshkol'nykh politicheskikh zaniatii" (n.d.), RGVA 9/13/97/169; M. Rafes and I. Korobochkin, "Instruktsiia o provedenii politicheskikh vneshkol'nykh zaniatii letom 1923 goda" (April 1923), RGVA 9/13/97/145–49; "Materialy dlia massovoi raboty k politustavu i prazdnikam," RGVA 9/13/97/248.

24. M. Lebedev, *Sud nad karaulom, dopustivshim sozzhenie ssypnogo punkta prodnaloga* (Kiev: izd. Politupravlenie Kievskogo Voennogo Okruga, 1921), RGVA 9/13/108/27–30ob. Other trials that aimed to teach army regulations included *The Political Trial of the Marauders (Politsud nad barakhol'shchikami)* (1922), RGVA 9/13/51/199–199ob.; *The Political Trial of the Military Employee Who Gave Away a Military Secret (Politsud nad voennosluzhashchim, vydavshim voennuiu tainu)* (1922), l. 200; *How to Put On the Trial of an Illiterate (Kak postavit' sud nad negramotnym)* (1922), ll. 224–25; D. Shirin, *Sud nad negramotnym chasovym (The Trial of the Illiterate Sentry)*, *Krasnaia Armiia*, July 23, 1922; *The Trial of the Soldier Who Violated His Oath (Sud nad krasnoarmeitsem za narushenie prisiagi)*, in *Klub! Pomogi komandiru i politruku!* supplement to *Krasnaia Rota*, 17, in RGVA 9/13/112/241–51.

25. "Prikaz Politupravleniia Zapsibvo," (October 6, 1922, Omsk), *Politrabotniku* (supplement to *Krasnoarmeiskaia zvezda*, No. 76–253), in RGVA 9/13/111/56–57.

26. "Tsirkuliar Politicheskogo Upravleniia Zapadno-Sibirskogo Voennogo Okruga" (December 23, 1922), RGVA 9/13/111/4.

27. Rozenshil'd, "Perspektivy klubnoi raboty" (draft article submitted to *Politrabotnik* but not published because of Korobochkin's criticisms) (April 1923), RGVA 9/13/111/269.

28. Ibid., ll. 269–71. The Eleventh Party Congress (March-April 1922) insisted that the military barracks, and by extension the clubs, should be turned into "a parallel division of the party schools." Political work should in fact be so well established that in a soldier's two years of military service he would attain the same level of political knowledge as that of a provincial party school. Later studies claimed that this was a blow against the "Trotskyists" who wanted political work in the army to have a "nonideological, recreational character." *Partiino-politicheskaia rabota v Sovetskoi Armii i Voenno-Morskom Flote* (Moscow, 1960), 15; "Protokol zaniatii klubnogo seminariia" (June 1922), RGVA 9/13/91/406–7.

29. E. J. Hobsbawm, "Revolution Is Puritan," *New Society,* May 22, 1969; Bruce Mazlish, *The Revolutionary Ascetic: Evolution of a Political Type* (New York, 1976); Michael Walzer, *The Revolution of the Saints: A Study in the Origins of Radical Politics* (Cambridge, Mass., 1965); R. P. Neuman, "The Sexual Question and Social Democracy in Imperial Germany," *Journal of Social History* 7 (1974): 271–86.

30. Zamnachpusa Grobov, Zamnachagitpropotdela Fridman, Vrid. Nachklubno-Khud. Otdeleniia Kazanskii, "Vsem podivam Politsekretariatam i t.d." (April 8, 1922), RGVA 9/13/91/229; Aleksei Kazanskii, Nachotdelenii, and Ivan Shcherbatykh, instruktor po klubnomu delu, "V Voensektsiiu GPP (otvety po klubnomu delu po ankete no. 5)" [1922], RGVA 9/13/91/505; I. Korobochkin, Nach. klubn. otdeleniia, "Ocherednye zadachi klubnoi raboty (Tezisy doklada NACHPURu)" (January 12, 1923), RGVA 9/13/97/9.

31. B. Zaits, zam. nach. klubno-khud. otdeleniia voennoi sektsii Glavpolitprosvet, "Svodka rabota Klubno-Khudozhestvennogo Otdleniia Voennoi Sektsii GPP za iiul' mes. 1922 g." (July 29, 1922), RGVA 9/13/91/338; Zaits, "Doklad o deiatel'nosti Klubno-khud. otdelenii Voensektsii GPP za iiul' mes. 1922 g.," RGVA 9/13/91/341.

32 I. Korobochkin, "Klub na puti k sisteme" (fall 1923), RGVA 9/13/97/294–300.

33. "Anketa sostavlennaia sektsiei obsledovaniia rab.-kr. teatra" *Vestnik teatra* 67 (September 7, 1920): 12; Aleksei Gan, "Sektsiia massovykh predstavlenii i zrelishch'," *ibid.,* 12–13; "Pervoe maia," *ibid.,* 13; R. Ginzburg, "Kampanii v massovoi rabote kluba," *Rabochii klub* 3–4 (1924): 34–36.

34. James von Geldern, *Bolshevik Festivals, 1917–1920* (Berkeley, 1993), 22–24; Katerina Clark, *Petersburg, Crucible of Cultural Revolution* (Cambridge, Mass., 1995), esp. 122–34; Rene Fulop-Miller, *The Mind and Face of Bolshevism* (London, 1927), 141–49. Immediately following the October Revolution, a number of works on French festivals were translated into Russian: V. S. [V. Smyshliaev], "Istoriia pervogo sotsialisticheskogo stsenariia," *Vestnik teatra* 62 (April 27–May 2, 1920): 6–10; Zhiul'en T'erso [Julien Tiersot], *Prazdnestva i pesni frantsuzskoi revoliutsii* (Petrograd: Parus, 1918). The premier source on the French festivals remains the work of Mona Ozouf, *Festivals and the French Revolution* (Cambridge, 1988), plus her "Space and Time in the Festivals of the French Revolution," *Comparative Studies in Society and History* 17, no. 3 (1975): 372–84.

35. Rita Dielmann, "Dramatic Representation as a Means of Popular Instruction in the French Revolution, 1789–1794" (Ph.D. diss., Cornell University, 1924), 17n., 23, 63 (my thanks to Yaakov Garb for this reference); Ozouf, *Festivals,* 197–203. In 1871 the Paris Commune also passed legislation declaring the theaters to be a means of education for virtuous citizens and placing them under the aegis of the delegations for enlightenment. N. A. Gorchakov, *Istoriia sovetskogo teatra* (New York, 1956), 45; V. Vidman, "Razvitie revoliutsionnoi bor'by na frantsuzskoi stsene," in *Teatr i revoliutsiia* (Moscow-Petrograd, 1923).

36. "Prikaz politicheskogo otdela Shestoi Moskovskoi Strelkovoi Divizii" (Novgorod, November 1, 1922), RGVA 9/13/91/436.

37. "Teatral'naia rabota v Krasnoi Armii (po dokladu tov. Smirnova)" (January 16, 1922), RGVA 9/13/93/155.

38. "Svodka PUR RVSR no. 67" (Moscow, January 4, 1923), RGASPI 17/84/633/1–2.

39. Sosnovskii and Kurdiumov, "Otzyv o materialakh Privo" [1923], RGVA 9/13/97/442; Korobochkin and Kurdiumov, "Otzyv o materialakh Privo ko dniu Parizhskoi kommuny i godovshchiny fevral'skoi revoliutsii" (April 24, 1923), RGVA 09/13/97/180–180ob.; 09/13/112/265–266ob. A number of other armies and units wrote in their reports that they were creating new plays for the holidays and organizing their club work around the new calendar: "Doklad kluba OKA za Oktiabr' mesiats" (November 11, 1922), RGVA 9/13/97/386; "Tezisy doklada teatral'noi sektsii klubota PUOKA na Tret'em armeiskom klubnom soveshchanii" [1922], RGVA 9/13/93/212; Shifres (Pom. Nach. Agitpropotdela) and I. Korobochkin, letter to Nach. PUR, Antonov-Ovseenko (March 15, 1923), RGVA 9/13/97/78; I. Korobochkin and Kurdiumov, letter to Politupravlenie Revvoensoveta Zapfronta (March 19, 1923), RGVA 9/13/97/79–79ob. Korobochkin and Kurdiumov also wrote to one of the political departments explaining that they were helping prepare a Glavpolitprosvet anthology of materials for the revolutionary holidays (letter to the Politupravlenie Revvoensoveta Zapfronta, March 6, 1923, RGVA 9/13/97/79ob.; also RGVA 9/13/112/94ob.).

40. "Sud nad Oktiabr'skim perevorotom 1917 goda" (kollektivnyi trud litkruzhka kluba im. "Karla Marksa" rukovoditelia kruzhka Bova i chlena Aleksandrova) (typescript) [1922], RGVA 9/13/93/143–44.

41. Borovich, *Instsenirovki kak metod prosvetitel'noi raboty* (Kharkov, 1923), 6–7.

42. D. Furmanov, "Formy agitatsii i propagandy," *Krasnoe znamia* 157 (October 28, 1920): 2–3.

43. E. I. Khlebtsevich, "Predislovie: O formakh vedeniia politiko-prosvetitel'noi raboty," in *Sud bespartiinykh rabochikh i krest'ian nad Krasnoi Armiei* (Moscow, 1923), 4; K. I. Abramov, *Bibliotechnoe stroitel'stvo v pervye gody Sovetskoi vlasti* (Moscow, 1974), 149.

44. Vl. Sarab'ianov, "Disputy o religii," *Pravda,* September 15, 1921.

45. I. Korobochkin and Kurdiumov, "Otzyv o materialakh k instsenirvannym sudam" [March 1923], RGVA 9/13/97/109. Korobochkin and Kurdiumov also commented in another review that the "outcome of the trial should not be too obvious from the outset": "Otzyv ob agitsude nad mezhdunarodnym imperializmom" (May 29, 1923), l. 214.

46. *Sud bespartiinykh rabochikh i krest'ian nad Krasnoi Armiei,* 5.

47. "Sud nad Sovetskoi vlast'iu," *Pravda,* December 21, 1920.

48. V. I. Lenin, "Rech' na Vserossiiskom soveshchanie politprosvetov" (November 1920), in *PSS,* 41:406–7.

49. *Biulleten' No. 15 Otdela TsK RKP po rabote sredi zhenshchin. Tezisy i rezoliutsii IV Vseross. soveshch. zavgubzhenotdelami* (Moscow, 1921), 21.

50. *Sud bespartiinykh rabochikh i krest'ian nad Krasnoi Armiei,* 12–15.

51. Korobochkin and Kurdiumov, "Otzyv o materialakh Privo ko dniu Parizhskoi kommuny"; "Agitsud nad Koalitsionnym Pravitel'stvom" (Privo, 1923), RGVA 9/13/112/182–83.

52. "Sud nad Oktiabr'skim perevorotom," ll. 143–44.

53. "Politsud nad Pil'sudskim," RGVA 9/13/51/135–37ob. Trotsky's comment (May 1920) is quoted in William Henry Chamberlin, *The Russian Revolution* (New York, 1935), 2:303.

54. "Kommuna 1871 goda (Stsenarii dlia samodeiatel'nogo tvorchestva)" (typescript, OKA, 1922), RGVA 9/13/51/66–68ob.; "Sud nad Parizhskoi kommuny," "Kommunary pered sudom," "Stsenarii Agitsuda 'nad T'erom'" in *Materialy k prazdnovaniiu 51–oi godovshchiny Parizhskoi kommuny* (Moscow: izd. Glavnoe upravlenie voenno-uchebnykh zavedenii, 1922); I. Gekhtman, "Sud v teatra Shatle," in *Proletarskie prazdniki v rabochikh klubakh*, 2nd ed., ed. N. K. Krupskaia (Moscow, 1924), 170–75. These trials were almost certainly conceived in response to the fiftieth anniversary of the Commune.

55. "Sud nad Parizhskoi kommuny," l. 38ob.

56. "Kommunary pered sudom," ll. 40–41 (lorgnettes and defendants' nobility); "Kommuna 1871 goda," ll. 68–68ob. ("they have no fear").

57. "Agitsud nad mezhdunarodnym imperializmom (izd. PUSKVO)" [1923], RGVA 9/13/112/252–64; reviewed, l. 361, 9/13/97/214.

58. "Sud nad okkupantami Rurskogo basseina" (1923) (typescript, OKA), RGVA 9/13/112/109–10.

59. Shifres, "Otzvyv o stsenariiakh OKA" March 23, 1923), RGVA 9/13/112/113–13ob; 9/13/97/127.

60. "Politsud nad Pil'sudskim," RGVA 9/13/51/135–37ob.

61. Sources on the trial of the Orthodox Church leaders include Arto Luukkanen, *The Party of Unbelief: The Religious Policy of the Bolshevik Party, 1917–1929* (Helsinki, 1994); Aleksandr I. Solzhenitsyn, *The Gulag Archipelago* (New York, 1973), 346–52; John Sheldon Curtiss, *The Russian Church and the Soviet State* (Boston, 1953), 106–28. On the trial of the Socialist Revolutionaries, Marc Jansen, *A Show Trial under Lenin: The Trial of the Socialist Revolutionaries, Moscow 1922* (The Hague, 1982).

62. A report from 1925 in the Polytechnical Museum's own archive notes that the auditorium in the museum could hold an audience of 1,000 and was considered the best auditorium in Moscow (Polytechnical Museum, f. 3, l. 33). The museum had been founded in 1870 as the Russian State Polytechnical Museum. Unfortunately, I was not able to obtain records of actual lectures or performances held except for the year October 1, 1924, to October 1, 1925, when two (presumably agitation) trials were held before a total audience of 1,700. Of all the events held that year including fifty-four lectures, twenty concerts, five debates and so on, the trials had the highest audience sizes, almost filling the house each time (f. 3, ll. 153–54).

63. Letter from PU Privo (Samara) to Nach. PUR (May 12, 1922), RGVA 9/13/51/85.

64. Jansen, *Show Trial under Lenin*; Solzhenitsyn, *Gulag*, 354–67.

65. "Soveshchanie nachagitpropov politorganov OKA" [fall 1922], RGVA 9/13/93/60.

66. "Put' na skam'iu prestupnikov" (1922), RGVA 9/13/51/94–106. The trial named several people as authors and editors including Boris Volin, listed as "responsible editor, commissioned by the Central Committee of the Russian Communist Party" for this trial; M. Rafes, head of the military section of PUR in Glavpolitprosvet; and I. Flerovskii, a journalist. Boris Mikhailovich Volin (real name, Fradkin) (1886–1957) had been a party member from 1904; from 1918 he served on the editorial board of *Pravda*. M. Rafes had a checkered, non-Bolshevik past. A former Menshevik, in 1919 he had been head of the Communist Bund (Kombund) in Ukraine, which sided with the Soviet regime rather than with the Petliura government. Ivan Petrovich Flerovskii (1888–1959) was an active member of the Communist Party from 1905; as a journalist, he had played a role in recording the events of Kronstadt.

67. "Politsud nad popom Obiralovym" (July 1922), RGVA 9/13/51/195–96.

Chapter 5. The Culture of Everyday Life, 1922–24

1. "Vnimanie k demobilizuemym tovarishcham-krasnoarmeitsam," *Pravda*, February 18, 1921.

2. "Organizatsiia politsuda v derevne" in *Samodeiatel'nyi teatr v derevne* (Leningrad: izd. Knizhnogo sektra GUBONO, 1924), 38.

3. "Politsud (Instruktsiia)," Rossiiskii Gosurdarstvennyi Voennyi Arkhiv (RGVA) 9/13/51/215–218; I. Korobochkin and Kurdiumov, "Otzyv," RGVA 9/13/108/13ob.

4. V. I. Lenin, "Rech' na Vserossiiskom soveshchanii politprosvetov gubernskikh i uezdnykh otdelov narodnogo obrazovaniia" (November 3, 1920), in Polnoe sobranie sochinenii (PSS) (Moscow, 1960–65), 41:400.

5. V. I. Lenin, "A Great Beginning," in The Lenin Anthology, ed. Robert C. Tucker (New York, 1975), 477–78.

6. On byt and its meanings, Svetlana Boym, Common Places (Cambridge, Mass., 1994), esp. 3, 29–40; Roman Jakobson, "On a Generation That Squandered Its Poets," in Language in Literature (Cambridge, Mass., 1987), 273–300; Eric Naiman, Sex in Public (Princeton, 1997), 185–88; Andrei Sinyavsky, Soviet Civilization (New York, 1990), 153–74; Gary Thurston, "The Impact of Russian Popular Theatre, 1886–1915," Journal of Modern History 55 (June 1983): 247–48.

7. Maksim Antonov, Sud nad plokhim krest'ianinom (Leningrad: Gos. izd-vo, 1924), 47.

8. Stephen P. Frank, "Confronting the Domestic Other: Rural Popular Culture and Its Enemies in Fin-de-Siècle Russia," and Joan Neuberger, "Culture Besieged: Hooliganism and Futurism," in Cultures in Flux: Lower-Class Values, Practices and Resistance in Late Imperial Russia, ed. Stephen P. Frank and Mark D. Steinberg (Princeton, 1994), 74–107, 185–203; Jeffrey Brooks, When Russia Learned to Read: Literacy and Popular Literature, 1861–1917 (Princeton, 1985), esp. 295–352; Glennys Young, Power and the Sacred in Revolutionary Russia: Religious Activists in the Village (University Park, Pa., 1997); William B. Husband, "Godless Communists": Atheism and Society in Soviet Russia, 1917–1932 (Dekalb, Ill., 2000).

9. Reginald E. Zelnik, "Russian Bebels: An Introduction to the Memoirs of the Russian Workers Semen Kanatchikov and Matvei Fisher," Russian Review 35, no. 3 (1976), 417–47; Zelnik, trans. and ed., A Radical Worker in Tsarist Russia: The Autobiography of Semen Ivanovich Kanatchikov (Stanford, 1986); Mark D. Steinberg, "Worker-Authors and the Cult of the Person," in Cultures in Flux, 168–84; Mark D. Steinberg, Moral Communities: The Culture of Class Relations in the Russian Printing Industry, 1867–1907 (Berkeley, 1992) and Steinberg, "Vanguard Workers and the Morality of Class," in Making Workers Soviet: Power, Class and Identity, ed. Lewis H. Siegelbaum and Ronald Grigor Suny (Ithaca, 1994), 66–84.

10. Peter Kenez, The Birth of the Propaganda State (Cambridge, 1985), 84–85.

11. I. M. Danilov, "K rabote krasnoarmeiskikh klubov," Kommunisticheskoe prosveshchenie 6 (November–December 1922): 77–78.

12. N. K. Krupskaia, "Vystuplenie na IV Kongresse Kommunisticheskogo Internatsionala" [1922], Pedagogicheskie sochinenii (Moscow, 1947), 9:90.

13. Dmitriev, "Kruzhki voennykh znanii v klubakh" [1923], RGVA 9/13/97/56; "Polozhenie o politchase" [May 1922], RGVA 9/13/51/146ob.

14. "Blizhaishie zadachi klubnoi raboty v Otdel'noi Kavkasskoi [sic] Armii (po dokladu t. Korobochkina)" [1922], RGVA 9/13/93/147.

15. Political scientist Jan Gross has made a similar point concerning the willingness of the state to accept people's denunciations. As both Gross and Sheila Fitzpatrick argue, the state found ways to allow (and, of course, to foster) preexisting practices of reporting. Jan T. Gross, "A Note on the Nature of Soviet Totalitarianism," Soviet Studies 34, no. 3 (1982); Sheila Fitzpatrick and Robert Gellately, "Introduction to the Practices of Denunciation in Modern European History," Journal of Modern History 68 (December 1996): 756–59.

16. B. Vetrov and L. Petrov, Agitsud i zhivaia gazeta v derevne (Moscow-Leningrad: Gos. izd-vo, 1926), 7–9.

17. Klubnoe otdelenie politupravleniia OKA, "Klub v dele likvidatsii bezgramotnosti" [1922], RGVA 9/13/93/198.

18. Klubnoe otdelenie politupravleniia OKA, "Tezisy doklada teatral'noi sektsii klubota PUOKA na 3[-em] armeiskom klubnom soveshchanii" [1922], RGVA 9/13/93/212; "Blizhaishie zadachi klubnoi raboty v Otdel'noi Kavkasskoi Armii, l. 147.

19. Klubnoe otdelenia politupravlenie OKA, "Metody vneshkol'noi raboty v oblasti strelkovogo dela (Tezisy)" [1922], RGVA 9/13/93/202.

20. Klubnoe otdelenie Politupravleniia OKA, "Rezoliutsii o klubnom stroitel'stve" [1922], RGVA 9/13/93/199.

21. Ia[kov] L[ozhkin], *Sud nad krest'ianinom, uklonivshimsia ot prizyva v Krasnuiu Armiiu* (Kharkov: izd. Voenno-Revoliutsionnogo Soveta Ukrkryma, 1922).

22. "Sud nad krasnoarmeitsem, ne pozhelavshim obuchat'sia voennomu iskusstvu," in *Sbornik. No. Pervyi. Vecher voennoi propagandy (Materialy dlia kluba)* (Nikolaev: izd. Podiv 15, 1922), RGVA 9/13/108/31–34ob.; *Sud nad Neriashkinym obvinenym v rasprostranenii zarazy sypnogo tifa* ([Kiev]: izd. Kievskogo Voennogo okruga, 1921).

23. "Sud nad politicheskim negramotnym" (1923), RGVA 9/13/108/36–37.

24. "Politsud nad krasnoarmeitsem ne poseshchavshim blagodaria svoei leni i pod-strekaniiam zlonamerennykh elementov, zaniatii kruzhka, i vernulsia domoi nichemu ne nauchivshis'" mentioned in "Tezisy dlia vedeniia klubno-kruzhkovoi raboty" [1922], RGVA 9/13/93/208.

25. In 1714 Peter the Great decreed that no nobleman could marry until he had learned ci-phering and geometry. Vasili Klyuchevsky, *Peter the Great* (New York, 1958), 96–97; Evgenii V. Anisimov, *The Reforms of Peter the Great* (Armonk, N.Y., 1993), 187–88.

26. "Politsud nad krest'ianinom, uklonivshemsia ot vneseniia podvornogo naloga" (August 1922), RGVA 9/13/51/228–231.

27. "Otzyv o materialakh Privo" (including review of *Sud nad neplatel'shchikom naloga*) (November 1923), RGVA 9/13/97/443.

28. Maksim Antonov, *Sud nad plokhim krest'ianinom* (Leningrad: Gos. izd-vo, 1924). Ro-goza's name comes from the word for "horn" (*rog*) which could refer to the horn of plenty (*rog izobiliia*) since he is a rich man. It is more likely, however, that peasant audiences would asso-ciate the name with the horns of a cuckold (*nastavit' roga,* to make someone a cuckold). Ukhva-tov's name comes from words meaning "to grasp."

29. Boris Vaks, "Tezisy-doklad po voprosu o politprosvetrabote v Krasnoi Armii. K Vseros-siiskomu S"ezdu Glavpolitprosveta" (September 15, 1921), Rossiiskii Gosudarstvennyi Arkhiv Sotsial'noi i Politicheskoi Istorii (RGASPI) 17/84/151/62.

30. James Bunyan, *The Origin of Forced Labor in the Soviet State, 1917–1921* (Baltimore, 1967), 172n.; Robert A. Lewis and Richard H. Rowland, *Population Redistribution in the USSR* (New York, 1979), 97. At its height the famine affected thirty-three provinces with a pop-ulation of over forty million. It resulted in some three million deaths from starvation and an ad-ditional one million deaths from epidemics. For a recent discussion of the range of estimates made by contemporaries, see Bertrand M. Patenaude, *The Big Show in Bololand: The Ameri-can Relief Expedition to Soviet Russia in the Famine of 1921* (Stanford, 2002), 196–99.

31. Solzhenitsyn disputes this claim, arguing that in fact the famine provided a convenient excuse to secularize church properties and seize valuables. *The Gulag Archipelago* (New York, 1973), 342–52. For more on the famine as a spur to attacks on the Russian Orthodox Church, see Husband, *"Godless Communists,"* 55–58; Arto Luukanen, *The Party of Unbelief: The Re-ligious Policy of the Bolshevik Party, 1917–1929* (Helsinki, 1994), 107–9.

32. "Sud nad vinovnikami goloda" (Kiev Voennyi okrug, 1922), RGVA 9/13/51/219–23; "Primernyi politicheskii sud nad tserkov'iu" (Privo, May 1922), RGVA 9/13/51/86–92; "Polit-sud nad popom Obiralovym" (July 1922), RGVA 9/13/51/183–96; "Neobyknovennoe sobytie v zhizni. Otets Evlampiia" (May 1922), RGVA 9/13/93/101–13.

33. "Neobyknovennoe sobytie v zhizni. Otets Evlampiia."

34. A variant of this trial, *The Trial of Priest Obiralov [Fleecer] (*Politsud nad popom Obi-ralovym*)* begins by telling the story of peasants in a village called Suffering (Stradalovka) who, beginning in the year 1903, are subject to the priest's deliberate obstruction of any real learn-ing. Not only does the priest Obiralov chase away the secular schoolteacher in the village, he also reports to the authorities the confessions of people who told him they had cursed the tsar or failed to report for military duty. As a sniveling informer, he thus is shown to have conspired with the tsarist authorities against the best interests of the villagers.

35. "Sud nad zhenshchinami, otkazavshimisia ot pomoshchi golodaiushchemu Povolzhiu," RGASPI 17/10/76/231–34; letter from Kibardina, zavobzhenotdela Kubano-Chernomorskoi oblasti and [illegible], zav. agitpropa Kubcheroblastkoma RKP(b), to all women's sections (July 29, 1921), RGASPI 17/10/6/22.

36. I. Korobochkin and Kurdiumov, review of "Sud nad nebrezhnem chitatelem," RGVA 9/13/258/3–4.

37. Interestingly, he was reading *Istoriia novogo vremeni* (*History of a New Time*) by R. Vipper, a historian whose work greatly interested Stalin as well. Robert C. Tucker, *Stalin in Power: The Revolution from Above, 1928–1941* (New York, 1990), 276–77.

38. "Politsud nad krest'ianinom, uklonivshemsia ot vneseniia podvornogo naloga."

39. E. Militsyna, *Sud nad negramotnym* (Rostov-na-Donu: Iugo-Vostochnoe kraevoe partiinoe izd. Burevestnik, 1925).

40. "Iazykom ne trepat'," *Krasnaia Armiia*, July 23, 1922, RGVA 9/13/51/227.

41. Zhogova's name also may have several referents—in polite language, a throw in the game of knucklebones *babki* known as "zhog"; in not so polite language, the posterior of a human being (*zhopa*).

42. D. Shirin, "Sud nad negramotnym chasovym," *Krasnaia Armiia*, July 23, 1922, RGVA 9/13/51/227.

43. "Negry pod 'sudom Lincha,'" *Krasnaia Armiia*, July 23, 1922.

44. B. Kanatchikova, "God raboty (na mestakh)," *Kommunistka* 16–17 (September–October 1921): 29–30; Anna Itkina, speech at the fourth national zhenotdel meeting (November 2–6, 1921), RGASPI 17/10/11/244; report from Ukraine, RGASPI 17/10/10/65–66; "Sud nad novoi zhenshchinoi," *Pravda*, February 20, 1921; "Zhenskii samosud," *Pravda*, November 21, 1921; Smeliakova, "Sud nad delegatkoi," *Rabotnitsa i krest'ianka* [Moscow] 1 (January 23, 1922); N. Tr-ii, "Rabota sredi zhenshchin v Sibiri," *Pravda*, January 13, 1923; Delegatka M. Genert, "Vypusk delegatok glavnogo Pochtamta," *Rabotnitsa i krest'ianka* [Petrograd] 6 (October 1923): 25. See chapter 7.

45. Boris Andreev, *Sud nad komsomol'tsem ili komsomolkoi narushaiushchimi soiuznuiu distsiplinu* (Leningrad: Knizhnyi sektor GUBONO, 1924); B. S. Sigal, *Sud nad pionerom-kuril'shchikom i sud nad neriashlivym pionerom* (Moscow: Zhizn' i znanie, 1927). See chapter 8.

46. A. Krupkov, "Klub imeni Kominterna. Fabrika Trekhgornoi manufaktury," *Klub* 9, no. 16 (1926): 55–58.

47. *Sputnik klubnogo rabotnika* (Moscow: Gos. izd-vo, 1922), 24–25, 46–48.

Chapter 6. Melodrama in the Service of Science

1. "Sudebnyi otdel: Bor'ba s prostitutsiei," *Pravda*, August 14, 1921.

2. "Popravka," *Pravda*, August 19, 1921.

3. A. Edel'shtein, "Neskol'ko slov o sanprosvetsudakh," introduction to A. I. Akkerman, *Sud nad prostitutkoi. Delo gr. Zaborovoi po obvineniiu ee v zaniatii prostitutsiei i zarazhenii sifilisom krasnoarmeitsa Krest'ianova* (Moscow-Petrograd: Gos. izd-vo, 1922), 4.

4. Letter from L. Rakovskii, Nachal'nik Politupravleniia Revvoensoveta Respublika, and Polonskii, Nachal'nik Lit.-izd. otdela, to Trotsky, January 23, 1920, Rossiiskii Gosudarstvennyi Arkhiv Sotsial'noi i Politicheskoi Istorii (RGASPI) 17/84/135/3.

5. A. Krylov, "Vtoraia armeiskaia kul't-prosvetitel'naia konferentsiia," *Krasnoe znamia*, October 29, 1920, 3.

6. "Pervoe Vserossiiskoe soveshchanie," *Sanitarnoe prosveshchenie* 1 (1924): 2–3.

7. Tsentral'nyi Gosudarstvennyi Arkhiv Oktiabr'skoi Revoliutsii i Sovetskogo Stroitel'stva goroda Leningrada (TsGAORL) 4301/1/798/400; 4301/1/801/188, 230; *Pervoe Vserossiiskoe soveshchanie po sanitarnomu prosveshcheniiu. 15–20 marta 1921 g. Tezisy, doklady, i rezoliutsii*, ed. L. M. Isaev ([Moscow]: GIZ, 1922); A. V. Mol'kov, "Sanitarnoe prosveshchenie, ego zadachi i metody," in *Sotsial'naia gigiena.* (Moscow-Petrograd, 1923), 43–44; "Sanitarnoe prosveshchenie v respublike," *Pravda*, March 17, 1921; "Pervoe Vserossiiskoe soveshchanie," 2–3.

8. Mol'kov, "Sanitarnoe prosveshchenie," 42. Al'fred Vladislavovich Mol'kov (1870–1947) was one of the earliest proponents of the study and practice of hygiene, especially for children and young people. He pioneered the creation of museums devoted to sanitation and hygiene topics in the prerevolutionary period and joined the Communist Party in 1919. He was also the first director of what later became known as the Institute of Social Hygiene.

9. *Sud nad Neriashkinym obvinenym v rasprostranenii zarazy sypnogo tifa* ([Kiev], 1921), 20–21.

10. Nancy Mandelker Frieden, *Russian Physicians in an Era of Reform and Revolution, 1856–1905* (Princeton, 1981); Frieden, "Child Care: Medical Reform in a Traditionalist Culture," in *The Family in Imperial Russia*, ed. David L. Ransel (Urbana, Ill., 1978), 236–59; John F. Hutchinson, *Politics and Public Health in Revolutionary Russia, 1890–1918* (Baltimore, 1990); Hutchinson, "'Who Killed Cock Robin?' An Inquiry into the Death of Zemstvo Medicine," in *Health and Society in Revolutionary Russia*, ed. Susan G. Solomon and John F. Hutchinson (Bloomington, Ind., 1990), 3–26; Susan Gross Solomon, "Social Hygiene and Soviet Public Health, 1921–1930," in *Health and Society*, 175–99; Neil Weissman, "Origins of Soviet Health Administration: Narkomzdrav, 1918–1928," in *Health and Society*, 97–120; Laura Engelstein, *The Keys to Happiness: Sex and the Search for Modernity in Fin-de-Siècle Russia* (Ithaca, 1992).

11. *Ocherki po istorii Sovetskogo sanitarnogo prosveshcheniia*, ed. I. S. Sokolov (Moscow, 1960), 78.

12. Quoted in M. V. Mirskii, "Zinovii Petrovich Solov'ev" in *Vrachi-Bol'sheviki: Stroiteli sovetskogo zdravookhraneniia*, ed. E. I. Lotova and B. D. Petrov (Moscow, 1970), 154.

13. Ibid., 150–59; see also Hutchinson, *Politics and Public Health*, 122–23 and *passim*, for more on Solov'ev. On November 25–30, 1920 the army held its first conference specifically devoted to sanitation education. *K s"ezdu rabotnikov sanitarnogo prosveshcheniia Zapadnogo fronta (tezisy dokladov)* (Smolensk, 1920).

14. Report of the sanprosvet otdel (March 23, 1921), TsGAORL 4301/1/801/188. In 1924 Strashun and A. O. Edel'shtein became editors of an important new journal, *Sanitarnoe prosveshchenie*.

15. A. Mol'kov, "Sotsial'naia gigiena," *Bol'shaia sovetskaia entsiklopediia* (Moscow, 1926–47), 41:1–38; Mol'kov, "Sanitarnoe prosveshchenie," 46–47. The sanitation education congress of March 1921 discussed other measures as well, including "sanitation satire," "sanitation rallies," and phonograph recordings on sanitation topics (TsGAORL 4301/1/798/400).

16. "Vsem Nachsanam frontov, okrugov i otdel'nykh armii," *Biulleten' Narodnogo Komissariata Zdravookhraneniia*, March 31, 1924, 6.

17. "Doklad voenkoma MOVSU za 1922 g.," Rossiiskii Gosudarstvennyi Voennyi Arkhiv (RGVA) 34/1/1/41, 165ob.–66.

18. "Doklad voenkoma okruzhnogo sanitarnogo upravleniia zap. sib. voennogo okruga" (late 1922), RGVA 34/1/1/81–89ob.

19. RGVA 34/1/10/38. The Ukrainian sanitation authorities also reported performances of trials in 1922, RGVA 34/1/1/175.

20. L. A. and L. M. Vasilevskie, *Sud nad samogonshchikami. Delo Karpova Tikhona i ego zheny Agaf'i po obvineniiu v izgotovlenii i tainoi torgovle samogonkoi* ([Moscow]: Oktiabr', 1923), i–ii. Numerous debates were held in Moscow in 1920–21 on sanitation education topics: "Brak i kommunisticheskaia moral'" (lecture/debate on communist morality and sexual issues), *Pravda*, February 20, 1920; "V poiskakh novoi morali" (lecture/discussion on Soviet power and prostitution), *Pravda*, December 26, 1920.

21. P. M. Vedernikov, "Sansudy i ikh postanovka na osnove kollektivizma ispolnitelei," *Krasnyi put* 19 (November 1924): 97–122, Gosudarstvennyi Arkhiv Rossiiskoi Federatsi (GARF) 9636/5/125/97–98; Vasilevskie, *Sud nad samogonshchikami*, i; Mol'kov, "Sanitarnoe prosveshchenie," 57; Edel'shtein, "Neskol'ko slov o sanprosvetsudakh."

22. Stephen P. Frank, "Confronting the Domestic Other: Rural Popular Culture and Its Enemies in Fin-de-Siècle Russia" in *Cultures in Flux: Lower-Class Values, Practices and Resistance*

in Late Imperial Russia, ed. Stephen P. Frank and Mark D. Steinberg (Princeton, 1994), 74–107.

23. The issue of the end of zemstvo medicine is thoughtfully considered in Hutchinson, "'Who Killed Cock Robin?'"

24. Frieden, *Russian Physicians,* 135–60, and "The Russian Cholera Epidemic, 1892–93, and Medical Professionalization," *Journal of Social History* 10 (1977): 538–59.

25. Hutchinson, *Politics and Public Health,* 29–30; also Engelstein, *Keys to Happiness.*

26. For rich discussions of Russian and Soviet melodrama that appeared after this chapter was written, see *Imitations of Life: Two Centuries of Melodrama in Russia,* ed. Louise McReynolds and Joan Neuberger (Durham, N.C., 2002), esp. Julie A. Cassiday, "Alcohol Is Our Enemy! Soviet Temperance Melodramas of the 1920s," 152–77, and Lars T. Lih, "Melodrama and the Myth of the Soviet Union," 178–207; E. Anthony Swift, *Popular Theater and Society in Tsarist Russia* (Berkeley, 2002), 34, 126, 206, 225–27.

27. Donald Fanger, *Dostoevsky and Romantic Realism: A Study of Dostoevsky in Relation to Balzac, Dickens, and Gogol* (Chicago, 1967).

28. For more on prostitution in the NEP era, see Elizabeth A. Wood "Prostitution Unbound: Representations of Sexual and Political Anxieties in Postrevolutionary Russia," in *Sexuality and the Body in Russian Culture,* ed. Jane T. Costlow et al. (Stanford, 1993), 124–35, and Wood, *The Baba and the Comrade: Gender and Politics in Revolutionary Russia* (Bloomington, 1997), 111–16.

29. "Novye prodelki Skapena," *Pravda,* October 13, 1921.

30. N. Semashko, "Novye formy prosveshcheniia," *Pravda,* October 18, 1921; for an interview with Semashko on the importance of sanitation education, see also W. Horsley Gantt, M.D., "A Medical Review of Soviet Russia" (Part V), *British Medical Journal* (February 19, 1927), 338–39. The court trial in which Semashko appeared as the prosecutor is reported in "Khronika: Delo akusherki Chervonskoi," *Pravda,* March 12, 1921.

31. "Pis'mo K. S. Stanislavskogo v khudozhestvenno-dramaticheskuiu gruppu studii NKZdrav o rabote etoi gruppy" (July 25, 1921) (unpublished letter), GARF 9636/5/111/1–2.

32. According to one source, two thirds of all civilian sanitation education staff people had been through the Red Army. N. T., "Sanprosvetchiki (Po materialam anket Sektsii sanitarnogo prosveshcheniia 8–go s"ezda bakteriologov, epidemiologov i sanitarnykh vrachei)," *Sanitarnoe prosveshchenie* 4–5 (1924): 18. A. O. Edel'shtein was head of the sanitation education department of the Main Military Sanitation Administration, and also head of the sanitation education department of political inspection in the army, in which latter position, he coauthored at least one set of instructions with Isaak Korobochkin, the head of the club section of the Political Administration of the Army. "Instruktsiia o vneshkol'noi sanitarno-vospitatel'noi rabote v Krasnoi armii i flote," in *Sbornik prikazov i tsirkuliarov,* no. 15, 7–26, RGVA 9/40/10/185–94ob.

Aleksandr Akkerman (b. 1894) received his medical education in the early 1900s in Lausanne, where Bukharin and other Russian Social Democrats were based in the prewar and war years, and then graduated from the Don University about 1916. From January 1919, he was in military service, including four months spent on the Austrian front. His official title in the early twenties was head of the agitation division of the sanitation education department under Edel'shtein (RGVA 34/2/44).

Aleksandr Shimanko (b. 1888), although by training a pharmacist, was an amateur playwright who managed to obtain a job in the early 1920s in the Moscow military sanitation administration after having written sanitation plays on the Western front during the Civil War (RGVA lichnoe delo n. 90–970). (My thanks to Nonna Tarkhova, archivist at the Russian State Military Archives, for her assistance in finding this biographical material).

V. M. Bronner (1876–1937) played a leading role in creating "social venereology," the study of the social and environmental causes of venereal diseases and prostitution. M. I. Aruin, "Vol'f Moiseevich Bronner," in E. I. Lotova and B. D. Petrov, *Vrachi-Bol'sheviki* (Moscow, 1970), 240–52.

N. A. Semashko (1874–1949) was one of Lenin's closest collaborators, having known him from 1907 and having helped him establish the Longjumeau school for workers in 1911. M. B. Mirskii, "Nikolai Aleksandrovich Semashko," in Lotova and Petrov, 65–83.

33. Sergei Eisenstein (1898–1948) also served on the Western Front near Velikie Luki, about 120 miles north of Smolensk. Here, as a twenty-year-old soldier from the Engineering Institute in Petrograd, he organized a drama circle in the club of the Eighteenth Military Engineering Corps in the Fifteenth Army. The drama circle put on a play in which an outsider pretends to be a communist. A. Fevral'skii, *Moskovskie vstrechi* (Moscow, 1982), 72–74.

34. Olga Vladimirovna Rakhmanova (d. 1943) was a Russian actress, director, entrepreneur, and theater pedagogue. She began her theatrical work in 1896 in Vilnius (teatr Nezlobina). After October 1917 she carried out theater-pedagogical and organizational work in Tula and other cities, until she became director of the Sanitation-Education Drama Studio in about 1922. (*Teatral'naia entsiklopediia* [Moscow, 1967], 14:545–46).

35. The Rogozhsko-Simonovskii neighborhood club had performed a *Trial of the Communist Party* in February 1921 (see chapter 3).

36. Archivists' introduction, GARF 9636/5.

37. Mol'kov, "Sanitarnoe prosveshchenie," 58; M. D. Utenkov, *Prostitutsiia v drame* (Moscow: izd. avtora, 1924); Mikhail Utenkov, *Prostitutsiia i besprizornost'* (Moscow: izd. avtora, 1925).

38. M. D. Utenkov's works were all self-published in Moscow: *Kholernyi god* (1924), *Prostitutsiia i besprizornost'* (1925), *Prostitutsiia v drame* (1924), *V tumane* (1924), *Zakleimennyi pozorom* (1923), *Znakharstvo—debri t'mi* (1924).

39. E. B. Demidovich, *Sud nad gr. Kiselevym po obvineniiu ego v zarazhenii zheny ego gonorreei posledstviem chego bylo ee samoubiistvo* (Moscow-Petrograd: Gos. izd-vo, 1922, 1923); L. A. and L. M. Vasilevskie, *Sud nad akusherkoi Lopukhinoi sovershivshei operatsiiu aborta, sledstviem chego iavilas' smert' zhenshchiny* ([Moscow]: Oktiabr', 1923); Vasilevskie, *Sud nad samogonshchikami*; B. S. Ginzburg, *Sud nad mater'iu, podkinuvshei svoego rebenka: Delo gr. Tikhonovoi po obvineniiu v 1) prestupno-nebrezhnom otnoshenii k svoemu rebenku, povlekshem za soboi riad tiazhelykh zabolevanii, [i] 2) ostavlenii rebenka na proizvol sud'by* (Moscow: Zemlia i fabrika, 1924).

40. Mol'kov, "Sanitarnoe prosveshchenie," 57–58; see also the discussion in Julie A. Cassiday, *The Enemy on Trial: Early Soviet Courts on Stage and Screen* (Dekalb, Ill., 2000), 69–71.

41. Edel'shtein, "Neskol'ko slov," 5–6; Vasilevskie, *Sud nad samogonshchikami*, v–vii.

42. No doctor in any of the agitation trials has a female name or is associated with female verb endings, suggesting that the working assumption was that they would have been male.

43. Edel'stein, "Neskol'ko slov," 6.

44. V. Bronner announced the impending appearance of the two trials in his article "Nekotorye ocherednye zadachi po bor'be s venericheskimi bolezniami," *Biulleten' Narodnogo Komissariata Zdravookhraneniia*, December 4, 1922, 5. Other sources that commented on the significance of the two trials include Vasilevskie, *Sud nad samogonshchikami*, viii–ix; "Sud nad prostitutkoi," *Kommunistka* 3–4 (1923): 55–56.

45. Akkerman, *Sud nad prostitutkoi*, 39.

46. Ibid., 43–44.

47. Ibid., 46–47.

48. Ibid., 53–54.

49. Ibid., 57.

50. Demidovich, *Sud nad gr. Kiselevym*, 53–54.

51. Akkerman, *Sud nad prostitutkoi*, 29.

52. Andrei Sinyavsky explains the distinction between "comrade" and "citizen" in *Soviet Civilization: A Cultural History* (New York, 1990), 212–18. A person in the workplace would be addressed as "comrade" at a public meeting, but a person under indictment had lost any rights to the title of "comrade" and was therefore called "citizen." Interestingly, the distinction between these terms had not yet entirely hardened at the time of these agitation trials. In the 1930s a person in the dock would never be allowed to refer to the judges as "comrades" since

he himself was under suspicion. Yet Kiselev begins his final speech with an appeal to "comrade judges." The prosecutor, by contrast, addresses the judges as "citizen judges," presumably to underline the fact that the two lay assessors are picked from the audience, that this is not a military tribunal, and that they are his peers, not his seniors.

53. Hutchinson, *Politics and Public Health*, 29–30.

54. Demidovich, *Sud nad gr. Kiselevym*, 29.

55. This last statement on the domestic production of Salvarsan suggests a new faith that in fact the country as a whole is becoming less dependent on Europe, more empowered to put an end to the debilitating illness of syphilis.

56. "Sanitarnyi sud nad sifilitikom" [1923], RGVA 9/13/108/2–12.

57. In the early 1900s the Russian Syphilological and Dermatological Society had argued that syphilis should be recognized as acceptable grounds for divorce. Engelstein, *Keys to Happiness*, 50–51. Of course, in the Soviet period no grounds were necessary beyond the "desire of one of the spouses." "Kodeks zakonov ob aktakh grazhdanskogo sostoianiia," art. 87, *Sobranie kodeksov RSFSR*, 3rd ed. [Moscow, 1925], 501.

58. For the prerevolutionary argument that syphilis should not be considered shameful, see Engelstein, "Morality and the Wooden Spoon," in *Keys to Happiness*, 192 and *passim*.

59. The doctor makes this claim in "Sanitarnyi sud nad sifilitikom," RGVA 9/13/108/8.

60. B. S. Sigal, *Sud nad grazhdaninom Fedorom Sharovym po obvineniiu v zarazhenii tripperom* (Leningrad: Zhizn' i znanie, 1925).

61. "Ugolovnyi kodeks R.S.F.S.R.," *Sobranie uzakonenii*, 1922, 15–153, art. 155, in *Sobranie kodeksov R.S.F.S.R.*, 3rd ed. (Moscow, 1925); *Izvestiia VTsIK*, July 10, 1923; *Sobranie uzakonenii*, 1923, art. 48–479; P. I. Liublinskii, *Prestupleniia v oblasti polovykh otnoshenii* (Moscow-Leningrad, 1925), 240–41.

62. "Ugolovnyi kodeks R.S.F.S.R.", arts. 166–171.

63. On prerevolutionary arguments in favor of a single moral standard for men and women, see Engelstein, *Keys to Happiness*, 223–25, 247–48, and *passim*. It is also interesting to contrast this notion of a woman's responsibility for her own behavior with Engelstein's persuasive findings that women in the nineteenth century were often not seen as full juridical persons. "Gender and the Juridical Subject: Prostitution and Rape in 19th-Century Russian Criminal Codes," *Journal of Modern History* 60, no. 3 (1988): 458–95, reprinted in *Keys to Happiness*, 56–95.

64. L. Vasilevskii, "Instsenirovka, kak metod sanprosvetraboty," *Profilakticheksia meditsina* 2 (February 1925): 69; R. Fronshtein, "Vvedenie," in Utenkov, *Zakleimennyi pozorom*, 1.

65. I. Sokolov, "Neskol'ko illiustratsii sanprosvetraboty v Krasnoi Armii (Iz itogov preds"ezdovskoi Konferentsii sanprosvetrabotnikov Moskovskogo Garnizona)," *Sanitarnoe prosveshchenie* 4–5 (1924): 66–67.

66. By the early 1910s large numbers of European texts on forensics, sexology, and psychiatry, including many of Freud's works, had been translated into Russian. For a representative list see Engelstein, *Keys to Happiness*, 132n; also see Alexander Etkind, *Eros of the Impossible: The History of Psychoanalysis in Russia*, trans. Noah Rubins and Maria Rubins (Boulder, 1997).

67. Liublinskii, *Prestupleniia*, 11–12. Pavel Isaevich Liublinskii was a psychiatrist and coeditor of the journal *Russkii evgenicheskii zhurnal*. Mark B. Adams, "Eugenics as Social Medicine in Revolutionary Russia: Prophets, Patrons, and the Dialectics of Discipline-Building," in *Health and Society in Revolutionary Russia*, 208.

68. Liublinskii, *Prestupleniia*, 22–23.

69. Ibid., 26–27. For more on the Russian and Soviet eugenics movements, see also Mark B. Adams, "Eugenics in Russia, 1900–1940," in *The Wellborn Science: Eugenics in Germany, France, Brazil, and Russia*, ed. Mark B. Adams (Oxford, 1989), 153–216; and Loren Graham, *Between Science and Values* (New York, 1981), 217–56.

70. Liublinskii, *Prestupleniia*, 234–35.

71. Doctors at this time held that victims of sexual crimes should be protected by holding such trials behind closed doors. Ibid., 241.

72. It should be noted, of course, that in the early Soviet years "the law" tended to be a bit vague anyway because judges were instructed to operate "according to revolutionary consciousness."

73. Wood, "Prostitution Unbound," 124–35.

Chapter 7. The Trial of the New Woman

1. "Sud nad novoi zhenshchinoi," *Pravda*, February 20, 1921. Some material from the first half of this chapter appeared in my article "The Trial of the New Woman: Citizens-in-Training in the New Soviet Republic," *Gender and History* 13, no. 3 (2001): 524–45. The article contains material about citizenship not included in this chapter.

2. The women's sections of the Communist Party were officially created in the fall of 1919 and served to draw women into the party until they were abolished in 1930. For more on their history, see Elizabeth A. Wood, *The Baba and the Comrade: Gender and Politics in Revolutionary Russia* (Bloomington, Ind., 1997); P. M. Chirkov, *Reshenie zhenskogo voprosa v SSSR (1917–1937 gg.)* (Moscow, 1978); Richard Stites, *The Women's Liberation Movement in Russia: Feminism, Nihilism, and Bolshevism, 1860–1930* (Princeton, 1978); Gail Warshofsky Lapidus, *Women in Soviet Society* (Berkeley, 1978); Carol Eubanks Hayden, "Feminism and Bolshevism: The Zhenotdel and the Politics of Women's Emancipation in Russia, 1917–1930" (Ph.D. diss., University of California, 1979); Mary Buckley, *Women and Ideology in the Soviet Union* (Ann Arbor, 1989); Carmen Scheide, "Einst war ich Weib und kochte Suppe, jetzt bin ich bei der Frauengruppe: Das Wechselverhältnis zwischen sowjetischem Frauenalltag und Frauenpolitik von 1921 bis 1930 am Beispiel Moskauer Arbeiterinnen" (diss., Historische Seminar der Universitat Basel, 1999).

3. A. Sergeev, "Zhenskii samosud," *Pravda*, November 21, 1921; B. Kanatchikova, "God raboty (na mestakh)," *Kommunistka* 16–17 (September–October 1921): 29; N. Tr-ii, "Rabota sredi zhenshchin v Sibiri," *Pravda*, January 13, 1923; Delegatka M. Genert, "Vypusk delegatok glavnogo Pochtamta," *Rabotnitsa i krest'ianka* 6 (October 1923): 25; Rossiiskii Gosudarstvennyi Arkhiv Sotsial'noi i Politicheskoi Istorii (RGASPI) 17/10/11/244, 17/10/20/2; *Biulleten' no. 15 Otdela TsK RKP po rabote sredi zhenshchin. Tezisy i rezoliutsii IV Vseross. soveshchaniia zavgubzhenotdelami* (Moscow, 1921), 21; V. Mikhail and A. Kollontai, "Ob oktiabr'skikh torzhestvakh. Vsem gubzhenotdelam," *Izvestiia TsK RKP(b),* November 15, 1921, 17.

4. Wood, *Baba and Comrade,* 49–52; *The Family in the USSR: Documents and Readings,* ed. Rudolf Schlesinger (London, 1949); Wendy Z. Goldman, *Women, the State, and Revolution: Soviet Family Policy and Social Life, 1917–1936* (Cambridge, 1993).

5. As Carol S. Nash has shown, this emphasis on mothers as educators dates at least to the eighteenth century. "Educating New Mothers: Women and the Enlightenment in Russia," *History of Education Quarterly* 21, no. 3 (1981): 301–16.

6. Wood, *Baba and Comrade,* 61–67.

7. One exception is the trial of Vertikhvostov discussed in chapter 6.

8. Judith Butler, *Gender Trouble: Feminism and the Subversion of Identity* (New York, 1990); Butler, *Excitable Speech: A Politics of the Performative* (New York, 1997); Rae Langton, "Speech Acts and Unspeakable Acts," *Philosophy and Public Affairs* 22, no. 4 (1993): 293–330; Mary Poovey, *Uneven Developments* (1988).

9. On "prereflective" views, which tend to include "taken-for-granted consensus about values and ends," see Nancy Fraser, "What's Critical about Critical Theory? The Case of Habermas and Gender," in her *Unruly Practices: Power, Discourse, and Gender in Contemporary Social Theory* (Minneapolis, 1989), 120, 139–40n.

10. For more on village healers, see Rose L. Glickman, "The Peasant Woman as Healer," in *Russia's Women: Accommodation, Resistance, Transformation,* ed. Barbara Evans Clements et al. (Berkeley, 1991), 148–62. On prerevolutionary notions of "backward" child-care practices, David L. Ransel, "Infant-Care Cultures in the Russian Empire," in *Russia's Women,* 113–32; and his *Mothers of Misery: Child Abandonment in Russia* (Princeton, 1988). Although

Ransel does a wonderful job of describing doctors' criticisms and fears of "bad" mothering, he does not explore in depth the possibility that much of what the doctors were seeing came from their own projections onto mothers, and their own hopes for the medicalization of the countryside.

11. Julia Kristeva, *Powers of Horror: An Essay on Abjection* (New York, 1982); see also Mary Douglas, *Purity and Danger: An Analysis of Concepts of Pollution and Taboo* (New York, 1966). In the Russian village specific rituals dictated both the separation of women giving birth and the purification for mothers rejoining the collective once the infant reached a certain age. See Eve Levin, "Childbirth in Pre-Petrine Russia: Canon Law and Popular Traditions," in *Russia's Women,* 44–59; Natalia Pushkareva, *Women in Russian History: From the Tenth to the Twentieth Century* (Armonk, N.Y., 1997), 36–40. It is also interesting to note that in the Soviet period hospitals sequestered women giving birth much more strictly than did their counterparts in Europe and America.

12. On this Section for the Protection of Mothers and Infants (known in Russian as Otdel okhrany materinstva i mladenchestva, OMM) and on Soviet views of motherhood see E. M. Konius, *Puti razvitiia sovetskoi okhrany materinstva i mladenchestva* (Moscow, 1954); Elizabeth Waters, "Teaching Mothercraft in Post-Revolutionary Russia," *Australian Slavonic and East European Studies* 1, no. 2 (1987): 29–56, and Waters, "The Modernization of Russian Motherhood, 1917–1937," *Soviet Studies* 44, no. 1 (1992): 123–35.

13. Sergeev, "Zhenskii samosud."

14. Of course, women in the audience may have clapped not in agreement with the defense but rather in hopes that clapping would bring an end to the performance. Until actual audience surveys can be found in the archives (if indeed they have been preserved), it will be impossible to gain a true sense of audience reception.

15. Sergeev, "Zhenskii samosud."

16. E. Kolokolova, "Svoimi rukami," in *Zhenshchiny v revoliutsii* (Moscow, 1959), 287.

17. On delegatki, Wood, *Baba and Comrade,* 85–93, 172; Scheide, "Einst war," 138–43, 240–48; Chirkov, *Reshenie,* 86–100; Buckley, *Women and Ideology,* 71–82; Hayden, "Feminism," 143–46, 151, 187–89, 199–203, 210–11.

18. Stites, *Women's Liberation,* 166–67.

19. Chirkov, *Reshenie,* 92.

20. The phrase "future perfect" comes from Svetlana Boym, *Common Places: Mythologies of Everyday Life in Russia* (Cambridge, Mass., 1994), 31; see also Eric Naiman, *Sex in Public: The Incarnation of Early Soviet Ideology* (Princeton, 1997), 13–14; Andrei Sinyavsky, *Soviet Civilization: A Cultural History* (New York, 1990), 28–53.

21. "Politsud nad krest'iankoi-delegatkoi" in *Mezhdunarodnyi den' rabotnits,* ed. G. S. Maliuchenko (Rostov-na-Donu, 1925), 31–51; T. Smeliakova, "Sud nad delegatkoi," *Rabotnitsa i krest'ianka,* January 23, 1922, 4; N. Bozhinskaia, *Sud nad krest'iankoi-delegatkoi* (Moscow-Leningrad: Gos. izd-vo, 1926).

22. "Sud nad chlenom fabkoma N.I. Egorovym," in *Sbornik Iskusstvo v rabochem klube* (Moscow: izd. Proletkul'ta, 1924), 101, 103, 114; *Sud nad krest'ianinom Medvedevym, sorvavshim vybory kandidatki ot zhenshchin v sel'sovet* (Leningrad: Priboi, 1925).

23. The rich historical literature on changing intelligentsia images of the peasantry shows how often members of the educated class tended to project their own ideas onto "the people." See especially Cathy A. Frierson, *Peasant Icons: Representations of Rural People in Late Nineteenth-Century Russia* (New York, 1993); Laura Engelstein, *The Keys to Happiness: Sex and the Search for Modernity in Fin-de-Siècle Russia* (Ithaca, 1992); Richard S. Wortman, *The Crisis of Russian Populism* (Cambridge, 1967); Esther Kingston-Mann, *Lenin and the Problem of Marxist Peasant Revolution* (New York, 1983). On images of peasant women, see Christine Worobec, "Temptress or Virgin? The Precarious Sexual Position of Women in Post-Emancipation Ukrainian Peasant Society," *Slavic Review* 49, no. 2 (1990); and her "Victims or Actors? Russian Peasant Women and Patriarchy," in *Peasant Economy, Culture, and Politics of European Russia, 1800–1921,* ed. Esther Kingston-Mann and Timothy Mixter (Princeton, 1991).

24. "Politsud nad krest'iankoi-delegatkoi," 32.

25. *Sud nad krest'ianinom Medvedevym*, 12, 6–8.

26. N. Glebova, *Sud nad delegatkoi: Delo po obvineniiu delegatki Tikhonovoi, ne vypol-nivshei svoego proletarskogo dolga* 2nd ed. (Moscow: Gos. izd-vo, 1925), 11.

27. Ibid., 27.

28. Stites, *Women's Liberation*; G. A. Tishkin, *Zhenskii vopros v Rossii 50–60e gody XIX v.* (Leningrad, 1984); Jane McDermid, "The Influence of Western Ideas on the Development of the Woman Question in Nineteenth-Century Russian Thought," *Irish Slavonic Studies* 9 (1988): 21–36; Derek Offord, "*Lichnost'*: Notions of Individual Identity," in *Constructing Russian Culture in the Age of Revolution: 1881–1940*, ed. Catriona Kelly and David Shepherd (Oxford, 1998), 13–25; Arja Rosenholm, "The 'Woman Question' of the 1860s and the Ambiguity of the 'Learned Woman,'" in *Gender and Russian Literature: New Perspectives*, ed. Rosalind Marsh (Cambridge, 1996), 112–28.

29. Wood, *Baba and Comrade*, 28–34, on the Bolsheviks' resistance to devoting attention to "the woman question." For comparisons to the German case, see Jean Quataert, *Reluctant Feminists in German Social Democracy, 1885–1917* (Princeton, 1979); Werner Thönnessen, *The Emancipation of Women: The Rise and Decline of the Women's Movement in German Social Democracy, 1863–1933* (London, 1973).

30. V. I. Lenin, "What Is to Be Done? Burning Questions of Our Movement" in *The Lenin Anthology*, ed. Robert C. Tucker (New York, 1975), 12–114.

31. "Politsud nad krest'iankoi-delegatkoi," 50–51. The name "Cherepanova" name comes from the word for skull (*cherep*). The name may have been chosen to emphasize her development from a skull—that is, a skeleton of a human being—to a full citizen and useful member of society. The play takes place in a Cossack village called "Glubokaia," meaning "deep."

32. Ibid., 34–35.

33. Boris Andreev, *Sud nad starym bytom* (Moscow-Leningrad: Doloi negramotnost', 1926), 15, 17–18. Her evolution is reminiscent of that of the title character in Gorky's novel *The Mother*.

34. Andreev, *Sud nad starym bytom*, 15.

35. "Politsud nad krest'iankoi-delegatkoi," 46.

36. Andreev, *Sud nad starym bytom*, 14.

37. One trial even brought a fictional woman to court "who did not use the rights given her by the October Revolution": "Sud nad zhenshchinoi, ne vospol'zovavsheisia pravami Oktiabria," *Rabochii klub* 7 (1924): 37.

38. "Politsud nad krest'iankoi-delegatkoi," 36–37.

39. Ibid., 39. The defense repeats this language at the end of the play, characterizing Cherepanova as a "very necessary, useful worker [*rabotnik*] for her society" (p. 49); the judge calls her a "useful member [*chlen*] of society." Once she has become useful, her "femaleness" falls away.

40. Ibid., 47, 49.

41. N. Bozhinskaia, *Sud nad krest'iankoi-delegatkoi* (Moscow-Leningrad, 1926). In parts of prerevolutionary Russia, the verb *gudit'* also meant to reproach, find fault with, or defame someone. V. Dal', *Tolkovyi slovar'* (Moscow-Petersburg, 1880), 1:405.

42. Bozhinskaia, *Sud nad krest'iankoi-delegatkoi*, 15–16; he uses the feminine form of the Russian word for "fool" (*dura*) rather than the masculine form (*durak*).

43. Gudkova's first name, Maria, may not be accidental. The author Bozhinskaia is probably descended from the clerical estate (since her last name contains the Russian word for God) and may have chosen the name Maria in order to create a secular heroine in place of Maria, the Mother of God.

44. Bozhinskaia, *Sud nad krest'iankoi-delegatkoi*, 17, 25, 21.

45. Ibid., 28. For an account of nineteenth-century female revolutionaries who are portrayed as saintly and therefore rather bloodless, see Christine Fauré, "Une violence paradoxale: Aux sources d'un défi, des femmes terroristes dans les années 1880," in *L'Histoire sans qualités*, ed. Christiane Dufrancatel et al. (Paris, 1979), 85–110.

46. Bozhinskaia, *Sud nad krest'iankoi-delegatkoi*, 10–11.

47. The play also betrays a perhaps unconscious fear on the part of the author that local delegates would take too much power for themselves. As part of her false claim that Gudkova received a bribe, Kosorotov's wife Varvara recounts that she saw Gudkova staggering down the street shouting, "It is my power. I can judge whomever I want and forgive whomever I want." Ibid., 12. The judge's disciplining of Gudkova both on the micro level of her speech acts and on the macro level of her general guilt or innocence thus establishes a hierarchy in which Gudkova may have power to uncover wrongdoing and denounce villagers, but she herself remains under the watchful eye of the state and the courts.

48. This type of "triptych" with good above and evil below would have been familiar to Russian churchgoers. For more on the relationship between prerevolutionary icons and postrevolutionary pictorial art, see Victoria E. Bonnell, *Iconography of Power: Soviet Political Posters under Lenin and Stalin* (Berkeley, 1997), and Stephen White, *The Bolshevik Poster* (New Haven, 1988). Bozhinskaia's own clerical background may have made her particularly cognizant of parallels to Russian hagio-graphy.

49. Bozhinskaia, *Sud nad krest'iankoi-delegatkoi*, 26. Another (probably unconscious) inversion can be seen near the beginning of the play when Kosorotov claims that this "baba" (Gudkova) has worn him out—literally, that she has "eaten" him up (*zaela menia baba*) (p. 7).

50. Ibid., 3, 9, 15, 14. While the judge addresses the witnesses using the formal "you" (*vy*), the people's assessors tend to use the informal *ty*, suggesting that they are closer to the witnesses than is the judge (presumably an outsider), who can therefore have more impartiality.

51. *Sud nad krest'ianinom Medvedevym*, 7.

52. Ibid., 19, 9, 18.

53. Ibid., 22–23.

54. The subject of citizenship is treated much more fully in my article "The Trial of the New Woman."

55. In some sense this ambivalence about women's participation in the public sphere is inherent in the Russian phrase "publichnye zhenshchiny," which means both "public women" and "prostitutes." For more on this, see Elizabeth A. Wood, "Prostitution Unbound: Representations of Sexual and Political Anxieties in Postrevolutionary Russia," in *Sexuality and the Body in Russian Culture*, ed. Jane T. Costlow et al. (Stanford, 1993); Julie A. Cassiday and Leyla Rouhi, "From Nevskii Prospekt to Zoia's Apartment: The Trials of the Russian Procuress," *Russian Review* 58, no. 3 (1999): 413–31; and Naiman, *Sex in Public*. For discussion of public women/prostitutes in the nineteenth century, see Laurie Bernstein, *Sonia's Daughters: Prostitutes and Their Regulation in Imperial Russia* (Berkeley, 1995); Engelstein, *Keys to Happiness;* Richard Stites, "Prostitute and Society in Pre-Revolutionary Russia, *Jahrbücher für Geschichte Osteuropas* 31 (1983): 348–64; Barbara Engel, "St. Petersburg Prostitutes in the Late Nineteenth Century: A Personal and Social Profile," *Russian Review* 48, no. 1 (1989): 21–44.

56. "Politsud nad krest'iankoi-delegatkoi," 50–51. For more on this issue of inner transformation, see Igal Halfin, *From Darkness to Light: Class, Consciousness, and Salvation in Revolutionary Russia* (Pittsburgh, Penn., 2000).

57. Ibid., 49. Even this formulation expresses some doubt that a woman like Cherepanova has become fully imbued with the light of Soviet power.

58. *Pravda* in Russian means both "truth" and "justice."

59. Bozhinskaia, *Sud nad krest'iankoi-delegatkoi*, 15.

60. Ransel, "Infant-Care Cultures in the Russian Empire," and *Mothers of Misery;* Nancy Mandelker Frieden, *Russian Physicians in an Era of Reform and Revolution, 1856–1905* (Princeton, 1981), and "Child Care: Medical Reform in a Traditionalist Culture," in *The Family in Imperial Russia,* ed. David L. Ransel (Urbana, Ill., 1978), 236–59; John F. Hutchinson, *Politics and Public Health in Revolutionary Russia, 1890–1918* (Baltimore, 1990); Engelstein, *Keys to Happiness;* Susan Gross Solomon, "Social Hygiene and Soviet Public Health, 1921–1930," in *Health and Society in Revolutionary Russia,* ed. Susan G. Solomon and John F. Hutchinson (Bloomington, Ind., 1990), 175–199; Samuel C. Ramer, "Feldshers and Rural Health Care in the Early Soviet Period," in *Health and Society,* 121–45; John F. Hutchinson, "'Who Killed Cock Robin?': An Inquiry into the Death of Zemstvo Medicine" in *Health and*

Society, 3–26; Neil Weissman, "Origins of Soviet Health Administration: Narkomzdrav, 1918–1928" in *Health and Society,* 97–120.

61. B. S. Sigal, *Sud nad babkoi znakharkoi* (Moscow: Zhizn' i znanie, 1925), cover.

62. *Kurynikha: Sud nad znakharkoi* (p'esa Leningradskogo Proletkulta) (Leningrad: Priboi, 1925), cover.

63. A famous Russian proverb also comments: "A chicken is not a bird, and a woman is not a person." On Baba Yaga, see Joanna Hubbs, *Mother Russia: The Feminine Myth in Russian Culture* (Bloomington, Ind., 1988), 36–51.

64. *Kurynikha,* 4.

65. Sigal, *Sud nad babkoi znakharkoi,* 5–6.

66. Ibid., 7–8.

67. B. S. Ginzburg, *Sud nad mater'iu, podkinuvshei svoego rebenka: Delo gr. Tikhonovoi po obvineniiu v 1) prestupno-nebrezhnom otnoshenii k svoemu rebenku, povlekshem za soboi riad tiazhelykh zabolevanii, [i] 2) ostavlenii rebenka na proizvol sud'by* (Moscow: Zemlia i fabrika, 1924), 39; Boris Sigal, *Sud nad mater'iu po obvineniiu v nevezhestvennom ukhode za det'mi i neprivitii ospy, povlekshem za soboi smert' rebenka (Sanitarno-prosvetitel'naia instsenirovka dlia derevni)* ([Omsk]: Omskii p/o okhrany materinstva i mladenchestva, [1925 or 1926]), 13.

68. Sigal, *Sud nad mater'iu po obvineniiu v nevezhestvennom ukhode,* 8–9.

69. On the alleged innocence of the peasantry in contrast to the "abuses bred by 'civilization,'" see Engelstein, *Keys to Happiness,* 254–99.

70. These examples are all taken from the trials. Many of these new rules of care were becoming well known in Western Europe and the United States at this time. See Anna Davin, "Imperialism and Motherhood," *History Workshop* 5 (Spring 1978): 9–56; Barbara Ehrenreich and Deirdre English, *For Her Own Good: 150 Years of the Expert's Advice to Women* (Garden City, N.Y., 1978), chs. 6–7; Molly Ladd-Taylor and Lauri Umansky, eds., *"Bad" Mothers: The Politics of Blame in Twentieth-Century America* (New York, 1998).

71. Ginzburg, *Sud nad mater'iu, podkinuvshei,* 44.

72. Sigal, *Sud nad mater'iu po obvineniiu v nevezhestvennom ukhode,* 4.

73. Ibid., 11.

74. B. Kanatchikova, "God raboty (na mestakh)," 29–30.

75. Anna Itkina, the fourth national zhenotdel meeting (November 2–6, 1921), RGASPI 17/10/11/244; 17/10/10/65–66; *Biulleten' No. 15 Otdela TsK RKP po rabote sredi zhenshchin,* 21; Mikhailov and Kollontai, "Ob oktiabr'skikh torzhestvakh."

76. Ginzburg, *Sud nad mater'iu, podkinuvshei.* This agitation trial seems to have been intended as particularly exemplary as it had an unusually large print run of one hundred thousand.

77. N. Semashko, "Sud nad mater'iu, podkinuvshei svoego rebenka," *Izvestiia TsIK SSSR i VTsIK,* April 18, 1924.

78. S. I. Andreeva, "Sud nad nevezhestvennoi mater'iu," *Rabotnitsa i krest'ianka* 3 (1923): 25.

79. Rabotnitsa Lez'enskoi volosti Lena [*sic*], "Kak u nas proshel sud nad nevezhestvennoi mater'iu v Lez'enskoi volosti," *Rabotnitsa i krest'ianka* 4 (1923): 19. In saying she will do what she did not do before, Lena is evidently promising to assist in the construction of day care for children, become more active politically, and perhaps even serve as a delegatka.

80. Sigal, *Sud nad mater'iu po obvineniiu v nevezhestvennom ukhode,* 20.

81. Glebova, *Sud nad delegatkoi.*

82. Theoretically both the judges and the doctors in these plays could have been played as women characters since women were now just beginning to enter both of these professions. The fact, however, that the legal and medical professionals are all either nameless (and use male verb endings in their speeches) or have male names suggests that the authors did not contemplate using women in these roles.

83. Joan W. Scott, "Gender: A Useful Category of Historical Analysis," *American Historical Review* 91, no. 5 (1986): 1053–75; Michel Foucault, *A History of Sexuality,* vol. 1, *An Introduction,* trans. Robert Hurley (New York, 1978).

Chapter 8. The Crisis of the Clubs and the Erosion of the Public Sphere

1. Between 1925 and 1928 the journals *Rabochii Klub* and *Klub* carried dozens of articles addressing these questions; see also Leon Trotsky, "Leninism and Workers' Clubs," *Pravda*, July 23, 1924, in Trotsky, *Problems of Everyday Life* (New York, 1973), 288–319. Even the party Central Committee acknowledged that adult workers were not participating in the clubs. "Kul'trabota soiuzov" (Fourteenth Party Congress, December 1925), in *KPSS v rezoliutsiiakh i resheniiakh*, 7th ed. (Moscow, 1954), 223. On the clubs in general, see John Hatch, "The Politics of Mass Culture: Workers, Communists, and Proletkul't in the Development of Workers' Clubs, 1921–1925," *Russian History* 13, nos. 2–3 (1986): 119–48; Hatch, "Hangouts and Hangovers: State, Class, and Culture in Moscow's Workers' Club Movement, 1925–1928," *Russian Review* 53, no. 1 (1994): 97–117; Gabriele Gorzka, *Arbeiterkultur in der Sowjetunion: Industriearbeiter Klubs, 1917–1929: ein Beitrag zur sowjetischen Kulturgeschichte* (Berlin, 1989).

2. "O rabote profsoiuzov" (October 1925), in *Kommunisticheskaia Partii Sovetskogo Soiuza v rezoliutsiiakh i resheniiakh s"ezdov, konferentsii i plenumov TsK, 1898–1953* (Moscow, 1953), 2:186–87; E. H. Carr, *Socialism in One Country, 1924–1926* (Baltimore, 1958–59), 1:420–29, 437–38; William J. Chase, *Workers, Society, and the Soviet State: Labor and Life in Moscow, 1918–1929* (Urbana, Ill., 1987), 239, 273–78.

3. "Protokol soveshchaniia klubnykh rabotnikov pri Agitprop" (March 24, 1922), Rossiiskii Gosudarstvennyi Arkhiv Sotsial'noi i Politicheskoi Istorii (RGASPI) 17/60/54; R. Ginzburg, "Nashi raznoglasiia v klubnoi rabote," *Rabochii Klub* 8 (1924): 3–7; "Vserossiiskoe soveshchanie klubnykh rabotnikov pri Glavpolitprosvete," *Rabochii klub* 8 (1924): 41; N. Krupskaia, "Vystuplenie na pervom s"ezde klubnykh rabotnikov," in *Pedagogicheskie sochinenii* (Moscow, 1957), 8:105–7; letters from representatives of both Glavpolitprosvet and the trade unions to Syrtsov, head of the party Agitprop section (1924), RGASPI 17/60/753/6–9, 51–52ob; R. Ginzburg, "XIV Parts"ezd o klubnoi rabote," *Rabochii klub*, 1 (25) (1926): 8; A. Seniushkina, "Vsesoiuznoe kul'tsoveshchanie," *Rabotnik prosveshcheniia* 5 (1926): 20; M. Tomskii, *Izbrannye stat'i i rechi, 1917–1927* (Moscow, 1928), 300–302; N. I. L'vov (theater historian), Gosudarstvennyi Tsentral'nyi Teatral'nyi Muzei im. A. A. Bakhrushina (GTsTM) 150, Nos. 33, 35, 61.

4. "Diskussii. Chem dolzhen byt' klub?" *Rabotnik prosveshcheniia* 1 (1926): 23–25.

5. Even in 1928 the national trade union budget prioritized recreation over utility: 42 million rubles for plays, concerts, and films; 16 million rubles for sports; 1.5 million rubles for eliminating illiteracy; and only 632,000 for production propaganda. *Istoriia kul'turno-prosvetitel'noi raboty*, ed. M. S. Andreeva et al. (Kharkov, 1970), 2:101–2. Narkompros and other political education organizations, on the other hand, wholeheartedly disapproved of dances, beer drinking, and the like: A. Polianskii, "Klubnaia rabota (Po informatsionnym materialam NKP)," *Narodnoe prosveshchenie* 6–7 (1924): 177–80; A. Egolin, "Politiko-prosvetitel'naia rabota v gorode," *Narodnoe prosveshchenie* 7 (1926): 86–92; Tsentral'nyi Gosudarstvennyi Arkhiv Oktiabr'skoi Revoliutsii i Sovetskogo Stroitel'stva goroda Leningrada (TsGAORL) 2552/1/1110/6–8ob., 63; 2552/1/1111/2–3, 5.

6. For evidence of the party ignoring the clubs, Degtiarev, in *Ocherednye zadachi politprosvetitel'noi raboty Glavpolitprosveta* (Kharkov: izd. Politupravleniia vsekh vooruzhennykh sil Ukrainy i v Krymu, 1921), 3. For renewed party interest, "Po voprosam propagandy, pechati i agitatsii" (Twelfth Party Congress, April 1923), in *KPSS v rezoliutsiiakh*, I:731 repeated at the Thirteenth Party Congress (May 1924), ibid., II:67. In 1925 Raisa Ginzburg commented that the Thirteenth Party Congress resolution on making mass propaganda the centerpiece of club work still had not been put into effect. R. Ginzburg, "Klub, kak on est'," *Rabochii klub* 1 (1925): 8. See also F. P. Andrichenko, *Partiinoe rukovodstvo kul'turno-prosvetitel'nymi uchrezhdeniiami (po materialam Moskovskoi oblastnoi i Moskovskoi gorodskoi partiinykh organizatsii 1917–1974 gg.)* (Moscow, 1975), 47.

7. *Klubnaia rabota. Prakticheskaia entsiklopediia dlia podgotovki klubnykh rabotnikov* (Moscow: Proletkul't, [1926]), 2:11–12; A. K. Kolesova, "Deiatel'nost' rabochikh klubov po kommunisticheskomu vospitaniiu trudiashchikhsia v 1917–1923 gg." (Diss., Kand. ped. nauk, Moscow, 1969).

8. Some of the new journals and their dates of first publication include: *Novyi zritel'* (trade union journal, December 1923); *Rabochii klub* (Proletkult, January 1924); *Rabochii i teatr* (the cultural department of the Leningrad trade unions and the state academic theaters, September 1924); *Klub* (the club division of Glavpolitprosvet and the Komsomol, 1925); *Klub* (monthly journal, the Down with Illiteracy Society [Doloi Negramotnost'], 1925); *Klubnaia stsena* (the trade union organizations VTsSPS and MGSPS, 1927–32, with a few subsequent name changes); *Kul'turnyi front* (journal of the Moscow trade unions [MGSPS]).

9. "Vserossiiskoe soveshchanie," 41.

10. Lynn Mally, *Culture of the Future: The Proletkult Movement in Revolutionary Russia* (Berkeley, 1990), 234–39. An extensive search of Proletkult theater materials in the files of Moscow oblast revealed almost no mention of agitation trials before 1924. Tsentral'nyi Gosudarstvennyi Arkhiv Moskovskoi oblasti (TsGAMO) 880/1/dd. 4–7, 25, 27, 34, 39–40, 50, 54, 58. The exceptions are brief mentions in the club materials of October 1922: "Zasedanie shirokoi klubnoi kollegii," Mosgubsovet prol. Kul'turno-prosvetitel'nykh organizatsii, Proletkul't October 2, 1922, TsGAMO 880/1/26/15–16; "Protokol No. 1 Zasedaniia konferentsii klubnykh rabotnikov rabochikh poligraficheskogo proizvodstva ot 19/X–1922 g.," TsGAMO 880/1/17/16; "Smeta kul'traboty obraztsovogo kluba (ca. October 1922), 880/1/ 353/57. See also R. Ginzburg, "Rabochie kluby pri novoi ekonomicheskoi politike," *Gorn* 6 (1922): 101–2.

11. "O rabote profsoiuzov" (Plenum TsK RKP(b), October 1925), in *KPSS v rezoliutsiiakh*, 2:184–87; "Kul'trabota soiuzov" (Fourteenth Party Congress, December 1925), in *KPSS v rezoliutsiiakh*, 2:222–23; "Itogi raboty i ocherednykh zadachakh profsoiuzov" (Fifteenth Party Conference, October–November 1926), in *KPSS v rezoliutsiiakh*, 2:325–27; Ginzburg, "XIV Parts"ezd o klubnoi rabote," 3–9.

12. Krupskaia, "Vystuplenie na pervom s"ezde," 102–11; Tsimmerman, "Rabochii klub i zadachi rabkorov," *Kommunisticheskoe Prosveshchenie* 3–4 (1924): 102–4. Raisa Ginzburg explicitly urged the use of dramatized trials and assizes court sessions for their role in "organizing public opinion." "Bor'ba s khuliganstvom," *Rabochii klub* 3 (1926): 12–13. *Istoriia kul'turno-prosvetitel'noi*, 2:101. By 1928, however, the party had reversed course and viciously attacked the leadership of the Central Committee of the Trade Unions (VTsSPS) for insufficient attention to political forms and excessive attention to entertainment.

13. *Klubnaia rabota*, 2:10; A. B., "O distsipline v rabochem klube," *Rabochii klub* 7 (1924): 34–35.

14. R. D., *Sud nad domashnei khoziaikoi* (Moscow-Leningrad: Gos. izd-vo, 1927), 14.

15. Boris Andreev, *Sud nad starym bytom* (Moscow-Leningrad: Doloi negramotnost', 1926), 21.

16. "Rech' tov. N. K. Krupskoi," in *Tri goda politprosvetraboty (ot 3–go S"ezda politprosvetov k 4–mu). Po materialam IV Vserossiiskogo S"ezda politprosvetov* (typewritten copy, [Moscow, 1926]), 65–67; Seniushkina, "Vsesoiuznoe kul'tsoveshchanie VTsSPS," 20.

17. A. B., "O distsipline," 34–35.

18. A. Petrov, "Boliachki ili bolezn'," *Rabochii klub* 9–10 (1928): 11–19; Gausman, *Pravda*, July 21, 1928; Comrade B., *Pravda*, August 9, 1928.

19. Peter H. Solomon, Jr. "Criminalization and Decriminalization in Soviet Criminal Policy, 1917–1941," *Law and Society Review* 16, no. 1 (1991–92): 9–43. As Joan Neuberger has skillfully shown, hooliganism in late tsarist Russia came to symbolize many larger social issues beyond direct questions of crime and criminality. *Hooliganism: Crime, Culture, and Power in St. Petersburg, 1900–1914* (Berkeley, 1993). On hooliganism in the Soviet context see Eric Naiman, *Sex in Public* (Princeton, 1997), esp. ch. 7 ("The Case of Chubarov Alley"); Anne E. Gorsuch, *Youth in Revolutionary Russia: Enthusiasts, Bohemians, Delinquents* (Bloomington, Ind., 2000), ch. 8 ("Discourses of Delinquency"); Vladimir Brovkin, *Russia After Lenin: Politics, Culture and Society, 1921–1929* (London, 1998), 108–16.

20. B. S. Sigal, *Sud nad mater'iu po obvineniiu v nevezhestvennom ukhode za det'mi i neprivitii ospy, povlekshem za soboi smert' rebenka* (Omsk: Omskii podotdel okhrany materinstva i mladenchestva, [1925]), 2.

21. "Zasedanie shirokoi klubnoi kollegii," Mosgubsovet proletarskikh kul'turnopros-

vetitel′nykh organizatsii, Proletkul′t (October 2, 1922), TsGAMO 880/1/26/15–16; M. Rastopchina, "Metodika: Rabota massovika v klube," *Rabochii klub* 1 (1924): 9–10.

22. Loginov, "Dorogie tovarishchi," *Rabochii klub* 2 (1924): 65.

23. *Materialy po soiuznoi kul′trabote*. vyp. 3: *Rabota klubnykh kursov-konferentsii pri kul′totdele MGSPS 1923–1924 g. (Programmy, tezisy, konspekty)* (Moscow: izd. MGSPS, "Trud i kniga," 1924), esp. 36–43, "Agit-sud [*sic*] (Konspekt lektsii t. Rebel′skogo)."

24. "Rabota Politiko-Prosvetitel′nogo instituta v Moskve," RGASPI 17/84/687/30–35ob. The report of this Institute of Political Education Work claimed that the old extracurricular education specialists (*vneshkol′niki*) who had worked out the original methods of political education work with adults could "no longer meet the political requirements of the day," while the new staffs were weak theoretically. The older extracurricular education experts appear to have been increasingly pushed aside as the clubs moved to more centralized methods of instruction.

25. "Org.-Instruktorskie kursy pri Tsentral′nom Komitete Proletkul′t," *Rabochii klub* 6 (1924): 55; A. Volkov, "K itogam perepodgotovki (Saratov)" *Rabochii klub* 11 (1926): 37–40; TsGAMO 880/1/47/116–21 (list of courses for club staffs in the Central Committee of the Textile Workers, including a group devoted to "The Dramatized Trial"); "K instsenirovaniiu politsudov," *Iskusstvo v rabochem klube* (Moscow: Vseross. Proletkul′t, 1924), 96–99.

26. TsGAORL 6276/12/469/143.

27. *Klubnaia rabota*, 6:13.

28. R. Ginzburg, "Letniaia rabota kluba," *Rabochii klub* 6 (1924): 9–10.

29. "Khudozhestvennaia rabota v klube," *Rabochii klub* 2 (1925), 19–22. In the third quarter of 1924–1925 the 245 club institutions in Ukraine allegedly performed some twelve hundred political agitation trials (together with over fifty-two thousand lectures and doklady). *Istoriia kul′turno-prosvetitel′ noi*, 50–51.

30. V. Gazar′iants, "God raboty klubov na Moskovsko-Kurskoi zheleznoi doroge," *Rabochii klub* 10–11 (1924): 63; the total number of clubs on this railway line was listed as twenty-two.

31. "Rabota kluba imeni Karla Libknekhta (Saratovskogo uchkprofsozha)," *Rabochii klub* 4–5 (1925): 77.

32. "Sud nad klubom," *Rabochii klub* 2 (1924): 30.

33. Rastopchina, "Metodika," 10; Kolesova, "Deiatel′nost′," 16–17.

34. "Samodeiatel′nost′," *Rabochii i teatr*, September 18, 1924, 20.

35. "Sud nad klubom," 30.

36. Ibid.

37. A. Abramov, "Kak my 'sdelali' sud (Klub Mytishchenskoi gruppy kirpichnykh zavodov Mossilikata)," *Rabochii zritel′* 22 (1924): 22.

38. "Sud nad shest′iu rabochimi zavoda 'Krasnyi Oktiabr' vedushchimi agitatsiiu protiv kluba," *Rabochii klub* 2 (1924): 30–32.

39. The Central Workers' Cooperative also organized a trial of a woman who had not joined a cooperative. The leadership claimed that the trial was a way to put "agitation pressure" (*agitnazhim*) on cooperative life and to "drag out into court all the deficiencies of the cooperatives." Through humor at the expense of the bazaar traders and through "the theatricalization of daily life," such a trial, the organizers claimed, had "completely justified itself." "Sud v Groznom," *Rabochii klub* 3–4 (1924): 85.

40. Aron Mil′shtein, *Prof-sudy (Profpropaganda)* (Moscow: izd. G. F. Mirimanova, 1924); M. Leizerov, *Instsenirovannye professional′nye sudy* (Moscow: Trud i kniga, 1925); L. Reinberg, *Instsenirovannye proizvodstvennye sudy* (Moscow, 1926).

41. Leizerov, *Instsenirovannye*, 4, 6, 13, 17–18; "Profsudy i profdisputy," *Rabochii klub* 12 (1926): 6.

42. "Sud nad rabotnitsei, ne poseshchaiushchei obshchikh sobranii," in Leizerov, *Instsenirovannye*, 37–53; "Sud nad neakkuratnym platel′shchikom chlenskikh vznosov v professional′nyi soiuz," ibid., 14–36; "Sud nad shest′iu rabochimi zavoda 'Krasnyi Oktiabr' vedushchimi agitatsiiu protiv kluba," *Rabochii klub* 2 (1924): 30–32; M. Polin, "Rabotnitsa ne poseshchaiushchaia obshchikh sobranii (Instsenirovannyi sud)," *Rabochii klub* 8–9 (1925):

20–28; "Professional'no-distsiplinarnyi sud nad rabochim, ne vstupivshim v chleny profsoiuza" and "Sud nad chlenom profsoiuza, ne plativshim chlenskii vznos," in Mil'shtein, *Prof-sudy*, 5–29, 30–32.

43. "Sud nad chlenom fabkoma N. I. Egorovym (Instsenirovka)," in *Iskusstvo v rabochem klube* (Moscow: Vserossiiskii Proletkul't, 1924), 100–16. The Komsomol stood for the All-Union Leninist Communist Union of Youth.

44. I use here Michael Holquist's translation of Bakhtin's term *dialogizm* because it conveys Bakhtin's sense of "dialogue" not only as an interaction between two individuals but also in the sense of a whole mode of interaction in which many voices were allowed to communicate with each other. M. M. Bakhtin, *The Dialogic Imagination*, ed. Michael Holquist, trans. Caryl Emerson (Austin, 1981), esp. Introduction, xv–xxxiv, and Glossary, 423–34.

45. "Sud nad chlenom fabkoma," 115.

46. E. A. Rees, *State Control in Soviet Russia: The Rise and Fall of the Workers' and Peasants' Inspectorate, 1920–1934* (New York, 1987); S. N. Ikonnikov, *Sozdanie i deiatel'nost' ob'edinennykh organov TsKK-RKI v 1923–1934 gg.* (Moscow, 1971); on women workers' participation, Elizabeth A. Wood, *The Baba and the Comrade: Gender and Politics in Revolutionary Russia* (Bloomington, Ind., 1997), ch. 2; on Rabkrin in the late 1920s, David R. Shearer, *Industry, State, and Society in Stalin's Russia, 1926–1934* (Ithaca, 1996), esp. ch. 3, "Rabkrin and the Militarized Campaign Economy," 76–107.

47. "Sud nad rastratchikom vremeni na zavode" and "Sud nad khoziaistvennikom, kotoryi svoim razgil'diaistvom, kumovstvom i rastochitel'nost'iu sposobstvuet razrukhe v proizvodstve i ponizheniiu zarabotnoi platy," in Reinberg, *Instsenirovannye proizvodstvennye sudy*, 14, 25.

48. "Sud nad proizvodstvennoi komissiei, kotoraia ne sumela vtianut' rabochie massy v ekonomraboty" and "Sud nad fabkomom, dopustivshim zabastovku na gosudarstvennom predpriiatii," in Reinberg, *Instsenirovannye proizvodstvennye sudy*, 11–13, 24. Other examples of trials of truants include A. Popov, "Sud nad progul'shchikom," *Rabochii klub* 11 (1927): 57–58; Nosovskii, "Kluby otstaiut," *Klub i revoliutsiia* 7 (1929): 33. In January 1929, the newspaper *Zavodskaia Pravda* reported, the shop administration of the copper shop of one factory put eleven individuals on trial for truancy using public trials (*obshchestvennye sudy*). TsGAMO 880/1/93/144ob.

49. "Sud nad vinovnikami porchi stanka, mashiny," in Reinberg, *Instsenirovannye proizvodstvennye sudy*, 18; also "Sud nad plokhim i dorogim traktorom, vypushchennym s zavoda," "Sud nad otdel'nymi mashinami," "Sud nad plokhim toplivom, syr'em," even "Sud nad proshedshim proizvodstvennym godom," ibid., 15–19, 23. According to V. Klyukin, this was all part of the Komsomol's efforts to introduce time management and the principles of the Scientific Organization of Labor (N.O.T.) "Komsomol i NOT v dvadtsatye gody," *Pozyvnye istorii* 1 (1969): 258–59.

50. "Sud nad shkoloi fabzavucha," in Reinberg, *Instsenirovannye proizvodstvennye sudy*, 30–44.

51. Ibid., 40.

52. Ibid., 42.

53. Ibid.

54. *Cultural Revolution in Russia, 1928–1931*, ed. Sheila Fitzpatrick (Bloomington, Ind., 1978).

55. T. P. Korzhikhina, *Obshchestvennye organizatsii SSSR v 1917–1936 gg.* (Moscow, 1981); *Obshchestvennye organizatsii v SSSR: Materialy k istochnikovedeniiu i istoriografii* (Moscow, 1992); Glennys Young, *Power and the Sacred in Revolutionary Russia: Religious Activists in the Village* (University Park, Pa., 1997); William B. Husband, *"Godless Communists": Atheism and Society in Soviet Russia, 1917–1932* (Dekalb, Ill., 2000); Peter Kenez, *The Birth of the Propaganda State: Soviet Methods of Mass Mobilization, 1917–1929* (Cambridge, 1985).

56. M. Epshtein, "XIII s"ezd partii i zadachi politprosvetraboty," *Kommunisticheskoe prosveshchenie* 3–4 (1924): 7, 10.

57. L. Alotin-E'lota, "Ekspromptnye sansudy," Gosudarstvennyi Arkhiv Rossiiskoi Federatsii (GARF) 9636/5/125/6–7.

58. Carr, *Socialism in One Country,* 1:424–25; Robert V. Daniels, *The Conscience of the Revolution* (New York, 1960), 308.

59. A. Nikolaev, *Avio-agitsud* (Moscow: Obshchestvo druzei vozdushnogo flota RSFSR, 1925).

60. *Ibid.,* 37.

61. The premier work on this is Golfo Alexopoulos, *Stalin's Outcasts: Aliens, Citizens, and the Soviet State, 1926–1936* (Ithaca, 2003).

62. "VI Vsesoiuznyi S″ezd RLKSM. Rech′ tov. N. K. Krupskoi," *Pravda,* July 13, 1924, 4, cited in Naiman, *Sex in Public,* 92.

63. Boris Andreev, *Sud nad komsomol'tsem ili komsomolkoi narushaiushchimi soiuznuiu distsiplinu* (Leningrad: Knizhnyi sektor GUBONO, 1924), 19–20.

64. "Informatsiia," *Rabochii klub* 8 (1924): 42–49; A. Irkutov, "Politsud nad bibliei" in *Sbornik Komsomolskaia Paskha* (Moscow: Novaia Moskva, 1924); I. Personov and G. Rybinskii, "Sud nad Troitsei: Komicheskoe sudoproizvodstvo v 1 d.," in *Sbornik "Troitsyn den'"* (Moscow: Novaia Moskva, 1924); "Sud kapitala nad Komsomolom" in *Sbornik "Karl Libknekht—nashe znamia"* (Moscow: Novaia Moskva, 1924); "Shemiakin sud (Postanovka komsomol'skoi dramstudii 1-i Obraztsovoi tipografii)," *Rabochii klub* 1 (1924): 36–37. I have not found any Komsomol trials before 1924, though there is evidence of numerous public debates.

65. Carr, *Socialism in One Country,* 2:100–20.

66. Andreev, *Sud nad komsomol'tsem,* 3. The title's reference to "union discipline" means discipline in the Komsomol as a union of youth.

67. Ibid.

68. "Obrashchenie TsK VKP(b) ko vsem chlenam partii, ko vsem rabochim o razvertyvanii samokritiki" (June 2, 1928), in *KPSS v rezoliutsiiakh i resheniiakh,* 4:94–98; I. V. Stalin, "Protiv oposhleniia lozunga samokritiki," *Pravda,* June 26, 1928. For recent discussions of the self-criticism campaigns in 1928 and their significance for political struggles, see Michael David-Fox, *Revolution of the Mind: Higher Learning among the Bolsheviks, 1918–1929* (Ithaca, 1997), 127–32; Catherine Merridale, *Moscow Politics and the Rise of Stalin: The Communist Party in the Capital, 1925–1932* (London, 1990), 211–15; Oleg Kharkhordin, *The Collective and the Individual in Russia: A Study of Practices* (Berkeley, 1999), 142–163; Alexei Kojevnikov, "Rituals of Stalinist Culture at Work: Science and the Games of Intraparty Democracy circa 1948," *Russian Review* 57, no. 1 (1998): 35–36.

69. One example (of many) is V. Ia. Ashanin, *Kritika i samokritika v zhizni i deiatel'nosti KPSS* (Moscow, 1966).

70. I. V. Stalin, "Ob osnovakh leninizma," *Sochineniia* (Moscow, 1952), 6:82. These "foundations of Leninism" were originally given as lectures at Sverdlov University and published in *Pravda* in April and May 1924, after which they were published as a brochure entitled "O Lenine i leninizme" in May 1924.

71. "Ob ocherednykh zadachakh partii v derevne. Rech′ na soveshchanii sekretarei derevenskikh iacheek pri TsK RKP(b)" (October 22, 1924), in Stalin, *Sochineniia,* 6:302–12.

72. "O zadachakh partii v derevne. Rech′ na plenume TsK RKP(b)" (October 26, 1924), in Stalin, *Sochineniia,* 6:319–20; also "O 'dymovke.' Rech′ na zasedanii Orgbiuro TsK RKP(b)" (January 26, 1925), in Stalin, *Sochineniia,* 7:19–24.

73. Andreev, *Sud nad komsomol'tsem,* 21.

74. V. Zamoskvoretskii, *Klub rabochei molodezhi* (Moscow: Novaia Moskva, 1924), 191–94.

75. Krylenko, "Chto takoe khuliganstvo," in *Khuliganstvo i prestupnost'* (Moscow-Leningrad, 1927), 16, cited in P. Kruglikov, "Kulturnaia revoliutsiia i pervoocherednaia zadacha sotsial'nogo vospitaniia (Pedagogicheskaia profilaktika prestupnosti v SSSR)," *Narodnoe prosveshchenie* 8–9 (1928): 25–26. Krylenko participated in a public debate (*disput*) on hooliganism on October 29, 1926, in Leningrad. Grigorii Avlov, *Sud nad khuliganami* (Moscow-Leningrad: izd. Doloi negramotnost', 1927), 8. On the campaigns against hooliganism, see Naiman, *Sex in Public,* ch. 7, "The Case of Chubarov Alley: Collective Rape and Utopian Desire"; Gorsuch, *Youth in Revolutionary Russia,* 167–76; Peter H. Solomon, Jr., *Soviet Criminal Justice under*

Stalin (Cambridge, 1996), 58–60. On Dymovka, see Steven R. Coe, "Peasants, the State and the Languages of NEP: The Rural Correspondents Movement in the Soviet Union, 1924–1928" (Ph.D. diss., University of Michigan, 1993), esp. 29–34.

76. G. Kochenova, "Bor'ba s khuliganstvom i alkogolizmom," *Klub* 9, no. 16) (1926): 37–40; A. Krutov, "Bor'ba s khuliganstvom v rabochikh klubakh," *Rabochii Klub* 12 (1926): 30–32. K. Tulina reported that a hooligan who had been convicted in a "show trial" and sentenced to eight days of forced labor found upon his release that his name was on the "black board" of those being shamed for harming the collective. He wrote a letter to the head of the club asking to have his name removed and promising to "demonstrate my activeness and to make up for my wrongdoing." "Rabkory i klubkory o khuliganstve (Obzor pechati)," *Rabochii Klub* 2, no. 26 (1926): 76–80.

77. Kochenova, "Bor'ba s khuliganstvom," 37. On the Muscovite and Imperial Russian practice of gaining signatures as part of collective responsibility, see Horace W. Dewey and Ann M. Kleimola, "Suretyship and Collective Responsibility in Pre-Petrine Russia,"*Jahrbücher für Geschichte Osteuropas* 18 (1970): 337–54; Horace W. Dewey, "Political *Poruka* in Muscovite Rus'," *Russian Review* 46 (1987): 117–34. Some anti-alcohol groups also had people sign collective promises that they would not drink anything alcoholic. A. Agienko, "Kluby v bor'be s alkogolizmom," *Klub* 8–9 (1928): 74–79.

78. Priokskii, "Sud nad khuliganstvom i izbieniem stenkora," *Rabochii klub* 11 (1925): 80; A. Krupkov, "Klub imeni Kominterna. Fabrika Trekhgornoi manufaktury," *Klub* 9 (1926): 55–58; Avlov, *Sud nad khuliganami*, 3.

79. R. Ginzburg, "Bor'ba s khuliganstvom," *Rabochii klub* 3 (March 1926): 11–14.

80. Iu. Bekhterev, "Khuliganstvo i klubnaia rabota v mestakh zakliucheniia," *Klub* 3 (1927): 45–53.

81. E. Karachunskaia, "Sud nad khuliganom," *Rabochii klub* 12 (1926): 37–38.

82. Avlov, *Sud nad khuliganami*; Avlov, *Klubnyi samodeiatel'nyi teatr: Evoliutsiia metodov i form* (Leningrad-Moscow: Teakinopechat', 1930), 92–104.

83. Eric Naiman suggests a similar conclusion in the Chubarov Alley case, where the defendants also revealed a distorted sense of collective responsibility and action. *Sex in Public*, 272–73, 283–84.

84. Avlov, *Sud nad khuliganami*. Hooliganism, of course, was also a crime that invaded the club from outside and against which the social body had to defend itself, a phenomenon that both Gorsuch and Naiman also see in this period. To my mind it is also related to the so-called war scare of 1927, when it was claimed that the Soviet Union was facing the threat of potential invasion and war. In both cases the "threats" proved extremely useful as an excuse for the authorities, be they at the club level or at the national level, to "invade" their subjects by investigating their behaviors and private lives.

85. On the increasing persecution of intellectuals, particularly in the "Changing Landmarks" (Smena vekh) movement, see Kendall E. Bailes, *Technology and Society under Lenin and Stalin: Origins of the Soviet Technical Intelligentsia, 1917–1941* (Princeton, 1978), 72.

86. P. M. Vedernikov, "Sansudy i ikh postanovka na osnove kollektivizma ispolnitelei," *Krasnyi put'* 19 (November 1924): 111, GARF 9636/5/124.

87. A. B. Zalkind, "Predislovie," in Doktor E. B. Demidovich, *Sud nad polovoi raspushchennost'iu* (Moscow-Leningrad: Doloi negramotnost', 1927), 3–5.

88. Ibid., 6.

89. Demidovich, *Sud nad polovoi raspushchennost'iu*, 38–39.

90. Ibid., 24.

91. Eric Naiman has a superb discussion of these cases in *Sex in Public*, 93–94. Many such cases were collected in volumes of articles from the press such as *Komsomol'skii byt*, ed. I. Razin (Moscow-Leningrad: Molodaia gvardiia, 1927).

92. B. Sigal, *Sud nad pionerom-kuril'shchikom i sud nad neriashlivym pionerom (dve instsenirovki)* (Moscow, 1927). Boris Samoilovich Sigal (b. 1893) was active in Leningrad sanitation education work and authored numerous sanitation trials. In 1924 he reviewed over 120 plays put on in Leningrad in the previous year. B. Sigal, "O sanitarno-prosvetitel'nykh ins-

tsenirovkakh [sansudakh]," *Sanitarnoe prosveshchenie* 3 (May 20, 1924): 2–3. He also wrote several books on sexuality in the 1920s, including *Polovoi vopros* (Moscow-Leningrad: Molodaia gvardiia, 1925).

93. This series, *Biblioteka "Narodnyi teatr,"* published a number of other staged agitation trial scenarios as well, all by Dr. B. S. Sigal: *Sud nad mater'iu vinovnoi v rasprostranenii skarlatiny* (Moscow, 1925); *Sud nad Stepanom Korolevym (posledstviia p'ianstva)* (Moscow, 1926); *Sud nad samogonshchikami* (Moscow, 1925); *Sud nad babkoi znakharkoi* (Moscow, 1925) ; *Sud nad grazhdaninom Fedorom Sharovym po obvineniiu v zarazhenii tripperom* (Leningrad, 1925).

94. Sigal, *Sud nad pionerom-kuril'shchikom*, 3.

95. Ibid., 15–16.

96. Ibid., 109.

97. There is a similar debate over conversion and whether it is sufficient for conditional acceptance into the collective in *The Trial of the Slovenly Pioneer*. At the end of that trial the prosecutor and defense argue whether Korovin, the twelve-year-old defendant, should have been able to overcome his bad habits in the three months he has served as a Pioneer. The prosecution wants to see him on probation for six months "until he reforms himself and ceases to be a carrier of infection." The defense, on the other hand, expresses the conviction that if the boy is not excluded and "you [the judges] give him the chance to become an honest Pioneer," then he will reform, and cease to be slovenly and dirty.

98. Andreev, *Sud nad komsomol'tsem*, 13–14.

99. Ibid., 15.

100. Avlov, *Sud nad khuliganami*, 47–48.

101. Boris Sigal, *Sud nad p'ianitsei* (Leningrad: Leningradskaia pravda, 1930), 47–48.

Chapter 9. Shaming Boys Who Smoke Cigarettes

1. L. Alotin-Elota, "Ekspromptnye sansudy" (unpublished typescript, 1926), Gosudarstvennyi Arkhiv Rossiiskoi Federatsii (GARF) 9636/5/125/6–7; an excerpt was published under the same title in *Profilakticheskaia meditsina* 12 (December 1925): 112–13.

2. Alotin-Elota, "Ekspromtnye sansudy," GARF 9636/5/125/2.

3. Ibid. The staging of the early agitation trials had been designed, as Nikolai Semashko put it, "to correspond to reality" (*instseniruetsia kakoe-nibud' deistvie otvechaiushchee real'noi deistvitel'nosti*). N. Semashko, "Introduction," in B. S. Ginzburg, *Sud nad mater'iu, podkinuvshei svoego rebenka* (Moscow, 1924), 3. Until mid-1924, however, such trials had never used real individuals as protagonists.

4. As was noted in chapter 4, trials of soldiers seen spitting were occasionally staged in the army. They do not, however, appear to have been a regular part of the practice of agitation trials at that time. Vrid. Nachagitprop Puokra Zap. Sib. Voennogo okruga and NachKlubotd. Semkov, "Dopolnenie k instruktsii o rabote krasnykh ugolkov" ([1923]), RGVA 9/13/111/92ob.

5. S. A. Markovich, "Iz opyta podgotovki budushchikh vrachei k sanitarno-prosvetitel'nomu delu," *Profilakticheskaia Meditsina* 1 (January 1925): 71–73; A. Z. Narodetskii, "Programma laboratorno-seminarskikh rabot po sanprosvetrampe" (zasedanie no. 8 rabotnikov tsentra Sanprosveta Moszdrava) (January 7, 1927), GARF 9636/7/24/4–6. Aleksandr Zinovievich Narodetskii was director of the sanitation education theater of the Moscow health division (Moskovskii teatr Sanprosveta) (GARF 9636/5/3).

6. "Protokol i rezoliutsiia Vsesoiuznogo soveshchaniia sanprosvetrabotnikov Krasnoi Armii i Flota, 27–30 maia [1924]," GARF 9636/7/20/2ob.; N. Tenenboim, "Iz opyta massovoi likvidatsii sanitarnoi bezgramotnosti (Po materialam konkursa na luchshuiu postanovku sanitarnogo vospitaniia v Krasnoi Armii i Flote)," *Sanitarnoe prosveshchenie* 2 (1924): 27. M. Belkin was a lecturer on sanitation education and a medical resident (*mladshii vrach*) in the Twenty-ninth Regiment of the Tenth Territorial Army. N. G. Tenenboim was an official in the Main Military Sanitation Administration of the Red Army (Glavsanupr).

7. Tenenboim, "Iz opyta," 27.

8. This venerable institution had been founded in 1798.

9. D. Lukashevich, "Kurs metodiki sanitarnogo prosveshcheniia v voenno-meditsinskoi akademii," *Sanitarnoe prosveshcheniia* 1 (1925): 56; Fishman, "Sanprosvetrabota slushatelei voenno-meditsinskoi akademii v Leningradskom garnizone," *Sanitarnoe prosveshchenie, sbornik* 1 (1925): 58.

10. Alotin-Elota, "Ekspromtnye sansudy," GARF 9636/5/125/2.

11. Ibid., l. 6–7.

12. Ibid.

13. Ibid.

14. The result was not unlike the "trial" staged by the boys in William Golding's novel *The Lord of the Flies.*

15. L.S. Ioff, "Obshchestvennyi sud nad bol'nym tripperom, zarodivshem zhenu i rebenka" (unpublished typescript, 1930), GARF 9636/5/127/21.

16. "Otchet po sanitarnomu prosveshcheniiu nauchno-metodicheskogo Kabineta g. Kieva za 3 mesiatsa 1927 g.," GARF 9636/7/26/3ob.; Sovetov, "Stsena, sansudy i sudebnye protsessy v dele anti-alkogol'noi propagandy," *Profilakticheskaia meditsina* (1927).

17. B. Sigal, "Pravila postanovki" (Introduction), in *Sud nad p'ianitsei* (Leningrad: Leningradskaia pravda, 1930), 4.

18. Tenenboim, at the All-Union Conference of Sanitation Education Workers in the Red Army and Navy in May 1924, spoke out against the way that money was spent on sansudy in the Northern Caucasus Military Organization, GARF 9636/7/20/3; also M. Frenkel', "Vnimanie k san-postanovkam!" *Sanitarnoe prosveshchenie* 2 (1924): 7–8.

19. I. Mil'man, "Opyt organizatsii sanitarno-dramaticheskogo kruzhka pri Dome Sanitarnogo Prosveshcheniia Zamoskvoretskogo raiona," *Sanitarnoe prosveshchenie* 3 (1924): 3.

20. B. Sigal, "O sanitarno-prosvetitel'nykh instsenirovkakh (sansudakh)," *Sanitarnoe prosveshchenie* 3 (1924): 3.

21. Ibid.

22. P. M. Vedernikov, "Sansudy i ikh postanovka na osnove kollektivizma ispolnitelei," *Krasnyi put'* 19 (November 1924): 97–122.

23. Lynn Mally discusses shaming by agitation brigades and "the war on the audience" during the First Five Year Plan in her *Revolutionary Acts: Amateur Theater and the Soviet State, 1917–1938* (Ithaca, 2000), 156–61.

24. Alotin-Elota, "Ekspromptnye sansudy," GARF 9636/5/125/2.

25. Vedernikov, "Sansudy i ikh postanovka," 97–98. Alotin-Elota, too, thought that the punishment for a character with venereal disease should be "placement under the strictest observation [*strozhaishchee nabliudenie*] of his comrades and of the medical personnel." Such a defendant should also, as part of his punishment, be required to attend lectures on sanitation education. Alotin-Elota, "Ekspromptnye sandsudy," l. 2ob.

26. Ioff, "Obshchestvennyi sud nad bol'nym tripperom," ll. 21–22.

27. Ibid., l. 27.

28. Ibid., l. 41.

29. Ibid., l. 47.

30. "Sansud nad rabochim Pavlovym I. S." [1934], GARF 9636/5/127/90–98.

31. A. A. Bogoslovskii, "Sami kolkhozniki daiut otpor ukloneniiam ot privivok" (unpublished typescript, 1933), GARF 9636/5/126/1–3. The Moscow oblast Institute of Sanitation Culture was founded in 1929 under the direction of Sofiia Volkonskaia. Volkonskaia (1889–1942) had worked in sanitation education from 1915 in the Sokol'niki neighborhood in Moscow, where several of the earliest agitation trials were held in 1920–1921. Gosudarstvennyi Arkhiv Oktiabr'skoi Revoliutsii i Sotsialisticheskogo Stroitel'stva Moskovskoi oblasti (GAORSS MO) 6890/1/4 (files of the Moskovskaia sanitarnaia chrezvychainaia komissiia during the Civil War); GARF 2315/1/41; archivists' introduction, GARF 9636/5.

32. Another agitation trial on vaccinations, one that informed the audience only at the end that it was fictional, was G. D. Van'ian, "Agitsud nad gr. Malkinym, Timokhinoi i Baikhovoi" (unpublished typescript, 1933), GARF 9636/5/127/1–19.

33. I. Blinkov, "Organizatsiia kachestvennogo ucheta," *Klub* 2 (1926): 62–68.

34. Admittedly, he was not above scripting some lines for speakers from the audience to express surprise and indignation when the case didn't seem to be going the way they thought it should.

35. S. Dolinskii, "Klubnaia vecherinka," *Klub* 3 (1926): 15–17; the original article, "Tret'ia zhena," appeared in *Rabochaia Moskva* 288 (December 17, 1925). Another trial allegedly taken from real life was *The Trial of a Wife Who Was Jealous of Her Husband for No Reason*. S. Moiseev, "Itogi letnei raboty klubov," *Klub* 10 (1926): 46.

36. D. Peniaev, "Sud nad pravleniem kluba (Stalingradskii rudkom, Donbass)," *Klub* 11 (1927): 68–69. The Donbas region, it should be noted, is where the famous Shakhty trial was staged a year later in 1928 (see chapter 10).

37. Other versions of the trial of the club included "Agitsud nad klubnikom" (April 1923), Rossiiskii Gosudarstvennyi Voennyi Arkhiv (RGVA) 9/13/111/14; "Sud nad klubom," discussed at a meeting of the club section of the Moscow Trade Union Council (MGSPS) (January 13, 1924), Tsentral'nyi Gosudarstvennyi Arkhiv Moskovskoi oblasti (TsGAMO) 880/1/45/183; "Tezisy obvinitelia" for "Sud nad pravleniem kluba," TsGAMO 880/1/47/30–32, 116–21.

38. A. Popov, "Sud nad progul'shchikom (Kozhraion im. Lenina)," *Rabochii klub* 11 (1927): 57–58.

39. It is conceivable that the whole episode was a fiction created by the author (A. Popov) for readers of *Rabochii klub* and there was no Dmitri Timofeev in the audience of the trial performance. Nonetheless, the fact that Popov chooses to claim that "everyone knew" who the "real" defendant was suggests a move away from trials where a particular behavior (say, drunkenness) was being discussed to trials of a known defendant.

40. Iakhnin, "Agitsud, kak forma bor'by s progulami," *Rabochii klub* 1 (1928): 67–69.

41. The Zlatoust Metal Factory was eventually to become known as "the cradle of the shock movement." Hiroaki Kuromiya, *Stalin's Industrial Revolution: Politics and Workers, 1928–1932* (Cambridge, 1988), 119.

42. For the birth of the prerevolutionary public sphere for professionals, see Laura Engelstein, *The Keys to Happiness: Sex and the Search for Modernity in Fin-de-Siècle Russia* (Ithaca, 1992); Edith W. Clowes, Samuel D. Kassow, and James L. West, *Between Tsar and People: Educated Society and the Quest for Public Identity in Late Imperial Russia* (Princeton, 1991).

43. Boris Andreev, *Sud nad komsomol'tsem ili komsomolkoi narushaiushchimi soiuznuiu distsiplinu* (Leningrad: knizhnyi sektor GUBONO, 1924), 7. The defendant was also charged with "carrying himself in an unseemly manner" (*nepodobaiushche podderzhal sebia*). Discipline thus takes priority over education and entertainment; the civilizing mission of the trials becomes central. "We were all very disturbed [*vozmushcheny*] by his behavior," says one young woman defendant in a prim tone.

44. Ibid., 8.

45. "Sud nad rabotnitsei, ne poseshchaiushchei obshchikh sobranii," in M. Leizerov, *Instsenirovannye professional'nye sudy* (Moscow: Trud i kniga, 1925), 37–38, 46, 52.

46. A. Nikolaev, *Avio-agitsud* (Moscow: Obshchestvo druzei vozdushnogo flota RSFSR, 1925).

47. R. Es-kii, "Propaganda knigi klubnoi biblioteki," *Klub i revoliutsiia* 3–4 (March–April 1929): 61–67; *Pisatel' pered sudom rabochego chitatelia. Vechera rabochei kritiki*, ed. G. Brylov, N. Veis, and V. Sakharov (Leningrad: LSPS, 1928); G. Nagornyi, review of *Pisatel' pered sudom, Rabochii klub* 7–8 (1928): 103–4.

48. Es-kii, "Propaganda knigi," 61–62.

49. Ibid.

50. The best source on worker correspondents is Steven R. Coe, "Peasants, the State, and the Languages of NEP: The Rural Correspondents Movement in the Soviet Union, 1924–1928" (Ph.D. diss., University of Michigan, 1993).

51. "Po povodu suda," *Rabochii zritel'* 30 (1924): 9. In a Smolensk club, workers' correspondents were also put on trial for allegedly slandering club activists and accusing them of carousing. Since the activists and the correspondents had "equal authority" in local people's eyes, the trial allegedly piqued everyone's interest. I. Emskii, "Interesnyi vecher," *Klub* 1 (1927), 66–67). This kind of trial reminds one of a gladiator sport. The organizers do not seem to have

cared what the outcome was. They did not even report who was found guilty and who was vindicated.

52. V. Ardov, "Po povodu odnogo suda (Fantaziia)," *Rabochii zritel'* 9 (1924): 6–8.

53. L. K. Kuvanova, "Furmanov i Babel'," *Literaturnoe nasledstvo* 74 (Moscow, 1965), 500–12. Budennyi's attack on Babel appeared in "Babizm Babelia," *Oktiabr'* 3 (1924); A. K. Voronskii then defended Babel in *Krasnaia nov'* 5 (August–September 1924): 276–91. The public debate was held on November 29, 1924.

54. Kuvanova, "Furmanov i Babel'." The verb "to call out" (*vyzvat'*) in Russian has many connotations including calling someone out to a duel, summoning a witness or defendant into court, calling a student to the blackboard, and calling for an actor to appear for curtain calls. The fact that Furmanov chose this verb (instead of the simpler verb "to call," *zvat'*) suggests that he was very much thinking of the event as a duel or summons into court.

55. Kuvanova, ibid., 500–504, mistakenly assumes that he was jotting down his own views in the notes that are in Rossiiskii Gosudarstvennyi Arkhiv Literatury I Iskusstva (RGALI) (f. 30, op. 1). From the context it appears clear that Furmanov was instead summarizing other people's views for his own use as "judge" in the debate.

56. No. 74.824, "Obraztsovyi litsud (Vysshaia Pogranichnaia shkola OGPU)," *Rabochii klub* 5 (1926): 58. The signature "No. 74.824" may refer to one of the students at the school.

57. Ibid.; also N. Vertinskii, *Literaturnaia rabota v klube* (Moscow: Proletkul't, 1927), 45–47. For the horrendous military trial of Babel inside the Moscow Butyrki prison in 1940, see Vitaly Shentalinsky, *The KGB's Literary Archive*, trans. John Crowfoot (London, 1993), 67–70. He was not allowed to have a defense lawyer or to summon witnesses. Immediately after the trial he was shot. The director Vsevolod Meyerhold was shot five days later.

58. *Vecherniaia Moskva* October 12, 1926, quoted in Anatoly Smeliansky, *Is Comrade Bulgakov Dead? Mikhail Bulgakov at the Moscow Art Theatre* (New York, 1993), 102–3. Other accounts of *disputy* were reported in *Zhizn' iskusstva* 44 (1926): 12; A. Orlinskii, "Protiv Bulgakovshchiny" *Novyi zritel'* 41 (October 12, 1926): 3–4; "Sud nad 'Beloi gvardii' (Disput v Dome Pechati)," *Novyi zritel'* 42 (October 19, 1926): 4. For discussion of this trial and the debates held on September 30 and October 2, 1926, plus February 7, 1927, see Smeliansky, *Is Comrade Bulgakov Dead?* 76–77, 99–114; G. Faiman, "Bulgakovshchina," *Teatr* 12 (December 1991): 82–102. My thanks to Edythe Haber for these and other references.

59. The most vicious of these attacks was Orlinskii, "Protiv Bulgakovshchiny," 3–4. Orlinskii at this time was head of the Artistic-Club Section of the Moscow Committee of the Communist Party and editor of *Novyi zritel'*. Also see Larisa Reisner, "Protiv literaturnogo banditizma," *Zhurnalist* 1 (1926): 26, quoted in Faiman, "Bulgakovshchina," 82. In a bitter letter addressed to the Soviet government in March 1930, Bulgakov wrote that in the ten years he had been writing, the Soviet press had carried 301 references to his work, 298 of which were "hostile and abusive." J. A. E. Curtis, *Manuscripts Don't Burn: Mikhail Bulgakov, A Life in Letters and Diaries* (Woodstock, N.Y., 1992), 104; Shentalinsky, *KGB's Literary Archive,* 72–94.

60. Public debates were not the only form of harassment. On May 7, 1926, Bulgakov's apartment was searched, probably in conjunction with a case against the editor of the journal *Rossiia*, which was publishing *The White Guard* in installments. And on the day of the dress rehearsal of *Days of the Turbines,* September 23, 1926, he was called into the OGPU for interrogation. By September 1929, after three years of attacks, all of Bulgakov's works had been banned and he described himself as "ruined, persecuted and completely isolated." Smeliansky, *Is Comrade Bulgakov Dead?* 163.

61. Ibid., 128.

62. M. Gorki, "Trata energii," *Izvestiia,* September 15, 1929, quoted ibid., 163–64.

63. Kochenova, "Bor'ba s khuliganstvom i alkogolizmom," *Klub* 9 (1926): 39.

Chapter 10. Fiction Becomes Indistinguishable from Reality, 1928–33

1. Eugene Lyons, *Assignment in Utopia* (New York, 1937). The Oxford English Dictionary lists Lyons's as the first use of "show trial": http://dictionary.oed.com/cgi/entry/00223609/00223609se70, accessed on October 1, 2004.

2. Walter Duranty, "Red Leaders Clash on Soviet Justice," *New York Times,* December 12, 1927, 6; Duranty, "Grim Soviet Court Opens Trial of 52," *New York Times,* May 19, 1928, 1; Duranty, "Anti-Semite Trial Opens at Minsk," *New York Times,* January 20, 1929, E3. In this last article he carefully explained a "show trial" as a trial "staged in the largest available hall and advertised throughout Russia." By November 15, 1933, he was referring to the German Reichstag fire trial as a "show trial" as well.

3. Duranty, "Cain-Abel Drama Grips Soviet Court," *New York Times,* May 28, 1928, 5; Duranty, "Moscow Has Thrill Daily in Red Trial," *New York Times,* June 3, 1928, E3. By the end of the Shakhty trial he was referring to "the duel" that had developed between Nikolai Krylenko, the state prosecutor, and one of the leading defendants, L. G. Rabinovich (*New York Times,* June 23, 26, 27, 1928).

4. Kendall E. Bailes, *Technology and Society under Lenin and Stalin* (Princeton, 1978), 69–94; Hiroaki Kuromiya, "The Shakhty Affair" *Southeast European Monitor* 4, no. 2 (1997).

5. "Obvinitel'noe zakliuchenie po delu ob ekonomicheskoi kontr-revoliutsii v Donbasse," Rossiiskii Gosudarstvennyi Arkhiv Ekonomiki (RGAE) 9474/7/181/204.

6. Peter H. Solomon, Jr., *Soviet Criminal Justice under Stalin* (Cambridge, 1996), 139–40.

7. N. V. Krylenko, "Uroki Shakhtinskogo dela," in *Ekonomicheskaia kontr-revoliutsiia v Donbase (Itogi Shakhtinskogo dela). Stat'i i dokumenty,* ed. N. V. Krylenko (Moscow: Iuridicheskoe izd. NKIu RSFSR, 1928), 55.

8. Lyons, *Assignment,* 118.

9. Roy A. Medvedev, *Let History Judge* (New York, 1971), 111–13; Kuromiya, "Shakhty Affair."

10. Lyons, *Assignment,* 370, 114–17, 120, 132.

11. Ibid., 114–15; Julie A. Cassiday, *The Enemy on Trial: Early Soviet Courts on Stage and Screen* (DeKalb, Ill., 2000), 110–33; Cassiday, "Marble Columns and Jupiter Lights: Theatrical and Cinematic Modeling of Soviet Show Trials in the 1920s," *Slavic and East European Journal* 42, no. 4 (1998): 640–60.

12. *Izvestiia TsIK i VTsIK,* March 12, 1928, cited in "Obvinitel'noe zakliuchenie," in *Ekonomicheskaia kontr-revoliutsiia,* 100–1; Lyons, *Assignment,* 117.

13. As Cassiday has pointed out, it is located near Theater Square, home of the Bolshoi and Malyi Theaters ("Marble Columns," 657n.). It was also the hall that had been used for the trial of the Socialist Revolutionaries in 1922 and where Lenin's body had been laid out in state in January 1924. Duranty, "Score Plead Guilty in 'Engineers' Plot'," *New York Times,* May 12, 1928, 6.

14. "Stenogramma po Shakhtinskomu delu," RGAE 9474/7/183–184.

15. Lyons, *Assignment,* 118.

16. It seems impossible to show causality or direction of influence here. Both the agitation trials and the show trials were bringing charges of "wrecking," which included accidents, harm done to machines, and so on. For more on wrecking, see Solomon, *Soviet Criminal Justice,* 139–40, 240–44.

17. For claims that this and later show trials were scripted, see Cassiday, *Enemy,* 115; Cassiday, "Marble Columns," 652; Robert C. Tucker, *Stalin in Power: The Revolution from Above, 1928–1941* (New York, 1990), 316–18, 497, 501, 551 (on the show trials of 1936–1938); *Stalin's Letters to Molotov,* ed. Lars T. Lih et al. (New Haven, 1995), 192, 195; cf. Robert Conquest, *The Great Trial: A Reassessment* (New York, 1990), who shows evidence that many episodes could not have been strictly planned (e.g., 353, 371–72).

18. Although Tucker writes extensively of a "scripted culture," he himself provides evidence that the trial victims in the 1936–1938 show trials were supposed to adhere to an outline (what was called a *skhema* or *kanva* in the agitation trials) rather than following an exact script. *Stalin in Power,* 416–17, 470.

19. As one methodology of agitation trials explained, "Any stiltedness, pathos in acting proves harmful in the agitation trial. . . . The witness must not act but rather truthfully represent [*pravdivo izobrazit'*] the character." M. Shishkevich, "Metodika agit-sudov," in V. Boichevskii, V. Malkis, and M. Shishkevich, *Sbornik agit-sudy* (Moscow: "Novaia Moskva"

(Moskovskii Gubpolitprosvet), 1926), 5. In 1920 Lenin had commented several times that the secret of Bolshevik agitation lay in its *pravdivost'*, i.e., its verisimilitude. "Rech' na bespartiinoi konferentsii rabochikh i krasnoarmeitsev Presnenskogo raiona 24 ianvaria 1920 g. Gazetnyi otchet," in *Sochineniia* (Moscow, 1935), 30:280; "Rech' pri zakrytii s"ezda 5 aprelia (IX s"ezd RKP(b), 29 marta–5 aprelia 1920 g.)," ibid., 454.

20. For many authors, using improvisation made agitation trials seem "natural" even though they were prepared in advance, Gr. Avlov, *Klubnyi samodeiatel'nyi teatr: Evoliutsiia metodov i form* (Leningrad-Moscow, 1930), 100; also Cassiday on antitheatricality in *Enemy*, 118.

21. "Shakhtinskoe delo i prakticheskie zadachi v dele bor'by s nedostatkami khoziaistvennogo stroitel'stva," *Pravda*, April 12, 1928.

22. Joseph Stalin, *Works* (Moscow, 1954), 11:57. Of course, this was not the first time that the party had "revealed" a threat that others could not see. The war scare of 1927 was another example of a crisis manufactured by the top leadership.

23. For more on this climate, Gabor Tamas Rittersporn, "The Omnipresent Conspiracy: On Soviet Imagery of Politics and Social Relations in the 1930s," in *Stalinist Terror: New Perspectives* ed. J. Arch Getty and Roberta T. Manning (Cambridge, 1993), 99–115.

24. *Pravda*, May 18, 1928, cited in Mikhail Heller and Aleksandr M. Nekrich, *Utopia in Power* (New York, 1986), 208.

25. A. Agranovskii, Iu. Alevich, and G. Ryklin, *Liudi-vrediteli: Shakhtinskoe delo* (Moscow-Leningrad, 1928).

26. Two such films were listed as "'Delo ob ekonomicheskoi kontrrevoliutsii v Donbasse' (Khronikal'naia, 437 metrov, proizvodstvo Sovkino; razreshena dlia vsekh po IV gruppe)" and "Shakhtintsy na skam'e podsudimykh. Protsess. Dokumental'naia fil'ma, godna dlia raboty v klube i derevne," in *Klub i revoliutsii* (June 1929): 73. It is interesting that the authorities thought carefully about when each film should be shown to. For more discussion, see Cassiday, *Enemy*, 126–27; Cassiday, "Marble Columns," 653–54.

27. B. Shneerson, "Spetsialisty, kul'trabota i bor'ba s vreditel'stvom," *Klub i revoliutsiia* 21–22 (November 1930): 6–14; Vyshinsky's concluding speech in *The Great Purge Trial*, ed. Robert C. Tucker and Stephen F. Cohen (New York, 1965), 525–26.

28. A trial in the southern city of Astrakhan, for example, charged local fishing firms with bribery and castigated local party organizations for failing to "carry out active struggle" against the private firms. *Pravda* coverage lasted from August 30 to October 29, 1929 (Solomon, *Soviet Criminal Justice*, 84). A summary of the case was provided in Iakov Grinval'd, *Klass protiv klass. Ekonomicheskaia kontrrevoliutsiia v Astrakhani* (Saratov: Gos. izd-vo Nizhne-Volzhskoe kraevoe otdelenie, 1930); this was also published as Iakov Grinval'd, I. Khankin and I. Chilim, *Sud nad "Astrakhanshchinoi"* (239 pp.).

29. Shneerson, "Spetsialisty," 7.

30. *Pravda*, June 3, 1928.

31. Stalin, "Protiv oposhleniia lozunga samokritiki," *Pravda*, June 26, 1928, 2, cited in *Bol'shaia Sovetskaia Entsiklopediia*, 2nd ed. (Moscow, 1953), 50:189.

32. KPSS o kul'ture, prosveshchenii i nauke (Moscow, 1963), 170, cited in *Kul'turno-prosvetitel'naia rabota v SSSR*, ed. T. A. Remizova (Moscow, 1974), 100; P. Kruglikov, "Kul'turnaia revoliutsiia i pervoocherednaia zadacha sotsial'nogo vospitaniia (pedagogicheskaia profilaktika prestupnosti v SSSR)," *Narodnoe prosveshchenie* 8–9 (August–September 1928): 23–33. "Cultural revolution" was the term that contemporaries used; cf. Michael David-Fox, "What Is Cultural Revolution?" *Russian Review* 58, no. 2 (1999): 181–201.

33. A. Krupnov, "Kluby i kul'turnyi pokhod," *Klub* 8–9 (1928): 65. Glavpolitprosvet, the Komsomol, and the Down with Illiteracy Society announced the new campaign by publishing a one-time newspaper entitled *Kul'turnyi pokhod*. M. S. Andreeva, A. P. Vinogradov, S. A. Pinalov, and G. I. Cherniavskii, *Istoriia kul'turno-prosvetitel'noi raboty v SSSR*, ch. 2, *Sovetskii period (1917–1969 gg.)* (Kharkov, 1970), 88–92; "Cultural Revolution as Class War," in *Cultural Revolution in Russia, 1928–1931*, ed. Sheila Fitzpatrick (Bloomington, Ind., 1978), 25–26.

34. Krupnov, "Kluby," 65; "Klub i byt: K Vsesoiuznomu klubnomu soveshchaniiu," *Klub i revoliutsiia* 4 (February 1930): 3.

35. Shneerson, "Spetsialisty," 6–14; Joseph Stalin, "The Tasks of Business Executives" (February 1931), excerpted in Robert V. Daniels, *A Documentary History of Communism in Russia* (Hanover, N.H., 1993), 180–83.

36. Syrtsov at the Nizhegorod regional party conference, in *Moskovskaia Pravda,* August 15, 1929, quoted in N. A. Selad'in, *Kul'trabota v rekonstruktivnyi period* (Moscow, 1930), 7.

37. Ia. Shitov, "Samokritika v kul'trabote," *Rabochii klub* 7–8 (1928): 59–62; "Kul'turnye nozhnitsy (Opyt obshchego analiza problemy)," *Narodnoe prosveshchenie* 10 (October 1928): 82–88.

38. Shitov, "Samokritika v kul'trabote," 59–62; "Kul'turnye nozhnitsy," 82–88. The attack on the clubs was probably part of Stalin's attack on the trade unions in conjunction with his move against the Right Opposition in 1928–29. Robert Vincent Daniels, *The Conscience of the Revolution* (New York, 1960), 344–48.

39. G. Nagornyi, "Klub v dele razvertyvaniia samokritiki," *Rabochii klub* 9–10 (1928): 3–4. On self-criticism as a form of pseudodemocracy in the 1930s, see Stephen Kotkin, *Magnetic Mountain: Stalinism as a Civilization* (Berkeley, 1995), 316–32; Oleg Kharkhordin, *The Collective and the Individual in Russia: A Study of Practices* (Berkeley, 1999); Hiroaki Kuromiya, *Stalin's Industrial Revolution: Politics and Workers, 1928–1932* (Cambridge, 1988), 35–49, 61–63, 118, 122.

40. Nagornyi, "Klub v dele razvertyvaniia samokritiki," 7; A. L., "Entuziasty kul'turnoi revoliutsii (Opyt Sormovskogo kul'tpokhoda)," *Klub i revoliutsiia* 21–22 (November 1930): 27–39; I. Aizenberg, "Samokritika na ushcherbe," *Rabochii klub* 11–12 (1928): 65–66; Nosovskii, "Kluby otstaiut," *Klub i revoliutsiia* 7 (1929): 27–37; Kul'trabotnik, "Sotsialisticheskoe sorevnovanie i klub," *Klub i revoliutsiia* 7 (1929): 18.

41. G. Grigor'ev, "Propaganda piatiletnego plana," *Klub i revoliutsiia* 6 (June 1929): 15.

42. Ibid.

43. The responsible historian must always add the caveat that it is possible that some trials or trial fragments have been overlooked.

44. *Vsesoiuznyi tekhnicheskii sud nad sbornym zhelezobetonom* (Moscow: Glavstroiprom, 1933).

45. R. G., review of S. Dolinskii and S. Bergman, *Massovaia rabota v klube, Rabochii klub* 8 (1924): 50–51.

46. R. Ginzburg, "Klub, kak on est'," *Rabochii klub* 1 (1925): 13.

47. V. Zamoskvoretsekii, *Klub rabochei molodezhi* (Moscow: Novaia Moskva, 1924), 96.

48. "Mezhdunarodnyi krasnyi den'," *Klub i revoliutsiia* 6 (June 1929): 3.

49. Ibid., 6. "Social fascists" was a derogatory term for social democrats in Western Europe. This appellation and the move of the Sixth Comintern Congress to divide the communist parties in Europe from the Social Democrats were to have disastrous consequences for the rise of fascism in Nazi Germany and Italy. For more on this congress see Adam B. Ulam, *Expansion and Coexistence: Soviet Foreign Policy, 1917–1973*, 2nd ed. (New York, 1974), 186–88; Stephen F. Cohen, *Bukharin and the Bolshevik Revolution* (Oxford, 1971), 291–95.

50. I. Lomskii, "Podgotovka klubov k oktiabr'skoi godovshchine," *Klub i revoliutsiia* 15–16 (August 1930): 44.

51. L. Reinberg, "Nashi khoziaistvennye zadachi i rabochii klub," *Klub i revoliutsiia* 3–4 (March–April 1929), 3–12; S. Krylov, "Na bor'bu s sektantstvom," *Klub i revoliutsiia* 5 (1929): 39–40.

52. A number of trials of this type were published by the Moscow Oblast Union of Consumer Societies (MOSPO), all with no author listed: *Agit-sud nad zaveduiushchim magazinom, nevypolniaiushchim ratsminimuma (minimum ratsionalizatorskikh meropriatii)* (Moscow: RIO MOSPO, 1930); *Agit-sud nad zaveduiushchim stolovoi (Za plokhoe obsluzhivanie potrebitelia)* (Moscow: RIO MOSPO, 1930); *Sud nad lavochnei komissiei* (Moscow: RIO MOSPO, 1930).

53. *Sud nad lavochnei komissiei,* 1–2.

54. B. S. Sigal, *Sud nad p'ianitsei* (Leningrad: Leningradskaia pravda, 1930), 47.

55. S. E. Chaiko, introduction to R. M. Mitel'man, *Sud nad gruppovodym kamenshchikom (pokazatel'nyi sud)* (Moscow, 1930), 3. Chaiko is listed as the deputy director of the sector of

mass cultural education work of the Central Committee. He also commented on the need for all aesthetic work to strive "to eliminate apoliticalness."

56. V. Vinogradov, *Sud nad muzykal'noi khalturoi* (Moscow, 1931), 36 (quote from Sixteenth Party Congress resolution); thanks to Amy Nelson for calling this trial to my attention.

57. *Sud nad lavochnei komissiei*, 7.

58. Ibid., 16.

59. A group leader was the one who hired workers in seasonal trades, made contact with employers, and handled all aspects of the job once it had been contracted for—in short, a kind of contractor or subcontractor.

60. Mitel'man, *Sud nad gruppovodym*, 29.

61. Sigal, *Sud nad p'ianitsei.*

62. Mitel'man, *Sud nad gruppovodom*, 25.

63. G. D. Van'ian, "Agitsud nad gr. Malkinym, Timokhinoi i Baikhovoi, po obvineniiu ikh v narusheniem dekreta Sovnarkoma ob obiazatael'nom ospoprivivanii" [1933] (typescript), Gosudarstvennyi Arkhiv Rossiiskoi Federatsi (GARF) 9636/5/127/19.

64. "Klub i byt (K Vsesoiuznomu klubnomu soveshchaniiu)," *Klub i revoliutsiia* 4 (February 1930): 6.

65. The one figure who seems still to have been advocating the performance of agitation trials in 1930 and after was Leningrad cultural activist Grigorii Avlov in *Klubnyi samodeiatel'nyi teatr*, 90–104, and in *Teatral'nye agitpropbrigady v klube* (Moscow-Leningrad, 1937), 28.

66. V. Pletnev, "Kluby v opasnosti," *Rabochii klub* 1 (1928): 7–10. Pletnev's use of the term "show trial" is confusing as it is unclear whether he has in mind agitation trial of fictional characters or small-scale trials of real individuals or both.

67. *Spisok materialov dlia raboty dramkruzhkov v klubakh*, ed. A. K. Mavrogan (Moscow: Mosk. Teatral'noe izd., 1925), 3.

68. *V pomoshch' dramkruzhku*, ed. K. K. Tverskoi (Leningrad, 1927), vyp. 1, 3.

69. Tat'iana Ippolitovna Andreeva, "Klubnyi samodeiatel'nyi teatr 1920-kh godov," (Kand. diss., Leningrad institut teatra, muzyki i kinematografii, 1977), 21; also Lynn Mally, *Revolutionary Acts: Amateur Theater and the Soviet State, 1917–1938* (Ithaca, 2000), 81–108, esp. 89 (Mally states that this turn was not dictated by the higher authorities but rather "came from within amateur theater circles themselves").

70. *V pomoshch' dramkruzhku*, vyp. 1, 3.

71. Lynn Mally, "The Rise and Fall of the Soviet Youth Theater TRAM," *Slavic Review* 51, 3 (fall 1992): 410–11.

72. *Spisok materialov*, 9–10; M. Konstantinovskii, "Klubnyi teatr i vliianie na nego obshcheteatral'noi kul'tury," *Klub i revoliutsiia*, 6 (1930): 40–44; V. Nikolaev, "O novykh organizatsionnykh formakh klubnoi raboty," *Rabochii Klub* 4 (April 1926): 48–49; Zil'berberg and Glan, "Bol'she smelosti," *Pravda* July 19, 1928, cited in A. Petrov, "Boliachki ili bolezn'," *Rabochii klub* 9–10 (1928): 14; Kul'trabotnik, "Sotsialisticheskoe sorevnovanie i klub," 18; Nosovskii, "Kluby otstaiut," 27, 32–33.

73. Aleksandr Afinogenov, "Za sotsial'no obosnovannym psikhologizm" (1929) in *Sovetskie dramaturgi o svoem tvorchestve. Sbornik statei* (Moscow: Iskusstvo, 1967), 51.

74. Aleksei Tolstoi, "Dramaturgicheskaia olimpiada" (1933) in *Sovetskie dramaturgi*, 44.

75. R. Pel'she, "Itogi sezona," *Repertuarnyi bulleten'*, 4 (1927): 7; Anatolii Glebov, "Odnoaktnaia p'esa" (1939), in *Sovetskie dramaturgi*, 165; V. Bliumenfel'd, "Smotr samodeiatel'nogo iskusstva (stat'ia 2-aia): Klubnyi teatr," *Rabochii Klub* 7 (July 1927): 23–27; A. A. Rub, "Ot mitinga-kontserta do agitbrigady (K istorii vozniknoveniia agitatsionno-khudozhestvennykh brigad-agitbrigad, 1917–1941 gg.)," (Diss. kand. iskusstvovedeniia, Moscow, Institut istorii iskusstv, 1975), 50–51. Living newspapers as a form also suffered from club members' desire to try their hands at acting and "high forms of 'recreation'" (K. Tiuliapin [Sverdlovsk], "Zhivaia gazeta v sisteme khudozhestvennoi raboty," *Klub i revoliutsiia* 19–20 [October 1930]: 36–42).

76. R. Ginzburg, "Klub, kak on est'," 13; Hatch, "Hangouts and Hangovers: State, Class, and Culture in Moscow's Workers' Club Movement, 1925–1928," *Russian Review* 53, no. 1 (1994): 106, 110–11.

77. Denise Youngblood, *Soviet Cinema in the Silent Era, 1918–1935* (Austin, 1991); Richard Taylor, *The Politics of Soviet Cinema, 1917–1929* (Cambridge, 1979).

78. Nik. Maslennikov, "Profteatr i samodeiatel'naia rabota v klube," *Repertuarnyi bulleten'* 7–8 (1927): 3–5.

79. A. A. Narodetskii (director of the sanitation theater), "Sanitarnoe prosveshchenie cherez stsenu (Opyt raboty Moskvskoi organizatsii)" at the Vsesoiuznyi s″ezd sanitarnykh vrachei i bakteriologov (March 6, 1928), GARF 9636/5/4/2; 9636/7/31/19–20. In 1928 F. Iu. Berman, chair of the so-called academic methodological bureau (*nauchno-metodicheskoe biuro*), also argued that the sanitation trials were dying out. "Podgotovka sanprosvet repertuara," GARF 9636/1/5/6–7.

80. For example, as was noted above, P. M. Vedernikov, the railway sanitation doctor, felt strongly that the performances of trials of the syphilitic lessened people's fear of adding their names to a list of those who turned to the doctors for assistance. "Sansudy i ikh postanovka na osnove kollektivizma ispolnitelei," *Krasnyi put'* 19 (November 1924): 97–98, GARF 9636/5/124.

81. Selad'in, *Kul'trabota*, 7. Selad'in is quoting here from *Kul'turnaia revoliutsiia* 12 (1929).

82. Selad'in, *Kul'trabota*, 25–27.

83. Ibid., 27.

84. For a rich description of the film, see Cassiday, *Enemy*, 89–94.

85. *Sud nad narushiteliami truddistsipliny po materialam kinofil'ma. Iz opyta kul'traboty Metrostroia* (Moscow: Profizdat, 1933).

86. Gr. Avlov, *Sud nad khuliganami* (Moscow-Leningrad: Doloi negramotnost', 1927), 6.

87. L. Alotin-Elota, "Ekspromptnye sansudy" (typescript, 1926), GARF 9636/5/125/6.

88. For example, after an agitation trial of an "unconscious" club member in the Artamanovskii tram park, many workers allegedly joined the club as members, a fact that was used to prove that the trial had indeed "attained the necessary effect." Krupnov, "Kluby i kul'turnyi pokhod," 68.

Conclusion

1. The formal titles for the Moscow trials were the trials of the "Trotskyite-Zinovievite Terrorist Centre" (August 1936), the "Anti-Soviet Trotskyite Centre" (January 1937), and the "Anti-Soviet Bloc of Rights and Trotskyites" (March 1938); *Sudebnyi otchet po delu antisovetskogo "Pravo-Trotskistskogo bloka": rassmotrennomu Voennoi kollegiei Verkhovnogo Suda Soiuza SSR 2–13 marta 1938 g.* (Moskva: Iuridicheskoe izd-vo, 1938); recently reprinted as *Sudebnyi otchet: Materialy Voennoi kollegii Verkhovnogo Suda SSSR* (Moscow, 1997).

2. Robert C. Tucker and Stephen F. Cohen, eds., *The Great Purge Trial* (New York, 1965), 515.

3. Ibid., 522.

4. Ibid., 522–23.

5. *Report of the Court Proceedings in the Case of the Anti-Soviet "Bloc of Rights and Trotskyites"* (Moscow, 1938), 625–26.

6. Ibid., 626.

7. Ibid., 697.

8. Ibid.

9. Robert Tucker cites these phrases from the trial of Zinoviev and Kamenev (1936) in his *Stalin in Power: The Revolution from Above, 1928–1941* (New York, 1990), 370–71.

10. Tucker and Cohen, eds., *Great Purge Trial*, 533.

11. Tucker, *Stalin in Power*, 403 (from the Piatakov-Radek Trial, 1937). The snake metaphor suggests also an analogy with the snake in the Garden of Eden, implying that the Bolsheviks' fall from a state of class harmony could be blamed on this one archenemy. One could in fact analyze the three show trials of 1936–38 as the trial of an absent Lucifer or Antichrist (Trotsky) who could be (conveniently) blamed for all of the country's problems. Bukharin is portrayed as a second Judas and also as Basil Shuisky, the traitor who ruled after Boris Godunov's demise (1606–10). Tucker and Cohen, eds., *Great Purge Trial*, 545, 556.

12. Vyshinsky insisted in 1938 that the defendants had to be seen as a "bloc of betrayers covered with eternal contempt, shame and [the] condemnation of millions of working people throughout the world." Tucker and Cohen, eds., *Great Purge Trial*, 522. The court had torn off their mask. "Their true colours, their real face are now clear for all to see; their shameful deeds are also clear to all, just as is their miserable and shameful fate." Now Bukharin and his codefendants were ending up "in the shameful prisoners' dock." Ibid., 527.

13. Aleksandr I. Solzhenitsyn, *The Gulag Archipelago* (New York, 1973), 374.

14. Eugene Lyons, *Assignment in Utopia* (New York, 1937), 116.

15. In this sense the agitation trials probably also contributed to the development of Soviet socialist realism, which Katerina Clark has so tellingly shown to have been based in ritual that focused on individuals' struggles, self-sacrifices, and rites of passage in the name of the larger Stalinist "family." *The Soviet Novel: History as Ritual* (Chicago, 1981).

16. A. I. Akkerman, *Sud nad prostitutkoi. Delo gr. Zaborovoi po obvineniiu ee v zaniatii prostitutsiei i zarazhenii sifilisom kr-tsa Krest'ianova* (Moscow-Petrograd: Gos. izd-vo, 1922).

17. Gr. Avlov, *Sud nad khuliganami* (Moscow-Leningrad: Doloi negramotnost', 1927).

18. Tucker and Cohen, eds., *Great Purge Trial*, 20.

19. *Report of the Court Proceedings*, 625.

20. Walter Duranty, *The Kremlin and the People* (New York, 1941), 86.

21. A good example is the trial of the Socialist Revolutionaries in 1922 (see chapter 4). The Communist Party organized discussions everywhere of the materials from the trial, "helping workers and peasants to understand the counterrevolutionary role of the Right SRs." T. A. Remizova, *Kul'turno-prosvetitel' naia rabota v RSFSR (1921–1925 gg.)* (Moscow, 1962), 163.

22. Tucker, for example, recounts the charges at the Piatakov-Radek trial that all the defendants were "members of a single community" (*Stalin in Power*, 399). The most graphic example of the notion of a new kinship came during two trials when sons stood up to denounce their fathers. In the Shakhty trial a young man named Kolodub denounced his father as a wrecker and claimed that from now on he, the younger Kolodub, was going to be known by the last name Shakhtin, i.e., one from Shakhty. In the Industrial Party trial in 1930 another defendant's son, Ksenofont Sitnin, also urged the death penalty for his father. Roman Brackman in his recent book *The Secret File of Joseph Stalin: A Hidden Life* (London, 2001) argues that Stalin had denounced his own father in a trial in Tbilisi in 1909 and hence was projecting onto others the very deeds he had himself committed (198, 216).

23. For an account of how these "organizations" were fabricated, see especially Roy A. Medvedev, *Let History Judge: The Origins and Consequences of Stalinism*, ed. David Joravsky and Georges Haupt, trans. Colleen Taylor (New York, 1971), 114–37. Throughout the purges of the 1930s tens of thousands of individuals were trapped primarily through guilt by association; their friendships and even their rivalries proved their guilt. Of the dozens of sources on this see, inter alia, Edward J. Brown, *Russian Literature Since the Revolution* (Cambridge, Mass., 1963), 169–75; Sheila Fitzpatrick, *Everyday Stalinism: Ordinary Life in Extraordinary Times. Soviet Russia in the 1930s* (New York, 1999), 194–99.

24. *Report of the Court Proceedings*, 157.

25. From the memoirs of A. M. Larina (Bukharin's wife), in Medvedev, *Let History Judge*, 174.

26. Tucker and Cohen, eds., *Great Purge Trial*, 656.

27. Arthur Koestler, *Darkness at Noon*, trans. Daphne Hardy (New York, 1941).

28. Solzhenitsyn calls the question of the defendants' confessions to crimes they obviously did not commit the "riddle" of the public show trials (*Gulag*, 408–412). Other considerations of this question of confession include Abdurakhman Avtorkhanov, *Stalin and the Soviet Communist Party* (New York, 1959), 231–37; Robert C. Tucker, "Introduction: Stalin, Bukharin, and History as Conspiracy," in *Great Purge Trial*, ed. Tucker and Cohen, ix–xlviii; Stephen F. Cohen, *Bukharin and the Bolshevik Revolution: A Political Biography, 1888–1938* (Oxford, 1971), 372–73; Tucker, *Stalin in Power*, 165, 314–16, 386, 494–95, 499; Nathan Leites and Elsa Bernaut, *Ritual of Liquidation: Bolsheviks on Trial* (Glencoe, Ill., 1954); F. Beck and W. Godin, *Russian Purge and the Extraction of Confession* (New York, 1951).

29. Among other sources on this see Cohen, *Bukharin*, 322–25, 335.

30. Tucker argues this in convincing detail in both his "Introduction" and in *Stalin in Power.* Roman Brackman also takes a psychological approach in *The Secret File of Joseph Stalin.* Stalin may also have particularly enjoyed the cat-and-mouse, hunter-and-prey games of the trials. In individual rounds of the debates Bukharin could and did best Vyshinsky. Vyshinsky himself described poor Krestinsky, a defendant who initially retracted his pretrial confession but who was then forced to reinstate it, by saying, "Like a mouse in a trap, he during the trial scurried hither and thither, trying to find a possible way of escape, but in vain." Tucker and Cohen, eds., *Great Purge Trial,* 548.

31. Tucker and Cohen, eds., *Great Purge Trial,* 532.

32. Stalin may in fact have latched onto the notion of staging the Moscow Show Trials after seeing how quickly the United Opposition capitulated in 1927 when they were threatened with expulsion from the party. Anna Larina, *This I Cannot Forget: The Memoirs of Nikolai Bukharin's Widow,* trans. Gary Kern (New York, 1993), 106.

33. Orlando Figes and Boris Kolonitskii, *Interpreting the Russian Revolution: The Language and Symbols of 1917* (New Haven, 1999).

34. Several words for gossip in Russian are based on the words for judgment—for example, *peresudy.*

35. I. V. Rebel'skii, *Instsenirovannye sudy (kak ikh organizovat' i provodit')* (Moscow: Trud i kniga, 1926), 10.

36. Catherine Bell, *Ritual: Perspectives and Dimensions* (New York, 1997), 224, drawing on Barbara G. Myerhoff, "A Death in Due Time" in *Rite, Drama, Festival, Spectacle,* ed. John J. MacAloon (Philadelphia, 1984), 149–78.

37. Contemporaries insisted that the trial was more convincing if the defendant's guilt was less obvious. "Otzyv" [1923], Rossiiskii Gosudarstvennyi Voennyi Arkhiv (RGVA) 9/13/97/109–110.

38. The failure of the tsarist government to create consensus can be seen most vividly in Hubertus Jahn's work on the disastrous shortfall in propaganda during World War I. *Patriotic Culture in Russia During World War I* (Ithaca, 1995).

39. Quoted in Bell, *Ritual,* 160; also Michel de Certeau, "Believing and Making People Believe" in de Certeau, *The Practice of Everyday Life,* trans. Steven F. Rendall (Berkeley, 1984), 115–30. Ritual also has the interesting aspect that you can participate in it even if you do not entirely believe in it (just as older children may go to visit Santa Claus in the department store).

40. The residue of this intellectual element of the trials can be seen in Leon Feuchtwanger's response to the show trial of 1937: "They drank tea, newspapers poking out of their pockets, and often looked at the audience. In general, it seemed more like an informal discussion among cultivated people trying to get at the truth, to establish exactly what happened and why. One had the impression that the accused, the prosecutor, and the judges were all caught up with the same, I almost want to say sportsmanlike interest in elucidating everything with maximum precision." Cited in Andrei Sinyavsky, *Soviet Civilization: A Cultural History,* trans. Joanne Turnbull (New York, 1990), 86.

41. Diane P. Koenker, "Factory Tales: Narratives of Industrial Relations in the Transition to NEP," *Russian Review* 55, no. 3 (1996): 384–411.

42. Sinyavsky, *Soviet Civilization,* 144–45.

43. "Doklad kluba OKA za Oktiabr' mesiats (November 11, 1922)," RGVA 9/13/91/386.

44. Moshe Lewin, *The Making of the Soviet System: Essays in the Social History of Interwar Russia* (New York, 1985); David L. Hoffmann, *Peasant Metropolis: Social Identities in Moscow, 1929–1941* (Ithaca, 1994); Stephen Kotkin, *Magnetic Mountain: Stalinism as a Civilization* (Berkeley, 1995).

45. Joseph Stalin, *Works* (Moscow, 1954), 11:57.

46. Robert Conquest, *The Great Terror* (New York, 1968), 130. Bukharin, for example, commented at his trial, "World history is a world court of judgment." Tucker and Cohen, eds., *Great Purge Trial,* 667.

47. Mikhail Tomsky, for example, noted at the Sixteenth Party Congress in 1930 that confession and repentance had become such requisites that they were the only permissible responses for those present. Still he resisted that notion, arguing that "repentance" was not a Bolshevik

term; it was a religious one (Larina, *This I Cannot Forget,* 107). As historian Maurice Bloch has argued, many rituals are structured in such a way that they imply an impermissibility of alternatives; only the ritual way is permitted. *From Blessing to Violence: History and Ideology in the Circumcision Ritual of the Merina of Madagascar.* Cambridge, 1986], 182; Bloch, *Ritual, History and Power: Selected Papers in Anthropology* (London, 1989); and the discussion in John D. Kelly and Martha Kaplan, "History, Structure, and Ritual," *Annual Review of Anthropology* 19 (1990), 119–50, esp. 125–26.

48. The fact that all the defendants in the so-called Industrial Party trial in November–December 1930 had confessed and that all five for whom Krylenko had sought the death penalty had had their sentences commuted may have given later defendants hope that confessions could result in prison sentences instead of execution.

49. Arkady Vaksberg gives an example of a prominent trial prosecuted by Vyshinsky in the spring of 1936 in which the defendants were acquitted, allegedly for lack of solid evidence. Then in the fall of 1936 the party announced that all charges had been dropped against Bukharin and Rykov because of the lack of evidence. *Stalin's Prosecutor: The Life of Andrei Vyshinsky,* trans. Jan Butler (New York, 1991), 75–76, 85; also Tucker, *Stalin in Power,* 375–76. Both Vaksberg and Tucker argue that the purpose was to make a show of impartial justice.

50. Cohen, *Bukharin,* 356–57; Tucker, *Stalin in Power,* 354–61.

51. Cohen refers to Bukharin as "Benjamin," ibid., 13 (but does not carry forward the analogy to the question of resistance).

52. As Cassiday notes, the defendants did not have the same access to information that the prosecution had. Julie A. Cassiday, "Marble Columns and Jupiter Lights: Theatrical and Cinematic Modeling of Soviet Show Trials in the 1920s," *Slavic and East European Journal* 42, no. 4 (1998): 640–60.

53. For a fascinating discussion of this issue in East European show trials, see Istvan Rev, "In Mendacio Veritas (In Lies There Lies the Truth)," *Representations* 35 (Summer 1991): 1–20.

54. J. Arch Getty, "Afraid of Their Shadows: The Bolshevik Recourse to Terror, 1932–1938," in *Stalinismus vor dem Zweiten Weltkrief: Neue Wege der Forschung,* ed. Manfred Hildermeier and Elisabeth Mueller-Luckner (Munich, 1998), 169–91; Alexei Kojevnikov, "Rituals of Stalinist Culture at Work: Science and the Games of Intraparty Democracy circa 1948," *Russian Review* 57, no. 1 (1998): 25–52. Nikolai Krementsov also discusses Andrei Zhdanov's creation of "honor courts" in 1947 in *The Cure: A Story of Cancer and Politics from the Annals of the Cold War* (Chicago, 2002), 109–26.

55. Kojevnikov and Getty do not say this explicitly, but their examples suggest it.

56. Kojevnikov, "Rituals," 32.

57. "Politsud (Instruktsiia)," RGVA 9/13/51/215; E. N. Medynskii, *Entsiklopediia vneshkol'nogo obrazovaniia,* v. 2: *Otdel'nye vidy sodeistviia vneshkol'nomu obrazovaniiu* 2nd ed. (revised) (Moscow-Leningrad: Gos. izd-vo, 1925), 159.

58. *Odinnadtsatyi s'ezd RKP(b), mart-aprel' 1922 g. Stenograficheskii otchet* (Moscow, 1961), 267.

59. He was expelled from the party in 1931, sent into internal exile in the mid-thirties, and executed in 1938.

60. *Izvestiia,* May 1, 1936, and July 6, 1936, cited in Cohen, *Bukharin,* 366–67; also discussed in Tucker, "Introduction," xxxvi–xxxviii; George Katkov, *The Trial of Bukharin* (New York, 1969), 94–96.

INDEX

Note: Page numbers followed by letters *f* and *t* refer to figures and tables, respectively.

abject issues: as focus of agitation trials, 7; women and, 130

absenteeism, agitation trials addressing, 183–86, 184f, 185f, 205

acquittal: absence in post-1928 agitation trials, 200, 202; in agitation trials of everyday life, 99; in earliest agitation trials (1919–24), 8; in medieval religious plays, 18; in sanitation trials, 113, 118, 122; in women's trials, 131

activeness. *See aktivnost'*

actors, in agitation trials, 4, 8, 12

Addams, Jane: on value of drama in education, 28; visit to Tolstoy, 27

advertising: for agitation trials, 4. *See also* publicity

agitation: during Civil War, 40; innovation at end of Civil War, 42–43; most effective forms of, 87; vs. propaganda, 234n4; tsarist trials and, 23

agitation trials: Achilles' heal of, 9; actors in, 4, 8, 12; advantages of, 5–6; advertising for, 4; allegorical characters in, 6; appeal of, 7, 9–10, 14; authors of, 4, 8; blurring of fact and fiction in, 220; cost of, 4; decline in, 202–5, 207; development of, 12–13; divide and conquer strategy in, 96; earliest (1919–24), 8; emotional impact of, 214; endorsement of, first formal, 250n54; evolution over time, 1–2; goals of, 6, 8, 65, 71, 84, 212; increasing harshness of, 215; last (1930–33), 200–202; legal consciousness undermined by, 219–20; length of, 63; loss of interest in, 176–77; moral agenda of, 6, 55, 71, 91, 110; organizers of, 12, 38, 215–16; origins of, 7–8, 12, 16–17, 233n3; power of the state in, 214–15; prerevolutionary roots of, 34–35; of real individuals (*see* impromptu trials); script for, 2; show trials compared with, 195; staging of, 6f, 7f; subjects of, 1, 7, 28–29, 213; as templates, 103–4; terms for, 2; types of, 4–5. *See also specific types and titles*

agricultural trials, 3f, 5, 88f

Akkerman, Aleksandr, 105, 111–12, 116, 266n32

Aksakov, Ivan, 22

aktivnost', principle of: army clubs and, 72; extracurricular education and, 35

alcoholism: agitation trials addressing, 15, 166–67, 166f, 206; campaigns combating, 205–6; prerevolutionary plays addressing, 26

Aleksinskii, M. A., 252n95, 253n100

Alexander II (tsar), 22

allegorical characters: in agitation trials, 6; in church-school plays, 18

Alotin-Elota, L., 174, 175–76, 178, 206–7

Andreev, Boris, 163–64

Andreev, Leonid, 239n50; *King Hunger,* 23–24; *The Trial of Anfisa,* 15–16

An-sky, S., 24, 240n57
antireligious trials, 5, 21
anti-Semitism, agitation trials addressing, 46–48
Antonov-Ovseenko, Vladimir, 240n67
Anuchin, Sergei A., 250n54, 253n100
Arbatov, B., 241n69
Ardov, Victor, 190
Armand, Lidiia, 241n69
army: Soviet (see Red Army); tsarist, theater programs in, 26
army clubs: education through agitation trials in, 71–73; New Economic Policy and pressures on, 74; utilitarian vs. recreational views on, 73–75, 259n28. See also political instructors
Artsybashev, Mikhail, 24–25
audience: acting learned by, 207; manipulation of, 64, 206; participation of, 205, 213, 214, 215; targeted by agitation trials, 63
authority, agitation trials and reinforcement of, 8, 11, 65–67
authority figures: in agitation trials on women's issues, 130, 146, 148, 273n82; in sanitation trials, 109, 114, 116, 119, 121, 127; in trials of sexuality, 169, 170
authors: of agitation trials, 4, 8; trials of, 189–91
avant-garde movement, influence on agitation trials, 31–34, 48–49
aviation agitation trial, 161–62
Avlov, Grigorii, 167

Babel, Isaac: literary trials of, 190–91; military trial of, 283n57
backwardness: overcoming through judgment, 215; Russia's, intelligentsia's concern about, 8, 25, 86–87, 106; women's, demonstrating in agitation trials, 129, 130, 131, 142–43
Bakhtin, Mikhail, 48, 158, 239n47
Belkin, M., 175
Bell, Catherine, 214
Bentovin, Boris, 27
Bliakhin, Pavel Andreevich, 49, 251n75
Bloch, Maurice, 291n47
Bolshevik culture: agitation trials and spread of, 10–11; returning soldiers and spread of, 42, 85; success in creation of, 86–87, 89
books: handling of, agitation trials addressing, 96–99. See also literary trials
Borovich, Boris Osipovich: on early NEP political trials, 77; as military instructor, 45–46, 48; and prerevolutionary extracurricular education, 29–30, 243n96; and Trial of Jewry, 46–48, 78

bourgeoisie, portrayal in agitation trials, 81–82
Briusov, Valerii, 32
Bronner, Vol'f Moiseevich, 111, 266n32
Budennyi, Semen, 190
Bukharin, Nikolai: in Moscow Show Trials, 209, 211, 212, 217–18, 290n46; on political fiction, 220; and "Stalin Constitution," 217
Bulgakov, Mikhail, hate campaign against, 191, 283n60

children's clubs, prerevolutionary, 27–30
church. See Orthodox Church; religion
Civil War: agitation during, 40; agitation innovation at end of, 42–43; agitation trials after, 86; challenges to Soviet leadership after, 68–69; drama circles during, spread of, 32; health issues during, 106, 107
club directors: and agitation trials, development of, 8, 10, 12, 216; pressure on, 216; training of, 152, 153; vulnerable position of, 213
clubs: children's, 27–30. See also army clubs; voluntary organizations; workers' clubs
Cohen, Stephen, 217
collective: rising power of, 188. See also compact collectives
collective creativity, agitation trials and, 49–50
collective discipline, agitation trials and, 50–51
collective guilt: in agitation trials of everyday life, 101–2; in production trials, 158; in sanitation trials, 113, 116, 117; in women's trials, 148
collective responsibility, 31, 216
collusion, in agitation trials, 214
communist culture. See society, new/Soviet
Communist Party: and agitation trials of real individuals, 192; "arraignment meetings" of, 218–19; authority of, agitation trials legitimating, 8, 11, 65–67; instructions for agitation trials (1921–23), 70–71; mock trials of, 58–59; problems in 1920–21, 62; show trials of 1930s foreshadowed by agitation trials, 12; and women, 134, 136, 142; women's sections of, 128, 133, 147, 269n2; and workers' clubs, new attention to, 150–51. See also leadership, Soviet
community values: in agitation trials of everyday life, 89, 91, 100; Bolshevik mobilization of, 87, 89
compact collectives (kompaktnye kollektivy), 214; agitation trials performed by, 161; arraignment meetings of, 218

comrades: vs. citizens, use of terms, 119, 267n52; women as, 124
confessions: in agitation trials of everyday life, 99, 100; function of, 217; in sanitation trials, 110; in show trials, 211–12, 217, 289n28; in women's trials, 148
conflict, in agitation trials, 214
cooperatives, agitation trials about, 276n39
Corney, Frederick, 65
courts: Lenin on, 1, 23; roles of, 1, 11; in tsarist Russia, 21–22
creativity, agitation trials and, 49–50
crimes, personification of, 71
Crimes in the Area of Sexual Relations (Liublinskii), 125–26
criminalization, in impromptu trials, 178
criticism and self-criticism: clubs' role in, 197–98; in earliest agitation trials (1919–24), 8, 78–79, 84; in party arraignment meetings, 218; pervasive culture of, in late 1920s, 164, 196–98; at root of agitation trials, 9
culture. See Bolshevik culture
Cummings, A. J., 256n42

Dal', Vladimir, 21
Days of the Turbines (Bulgakov), hate campaign against, 191
debates *(disputy):* agitation trials compared with, 16; discouraged in later trials, 210; in early NEP political trials, 77; early postrevolutionary, 78; literary, 191; party arraignment meetings and illusion of, 219; political trials' kinship with, 60; on sanitation topics, 108
deception: in agitation trials, 64, 105, 108, 206; in impromptu trials, 181
defendants: absentee, 179–80; acquittal of *(see* acquittal); confessions of *(see* confessions); dehumanization in show trials, 196, 208–9, 211, 289n12; guilt of *(see* guilt); participation in show trials, 217; separation from audience, 214
defense lawyers: in later agitation trials, 8; in tsarist trials, 22
defense strategies: collective guilt as, 101–2; ignorance as, 179; peasants', 99–100
dehumanization of defendants, in show trials, 196, 208–9, 211, 289n12
delegatki, agitation trials of, 130–42
Demidovich, E. B., 111, 168–69
deserters, trials of, 50–51, 94, 100
Dewey, John: influence on prerevolutionary Russian educators, 28, 242n82; Soviet attacks on, 34, 245n126; on value of drama in education, 28
dialogic imagination, in agitation trials of early 1920s, 158–59

discipline: agitation trials and, 12, 50–51, 161, 163, 213; Komsomol agitation trials focusing on, 163–65; among railroad workers, approaches to, 61; in Red Army, approaches to, 41, 50–51; in workers' clubs, agitation trials addressing, 152–53
divide and conquer strategy: in agitation trials, 96; in impromptu trials, 192
doctors: and agitation trials, development of, 8, 10, 12, 106, 108; as expert witnesses in sanitation trials, 109, 114, 119, 121, 127; on folk healing *(znakharstvo),* 142; hopes regarding sanitation trials, 108–10, 178–79; and prerevolutionary theater programs, 26, 27; as representatives of new Soviet order, 127; in women's trials, 146
Dolinskii, Semyon, 182
Dostoevsky, Feodor: dramatization of novels of, 27; trial scenes in novels of, 23
Duranty, Walter, 193, 211
The Dybbuk (An-sky), 24

Edel'shtein, A. O., 105, 111–12, 266n32
education: agitation trials and, 6, 8, 11, 71–73, 161, 163, 199; international cultural exchanges in, 27–28; librarians' revolution in, 29–31; peasants' prejudices against, Soviet efforts to overcome, 89; in Red Army, 71–73; sanitation, 106–7; state and, 11; theater and, 26, 241n69; tsarist trials and, 23; use of drama in, prerevolutionary educators' interest in, 27–29. See also extracurricular education; political education
Eisenstein, Sergei, 244n111, 267n33
Elkina, D., 16
enemies: eliminated in agitation trials, 84; focus on, in late 1920s, 197; Stalin on, 216; unity around persecution of, 212–13
entertainment: agitation trials and, 6, 8, 199. See also rational recreation
Epshtein, Moisei Solomonovich, 253n100
Esenin, Sergei, 32–34
everyday life *(byt),* agitation trials of, 86–87; book harming in, 96–99; collective guilt in, 101–2; community values in, 89, 91, 100; confessions in, 99, 100; forms of influence in, 89; peasant self-defense in, 99–100; peasant soldiers in, 90–91; rituals in, 102–4; tax evaders in, 92–93
Evreinov, Nikolai, 31–32, 245n113
expert witnesses: in sanitation trials, 109, 114, 116, 119, 121, 127; in sexuality trials, 169, 170
extracurricular education: attacks on activists, in late 1920s, 199–200; in early Soviet state, 239n55, 240n57; prerevolutionary, 25–31, 35; principles carried over

extracurricular education (*continued*)
to agitation trials, 35; in Red Army, trial
forms used in, 45–48

famine of 1921–22: agitation trials assigning
blame for, 94–96; trauma of, 93–94; trials related to, 82–83
Fanger, Donald, 109
fantasy, in agitation trials, 81, 199
Fedotov, Georgy, 216
films, and demise of agitation trials, 204
Finlay-Johnson, Harriet, 28
First Moscow Settlement, 27–28
Fitzpatrick, Sheila, 70, 262n15
Five Year Plan, First: agitation trials as pro-
paganda for, 198; and focus on enemies,
197
Flerovskii, Ivan, 261n66
Foucault, Michel, 149
Frank, Stephen, 108
freedom: individual, public forums encour-
aged at expense of, 157; women's, public
work associated with, 135–36
Frieden, Nancy, 107
Furmanov, Dmitrii, 70, 250n54; on rallies,
247n9; in trial of Isaac Babel, 190; and
Trial of Wrangel, 52–54; on witnesses'
testimony, 77
Furmanova, Anna, 53, 70

Gaideburov, Pavel, 243n94
Garin, Artemii, 70
Geertz, Clifford, 11
gender. *See* women
Gernet, Mikhail, 27
Getty, J. Arch, 218
Ginzburg, B. S., 147
Ginzburg, Raisa, 153, 199, 275n12
glasnost': later agitation trials and, 202; Tsar
Alexander II's programs of, 22
God, placed on trial, 21, 24
good and evil: in agitation trials, 217; in religious school plays, 17–18
Gorky, Maxim: on courts, 23; on hate campaign against writers, 191–92; on prerevolutionary theater, 27; quoted in Moscow
Show Trials, 209
graduation ceremonies, agitation trials as
part of, 102–3
Gramsci, Antonio, 11
Griboedov, Aleksandr, 220
Gross, Jan, 262n15
guilt: in agitation trials of everyday life, 99,
100; collective (*see* collective guilt); emphasis on, in later agitation trials, 8, 172,
200; initial denial of, in early agitation trials, 4, 214; in show trials, 210

Hall, G. Stanley, 28
healers (*znakharki*), in sanitation trials, 124,
129, 130, 142–46, 144f, 145f
heroic trials: of Soviet leadership, 57–59,
64–67, 77–81; turn away from, 199; of
women activists, 130–42
Herzen, Alexander , 238n35
hooliganism: agitation trials addressing, 9,
165–68, 172; prerevolutionary concern
with, 29, 275n19; rapid urbanization and,
216
Hull House, Chicago, Russian visitors to, 27
humanization: of women, emancipation as,
134–36, 142. *See also* dehumanization of
defendants
human nature, agitation vs. show trials' understanding of, 211
humiliation. *See* shaming of defendants
humor, disappearance from agitation trials, 200
Hutchinson, John, 107, 109

ignorance, demonstrated in agitation trials:
as mitigating circumstance, 179; overcoming through judgment, 215; of peasants,
90–91, 99–102; of Pioneers, 171; on sanitation issues, 118, 120, 122; of women,
130, 143, 146, 148
illiteracy, agitation trials addressing, 99–103
illusion, in agitation trials, 64, 105, 108, 206
imagination, in agitation trials of early
1920s, 158–59
Imperial Russia. *See* tsarist Russia
impromptu trials (*ekspromptnye sudy*), 174–
75; of authors, 189–91; in clubs, 181–83;
deception in, 181; motivations for turn toward, 176–78, 192; public work required
in sentencing, 180–81; shaming of defendants in, 176, 178, 182, 183, 186; show
trials compared with, 195; in trade unions,
183–86; transition to, 179–80, 183
improvisation, genuine vs. simulated, 182
independent activity. *See* samodeiatel'nost'
Industrial Party trial, 289n22, 291n48
intelligentsia: concern about Russia's backwardness, 8, 25, 86–87, 106; legal reform
of 1864 and hopes of, 22; "new," and origins of agitation trials, 38; as subject of
agitation trials, 106, 108; as subject of agitation trials, 95–96, 97–99, 101–2, 117, 167–68;
tsarist trials and, 23; on woman question,
134, 149
Ioff, L. S., 179
Iuzhin, Aleksandr, 111

Jesuit mystery/morality plays, 236n14,
236n16; influence on prerevolutionary
adult education, 30–31

S

Jewish tradition: God on trial in, 21, 24; Heavenly Tribunal in, 18–21
jury trials, introduction of, 21, 22
justice: in agitation trials, 220; political, 1

Karzhanskii, Nikolai, 49–50, 52, 57, 63, 244n111, 251n78
Kenez, Peter, 87
Khersonskaia, E., 35
Khlebnikov, Velimir, 34
Khlebtsevich, Evgenii I., 77
Kingston-Mann, Esther, 25
kinship, vs. state allegiance, 211, 234n8, 289n22
Koestler, Arthur, 211–12
Kojevnikov, Alexei, 218
Kollontai, Aleksandra, 39
Komsomol, 162–63; cultural campaign of 1928, 197; discussions of real court cases, 170; pressure on, in mid-1920s, 8–9, 161, 163; vulnerability of, 216
Komsomol agitation trials, 103, 163; disciplinary focus of, 163–65; harsh language in, 164; humiliation of defendants in, 163, 168–69, 172; linguistic vagueness in, 188; sexuality as subject of, 168–70
Konopnicka, Maria, 47
Korobochkin, Isaak, 75, 79, 266n32
Kotkin, Stephen, 10
Kristeva, Julia, 7, 130
Kronstadt mutiny, agitation trial addressing, 54–55
Kropotkin, Petr, 27
Krupskaia, Nadezhda: on agitation, most effective forms of, 87; on clubs, 151; Dewey's influence on, 28; on extracurricular education, 245n128; on political education, 69; on prerevolutionary theater, 27; on rally-style agitation, 40; on school-based courts, 35–36; on school self-government, 246n134; at Sixth Komsomol Congress, 163; Tolstoy's influence on, 243n94
Krylenko, Nikolai, 165, 193, 214
kulaks, portrayal in agitation trials, 92–93, 94, 137, 140, 162; women, 95–96
Kurdiumov, Vsevolod, 79

Last Judgment, frescoes of, 18, 19f, 20f
law students: moot trials practiced by, 17; reform of 1864 and hopes of, 22
leadership, Soviet: challenges after end of Civil War, 68–69; legitimacy of, agitation trials fostering, 65–67; mock trials of, 57–59, 64–67, 78–80 (see also The Trial of Lenin). See also Communist Party; state, Soviet

lectures, agitation trials' advantage over, 77
legal consciousness: agitation trials and, 219–20; Russian public's lack of, 15–16
legal debates, in sanitation trials, 123–27
Lenin, Vladimir Ilich: authority of, agitation trials legitimating, 65–67; on church, 83; on control from below, 159; on courts, 1, 23; on criticism and self-criticism, 164; on Kuban Cossacks, 53; on lice, 107; on literacy, 69; on main battle in postwar period, 69, 86; mock trial of (see The Trial of Lenin); on post-Civil War challenges, 68; on prerevolutionary theater, 27; public speeches by, 39; reaction to criticism, 62; on revolutionary trials, 23; "What Is to be Done?" 134
librarians: and literary trials, 189; and prerevolutionary extracurricular education, 29–31; as subjects of agitation trials, 97–99
literacy: Lenin on importance of, 69; prerevolutionary societies promoting, 25. See also education; illiteracy
literary trials, 4; adaptation to political subjects, 55; authors as defendants in, 189–91; benign form of, 190; favorite material for, 48; prerevolutionary, 24–25; in Red Army, 47–48; by Symbolist poets, 32–34, 33f
Liublinskii, Pavel, 125–26
living newspapers, 43
localization, in agitation trials, 35
Lotman, Yuri, 235n19
Lunacharsky, Anatoly, 31, 32, 39, 43, 111, 250n65
L'vov, Nikolai, 239n50
Lyons, Eugene, 193–94, 210

Mally, Lynn, 203
Mandelshtam, Osip, 34
marginal figures/behaviors, as targets of agitation trials, 28–29, 213
McConachie, Bruce A., 234n14
medicine: in tsarist Russia, 106–7, 108. See also doctors; sanitation trials
melodrama: in sanitation trials, 109–10, 112–13, 114; in show trials of 1930s, 194
membership: agitation trials and, 162, 212; confession as ritual marker of, 212; party arraignment meetings and, 218; Pioneer trials and, 171–72
Meyerhold, Vsevolod: and development of agitation trials, 31–32, 52, 111, 244n11, 252n95; execution of, 283n57; imaginary trial of, 190
midwives, as characters in sanitation trials, 129, 130, 142, 143

Mol'kov, Al'fred Vladislavovich, 106, 265n8
Molotov, Viacheslav, 211
Montessori, Maria, 28
moral issues: agitation trials devoted to, 71; in agitation trials of everyday life, 91; in sanitation trials, 110; Soviet authorities appropriating, 126–27
morality plays, agitation trials as, 6, 55, 110
Moscow Show Trials of 1936–38, 9, 208–11; anti-trial in, 217–18; biblical analogies in, 209, 288n11; Bukharin's confession in, 211, 212, 217–18; Dewey's criticism of, 245n126; fantastic nature of, 199
mothers, agitation trials of, 142, 143–46; audience's reaction to, 147–48
Mueller, Georg, 24
Myerhoff, Barbara, 214

Nemirovich-Danchenko, Vladimir, 111, 191
Nevskii, Vladimir A., 30–31, 49, 244n101
New Economic Policy: and army clubs, pressures on, 74; and Bolsheviks' quest for legitimacy, 68; voluntary organizations during, 151
newspapers, living, 43
Nicholas II (tsar): absence of trial of, 64–65; sobriquet for, 212

October Revolution, agitation trial of, 79–80
Office Hours of the Criminal Chambers: Court Scenes from the Notes of an Eyewitness Bureaucrat, 22
Old Bolsheviks, demise of, 9
Ordzhonikidze, Sergo, 217
Orthodox Church: famine of 1921–22 and blame on, 82–83; priests as characters in agitation trials, 94–95, 101, 140, 162; school plays with trial scenes in, 17–18; trial of leaders of (1922), 82, 83. See also religion

Paris Commune of 1871, agitation trials of, 80–82
peasants: misogyny of, 133–34; recalcitrant, agitation trials featuring, 90–93; rich (see kulaks); self-defense in agitation trials, 99–100
peasant soldiers: characteristics of, 87; psychology of, 43; as subjects of agitation trials, 86, 90–91, 97
Peretz, Isaac Loeb, 239n52
Peter the Great (tsar): disputations and school plays under, 244n103; forced enlightenment of nobles under, 91, 263n25
Piatakov-Radek trial, 289n22
Pilsudski, Jozef, agitation trial of, 80, 82
Pioneers, agitation trials for, 170–72

Plekhanov, Georgii, 23
Podvoiskii, Nikolai, 251n78
Poland, relations with, agitation trial addressing, 80
political education (politprosvet): agitation trials as, 55; functions of, 41–42; Krupskaia on, 69; in postwar period, 86; prerevolutionary roots of, 35; Red Army experimentation with, 41, 42
political instructors (politruki): activities at end of Civil War, 42–43; adaptation of literary trials to political subjects, 55; and agitation trials, development of, 8, 12, 35, 38; interest in theater, 43–44; prerevolutionary trends influencing, 35; pressures on, 35, 38, 51; red calendar and, 77; role of, 40–41; on soldiers' psychology, 43; Vishnevskii's work as, 54–55; vulnerable position of, 213
political justice, 1
The Political Trial of the Peasant Evading Payment of the Household Tax, 92, 99
The Political Trial of the Peasant Woman Delegate, 134–35, 142; cover illustration of, 139f
political trials, 4; heroic, 57–59, 64–67, 77–81 (see also The Trial of Lenin); rationale for, 64; red calendar and, 76–77; of women (delegatki), 130–42
Popov, Nikolai, 21–22
Preobrazhenskii, Evgenii, 40
priests, portrayal in agitation trials, 94–95, 101, 140, 162
privacy, erosion of: in agitation trials after 1928, 202; in impromptu trials, 178; in Komsomol trials, 169–70, 172; in show trials, 210
production trials, 5; of mid-1920s, 156–59; of late 1920s, 159–60
propaganda: after end of Civil War, 69; vs. agitation, 234n4; trials and, 12
prostitution: agitation trials addressing, 105, 111, 114–18; prerevolutionary plays addressing, 27; Soviet authorities on, 126–27; and venereal disease, link between, 119–20
publicity: in show trials of 1930s, 194, 195–96; in tsarist trials, 22–23. See also advertising
public speaking, agitation trials and practice in, 63, 190, 282n51

Rafes, M., 261n66
railroads: and agitation trials, 57, 61–62; disciplinary problems on, 61; militarization of, 61; political agitation work on, 62
Rakhmanova, Olga, 111, 112, 267n34
rallies: agitation trials compared with, 63,

77; public weariness with, 39–40, 247n9; sanitation, 107, 108

rape, discussed in agitation trial, 123–24

Rastopchina, M., 154

rational recreation: army clubs and, 72; pre-revolutionary activists' interest in, 26, 29, 240n67

realism: romantic, in sanitation trials, 109–10; socialist, development of, 289n15

Red Army: agitation trial of, 78–79 (see also Red Army, agitation trials in); calendar of patriotic events, 75–77; deserters from, trials of, 50–51, 94, 100; experimentation in political education (politprosvet), 41, 42; extracurricular education in, trial forms used in, 45–48; failure of old methods for rousing soldiers in, 38, 39–40; health/sanitation issues in, 106, 107; recruits of 1921, 85–86, 87; returning soldiers and spread of communist culture, 42, 85. See also army clubs

Red Army, agitation trials in: appeal to soldiers, 44; early (1919–20), 52–56, 69–70; later (1921–23), 69, 70–71; on literary topics, 47–48; party instructions for, 70–71; precursors of, 35; of real individuals, 175; on sanitation topics, 107–8; spontaneous origins of, claims about, 37–38

religion: agitation trials targeting, 5, 21; moral functions of, Soviet authorities appropriating, 126–27; and origins of agitation trials, 17–18; Soviet propaganda against, 187f. See also Orthodox Church

revolutionaries: tsarist trials of, 22, 66

Revolution of 1905, trials during, 22–23

Riazanov, David, 220

rituals: agitation trials and, 11, 14, 63–64, 102–4, 212, 213–14; avant-garde movement's interest in, 32

Rolland, Romain, 31

romantic realism, in sanitation trials, 109–10

rumors, combating with agitation trials, 58–59

Rykov, Aleksei, 217, 218

Safran, Gabriella, 24

samodeiatel'nost' (independent activity): American influences on, 242n82; army agitation trials and, 37–38, 69, 74–75; impromptu trials and, 176; vs. planning and systematization, problem of, 74–75; pre-revolutionary extracurricular education and, 26, 29, 35

Sanin (Artsybashev), 24–25

sanitation rallies, 107, 108

The Sanitation Trial of a Syphilitic, 120–22

sanitation trials (sansudy), 4–5, 105–6; ab-sentee defendant in, 179–80; acquittal of defendants in, 113, 118, 122; advantages of, 108; collective guilt in, 113, 116, 117; criticism in mid-1920s, 177–78; doctors' hopes regarding, 178–79; expert witnesses in, 109, 114, 116, 119, 121, 127; first, 105, 114–18; goals of, 110; legal debates in, 123–27; melodrama in, 109–10, 112–13, 114; military metaphors in, 117; as morality plays, 110; party endorsement of, 111–12; popularity of, 111; of real individuals, 174–75, 180–81; in Red Army, 107–8; topics of, 106, 113; women in, 110, 128, 142–48

school plays: under Peter the Great, 244n103; religious, 17–18

Scott, Joan, 149

script: for agitation trials, 2; for show trials, 195

Semashko, Nikolai, 111, 147, 266n32

sentencing: in agitation trials after 1928, 200, 202; in agitation trials of everyday life, 91. See also acquittal; guilt

sexuality: agitation trials on subject of, 168–70; crimes of, law on, 123, 126–27; forms of restraint in area of, 126

Shakhty trial (1928), 193–96; Krylenko's clothing in, 214; publicity surrounding, 194, 195–96

shame: false, in show trials, 211; false vs. true, in early sanitation trials, 124–25, 172, 178; as regulator of mass behavior, 125

shaming of defendants: absentee, 180; impromptu trials and, 176, 178, 182, 183, 186; Komsomol trials and, 163, 168–69, 172; in late agitation trials, 206; Pioneer trials and, 170–72; in sanitation trials, 122; voluntary organizations' agitation trials and, 162

Shatskii, Stanislav, 27

Shcheglov, Ivan, 26

Shemiakin sud, 21–22

Shershenevich, Vadim, 34

Shimanko, Aleksandr, 111–12, 266n32

Shleger, Luiza, 27

show trials: blurring of fact and fiction in, 220; defendants' participation in, 217; first use of term, 193; mysterious power of, 214–15; scapegoats provided by, 216

show trials of 1922, agitation trials based on, 82–84

show trials of 1930s: agitation trials as preparation for, 12; agitation trials overshadowed by, 204; appearance of free speech in, 256n42; attention to ceremony in, 195; conventions shared with earlier agitation trials, 211; dehumanization of

show trials of 1930s (*continued*)
  defendants in, 196, 208–9, 211, 289n12;
  early agitation trials contrasted with, 209–
  11; melodrama in, 194; new kinship
  demonstrated in, 211, 289n22; publicity
  surrounding, 194, 195–96; residual intellectual elements in, 290n40; script used in,
  195; tsarist trials contrasted with, 217,
  218. *See also specific trials*
Sigal, Boris, 170, 177
Sinyavsky, Andrei, 216
smoking, agitation trials targeting, 170–71,
  174, 206–7
Social Fascists, trial of, 200
socialist realism, development of, 289n15
Socialist Revolutionaries, trial of, 82, 83–84
society, new/Soviet: agitation trials as instru-
  ment of, 10–11, 110; exclusion from
  membership in, 162, 212; returning soldiers and, 42, 85; sanitation trials and,
  110, 122; success of Bolshevik efforts to
  create, 86–87, 89
Society of Friends of the Air Force, agitation
  trial published by, 161–62
soldiers. *See* peasant soldiers; Red Army
Solov'ev, Zinovii, 107
Solzhenitsyn, Aleksandr, 210, 263n31,
  289n28
Sosnovskii, Lev, 111
Stalin, Joseph: and agitation trials of real individuals, 192; confessions required by,
  212; on criticism and self-criticism, 164,
  196; denunciation of father, 289n22; on
  enemies, 216; on Shakhty trial, 195; and
  show trials, 10, 217; on voluntary organizations, 161
Stanislavsky, Konstantin, 111
state, domination vs. hegemony of, 11
state, Soviet: ability to overcome defendant's
  resistance, 218; allegiance to, vs. kinship,
  211, 234n8, 289n22; theatrical nature of,
  11, 14, 220
Strashun, I. D., 107
study circles (*kruzhki*): criticism in mid-
  1920s, 151; military, 72
Swift, E. Anthony, 241n70
Symbolist poets, literary trials by, 32–34,
  33f
Syrtsov, Sergei, 197

tax evasion, agitation trials addressing, 92–
  93
teachers, as characters in agitation trials,
  95–96, 101–2
theater: appeal to Red Army soldiers, 43–44;
  appeal to Russian people, 32; educational
  value of, 26, 241n69; French revolutionaries on, 76, 260n35; prerevolutionary, 26–
  27

theatrical state, early Soviet Union as, 11,
  14, 220
Tolstoi, Aleksei, 203–4
Tolstoy, Leo: on courts, 23; cultural exchanges with West, 27; Yasnaia Poliana
  experiment of, 29, 36
Tomsky, Mikhail, 217, 290n47
trade unions: and clubs, 150–51; and im-
  promptu trials, 183–86; party pressure
  on, 8–9, 150, 151, 161, 197; and produc-
  tion trials, 156–60; vulnerability of, 216
The Trial of Anfisa, 15–16
The Trial of the Bad Peasant, 92–93
The Trial of the Careless Reader, 96–99
*The Trial of Citizen Kiselev Accused of In-
  fecting His Wife with Gonorrhea Which
  Resulted in Her Suicide*, 115–16; front
  cover of, 5f; ignorance demonstrated in,
  118, 120
The Trial of a Cow, 3f
*The Trial of Factory Committee Member
  N. I. Egorov*, 157–59
The Trial of Fedor Sharov, 126
The Trial of the Ignorant Mother, audience's
  reaction to, 147
The Trial of the Illiterate, 99–102
The Trial of Jewry, 46–48, 78
*The Trial of the Komsomolets or Komso-
  molka Who Has Violated Komsomol Dis-
  cipline*, 163–64, 172
The Trial of the Kronstadt Mutineers, 54–55
The Trial of Lenin, 57–58; audience at, 63;
  multiple accounts of, 59–61; participants
  in, 61, 63
The Trial of Neriashkin, 90, 91, 106, 114
The Trial of the New Woman, 128, 131–32
The Trial of the October Revolution, 79–80
The Trial of the Old Way of Life, 135–36
*The Trial of the Peasant Medvedev Who
  Wrecked the Election of the Women's
  Candidate to the Village Council*, 140–41
*The Trial of the Peasant Who Avoided Con-
  scription into the Red Army*, 90
The Trial of the Peasant Woman-Delegatka,
  136–40
The Trial of a Pig, 88f
The Trial of Pilsudski, 80, 82
The Trial of a Pioneer-Smoker, 170–71
*The Trial of Prefabricated, Reinforced Con-
  crete*, 199
The Trial of a Prostitute, 105, 111, 114–18;
  advertising for, 3; expert testimony in,
  119; sensationalism of, 113
The Trial of the Red Army, 78–79
*The Trial of a Sentry Who Allowed the
  Burning of the Grain Collection Site*, 73
The Trial of Sexual Depravity, 168–70
*The Trial of Six Factory Workers Who Agi-
  tated against the Club*, 156

The Trial of a Slovenly Pioneer, 170, 280n97
The Trial of Smut Fungus, 44f–46f
The Trial of the Soldier Who Didn't Want to Learn Military Arts, 90–91
The Trial of Those Guilty of the Famine, 94
The Trial of Vodka, 15
The Trial of the Women who Refused to Aid the Starving Population in the Volga Region, 95–96
The Trial of Wrangel, 52–54; authorship of, 253n100
The Trial of the Young Men Who Did Not Enroll in the Komsomol, 165
Trotsky, Leon: authority of, agitation trials legitimating, 65–67; Civil War slogan of, 152; on Kuban Cossacks, 53; in Moscow Show Trials, 209, 245n126, 288n11; on Pilsudski, 80; on political instruction, 43; public speeches by, 39
truancy, agitation trials addressing, 183–86, 184f, 185f, 205
tsarist Russia: court corruption in, 21–22; disputations and school plays in, 17–18, 244n103; as enemy in early agitation trials, 212–13; jury trials in, introduction of, 21, 22; legacy of ignorance, brutishness, and inequality, 133; medicine in, frustrations of, 106–7, 108; trials in, contrasted with Soviet show trials, 217, 218; trials of revolutionaries in, 22, 23, 66
Tucker, Robert, 217
Tukhachevsky, Marshal, 217
Turgenev, Ivan, 23
Turner, Victor, 11

Ulianova, Maria, 60, 151
Ulrich, Vasilii, 218
An Unusual Life Event—Father Evlampiia, 94–95
Uspensky, Boris, 235n19
Utenkov, Mikhail, 112

vaccination, agitation trials addressing, 180–81
Vedernikov, P. M., 178–79
venereal disease: advances in treatment of, 122; agitation trials addressing, 115–16, 119, 120–22; legal debates about, 123; prostitution and, link between, 119–20; shame associated with, 125
Vinogradskaia, Sofia, 59, 60
Vishnevskii, Vsevolod: and *The Trial of the Kronstadt Mutineers,* 54–55; and *The Trial of Wrangel,* 52–53, 253n100
Volin, Boris, 84, 261n66

Volkonskaia, Sofiia, 281n31
voluntary organizations, 214; and agitation trials of mid-1920s, 161–62; conditional membership in, 188, 212; dilemmas faced by, 151; pressure on, in mid-1920s, 9, 150, 151. *See also* army clubs; Komsomol; Pioneers; workers' clubs
von Geldern, James, 65
Vyshinsky, Andrei, 208–9, 212, 217, 218, 290n30, 291n49

witches, folk healers compared with, 143
women: and the abject, 130; delegatki, 132–33; emancipation as "humanization" of, 134–36, 142; freedom and rights of, public work associated with, 135–36; Soviet ideology on, 124, 129
women, agitation trials relating to, 103, 128–49; assumptions about public work and service in, 133, 135–36; audience's reaction to, 147–48; criticism of backward woman *(baba)* in, 129, 130, 131, 142–43; criticism of intelligentsia representatives in, 95–96, 97–99, 101–2; heroine-delegatka in, 130–42; male authority figures in, 130, 146, 148, 273n82; male characters in, 133–34, 138–40; mixed messages in, 129–30; negative stereotypes reinforced by, 100, 129, 130, 133–34, 136–37, 142, 148–49; on sanitation topics, 110, 128, 142–48
workers' clubs: activities offered in, 154t, 155t; agitation trials of, 152–56; campaign against hooliganism, 165–68; criticism of, 151–52, 197; cultural campaign of 1928, 197; disciplinary problems in, 151, 152, 192; drama circles in, evolution of, 203, 204; impromptu trials in, 181–83; literary evenings in, 189–90; prerevolutionary, 25, 26–27, 30–31; rites of passage in, agitation trials marking, 154–55; and self-criticism, 197–98; strict program of activities, in late 1920s, 200
worker correspondents, 190, 282n51
Wortman, Richard, 58
Wrangel, Baron Peter: mock trial of, 2, 52–54; threat perceived in, 53

youth organizations. *See* Komsomol; Pioneers

Zalkind, A. B., 168
Zelenko, Alexander, 27
Zelenko, V. A., 29, 243n92